THE THING HAPPENS

THE THING HAPPENS

Ten Years of Writing About the Movies

Terrence Rafferty

GROVE PRESS
NEW YORK

Published by Grove Press
A division of Grove Press, Inc.
841 Broadway
New York, NY 10003-4793

Grateful acknowledgment is made to the following for permission to reprint copyrighted materials:

Film Quarterly, vol. 36, no. 2 (Winter 1982), The Regents of the University of California: "Barbarosa," 1982.

The Nation magazine/The Nation Company, Inc.: "Blue Velvet," 1986; "The Color of Money," 1986; "Housekeeping," 1988; "Sid and Nancy," 1986; "The Stepfather," 1987; "The Untouchables," 1987.

Sight and Sound, The British Film Institute: "Brian De Palma," 1984; "Casualties of War," 1989–90; "Chris Marker," 1984; "John Huston," 1985; "Martin Scorsese," 1983; "Philip Kaufman," 1988; "The Purple Rose of Cairo," 1985; "Stanley Kubrick," 1987.

Other essays and reviews were originally published in *The Atlantic* and *The New Yorker*.

Library of Congress Cataloging-in-Publication Data

Rafferty, Terrence.
    The thing happens: ten years of writing about the movies/
Terrence Rafferty.—1st ed.
        p.   cm.
    Includes index.
    ISBN 0-8021-1485-7 (acid-free)
    1. Motion pictures—United States—Reviews. 2. Motion picture producers and directors—United States. I. Title.
PN1995.R28   1993   92-25769
791.43′75—dc20   CIP

Manufactured in the United States of America

Printed on acid-free paper

Designed by Eve Kirch

First Edition 1993

1   3   5   7   9   10   8   6   4   2

For
Mom and Dad
Penelope Houston
and
Diane

Contents

Introduction

The title of this book comes from James Agee's 1950 *Life* magazine profile of John Huston, "Undirectable Director." Huston, who was a writer before he was a director, says to Agee: "On paper, all you can do is say something happened, and if you say it well enough the reader believes you. In pictures, if you do it right, *the thing happens, right there on the screen.*" (The italics are Agee's.) To an academic theorist, this casual formulation of the nature of film-making might sound weak, vague, unhelpful. To Agee, who merely loved movies, Huston's words have the terse suggestiveness of a memorable line of poetry, and I hear them that way, too. You can spend your whole life making movies, or watching them and writing about them, without ever exhausting the possible meanings of Huston's simple phrase. The great French critic André Bazin collected his essays under the title *What Is Cinema?*—even his writings don't add up to any sort of definitive answer, and aren't meant to. Every fresh occasion of the thing happening on the screen poses the question in a different way. If I were French, I'd say that *The Thing Happens* is an interrogative sentence in the guise of a declarative sentence. Since I'm not, I'll just say that this book's title means to suggest the mysteriousness, the elusiveness, and the unpredictability of the movie experience—the qualities that made me want to write about films in the first place and that keep me going now.

*   *   *

I've laid out this selection of essays and reviews in three parts. The first is a single long essay on Jean Renoir's 1939 film *The Rules of the Game*, which ran as a "Critic at Large" piece in *The New Yorker* in 1990. I begin with it because for me *The Rules of the Game* is the richest movie in the short history of the art: the film that most fully embodies what the medium is capable of. It's a work that draws from the best of its (European) cultural tradition; points forward to new, and freer, forms of expression; and is also entirely of its own time, its specific and frighteningly uncertain historical moment. For most of my moviegoing life, *The Rules of the Game* has been my standard, and in trying to evoke the complex pleasures it gives me as thoroughly and as accurately as possible I found myself writing something that's probably as close to a comprehensive statement of my aesthetic principles as I'll ever get. The essay doesn't come anywhere near doing justice to Renoir's film, but it frames the essential questions of what happens to us when we look at movies as clearly as I know how to frame them.

The second section consists of essays on individual filmmakers, most of which I wrote as a free-lance critic for *Sight and Sound* and *The Atlantic. Sight and Sound* (published by the British Film Institute) gave me vast amounts of space to range over the careers of some major directors, for a movie-knowledgeable readership. These pieces are heavier on visual analysis than most of my writing for other magazines: I was able to explore ideas and develop lines of argument that I couldn't have expected the readers of a general-interest publication to sit still for. The career-overview kind of essay—in both the extended form of the *Sight and Sound* pieces and the more concise form of the *Atlantic* and *New Yorker* articles in this section—has always seemed to me a uniquely fruitful way of thinking about movies. It forces you, in a sense, to consider a filmmaker's work as a series of personal responses to experience, which change over time. In a movie climate that seems increasingly geared to the production of impersonal artifacts, it's good to be reminded periodically that films can also speak to us in identifiable human voices.

The final section gets down to the nitty-gritty of movie criticism:

reviewing, the week-to-week coverage of what's playing. I've made a selection from reviews written for *The Nation* from 1986 to 1988 and for *The New Yorker* from 1988 to the present. (There are a few pieces from *Film Quarterly* and *Sight and Sound*, too.) I didn't make a conscious choice to include more positive reviews than negative ones, but that's the way it seems to have worked out. Partly, I suppose, I've skewed positive because I felt it was more valuable to have a book that celebrates the ways movies can go right than one that keeps lamenting the ways they go wrong. In any event, bad movies—big-budget Hollywood productions, especially—tend to be bad in depressingly similar ways, and finding fresh language to deplore them in is not very rewarding work. Sounding like a witty, imaginative crank rather than a ranting radio-call-in-show blowhard is a challenge of sorts; but you can meet the challenge and still not feel that the prize was quite worth the effort. Good movies are simply more interesting, more *fun* to think about and to write about than bad ones; in general, only the most ambitious and the most pernicious stinkers provide me with the incentive to demolish them at length. As consumer guides, reviewers can't really be choosers: you have to take a shot at every big turkey that gobbles into view. But you don't have to keep all the heads as trophies.

Anyway, nothing in this book—neither the subjects of the pieces nor the pieces themselves—was ever meant to be stuffed and mounted (with the possible exception of the works of Peter Greenaway and Arnold Schwarzenegger). All I really want to do here is convey some sense of the pleasure and stimulation that movies can supply, even at this relative low point in their development. There's still plenty of vitality and variety in the art. Somehow, the thing keeps happening, and differently all the time.

Criticism isn't a collaborative activity, but every writer needs help, and I've had plenty over the years. I've been very lucky in the editors I've worked with, beginning with Ernest Callenbach of *Film Quarterly*, who published my first attempts at movie criticism. For my pieces at *The Atlantic*, I benefited from the intelligent, meticulous editorial support of Corby Kummer and William Whitworth. Elizabeth Pochoda of *The Nation* gave me the opportunity to review movies regularly, and Maria Margaronis helped with the editing. At

The New Yorker, there's a long list of people I'm grateful to. William Shawn accepted my unsolicited piece on Truffaut; his successor, Robert Gottlieb, allowed me, a couple of years later, to appear frequently in the magazine's pages; and in both cases, Pauline Kael brought my work to their attention. Most of the pieces I've written for the magazine have been edited—expertly—by Nancy Franklin. When I've been edited by someone else—John Bennet, Chip Mc-Grath, Hal Espen, Ann Goldstein, or Elizabeth Pearson-Griffiths—the experience has always been a happy one. For every piece I've enjoyed the security provided by the magazine's fact-checkers and proofreaders, and its wizardly, infinitely subtle grammarian, Eleanor Gould Packard. And I'd like to express my appreciation for the friendship and practical support of other *New Yorker* colleagues: Bruce Diones, Vic Webb, Edith Oliver, Joseph Cooper, and Sally Ann Mock. With no disrespect to anyone named above, I'd like to give special thanks to my editors at *Sight and Sound*, Penelope Houston and John Pym: great film lovers and terrific people who put out (until their recent departures from the magazine) the best movie journal in the world. No matter what other publications I was writing for, I always felt particularly proud to appear in *Sight and Sound*, and privileged to be working with John and Penelope.

For the *Rules of the Game* piece, I drew on a variety of sources which I wasn't able to acknowledge in the text. Works by Alexander Sesonske, Claude Gauteur, Célia Bertin, Christopher Faulkner, and the editors of *L'Avant-Scène Cinéma* were especially helpful in supplying details of the film's production, reception, and subsequent fate at the hands of both censors and restorers. Particular thanks to Mr. Faulkner, who took the time to respond personally to inquiries from the fact-checking department; his aid was invaluable. Many of the quotes from Renoir came from collections of writings and interviews which, at the time of my writing, had appeared only in France. I should mention that one of my primary sources, a volume called *Jean Renoir: Entretiens et Propos,* has been translated into English, by Carol Volk, as *Renoir on Renoir* (Cambridge University Press, 1990); the translations here, however, are my own.

Then, those who have provided, at various times, encouragement, inspiration, instruction, or just good movie talk: my parents, Terrence and Lucy Rafferty; Ellen Williams; Ann Smith; Rose Coviello; Joan Cuomo; Roger Tourangeau; Bill and Kay Gilcher; Hal Hinson; Lloyd Rose; Pat LoBrutto; Estelle Peisach; Billy and Joyce Altman; Howard Rodman; Martine Aballéa; and my colleague in "The Current Cinema," Michael Sragow. This is the short list.

I'd also like to thank my scrupulous editor at Grove Press, Jim Moser; and Peter Schneider, who is no longer at Grove but had a lot to do with the publication of this book. And I want to acknowledge the support of the John Simon Guggenheim Memorial Foundation, which gave me a generous grant in 1987 to write a book that in no way resembles this one. I'm very, very grateful to the foundation, and I hope it will consider *The Thing Happens* an acceptable substitute for the project it thought it was funding.

Finally, there is no kind of support—editorial, moral, you name it—that I haven't received in abundance from my wife, Diane. She's a miracle, a constant wonder, like *The Rules of the Game*; only better.

June 1992

Part One

The Essence of the Landscape

For François Truffaut it was "the film of films." Another, very different filmmaker, Alain Resnais, says his first viewing of it was "the single most overwhelming experience I have ever had in the cinema." But when Jean Renoir's *The Rules of the Game* (*La Règle du Jeu*), a dramatic comedy about a week-long party at a château in the Sologne, was first shown to the public—on July 7, 1939, at the Colisée and Aubert cinemas, in Paris—the reaction wasn't quite so enthusiastic. According to Renoir, one opening-night spectator at the Colisée put a match to his newspaper "with the obvious intention of setting fire to the auditorium"; others "wanted to smash the seats." Even a friend of Renoir's, the director René Clair, felt compelled to ask him, "In fact, what, exactly, was it you wished to do?" (The depressed filmmaker replied, "I don't know—I no longer know.")

Not an auspicious beginning for "the film of films," and things didn't get better any time soon. The reviews in the most important papers were abusive (the film got good notices in some smaller publications, though), the public mostly stayed home, and Renoir and his editor hacked away at the movie in the hope of averting financial disaster: *The Rules of the Game*, which had already been cut for its premiere, at the urging of its nervous distributor, from 107 minutes to ninety-seven, dwindled to ninety minutes, then eighty-five. It's as if the film had begun to disappear the moment Renoir stopped shooting. Three weeks after that clamorous first screening

3

at the Colisée, *The Rules of the Game*—what remained of it—was pulled from distribution, and it was rarely seen in the years that followed, because it was banned at various times by both the Vichy government and the occupying Germans. And in 1942 Allied bombers wiped out the G.M. Film Laboratories at Boulogne-sur-Seine, destroying the only negative of the complete, 107-minute version. By then, Renoir himself had disappeared. He left for America in 1940; *The Rules of the Game* was the last movie he made in France until 1954.

Now, at the end of the movie's fiftieth-anniversary year, July 7, 1939, has for us the aura of a special day, an important occasion in film history; but the date commemorates a catastrophe, not a triumph. In 1939, no one had really seen the movie we now know as *The Rules of the Game*, and those few who attended screenings of the incomplete versions watched them through a haze of doubt, fear, and anxiety: France was on the verge of war (it had begun to mobilize in March, soon after Renoir started filming), and not many people were in the mood for a devastating analysis of the society they would have to fight to defend. To make matters worse, the first public showing of the film was preceded by a long patriotic documentary. And, in any event, *The Rules of the Game* was like nothing anyone had ever seen in a movie theater before. No one—not Renoir himself, in his twenty-two previous films—had ever used the medium to express such a dense, complex vision of life; had ever challenged his audience with so rich an assortment of characters and so intricate and subtle a play of ideas; or had ever deployed the resources of film technique with such abandon and command. The movie was, even in its diminished state, just too much for the audiences of the time—and the cuts probably made it even more confusing.

It's still a difficult film, not because there's anything obscure or abstract about it—dramatically, it is always strong and lucid—but because it never lets us rest, never allows us the comfort of knowing that we're responding "correctly." A single scene in *The Rules of the Game* gives us more for our senses, emotions, and intellect than most whole movies do, yet Renoir never tells us what to feel or think, or even what to see and hear: the images are composed with extreme depth; the camera is always moving, reframing the action; and the soundtrack is crowded with voices and natural sounds. There isn't a true protagonist, either: Renoir, a genuine democrat, encourages us to pay attention to a dozen or so characters, from every class of French society, and to find them all equally interesting. Renoir's style couldn't be less coercive—which means that we can't just sit there passively. Truffaut wrote in 1967, after countless viewings, "We look at this movie with a strong feeling of complicity; I mean that, instead of seeing a finished product handed to us to satisfy our curiosity, we feel we are there as the film is made, we almost think that we can see Renoir organize the whole as we watch the film projected." *The Rules of the Game*, the story of a group of people caught in the machinery of European culture, is a movie about freedom. The making of the film was a loose, intuitive, collaborative process (it was, Renoir said, the most improvised of his movies), and the director was clearly offering the same freedom to his audience that he had extended to his cast and crew; he couldn't imagine that anyone wouldn't want it.

Obviously, *The Rules of the Game* wasn't what the French public wanted in the anxious days before the war. And despite the movie's current status as an official classic of world cinema, no one in this country threw any parties for its fiftieth birthday. Over and over last year, we were told by virtually everyone in the American "entertainment news" media that 1939 was the best year in the history of the movies, a conclusion based on a handful of Hollywood pictures that had remained audience favorites for five decades: *Stagecoach*, *Wuthering Heights*, *Gunga Din*, *Mr. Smith Goes to Washington*, *Young Mr. Lincoln*, *The Wizard of Oz*, and, preeminently, *Gone with the Wind*. In the fan-historians' celebrations of the way things used to be, there's no mention of *The Rules of the Game*. In a way, the omission seems appropriate. The classic Hollywood films of 1939 are all, in varying degrees, products of a system rather than expressions of individual sensibilities: to cite those movies as the collective high point of movie history is to accept a limited conception of the nature of the art.

As richly enjoyable as *Gone with the Wind* is, it is also, intentionally, impersonal—a triumph of planning and traditional, anonymous studio craftsmanship. Famously, it's a producer's film: the director whose name is on the picture—Victor Fleming, a versatile, reliable type—wasn't even around when shooting started (he was the second man in, after George Cukor was fired by David O. Selznick); and the movie had nearly as many writers as it had extras. *Gone with the Wind* is a cathedral—a humble monument to the unseen, all-powerful Architect, the Hollywood studio—and for most of us it's a very comforting place to retreat to. Whether we attend the full four-hour service or just drop in for a few minutes of meditation, we know we'll walk out reassured of American movies' eternal verities: the narrative conventions, the fine production values, the iconlike stars—the articles of faith that we grew up with, and know almost better than we know ourselves.

The Rules of the Game has an altogether different effect. It glories in all that's variable, unplanned, unsystematic; no matter how many times you've seen it, each new viewing provokes fresh, unfamiliar responses. No less than *Gone with the Wind* and the other certified miracle movies of 1939, *The Rules of the Game* represents the culmination of great traditions, but Renoir's film feels like a turning point, not an end point. The American movies that came out on the eve of the Second World War set a kind of standard, and they function now as a reproach: the studio system that produced those strong, confident popular entertainments hasn't worked as well since. (When Selznick himself tried to equal *Gone with the Wind*, only seven years later, what he came up with was *Duel in the Sun*.) The Hollywood system of moviemaking was able—because it *is* a system—to perfect itself in the prewar years, to achieve an ideal form; from then on, the product could be new but not (except technically) improved.

When we watch the studio pictures of fifty years ago, time seems to stop. If we accept the notion of a true golden age of movies, the history of the art turns static, as unalterable as Scripture: the revelation of absolute truth has a tendency to discourage the development and free exploration of ideas. (Let's not forget that even in the thirties and forties there were people for whom the *silent* cinema represented the ultimate truth, the never-to-be-recaptured peak of pure film art.) We don't watch *The Rules of the Game* that way. It never presents itself as ideal or unsurpassable; it expands our ideas of what movies can be, and enriches our sense of what they have been, both before and after it. We can't see Renoir's film today without seeing in it as well the shadows of the artists it has inspired: De Sica and Rossellini, Satyajit Ray, Truffaut, the early Godard, Robert Altman, the Visconti of *The Leopard*, and even, in one beautiful film (*Smiles of a Summer Night*), Ingmar Bergman. *The Rules of the Game* doesn't stand out like a monument. It's the image, and the embodiment, of a profound sense of continuity; whenever we see it, it seems somehow to have inserted itself in the flow of history—to have matched exactly the rhythm of our lives. *The Rules of the Game* is one of the rare movies that will always look as if they had been made just yesterday. We can't watch it with they-don't-make-'em-like-they-used-to nostalgia, because no one but Renoir made them like that even then. This movie could never have fitted comfortably into the film-history canon of ruined masterpieces, alongside *Greed* and *The Magnificent Ambersons*. The work of flamboyant, obsessive artists like Stroheim and Welles can retain its force even in fragments, in brilliant individual sequences, but the natural, unobtrusive flow of Renoir's images can't be interrupted without violating something essential. (Among his thirties films, the only ones that refuse to come to life are those which remain incomplete: his 1934 *Madame Bovary*, cut from over three hours to just two; and the 1932 *La Nuit du Carrefour*, three reels of which were lost before editing.)

What is worth celebrating now, in this generally dispiriting time for movies, is that *The Rules of the Game* has survived. The vision that Jean Renoir committed to film between February and May of 1939 was finally, almost miraculously, restored twenty years after the catastrophe of its premiere, and the audience was at last ready for it. In 1958, the movie's new distributors, Jean Gaborit and Jacques Maréchal, discovered that not all had been lost in the bombing of the G.M. Laboratories: there remained some two hundred cans of film which contained bits and pieces of *The Rules of the Game*. Under Renoir's supervision, Gaborit and Jacques Durand began to assemble the footage, and when they were finished they had something very close to the movie he had actually made—the one he had originally intended to unveil at the 1939 World's Fair in New York.

This 106-minute patchwork version (several scenes had to be printed from positives, because no negatives of them existed, and one minute-long sequence couldn't be located in any form) had its premiere at the Venice Film Festival on August 31, 1959, and the only fire this time was in the minds and hearts of the grateful spectators. Renoir was then sixty-four years old, and past his peak as an artist (he made only two more pictures before his death, in 1979), but the restoration of *The Rules of the Game* was more than a vindication for an old man, or even a delayed fulfillment of the younger man's dream. It must have seemed to the fortunate audience as if a twenty-year gap in movie history had suddenly closed up—as if a rip in time had been repaired.

It wouldn't be strictly accurate to claim that the renovation of *The Rules of the Game* was the impetus for the revolution in French filmmaking that became known as the New Wave: by the autumn of 1959, many of those young *cinéastes* had shot their first films, and Renoir was already, in varying degrees, the spirit presiding over them. There was, after all, more than enough in the rest of his work to draw inspiration from. He had made great films before 1939 (*Boudu Saved from Drowning*, *A Day in the Country*, *The Crime of Monsieur Lange*, *Grand Illusion*), and he made them after (*The River* and *The Golden Coach*); even his lesser movies were vibrant and energetic—evidence of a complex moviemaking intelligence.

When Renoir began shooting *The Rules of the Game*, he had been making movies for fifteen years—a career he stumbled on, and then pursued with the innocent passion of an amateur. Born in 1894, the son of the Impressionist painter Pierre-Auguste Renoir, he was, by his own account, a rather aimless young man. After serving in the First World War (he was wounded), he returned to his father's house and contented himself with dabbling in various arts; as he approached thirty, he had more or less settled on pottery as his métier. But one last dilettantish impulse intervened. He and his young wife, Catherine Hessling, were avid moviegoers, and Renoir thought that Catherine was every bit as beautiful as Gloria Swanson or Mary Pickford. He later wrote, "I set foot in the world of the cinema only in order to make my wife a star, intending, once this was done, to return to my pottery studio." The film he wrote and produced, *Catherine*, was directed by Albert Dieudonné (who would later play the title role in Abel Gance's *Napoléon*), and it was, Renoir said, "a total failure." (It remained unreleased for three years.) But Renoir was hooked, and decided to try again, this time directing his wife himself: the result, *La Fille de l'Eau* (1925), was the real start of his filmmaking life. He made seven more silent movies, and never quite managed to turn Catherine Hessling into a star. The marriage fell apart at the beginning of the thirties, but Renoir kept on making films, and started to hit his stride around the time sound was coming in. *La Chienne* (1931), with Michel Simon, was his first commercial success, and his first great film. His reputation grew throughout the thirties. By 1935, he was France's best filmmaker. (René Clair and Abel Gance had made their most memorable pictures in the silent era, and Jean Vigo died in 1934—at the age of twenty-nine—after making his two extraordinary movies, *Zero for Conduct* and *L'Atalante*.) And by 1937 he was even its most respected: his classic antiwar movie, *Grand Illusion*, was a huge international hit (except in Germany and Italy, where—not surprisingly—it was banned). Two years later, the scandalous failure of *The Rules of the Game* destroyed his reputation in a stroke, and nearly broke his spirit; it left him, he wrote, "so depressed . . . that I resolved either to give up the cinema or to leave France."

After the war, Renoir slowly became—in absentia—an important figure in French film again, his influence having been kept alive by the critic André Bazin. Renoir's work in the thirties was the touchstone of the sophisticated film aesthetic that Bazin passed on to the young critics who wrote for his new magazine, *Cahiers du Cinéma*: François Truffaut, Jean-Luc Godard, Maurice Schérer (better known as Eric Rohmer), Claude Chabrol, Jacques Rivette. The support of Bazin and his protégés probably encouraged Renoir to try making films in his native country once more. When *French Cancan* and *Eléna et les Hommes* were released, in the mid-fifties, the *Cahiers* writers were their most vigorous champions. By the time *The Rules of the Game* was reborn in Venice, there was, perhaps for the first time, an audience that was ready, and eager, to learn from it. Although Bazin died in 1958, before the restoration was complete (and before he could finish his book on Renoir), he was the crucial link between Renoir and succeeding generations of filmmakers. His teachings encouraged the continuity of what was best in movies, and stimulated his younger colleagues to see and take advantage of the remarkable liberation that Renoir's thirties films proposed—to carry on the explorations that had stopped abruptly on the terrible night of the premiere of *The Rules of the Game*. Renoir dedicated the version unveiled in 1959 to the memory of Bazin.

In any event, the mutilated *Rules of the Game* was probably more impressive to aspiring filmmakers than to anyone else—they were better equipped to understand the impulse behind Renoir's technical innovations, to appreciate the audacious beauty of his experiments with film form. What no one could have seen before Venice was that *The Rules of the Game* wasn't just a brave attempt, a series of provocative suggestions, a radical but not quite articulate manifesto of cinematic freedom. The integral version showed that all Renoir's gambles had paid off: that in movies the willingness to remain open to chance—the vagaries of the weather, the stray discoveries of improvising actors, the flickering intuitions of correspondence between the great art of the past and the wholly new forms of expression demanded by a shifting, uncertain present—could sometimes uncover a deeper kind of order, make us hear harmonies in what had once seemed only noise.

An achieved masterpiece is a different sort of inspiration from a failed one: it gives other artists something to aim for, provides them with the confidence (which might otherwise be hard to sustain) that everything is possible. Truffaut believed that "along with *Citizen Kane*, *La Règle du Jeu* is certainly the film that sparked the careers of the greatest number of directors." And Resnais reported that after seeing the movie for the first time "all my ideas about the cinema had been challenged." He added, "Since then, of course, I've seen it at least fifteen times—like most filmmakers of my generation." For these filmmakers *The Rules of the Game* was a *useful* classic, just the movie they needed. Physically, there's no more restoration to be done, but the fiftieth anniversary of *The Rules of the Game* gives us an occasion for renewing our acquaintance with this great film, for learning to use it again. We've never needed it more.

Renoir was a master of taking what he needed from the art he loved. In his autobiography, *My Life and My Films*, he begins the chapter on *The Rules of the Game* this way: "You spend an evening listening to records and the result is a film. I cannot say that it was French Baroque music that inspired me to make *La Règle du Jeu*, but certainly it played a part in making me wish to film the sort of people who danced to that music. I based my thought on it only at the beginning. . . . I was entering a period of my life when my daily companions were Couperin, Rameau, and every composer from Lulli to Grétry. By degrees my idea took shape and the subject became simplified, and after a few days, while I lived to Baroque rhythms, it became more and more clearly defined." None of the music he cites actually wound up in the film—he used Mozart and Monsigny instead—but his recollection is plausible: there's a lot of this music on the soundtrack of Renoir's film about the Revolution, *La Marseillaise* (which was finished just a few months before he began writing the scenario of *The Rules of the Game*), and the "Baroque rhythms" are still very evident in the final product.

Renoir often spoke, too, of literary and theatrical sources for the style of *The Rules of the Game*. In a 1966 television interview, he said, "I looked for inspiration in Beaumarchais, in Marivaux, in the classical authors, in comedy," and he frequently acknowledged the importance to him of Alfred de Musset's *Les Caprices de Marianne*, a tragic farce, written in 1833, in which a young man hopelessly in love with a married woman is killed in a garden because he has been mistaken for someone else. Something like this happens at the end of *The Rules of the Game*, and the unlucky hero of Musset's play, like his counterpart in Renoir's film, has a confidant named Octave, but Renoir took little else from the classical source, and he never thought of his film as an adaptation. His reading and rereading of classical texts, like his listening to Baroque music, was essentially a matter of putting himself in a specific frame of mind, of immersing himself in a particular form of thinking and feeling about the world. "My ambition," he once said, "was to find again a certain elegance, a certain grace, a certain rhythm which is typical of the eighteenth century." What he cared about, even before he knew what his story was going to be, was "the classical spirit, which is a spirit in which one keeps things on the inside rather than show them on the outside"—a spirit that he felt was "apparently extremely difficult to understand for a public that has been submerged in romantic tears for a hundred years."

The film that immediately preceded *The Rules of the Game* wasn't at all in the classical spirit. It was an adaptation of Zola's novel *La Bête Humaine*, with the very popular Jean Gabin as its star, and it was one of Renoir's greatest commercial successes. (It opened in December 1938, and was still playing when Renoir began shooting *The Rules of the Game*, almost three months later.) Watching the movie today, we can see that the claustrophobic, fatalistic material doesn't really suit the director's temperament. His adaptation isn't slavish, but in trying to be faithful to Zola's spirit he's as trapped as Jacques Lantier, the novel's unfortunate hero. Lantier, a railroad engineer (and, like many Zola protagonists, the inheritor of some powerfully bad genes), kills his mistress in a spasm of rage and commits suicide to atone for his crime. Two of Renoir's best movies, *La Chienne* and *The Crime of Monsieur Lange*, also have heroes who are murderers, but the director can't bring himself to punish them: to our great satisfaction, both of those sympathetic killers are allowed to escape. Lantier's fate is determined, inexorable, as rigidly laid out as the tracks his engine runs on. (It's also determined to some extent by the presence of Gabin, who achieved stardom by dying splendidly in doomed-love poetic melodramas like *Quai des Brumes*.) Renoir's open style comes close to subverting Zola's ideas: the long scenes of Lantier driving his locomotive, which should probably give us a sense of the hero's entrapment by the Machine or Fate or History, or whatever, are instead peculiarly exhilarating.

Years later, Renoir said, "I had wanted to make *The Rules of the Game* for a long time, but that desire became more distinct while I was shooting *La Bête Humaine*. . . . Working on that scenario made me want to change course, and perhaps to escape naturalism completely." And in order to escape other, more practical sorts of constraints he formed his own production company. In an interview he gave in January 1939, Renoir spoke exuberantly about his new organization, La Nouvelle Édition Française: "The NEF—that's what I call my production company—is directed by old friends." Actually, they were three friends—André Zwobada, Camille François, and Olivier Billiou—and the director's brother Claude. "The five of us get along like the five fingers of a hand," Renoir went on. "I will make two films a year, and I'll be able to keep my crew: de Bretagne, the sound engineer; Bachelet, the cameraman; Lourié, the designer; and the others." The first project of this merry band, he announced, would be *The Rules of the Game*. Neither the screenplay nor the cast was yet complete, but he knew what he wanted the film to be: "a precise description of the bourgeois of our age." Later, puzzled and chastened by the public's response to the film, Renoir affected a certain modesty in speaking of his ambitions for *The Rules of the Game*, and expressed astonishment that this "pleasant" film, with its "charming story," could arouse such strong feelings. But it's clear that his own feelings were running pretty high at the time he made it. He was breaking away from a set of aesthetic principles he had become uncomfortable with, declaring his independence from the French film industry, gathering his dearest friends and most respected colleagues into an almost utopian experiment in communal filmmaking, paying homage to the art and literature he felt closest to, and attempting to portray the true nature of European culture at the moment of its most profound unease—the moment when it was about to be transformed forever.

The circumstances and the impulses that combined to produce *The Rules of the Game* were perhaps so strong, so deep, and so complex that even its author wasn't fully conscious of everything the film meant to him (and would later mean to us). Yet he obviously had more than an inkling that he was onto something. The movie was, for its time, very expensive to make, and Renoir was willing to gamble the future of his new company on it. He was willing, too, to expose himself onscreen in a central role, to let the audience have a good, long look at him, whatever the consequences. *The Rules of the Game* represents an extraordinary gesture of faith; it tests all that Renoir values as an artist and as a man.

In February 1939, Renoir took his cast and crew to the Sologne, a marshy region (not far to the south of Paris) known for excellent hunting. The story he had come up with, to satisfy his desires to express the classical spirit and to describe precisely the bourgeois of his age, was set mainly on a large country estate belonging to the Marquis de la Chesnaye, who has invited several of his friends for an extended houseparty. The planned entertainment includes a musical revue, endless card games, the unveiling of a spectacular mechanical toy (the Marquis is a passionate collector of automatons), and a hunt. The unplanned entertainment is farce—the working out of a variety of amorous intrigues involving the host, his guests, and the servants. The catalyst of all the romantic confusion is a young pilot named André Jurieu, who, as the film begins, has just completed a solo transatlantic flight, landing in Paris to a hero's welcome. On being accosted by a radio interviewer as he walks across the tarmac, Jurieu blurts out, for the nation to hear, that his great feat means nothing to him: "I undertook this exploit because of a woman. She isn't even here waiting for me." The woman, as everyone in Paris seems to know, is Christine, the wife of the Marquis. Christine reassures her husband (truthfully) that there has never been anything but warm friendship between her and the aviator; La Chesnaye is so moved by her fidelity that he decides to break with his longtime mistress, Geneviève. ("My darling, yesterday evening, quite suddenly, I decided to be worthy of my wife.") Jurieu, almost suicidal with disappointment, begs his friend Octave to speak with Christine, and Octave, who has known her since she was a little girl, persuades her to invite the lovesick hero to the Marquis's country house, La Colinière (in reality, the Château de la Ferté-Saint-Aubin). Christine and her husband are reluctant, of course. But she's genuinely fond of Jurieu, and feels guilty for having been, however innocently, the cause of his misery. La Chesnaye wants to please his wife, and his image of himself is of someone who believes in freedom, who is "against barriers . . . against walls"; and besides, everyone involved "has class" (as one of the Marquis's guests later pronounces)— people like them know how to handle awkward situations.

Everything in the first few minutes of the film is laid out with a splendid, classical economy. (According to most sources, these expository passages were the only part of the film's scenario which was finished when shooting began.) Yet we barely notice how carefully the plot is being set in motion; nothing feels obligatory or purely formal. The camera moves fluidly through the beautiful set (designed by Eugène Lourié) of La Chesnaye's Paris apartment, and the actors seem to be gliding through their scenes with equal ease. There's an almost insolent grace in these passages: Renoir and his company have the nerve to play this Comédie Française material as if nothing could be more natural. It goes down as easily as the Mozart we hear over the opening credits. Every line, every gesture, looks as if it had been invented on the spot. And more than one probably was. The screenplay credit for the film reads, "Jean Renoir, with the collaboration of Karl Koch, Camille François . . . and the actors." "I improvised a lot," Renoir said in an interview. "The actors are also the authors of a film, and when you're in their presence they give you reactions you couldn't have foreseen; these reactions are often good, and you'd be crazy not to take advantage of them. . . . I have a certain tendency to be a little theoretical when I begin work: I say what I mean a bit too clearly, rather like a lecturer, and it's extremely tedious. Little by little (and contact with the actors helps me enormously in this), I try to get closer to the way in which, in real life, people are able to incorporate their theories while still being subject to the thousand impedimenta of life, the thousand little events, the thousand little feelings that make it impossible to remain theoretical."

The actors who collaborated with Renoir on *The Rules of the Game* were in most cases not his first choices for their roles. His original choice for La Chesnaye was the polished Claude Dauphin; the role finally went to Marcel Dalio, who had played Rosenthal, the urbane Jewish banker's son who escapes from the prisoner-of-war camp with Maréchal, the working-class Parisian played by Gabin, in *Grand Illusion*. Dalio's warm and rather excitable manner transforms the character of the Marquis from a chilly, "theoretical" creation into a remarkably vivid and ambiguous presence on the screen. His Marquis is in many ways a hypocrite—an empty, superficial man—but he's also touching and likable, and his superb manners aren't entirely meaningless gestures; they're evidence of a sincere, if unfocused, benevolence. Renoir wanted Gabin for André Jurieu, but he wound up with a young leading-man type named Roland Toutain, whose open, boyish features suggest—perhaps better than Gabin's would—the hero's profound unworldliness, his head-in-the-clouds romanticism. Christine was to have been played by Simone Simon, the femme fatale of *La Bête Humaine* (and later, appropriately, the heroine of Val Lewton and Jacques Tourneur's eerie *Cat People*). Renoir settled for Nora Grégor, an Austrian actress who happened to be an aristocrat—the Princess Starhemberg. She spoke very little French, and Renoir later expressed regret at having cast her, but the stiffness of her movements and the halting, uncertain quality of her line readings seem right for Christine, who is a true innocent—a woman whose emotional directness makes her an alien in the smoothly mendacious social world she inhabits. And

Grégor's German accent provides a subtle link to another character whose sense of rectitude sets him apart—the grim-faced, upright Alsatian gamekeeper, Schumacher, who is married to the Marquise's flirtatious maid, Lisette. Schumacher is a conscientious servant and a firm believer in (and enforcer of) the rules of sport and marriage, but he's so rigid that virtually everyone—even the tolerant Marquis—finds him unendurable. The only person who shows any respect for him is Christine; she's also the only one who pronounces his name in the German, rather than the French, way. When Fernand Ledoux was unable to play the role, Renoir turned to the taller, much more severe-looking Gaston Modot, who makes the gamekeeper both pathetic and frightening. A *Rules of the Game* with Dauphin, Gabin, Simon, and Ledoux now seems unimaginable. It might have been just as great, but it wouldn't have been *this* film—the one we know, and whose vision is so consistent and so powerful that its every detail has retrospectively taken on the glow of inevitability.

The key role of Octave, the confidant, was no easier to cast. Originally, it was to have been played by Pierre Renoir, Jean's older brother—an accomplished actor, who had starred in three of Renoir's films (*La Nuit du Carrefour*, *Madame Bovary*, and *La Marseillaise*). When theater commitments forced Pierre to drop out, Jean decided to take the role himself. Although he had played bit parts in some of his previous movies (and in each case had hammed it up energetically), he had never before given himself such an important role. His performance turned out to be one of the most controversial aspects of the film. A representative of Gaumont, which had agreed to distribute the film, was reported to be so unhappy with Renoir's playing of Octave that he prevailed on the director to cut some of his own scenes. (Renoir, ever adaptable, proposed replacing himself with Michel Simon and reshooting Octave's scenes, but the filming was too far along for that to be practical.) When the picture opened, the many critics who disliked it singled out Renoir's acting for particular scorn. The tendency since has been to ascribe perhaps too much significance to the director's presence in front of the camera, to assume that the role of Octave—a failed musician who never emerged from the shadow of the great conductor (Christine's father) who was his mentor and father figure—somehow had special meaning for Jean Renoir. But the father theme is a minor resonance at best—no more striking than dozens of others and, in any event, Renoir's casting of himself as Octave was unplanned, just one of many accidents he took advantage of. (Besides, there is no evidence that Jean's relationship with his famous father was especially anguished; in his sixties, he wrote a wonderfully sane, perceptive book called *Renoir, My Father*.) The real importance of Renoir's playing Octave in *The Rules of the Game* is that it puts him in the middle of things, right in there with his actor-collaborators. His character— rumpled, amiable, and unthreatening—is everyone's friend. He flirts with the women, jokes with the men, acts as go-between and peace- maker in volatile situations. Everybody trusts him; everybody seems to loosen up a little in his company. And he speaks the line that is probably the most succinct expression of the movie's spirit: "In this world there is one terrible thing, and that is that everyone has his reasons." It's a perfect role for Jean Renoir, and he throws himself into it happily, recklessly. He looks delighted, as if he were breaking down a barrier, knocking down walls.

In an interview with Truffaut and Rivette (in the fifties, when both were critics for *Cahiers du Cinéma*, and not yet filmmakers), Renoir gave a lovely metaphorical description of his working meth- ods: "You walk in the country, you know that you're going to arrive at a certain spot near the path, and that there will be a meadow with poplars there; you see the meadow and the poplars, first in your imagination, then for real, you stop, you look; at first you see only a meadow and poplar trees; little by little, subtler emanations, tricks of light, certain contrasts, certain relationships appear, which are the essence of the landscape, much more important than the meadow and the poplars, but you can only see them after having seen the meadow and the poplars." This approach to artistic practice, based on intuition and a highly developed receptiveness to experience, served Renoir well throughout his career. It's what enabled him in *Grand Illusion* to aim for a simple antiwar message and the illustra- tion of the democratic ideals of the leftist Popular Front, and to arrive at something far richer—a lucid and stirring dream of comradeship, heroism, and freedom. He had the rare gift of making ideals palpa- ble, giving them flesh and texture; watching *Grand Illusion*, with its abundance of exactly rendered physical details and vibrantly ambiguous human relationships, we actually believe, at least for the duration of the film, that this vision of courage and integrity and mutual tolerance corresponds to something real—that Renoir's camera has led us to an elusive place where the light hits the landscape just right and everything we didn't think existed is suddenly there before our eyes. In *The Rules of the Game* he takes himself, and us, even farther. After the classically precise exposition, the Marquis's guests begin arriving, in a driving rain, at La Colinière, and the emanations and tricks of light, the contrasts and relationships hit us almost faster than our eyes can register them: from here on, every moment is radiant. And, with Renoir shambling through the movie in the baggy disguise of Octave, it's as if he were looking at this landscape and finding, to his surprise, that he's in it, too—one of the poplars. What we're looking at in *The Rules of the Game* is the sum of Renoir's knowledge of the culture that produced him, seen from the outside and from the inside: the path and the meadow.

It seems a small thing, but the downpour that greets the guests at the château is somehow emblematic. In a sense, they're taking their places on the stage, assembling for the second act of a farce whose machinery is already humming with the assurance that its classical operations will be carried out smoothly, but their entrances are unexpectedly messy, disrupted, chaotic. It's at this point, perhaps, that we realize that Renoir's classicism isn't going to be of the sort we're accustomed to. As much as these European literary and theatrical traditions are in his bones, as much as he loves the art that shaped him, this rain is in his bones, too: the common accidents of nature that foul up the works—disturb the poise of people striding confidently to their assigned spots, force them to hurry their pace, slip, stumble, mutter breathless inanities, and forget the speeches they've prepared—and that film alone can show us in the most essential, physical way. This is not to say that Renoir is doing anything as straightforward as setting up classical structures in order to subvert them. Even in this scene of wet, flustered arrivals, order quickly reasserts itself. After greeting Jurieu, Christine commands everyone's attention with the announcement "Dear friends, I must let you in on a little secret about my relationship with André Jurieu." Smiling warmly (if a bit self-consciously), she gives a short, elegantly phrased speech about her "small part in the success of his exploit."

She says, "We spent many hours together—very pleasant hours—hours passed under the sign of that rare thing friendship. He told me about his plans and I listened to him. . . . I'm very proud of it! And I felt the need to tell you about it now." It's quite a performance, and her listeners respond with bravos and appreciative laughter, as if she were an actress who had just carried off a particularly tricky scene in a Molière play. Later, La Chesnaye thanks her: "It was an unbearable test in which you acquitted yourself admirably. I must compliment you on it." The inconvenient emotions having been disposed of by Christine's tact and self-control, the guests—except for the disconsolate Jurieu—are free to go about the business of amusing themselves: they break into groups for cards and billiards, talk about the upcoming hunt, plan a fancy-dress celebration for the following week. "We'll put on a comedy!" La Chesnaye exclaims.

From here on, as the real comedy—Renoir's, not La Chesnaye's—plays itself out, the movie keeps veering, with thrilling abandon, between the poles of pure formality (social and aesthetic) and something wild and unpredictable: the ungovernable forces of love and nature. Renoir is trying not to undermine classicism but, in a way, to reinvent it—to explore whether it's possible to retain its elegance, its grace, its serene rhythms while making full use of the riskier and less disciplined energy of film. In his book about his father he quotes these aphorisms from Auguste Renoir's notebooks:

> It is impossible to repeat in one period what was done in another. The point of view is not the same, any more than are the tools, the ideas, the needs or the painters' techniques.
>
> An artist, under pain of oblivion, must have confidence in himself, and listen only to his real master: Nature.
>
> The greatest enemy of the worker and the industrial artist is certainly the machine.
>
> There are people who imagine that one can redo the Middle Ages and the Renaissance with impunity. One can only copy: that is the watchword. And after such folly has continued long enough, go back to the sources. You will see how far away we have got from them.
>
> Consider the great masters of the past. They were aware that there are two regularities: that of the eye and that of the compass. The great masters rejected the latter.

Jean Renoir interprets his father's remarks this way: "He was torn between two procedures: direct perception, on the one hand, and tradition, on the other; it was a question of method and not of principle." *The Rules of the Game* might almost have been designed to test the beliefs that Auguste Renoir passed on to his son. The whole import of this film, the great theme that emerges from the dazzling play of light on this landscape, is that the social and aesthetic forms of the past—the traditions that shaped Jean Renoir and his generation—have become mechanical, inhospitable to life. Their regularity is that of the compass, not the eye. The people gathered at La Colinière, all of whom Renoir loves even when they behave badly (perhaps because he makes so little distinction between the actors and the characters), are struggling inside various machines—structures that appear sometimes hostile to them, sometimes accommodating, but are in fact always fundamentally indifferent.

It's no accident that the Marquis has a passion for automatons. (They were all the rage in the eighteenth century, too.) His Paris apartment is filled with mechanical figurines: warbling birds, a musical doll in the form of a black girl. ("It's a little romantic Negress," La Chesnaye says delightedly. "The mechanism is perfect.") During the musical-comedy revue that the Marquis and his guests perform on the last night of their week-long house party, there's a remarkable shot of a player piano, its keys moving up and down by themselves in the darkened drawing room: it's playing Saint-Saëns's *Danse Macabre*, and the camera pans to the stage, where, against a black background, figures in ghost costumes appear, followed by one in a skeleton suit, and begin to dance. This is one of the most astonishing shots in movie history, and Renoir tops it just a few seconds later with a long pan across the back of the room which catches various characters running off with other people's partners and hiding from their own as the eerie light flickers across the spectators' faces. (In one of the brief shots linking these two virtuoso camera movements, we see an ornate mirror, and for an instant we find among the guests the reflection of the ghosts and the skeleton dancing on the stage.) Soon afterward, La Chesnaye, who has been dashing madly around the chateau looking for Christine, appears onstage to present the climax of the evening's entertainment—"the culmination," he says, "of my career as a collector of musical and mechanical instruments."

The curtain opens to reveal a gigantic mechanical organ, called a *limonaire;* it's a ridiculous-looking contraption, decorated with elaborately kitschy paintings and carvings and, in the center, three little statues of boys. As the organ begins to play (a jangling, monotonous rendition of a melody from *Die Fledermaus*), the camera pans again, discovering, in close-up, first one mechanical boy, striking a bell, then a second, beating time, then the last, striking another bell, and, finally, La Chesnaye, in his dinner jacket, nervously dividing his attention between his great acquisition and the audience he so desperately wants to please.

In a 1966 television program, Renoir and Dalio, two old men sitting on the steps of the Château de la Ferté-Saint-Aubin, reminisce about the making of *The Rules of the Game*. Renoir says of the character of the Marquis, "We discovered it as we went along. What excited me about that story, and excites me still in my memory of it, is that we produced your character and the whole story of the film—since it revolves around your character—as we went along; we didn't follow a plan or a map. You see, what I think is deadliest in our times is the plan, the architect's blueprint. . . . The Marquis de la Chesnaye wasn't produced by the work of engineers, it was produced by memories; I have known many Marquis de la Chesnaye." Then Renoir reminds Dalio of the pan across the *limonaire,* and the actor recalls how much trouble he had playing that scene, how many takes he needed to get the Marquis's expression just right. Renoir cuts him off: "But what a shot! I think it's the best shot I did in my life. Oh, it's fantastic! The mixture of humility and pride, of success and doubt. Nothing definite—on the margin of many things." The director's enthusiasm is charming, and so is his graciousness in attributing the greatness of the shot to Dalio's performance, and not to his own conception, his own plan. "At first, I had the wrong idea," he says. "I thought it could be an improvised shot. But it couldn't be; it had to be worked at, in shooting and reshooting." What Renoir seems to have discovered in the course of making the shot he considered the best of his career are the things he spent his life discovering and rediscovering, in shot after shot and film after film: that nothing is, or should be, predictable; that you have to attend always to what is actually before your eyes, and be willing to discard any notions you elaborated in advance; and that in movies (and elsewhere) repetition is sometimes the only route to the unexpected, the unforeseeable.

The shot that Renoir and Dalio remember so vividly almost thirty years later is one of those startling moments in which the essence of the landscape is revealed: both the film's meanings and its processes are abruptly flooded with light. The idea of the shot couldn't be clearer: that there's a fundamental connection between the Marquis and the silly little figures on the *limonaire*—that he is, like them, in some sense an automaton, a parody of something, a copy, a triumphantly useless product of engineering. Even if all we took from the scene were this satiric point, that would still be quite a bit. It might help us to understand, for instance, why the first shot of *The Rules of the Game* is of a radio sound engineer surrounded by his equipment; the camera escapes from this maze of machinery by following the path of a cable to its end, a microphone in the hands of the announcer reporting Jurieu's historic landing at Le Bourget. And why the second shot is of the airplane—why our first look at the hero is this image of a tiny, fragile machine approaching from a distance. We may understand, too, the full significance of Jurieu's revealing his most intimate feelings to the reporter's inert, indifferent microphone, and of Christine's learning of his love for her by listening to his faint, static-distorted voice on the radio. And we may begin to recognize—if we haven't done so already—the extraordinary intricacy of the film's metaphors. The Marquis's mechanical creatures, Jurieu's flying machine, the birds and rabbits that are hunted for sport, the servants who go through their paces so that their masters' lives can run like clockwork are all variations on a single, infinitely complex theme: the relationship between culture and nature, between the arts we've acquired and the world that makes sport of our proud inventions. All these metaphors and suggestions are present in the design of the *limonaire* shot, in the idea of it—and for that reason they're not enough for Renoir. He wouldn't settle for what planning, even at its most inspired, could give him. He kept exploring, in take after take, until his actor at last came through with that miraculous expression: a look that, in its human complexity, transcends the satiric content of the scene—that smudges the blueprint's elegant lines and somehow makes them more beautiful.

* * *

The genius of Renoir is that, like so many of his characters, he has two loves: to him reality and artifice are equally irresistible. He embraces his own contradictions; they put him where he wants to be, on the margin of many things. Late in his life, he often sounded as if he dogmatically loathed anything artificial or mechanical. In an interview published in 1959, the year of the restoration of *The Rules of the Game* (it was also the year in which he made *The Testament of Dr. Cordelier* and *Picnic on the Grass*, both of which are rather single-minded attacks on modern science), he said, "All technical refinements depress me. The perfection of photography, the big screens, the stereo sound, all of it makes possible a servile reproduction of nature; and that reproduction bores me. What interests me is the interpretation an artist makes of life. The artist's personality interests me more than the copying of an object." Like his father, Renoir has nothing but contempt for the notion that nature could, or should, be copied; the object will always be finer and more mysterious than its reproduction. But he isn't—or, in any event, wasn't at the time of *The Rules of the Game*—a pure Luddite, an unthinking enemy of technology. Although his work as a filmmaker began in the silent era, he welcomed sound, and made more imaginative use of it than anyone else in the thirties; he worked brilliantly with the improved lenses that allowed greater depth of focus; and he didn't resist color, either. (At one point, he considered shooting *The Rules of the Game* in color.) In his autobiography, which appeared in 1974, he makes the surprising statement that he has become "a worshiper of the artificial." What he hates isn't so much the machine itself as the attitude it engenders—the feeling that nature can be trapped, conquered, brought under our control by technical ingenuity. Everything that the characters possess in *The Rules of the Game* and all the activities they undertake have been engineered to keep the real world, and their own natures, at a distance. Everything that Renoir does in this picture—with the camera, with the actors, and in his own performance—is designed to reduce that distance.

The subtlety of his means of closing the gaps—between culture and nature, between what we've mastered and what we never will, between the reassuring past and the elusive, confounding present— is nowhere clearer than in the famous sequence of the hunt, which is in every sense the film's centerpiece. It depicts a traditional pastime of the class Renoir is examining ("a sport which I detest . . . an abominable exercise in cruelty," he once wrote), and it's also, in technical terms, the sequence in the film which is most closely linked to the silent-movie aesthetic of montage. Elsewhere in *The Rules of the Game* Renoir films the action with very long takes, lots of camera movement, and extremely deep focus; he cuts only when he has to. André Bazin, who understood Renoir better than anyone else, wrote that the director "forced himself to look back beyond the resources provided by montage and so uncovered the secret of a film form that would permit everything to be said without chopping the world up into little fragments, that would reveal the hidden meanings in people and things without disturbing the unity natural to them." But while the rabbits and birds are being slaughtered the shots are brief and the editing is fast. (In the three-and-a-half-minute sequence in which the animals are killed, there are fifty separate shots, out of only 337 in the entire film.) This scene represents a conscious break in the movie's easy, flowing rhythm, and it occurs at virtually the midpoint of the narrative: we experience it viscerally as something jarring, unnatural—the intrusion of a kind of technical artifice our senses told us had been abandoned. And the scene is overwhelming. The killing seems interminable, as if time had halted in its tracks, and the uncharacteristic abruptness of the cutting expresses precisely the essence of our sense of violation. Many of the shots are in fact truncated examples of the fluid camera style we see elsewhere in the movie. The camera gets a rabbit in its sights and tries to follow it as it runs, panicked, from the beaters and the hunters, and after a few, blurry seconds we hear the report of a rifle and everything stops: the brief exhilaration of high-speed movement is arrested with terrible suddenness and finality, the moving camera pulls up like a dog jerked back by its leash, and the shot has, within a sickeningly short time, become what it never meant to be—a fixed, stunned close-up of a lifeless object.

It's as if Renoir, having set himself the task of recording this time-honored ritual in which the upper classes express their power over the natural world, found himself forced into a style at odds with his own nature. For three and a half frantic minutes, he is trapped in the stern mechanism of classic montage and can't escape: no matter how fast he moves, every shot seems to end with something dead, and he has to keep cutting. The reason the sequence is so wrenching is that Renoir makes us feel the frenzy of his struggle not to give in to this imposed rhythm. The last rabbit the camera follows is, like the others, brought up short by a burst of gunfire, but, since there are no further sounds of shooting, Renoir allows himself to linger on the image of the dead animal, to show us that it continues to twitch, weakly, for a few seconds—a mysterious persistence of the nerves and the muscles, a reminder of the stubborn need of living things to remain in motion.

In those three or four extra seconds, the movie begins to breathe again, to recover—with tremendous relief—the natural rhythm of its unique sense of life. The sequence isn't over yet, and the longer, more flowing takes that follow fill us with a kind of melancholy joy. After the spectacle of organized destruction—sanctioned by tradition and not questioned by those who participate in it—Renoir's openness and ease seem even more precious. The stakes have been raised: the tension between the old forms inherited by the people of Renoir's time and the new forms he is trying to discover in his filmmaking has become something far more fundamental and more passionate than a theoretical opposition. The textures of the vast gray sky and the slender trees, the glimpse of a bird in flight, the way the actors move, and the way the camera moves with them all seem to matter more than they did before.

It's at this point, as the servants retrieve the carcasses, and the characters search for each other and begin to resume their normal social intercourse, that the mechanism of the farce starts to break down, that the warps in the classical structure of the comedy are unmistakably exposed. Here, in the open air of the estate, Christine discovers her husband's infidelity. As La Chesnaye and his mistress, together on the bank of a marsh, discuss his decision to end their affair, Christine, far away, is amusing herself with a small telescope that one of the guests has lent her. Through it she first watches a squirrel in a tree: "I can see it as though I could touch it!" she exclaims (as the camera holds the animal in a close-up that, disconcertingly, recalls to us our vision of the dying rabbit). The owner of the telescope boasts that the instrument allows its user to share the animal's "intimate life." It allows the Marquise, a few moments later, an unexpected view of the intimate life of her husband, who is saying farewell to his mistress with an especially warm embrace. (And, while Christine watches, Renoir, as Octave, is at her side, pestering her to let him see what she's looking at.)

In the heady aftermath of the shoot—that graphic display of her class's illusion that it has mastered the world—Christine, by chance, has a glimpse of something real: evidence that her husband's beautiful manners, his exquisitely correct behavior, don't tell quite the whole story of his nature. And the recognition of this bit of dirt inside her smooth-running life is enough to send her spinning out of control. She becomes volatile, erratic, as if her internal compass had gone haywire. On the last night of the party—the night of the amateur theatrics and the unveiling of the *limonaire*—she whirls through La Colinière in a kind of moral panic, disrupting everyone else's plans and expectations as she gives in to a series of capricious attractions, looking frantically for the one that will stabilize her again. She allows herself to be carried off by one of the guests, a rather oily Casanova named Saint-Aubin; then she begs Jurieu to take her away from her husband; then she falls, awkwardly, into the arms of Octave (who eventually gives her back to Jurieu). The men, including La Chesnaye, chase her, plead with her, fight over her, lose her, run after her again, while the camera, serenely intoxicated with its freedom in the midst of this havoc, moves gracefully through the rooms and hallways of the château and, finally, outside, missing nothing, although everything is happening at once. In a sense, all this activity is just the playing out of the classic door-slamming farce that was set up so expertly in the film's first third. The difference is that in Renoir's world the doors are all wide open, and remain that way. There's no place for anyone to hide: we catch sight of the characters through receding doorways, and they're in focus even when they're far in the background.

And while Christine's unpredictability is forcing everyone around her into frenzied motion her counterpart, Schumacher, is also on a rampage: waving a handgun, the gamekeeper is stalking a servant named Marceau (a former poacher, whom the Marquis has recently put on the domestic staff), because he has been flirting with Lisette. This slapstick chase starts in the kitchen but quickly spills over into the rooms where the Marquis's guests are enjoying their civilized amusements. In the drawing room, where the guests are by now playing cards, Schumacher fires at Marceau (marvelously played by Julien Carette, whose movements are as nimble as a rabbit's). After the initial shock, the ladies and gentlemen decide that this ludicrous melodrama must be part of the evening's entertainment, a bit of theater arranged by their charming and ingenious host. At the height of the chaos, La Chesnaye orders his butler, Corneille, to "put a stop to this comedy," and Corneille replies, "Which one, Monsieur le Marquis?" No one can quite accept that all the evening's fierce emotions are real: La Chesnaye, who has been screaming and flailing about and throwing punches at Jurieu, ruefully compares the drama he has been taking part in with something he might read in the papers about "an Italian laborer" who "tried to carry off the wife of a Polish worker and . . . it finished up with a stabbing." He says, "I didn't believe such things possible." These lower-order emotions not only are possible but are capable of fouling up even the most precisely regulated mechanisms: in the midst of the shooting and carrying on, the Marquis's *limonaire* has gone berserk, its monotonous tune transformed into a horrible, dissonant clanging of parts.

The harmonies of the characters' lives have dissolved in cacophony, yet we watch and listen to the resolution of this tragic farce with a strange sense of calm, as if—like the bum, at the end of *Boudu Saved from Drowning*, who allows the Seine to carry him away from the respectable bourgeois world—we were abandoning ourselves to a sudden, strong current, forgetting everything in the euphoria of headlong motion. The rhythm that Renoir discovers in the hectic final act of *The Rules of the Game* isn't exhausting; it's varied, virtuosic—as light and as inexplicably moving as a great piece of chamber music. Among all the wild, hilarious scenes of servants in uniform dashing about maniacally and trying to keep their footing on the superbly polished floors, and of the upper classes, in formal dress or still in their music-hall costumes, bellowing and taking inept swings at each other, there are a number of slow, contemplative passages in which one character finds himself or herself alone with another, away from the rest. Jurieu and La Chesnaye apologize to

each other; Schumacher and Marceau console each other for the loss
of their jobs; Christine and Octave reminisce about her father, the
famous conductor—Octave standing on the steps of the château,
facing the house in which the chaos is still going on, and raising his
arms as if to begin conducting, then stopping, defeated. (This scene
was among those eliminated before the film's premiere.) Octave, the
genial failure, seems to know what the man who plays him knows:
that his gestures are worthless if they're only imitation, only a repetition of something learned long ago. At the moment when his arms
freeze in the air, Renoir looks as if he were hearing the voice of his
father: "Go back to the sources. You will see how far away we have
got from them."

   The gestures of Jean Renoir the filmmaker, conducting his ensemble of actors and technicians, are never arrested in this way.
Every movement he makes, every direction he gives, seems to produce a pure, clear tone—something we have never heard before
and yet recognize immediately. His subject is how far we've gone
from our sources while clinging to their forms. The miraculous
paradox of *The Rules of the Game* is that Renoir, while examining the
distance between the powerful emotions of these cultured Euro-
peans and the feeble, tinny expressive means at their disposal, has
somehow managed to reanimate the classical spirit—to make the
music of reason seem once again the music of the heart. And we feel,
throughout, that what he has done wouldn't have been possible in
any medium but film—that his rediscovery of the sources of his
culture is in some sense a consequence of his exploration of the
resources of this still young art. Renoir often expressed his admiration for the cinema's pioneers, the inventors and improvisers—
those who used the art, unself-consciously, as a thrilling new form
of play, a game whose rules you could make up as you went along.
He was especially awed by Mack Sennett, who, he said, would
gather his company around him every day and say to them, "What
are we going to do this morning?" Renoir wrote in his autobiography, "The earliest films were the direct expression of the dreams of
the filmmaker and bore his unmistakable signature, together with all
the influences that had combined to shape him." Renoir carried a
much heavier load of influences—he could hardly have willed him-

self to be a primitive artist, to undo the tradition and history that shaped him—but he was able to express himself, in all his complexity, on film as directly and unmistakably as his distant predecessors had done. The cinema, not burdened with much of a past, was the ideal field for him to play in, and the joy of playing is in large part what *The Rules of the Game* is about. The French title is richer, more apt, and more ambiguous, since *jeu* means more than a game: it can also refer to the playing of music, and to acting, the playing of scenes—that is, to the varieties of play that Renoir loves the most.

In *The Rules of the Game* Renoir, working equally out of his own memories and out of what must have seemed the infinite possibilities of film, discovers a classicism that isn't confining or mechanical. We can be open to anything, as mobile and receptive as the eye of the camera, the movie says, and yet remain lucid. The sadness that overtakes us at the end of the film comes from the recognition that its attractive, sympathetic characters are playing their lives very poorly—by rote or not at all. The ones who can't seem to manage with any kind of skill, like Jurieu, pay the heaviest price: trying to escape with Christine, in the darkness outside the château, he's shot and killed by Schumacher. (The inept gamekeeper thinks that Christine, who's wearing Lisette's hooded cape, is his wife, and that Jurieu is Octave.) On the run, the victim crumples with shocking suddenness, in a plain, startled medium shot: as Marceau reports, "he rolled over like an animal." The fatal accident is absurd, and a violation of the rules of farce, yet it feels inevitable—the ultimate expression of a world in which no one sees anything for what it is. As people gather on the steps of the château, everyone looks lost, shattered, confused, few of them knowing what has happened and none of them knowing why. For the last time, the Marquis, standing at the top of the steps (at the spot where Octave attempted to conduct the phantom orchestra), marshals his considerable skills to carry off a difficult moment. Having instructed the butler to "deal with the formalities," La Chesnaye, hollow-eyed and weary, tells the guests that the gamekeeper "thought he saw a poacher, and fired, since that is his duty," and briefly eulogizes the dead aviator.

As in the *limonaire* shot, the actor's expression is on the margin of many things, now showing sadness and relief at once, along with a desperate emptiness. We can't look at him without recalling that earlier shot: the image that revealed this elegant man as a fidgety, helpless mechanical doll is lodged in our minds, and its memory complicates our reactions to the Marquis's glib performance on the steps. We can't condemn him, somehow, for the ease with which he lies. For the Marquis and his kind the denial of reality is simply a reflex, a tic, no more willed than the ghostly twitching of an animal that has been shot—movement that once gave evidence of the presence of life but now signifies nothing at all. And Dalio's playing has a sorrowful eloquence: his deadened eyes and his limply grace-ful gestures are a terrifying, melancholy image of an exhausted spirit. He's like a puppet wearing out from the strain of repetition: he has been required to perform his limited repertoire of moves too many times.

As the Marquis finishes his speech—having discharged his duty of providing the assembled guests with the illusion of closure, the comfort of resolution—we begin to hear music, a melody resonant with the exalting clarity of the eighteenth century. It's from *Le Déser-teur*, an opera by Monsigny, and it's incomprehensibly moving: how is it possible for something so precise, so deftly measured, to stir us so profoundly? Its formal beauty seems to come from somewhere deep in our memories, as if everything that came before us, and made us, were present again in the most immediate way. We can almost believe that sounds like these are capable of reanimating parts of our imaginations we've never known how to use, of re-storing power to rooms that were closed up before we were born. In *The Rules of the Game* Renoir makes the world look larger, less constricting, with more space to live and play in. The final image is inseparable from the music that accompanies it, just as the film is inseparable from the music that inspired it: a stately procession of trembling shadows moves across the walls of La Colinière as the characters go back inside. Like so many other moments in this film, the image is simple yet fathomlessly suggestive, filling our minds with echoes and ideas. It tells us most obviously that the world these people live in is spectral, bodiless, vanishing before our eyes in an involuntary danse macabre. But the sheer loveliness of the image and its unearthly serenity are difficult to account for. We feel in it, perhaps, some of Renoir's sadness at the end of play: his reluctance to leave the world he has been immersed in; his knowledge that the people and things he has lived with have now become, irrevocably, shadows on a screen. The movement of the dark forms has a dream-like, reflective rhythm, the deliberate pace of memories drifting behind closed eyes. It's as if in becoming shadows the Marquis and his guests and his servants had achieved the dignity, the true grace, that their worldly manners could only imitate. The distance between what these people could be and what they allow themselves to be is heartbreaking, but they have at least served as the instruments for measuring that distance, for enabling us to see ourselves more clearly, and Renoir, in this last shot, pays them homage for their service. As their shadows file across the screen, returning home, they merge, somehow, with all the spirits that *The Rules of the Game* has summoned up—Baroque composers, classical dramatists, the artist's father—and with the members of the audience rising from their seats to leave the theater, carrying these images now as part of themselves. The shadows are everything that Jean Renoir found in himself and exposed to light.

The New Yorker, June 25, 1990

Part Two

DIRECTORS

Martin Scorsese

Martin Scorsese has stopped moving. The whirling, volatile camera of *Mean Streets, Alice Doesn't Live Here Anymore, Taxi Driver* has been slowing down gradually over the years, steadying itself, settling into the fixed position it finally assumes in *The King of Comedy*: an almost classical *mise en scène,* cut to the stately, regular editing rhythms of the traditional American narrative film. *The King of Comedy* isn't a dull movie: the story of an aggressive aspiring comedian named Rupert Pupkin (Robert De Niro) who besieges talk-show host Jerry Langford (Jerry Lewis) in the hope of landing a spot on his show, it has—like *Taxi Driver*—a built-in, grotesque fascination, and Scorsese's newly stripped-down style serves it well. But it's a static situation. Scorsese explains his conception of the film this way: "I can make each shot moving, but I didn't find any reason for it. Everybody in this movie is impassable, they're like rocks: Lewis is here, he ain't going to budge; Rupert is here, *he*'s not going to; Shelley Hack [who plays Jerry Langford's assistant] is here. . . . Everybody's so rigid that just a medium shot of them talking to each other would do." This fixed quality isn't new in Scorsese's work, but in the past it has been his characters' *final* state—the earlier films' furious movement often culminated in stasis, immobility, even death. In the new film, the characters are dead right from the start. *The King of Comedy* is a message from beyond the grave of ambition, from the afterlife of achieved success.

Scorsese describes the new film as a "reassessment." "It's like

35

looking back on the years before. Jerry Langford is what I am now, to a certain extent. The film is a kind of bridge—to where, I don't know. It's like starting all over." Though *The King of Comedy* doesn't feel as passionate and personal as Scorsese's description—it seems more an epilogue than a climax—the film does recapitulate the themes of the director's post–*Taxi Driver* work: the establishment of identity in public and the ambiguous relationship of self to performance.

The real climax of the story that Scorsese has been telling in his recent work is the complex, unnerving final scene of *Raging Bull*, in which the retired Jake La Motta, encased now in evening clothes and his own massive flesh, sits before a mirror in his dressing room rehearsing a speech for his one-man stage show. The reading is Brando's famous taxicab scene from *On the Waterfront*, the eloquent monologue in which Terry Malloy accuses his brother of ruining his career by encouraging him to throw a fight. It's a scene that La Motta has lived through—he, too, has taken a dive, sacrificed his pride at the instigation of his pragmatic brother—but there's no conviction in his reading. La Motta is an entertainer now, a glossy abstraction of his former self, his fighter's body gone to comfortable flab, a cushion against the pain and punishment that have defined his life. His flat reading tells us that he's not feeling the pain any more, but is simply alluding to it, *using* it because it's what the audience expects, it's how they recognize a "Jake La Motta" who's nearly unrecognizable otherwise.

Scorsese refers to this as the "redemption scene" in *Raging Bull*. "We should all have such peace," he says, and it's true that there's a resignation in La Motta that contrasts sharply with the uneasy, combative persona of the younger man (and that contrasts, too, with his transitional stage as nightclub owner and comedian, making hostile, unfunny jokes based on his own sexual paranoia and his contempt for the audience). But the toneless reading, the distance from reality (De Niro as La Motta as Brando as Terry Malloy, reading a movie-script version of one of the most painful experiences in the fighter's life), and the vacancy of La Motta's slitted eyes, nearly invisible in the fleshy mask of his face—all make this, at best, an ambiguous redemption. La Motta hasn't died and gone to heaven; he's died and gone onstage.

The chill in the last scene of *Raging Bull* pervades *The King of Comedy*. The film confines itself to a stifling, hermetic show-biz world: there isn't a scene in the film that is not related to celebrity and its pursuit. It begins with television—the introduction to Jerry Langford's late-night talk show; a caricature of Jerry against a hideous purple curtain, an oozing voice-over announcing his entrance before the "live" star walks on—and ends with television, as a stiff, glassy-eyed Rupert Pupkin is introduced as the star of his own show. These scenes are like quotation marks, distancing with irony everything in between them: the "real-life" action of the film can't shake off the insidious, glossy inauthenticity of the images that frame it.

The basement where Rupert spends his time when he's at home is done up in the bright, anonymous decor of a talk-show set, and he hosts his own "show" there every morning before work, trading show-biz banter with life-size cardboard cutouts of Liza Minnelli and Jerry Langford, kissing their flat, grinning faces when he's "gotta run." Except for brief bursts of anger at his mother (unseen but very clearly heard) and at the crazed fan Masha, who helps him kidnap Jerry, Rupert never slips out of the TV-smoothie persona he's created for himself: his loud clothes (he wears a red-white-and-blue outfit through the first half of the picture) and hard, manufactured-looking hairdo and mustache are like armor protecting him from the difficulty of the world, from reality itself—the kind of armor that the fat, tuxedoed La Motta has acquired by the final scene of *Raging Bull*, after years of standing almost naked in the boxing ring, absorbing punishment.

This anesthetized quality isn't unique to Rupert. It's shared by all the characters in *The King of Comedy*, including Jerry Langford, the character Scorsese claims is what he is now. Langford seems to have no human relationships; he has only fans and employees. Instead of friends, he has the "guests" at his endless talk-show party—human intimacy only marginally less illusory than Rupert's cardboard fantasies in his basement. Langford is as isolated in his celebrity as Rupert is in his illusions of celebrity: the most basic kinds of human communication are missing from their lives, or distorted into parody. When someone knits a sweater for Jerry, it's not a wife or a girlfriend or a mother, it's crazy Masha; when Rupert shows Jerry a picture of his "pride and joy," it turns out to be a dumb joke, a wallet-size picture of the furniture polish Pride and the dishwashing liquid Joy. And every stage of Rupert's courtship of Rita, the girl he had a crush on in high school, is mediated by his show-biz obsessions: on their first date, he shows her his collection of celebrity autographs; their second date is a trip to Langford's country home, where Rupert thinks he has been invited for the weekend; their last meeting, in the bar where Rita works, consists of watching Rupert's monologue on the bar TV. Langford's Manhattan apartment is as elegantly desolate as his talk-show set or his corporate offices, where Rupert waits to see him. For company, as Langford sits down to dinner, he has a TV set (showing *Pickup on South Street* with the sound off); when he answers the phone, it's Masha.

Scorsese calls attention to the absences, the vacancy of these lives through the absence of his characteristically extravagant visual and narrative techniques. It's a far cry from the teeming, anecdotal narrative of *Mean Streets*, the camera that wouldn't stay still, framing and reframing the action as if it couldn't see *enough*. In *The King of Comedy*, Scorsese operates from a minimalist aesthetic, taking more and more away until only the barest plot, the most functional and abstract compositions are left. "I kept saying to myself, 'Maybe I should move the camera. People are going to say I didn't direct this because the camera's not moving.' And then I said, 'Don't be a schmuck, the director doesn't have to be a person who moves the camera.' You have to know when *not* to move the camera. I wanted the material and the characters to carry the depth of the story—the size of the frame, too. The camera moves with people, either tracks or pans, but that's about it. I wanted the characters to hold the frame." And just as camera movement is reduced to a minimum, so is narrative information. Scorsese admits, "I had trouble with the film because it was a straight story line. I had difficulty directing certain key story images to help the story along, and sure enough a lot of them were cut out of the picture. . . . At times I couldn't understand why I had to take a shot of a guy walking through a doorway to explain that he was in there. Certain connective shots bother me, they bother me."

So he keeps reducing, abstracting, eliminating even crucial information, like what kind of performer Jerry Langford is: "I shot a [Jerry Langford] monologue, but I took it out. If you show him performing, if you show any real comedy in the picture, you're testing what's funny to me and what's funny to you. I mean, I may find a Jerry Lewis monologue funny and the film audience may not, and that may take away from the validity of the main character, Rupert Pupkin, who idolizes this guy's comedy. The audience may say 'What do you want to be like him for? *We* don't like his jokes.' So I thought I'd take any chance of that away." So it "doesn't matter, not at all," whether Jerry Langford's funny or not—all that's left, then, is that he's "Jerry Langford," a star, a fully achieved, self-contained, rocklike identity. That's paring it down pretty far.

Scorsese's techniques in *The King of Comedy* produce a world in which everything and everyone is hard, inscrutable, opaque. There's nothing for the camera to search out, nothing more to tell us about the characters or the culture they live in, nothing that matters beyond the placement of objects and bodies in the fixed frame. The most memorable image in the film is of Lewis taped from head to toe, immobile and silent, like a mummy, in Masha's creepy, candlelit, opulent town house. Masha circles around him, caressing, crazy, seductive, taking him in from every angle, as the flickering light shows us new, unexpected contours of their faces and bodies. Scorsese's films have always been fascinated by stasis, but he has always hovered around his characters, exploring, playing with them as Masha does, predatory, voracious. But there's no appetite in *The King of Comedy*. If Jerry Langford is Scorsese's metaphor for his current self, then this film's metaphor for itself might be Jerry's solitary dinner in his Manhattan apartment: he eats without much interest, picking at his food, in a barren, featureless, too-bright room, in medium shot, the only flicker of interest in the background an old movie on TV, deprived of sound, image reduced, unwatched, simply there.

Some of the old movies in the background of *The King of Comedy* are Hollywood classics—and some are Scorsese's own. Scorsese is knowledgeable and enthusiastic about the old Hollywood, almost reverent: describing a meeting with André De Toth, he refers to him throughout as *Mr.* De Toth; he never cites a film without attaching the director's name, in a kind of academic incantation ("*Northwest Passage*, King Vidor . . . *Public Enemy*, William A. Wellman"). In some sense, *The King of Comedy* is an experiment for Scorsese, an exercise in the classical style of the American directors he loves, like John Ford. "From Ford, you kind of notice when not to cut. When it's so damn beautiful—what's the sense? What, are you crazy, move the camera? Just *leave* it there, look how beautiful it is." Scorsese's work in *The King of Comedy* may be a kind of homage to old masters, but he can't quite disguise his ambivalence: he holds the camera on his minimalist compositions, the rocklike figures set against stark and cheerless decor, but it's not because they're so damn beautiful. This isn't Monument Valley; it's Death Valley.

This may be deliberate, or it may not. Scorsese admits that the style of the Hollywood masters is dead: "The way we make films these days is totally different, naturally—different setup, different systems, different studio system and everything else. They were making three films a year and they never saw the editor, so they had to shoot the film in such a way that the editor wouldn't use certain cuts." We can read the dry, academic style of *The King of Comedy* as something self-consciously vestigial, a reminder of a tradition that was once vigorous but has lost its energy—weakened by the death of its masters, the collapse of the system that supported it, and perhaps the whole culture's lack of the shared assumptions neces- sary to keep a tradition alive. Or perhaps the tradition is a victim of its own success, as Jerry Langford is, turned into something too solid, too perfect, too *recognizable* to be very expressive any more. The film by itself doesn't quite support this reading: Langford isn't fully articulated as a metaphor for the old tradition—we'd need to see him perform, to have some sense of his place within his own art, not simply his place in the hearts of his uncritical fans. Still, the face of Jerry Langford in *The King of Comedy* is just the sort of portrait of death-by-success in America that has been the focal point of all Scorsese's recent films.

Unlike the director's earlier films, which are concentrated studies of characters in moments of crisis or transition, of identities in the process of definition, the four remarkable films between *Taxi Driver* and *The King of Comedy* have included, or alluded to, such mo- ments without making them the sole focus of the narrative. From *New York, New York*, through the documentaries *The Last Waltz* and *American Boy*, to *Raging Bull*, Scorsese has been working out an idiosyncratic form of film biography based on narrative ellipsis—a form which assumes a huge gulf between the intense, critical moment when an identity is defined and the long haul of living within the definition. The protagonists of Scorsese's early pictures—J.R. in *Who's That Knocking at My Door?*, Charlie and Johnny Boy in *Mean Streets*, Alice in *Alice Doesn't Live Here Anymore*, Travis in *Taxi Driver*—have the impulsiveness and volatility of personalities that haven't quite jelled yet: their responses to experience haven't taken on the systematic, predictable quality that comes from a solid sense of one's place in the world. The restless camera and the variable, unsettling editing rhythms of these films are largely functions of their protagonists, characters who can't seem to find a point of rest within the frame.

There's a precise moment when Scorsese's work enters its second phase: it's the controversial denouement of *Taxi Driver*. Having last shown us Travis immobile, apparently dying, amid the carnage he has wrought, Scorsese jumps several months forward, panning across a wall filled with newspaper clippings which proclaim Travis a hero, the savior of a teenage prostitute. Travis has risen from the dead and been reborn in public, given an identity that we know is purely external, that has nothing to do with his psychotic nature. For the last few minutes of the film, Scorsese lets us take in the effects of Travis's new celebrity: the respectful attitude of his fellow cabbies; the warily friendly, almost chastened behavior of Betsy, the blond dream girl who'd spurned him earlier; the quiet, dignified manner that Travis has now assumed. Scorsese's manner in these final scenes is quiet, too, a chilling reserve that allows us plenty of room to consider the gap between the public, heroic Travis and the dangerous sociopath we've been watching for almost two hours, plenty of room to ponder how Travis might attempt to live up to his socially approved identity as avenging angel.

From this point on, from the abrupt freeze-frame of Travis's eyes in the rearview mirror, the image that snaps shut the tight, internalized world of *Taxi Driver*, the focus of Scorsese's work shifts to the public world, where identities must be sharply defined, where personal conflicts and confusions resolve themselves into a distinctive music, an *act*—whose success is determined less by the internal demands of the performer than by the external demands of the audience, by how well the act "plays." Scorsese's next film, *New York, New York*, not only explores these themes, it embodies them: "We made up scenes as we went along," the director says, "and as our personal lives started to disintegrate also. We'd say, 'Hey, let's put this in,' and in the meantime, the sets were built and we had to work within the sets." But for all the passionately personal material being worked out on the screen, the film didn't do well with audiences. "It's quite ambitious," Scorsese says, "but it was never marked for amazing success." It didn't *play*.

But *New York, New York* is one of Scorsese's richest films, a work that's almost too dense with ideas. The film intends to be a thorough critique of American values and culture after the Second World War; Scorsese pours into it everything he knows about postwar society, about movies, music, violence, sex, money, ambition—and does it in a mixture of styles and tones that's equally varied, encyclopedic. Of course it doesn't work—Scorsese admits that, at two hours and forty minutes, the picture is a good half hour too long—but it has the power, the emotional heat, that unresolved arguments often have. *New York, New York* is like the intense moment of intellectual excitement when *all* the implications of a question have suddenly come into view, long before they've been narrowed down to a manageable conclusion.

New York, New York begins on VJ Day in New York, and introduces its characters in the context of a big-band celebration that consciously evokes the "innocent" style of forties musicals: a huge studio set with a fake New York visible through the windows; a famous band, Tommy Dorsey's; the celebration used as backdrop for the meeting of the hero and heroine, as if the setting and the music were merely a pretext for the important thing, the love story. The innocent style suits the characters, who seem newly born into this wild, joyful night—they haven't even begun to imagine their lives, the people they'll become.

The tone of this long opening sequence is very cunning: Jimmy Doyle (Robert De Niro), out of uniform, makes a long pass at Francine Evans (Liza Minnelli)—who *is* in uniform—and they play out their meeting scene as just slightly exaggerated versions of the optimistic, energetic boy and girl of the forties musical. He's brash, aggressive, amusingly persistent; she's reluctant, but with a highly developed skill at snappy putdowns. He's all naked ambition, she's all armor, and they're perfect images of American values after the war, values that inform every aspect of the characters' lives, that determine both their very different musical styles (Jimmy plays bebop-flavored jazz saxophone, Francine's a big-band singer) and the course of their personal relationship. But the sexual antagonism that Scorsese, in the Hollywood tradition, uses for charm and comedy in the opening sequence is progressively stripped of its appeal in the course of the picture until nothing's left but the antagonism, an unbridgeable gap between individuals in a culture that appears seamlessly connected, a perfect success.

Early in the film, Jimmy Doyle explains his priorities to Francine: music, money, and love (or sex—he doesn't use either word, just mimes a kiss)—not always in that order, he claims, though we never sense that his hierarchy has changed. His music is his expression of self, his identity, but a more fragile identity than his arrogant manner suggests—his dissonant, slightly abrasive, highly emotional style of playing is borrowed from black music. He's in the vanguard, perhaps, but he's not an innovator, and in some fundamental way he lacks conviction: although he despises the dominant form of popular music, the big-band sound, he can't stop envying its success. He needs to feel independent *and* he needs to feel recognized; the conflicting demands give a nasty, competitive edge to his personality and a reckless, almost nihilistic intensity to his playing. Slowly, his art becomes inseparable from his ambition, his need for a public identity.

Recognition comes more easily for Francine Evans. Her performing self, like Jimmy's, is an extension of the personality she shows in her first scenes: cheerful, good-natured, unthreatening. She doesn't stick out in the crowd the way Jimmy does, loudly dressed, moving against the flow of the dancers—she's in uniform, unselfconsciously and unobtrusively, tapping her foot to the music as if its rhythms were precisely hers. Francine turns out to be a perfect big-band singer, a performer in complete harmony with the majority culture. Her music is postwar America's song of itself, a confirmation and a celebration of its identity—a music that's spirited, optimistic, dreamy, and clear.

Jimmy Doyle and Francine Evans are made to represent quite a lot about America in the forties and fifties. And what's most startling about *New York, New York*'s very complicated structure is that they *keep* representing even after their story, on the dramatic level, has ended: they persist as metaphors. The narrative reaches its emotional climax when, in a swift, brutal rush of events, Jimmy and Francine have a terrifying fight in their car, Francine goes into labor, their son is born, and Jimmy leaves her even before she's out of the hospital. There's nothing more to say about them, as characters, after this exhausting sequence; the failure of their relationship couldn't be more final. But *New York, New York* goes on. Jimmy all but disappears, and Francine just *performs,* three big numbers right in a row: the first in a recording studio; the second, an elaborate Hollywood production number; the third, a "live" club performance of "New York, New York," the official showstopper. This looks like a serious structural flaw, a shockingly obvious one for a director as meticulous as Scorsese; but it's also an index of the complexity of his intentions.

The orgy of performance that closes out *New York, New York* means to tell us a great many things. It wants to say that Francine Evans now exists only as a performer; that public success, in the terms of postwar America, is inevitably an overdetermination of identity, the reduction of self to a performing style, a recognizable product; that any human quality, even energy, can be refined to lifeless self-parody, packaged and sold, like Francine's grotesquely calculated performance of the title song, her body jerking from one exaggerated pose to another, as if electric shocks were running through her every third or fourth beat. It means to say, too, that Jimmy Doyle's aggressive style, the rage he borrowed from the underclass, has begun to find its place in the postwar society, transformed, assimilated into America's optimistic image of itself: the song "New York, New York" is Jimmy and Francine's collaboration, but it has to be Francine who performs it, who makes it a rousing anthem to the competitive spirit, a love song to success.

What *New York, New York* means to say, finally, is that the reconciliation of what Jimmy and Francine represent can take place solely on the level of representation, of image, of performance, only after Jimmy and Francine and their tangled personal histories don't exist anymore: the song "New York, New York" is an anthem for postwar America, but it's an elegy for Jimmy and Francine. The film

New York, New York is an attempt at reconciliation, too, a fusion of diverse movie traditions—film noir, MGM musical, documentary, underground-movie realism—that tells the story of our distance from what those traditions once meant: it's an elegy read over the grave of fifties America.

"It's a whole world changing," Scorsese says of *New York, New York*. "It's also a goodbye to a certain kind of filmmaking. When Jimmy Doyle sees the two people dancing under the El—it's finished." What the world changed into—the next dance—is the subject of *The Last Waltz*, Scorsese's record of the Band's final concert, in 1976, their "farewell to the road." It's an elegy, too: Scorsese jumps forward twenty years from the end of *New York, New York*, to catch the generation of the sixties at its very end, making its own elegy, its retrospective image of itself. *The Last Waltz* is a documentary, but there's nothing accidental about it: the site of the concert, Winterland in San Francisco, was chosen because it was the site of the Band's first major-league concert in 1969; the guests—Ronnie Hawkins, Muddy Waters, Doctor John, Eric Clapton, Van Morrison, Bob Dylan, and more—were selected to illustrate the Band's history and the history of the kind of music they've made; the stage was decorated and lighted to evoke the faded-ballroom ambiance of the "last waltz" theme; the camera positions were set, and their moves planned, in advance; interviews, conducted by Scorsese, with the members of the Band were shot to fill in their history and record their reflections at the end of the road; and three additional numbers were shot in a studio.

The Last Waltz is a calculated document, as conscious and reflective as *Woodstock* was unconscious and immediate. The Woodstock festival in 1969 was the rock culture's definition of itself at its peak; the Band and many of its guests had been there, and Scorsese was one of the editors of the film that emerged from the concert. In that film, the rural openness, the torrents of music, the overflowing crowds merged into a single definitive image: a huge community drawn together by its music, a culture overwhelming in size and dedicated to the experience of being overwhelmed, of losing personal identity to a transcendent group identity. What *Woodstock* gave a name and an image to was the set of values that succeeded the ones frozen in place at the end of *New York, New York*.

The Last Waltz doesn't find this image in the audience; the performers will it into being on the stage, and Scorsese fixes it on the screen. The audience might almost not be there: we hear their applause, faintly, and the brief glimpses of them at the beginning and the end of the concert are ghostly, indistinct. The calculated *mise en scène* tells us that the values celebrated by *Woodstock* no longer bind the performers to the audience, but only bind the performers to each other. The group identity is all on stage now, it's the Band and their guests, now no longer an image of community so much as a community of images, perpetuating onstage what recently existed on a much larger scale beyond it. What *The Last Waltz* is celebrating, after all, is the end of the Band's "live" relationship to the audience.

Their connections to each other, however, are still alive: that's what distinguishes the exhilarating performances in *The Last Waltz* from the deadening numbers that end *New York, New York*, and that's what Scorsese focuses on in the confined space of Winterland. His camera is as mobile as *Mean Streets'*, his editing as quick and precise as *Taxi Driver*'s, sometimes with the rhythm of the music and sometimes with a rhythm entirely its own, framing the members of the group individually, as a whole, and, it seems, in every possible combination. The wide shots place the musicians in their elegant, elegiac setting; the two-shots catch the fast, mysteriously familiar messages that pass between them; the close-ups record their exhausted, end-of-the-party joy. Scorsese's portrait of the group performing at Winterland is both lyrical and thoroughly analytic, a triumph of style for him (and his team of cameramen) that matches the musicians' triumph on stage.

But Scorsese is also telling a story in *The Last Waltz*, in his elliptical, retrospective manner, the story of what happened to everybody between the fifties and the seventies. As in *New York, New York*, he's telling the story of a culture and he's again locating the culture's defining image at its endpoint, the point of exhaustion, of death. His interviews with the Band impose a rough biographical structure, but everything we see is in the present, a re-creation, a copy with no original to compare it to—or an original that exists only in our own memories. What Scorsese is trying to create in *The*

Last Waltz, in all his films since *Taxi Driver*, is a narrative of infer-
ence: he gives us the images, the re-creations, the achieved identities, and we tell *ourselves* the story. For this purpose, of course, the
best images are those that are densest with associations, the best
identities those that are highly defined.

When Bob Dylan appears onstage in *The Last Waltz*, a small,
opaque presence, his face half hidden underneath an incongruously
dandyish white hat, our story-making machinery goes into high
gear. We tell ourselves how his stardom—based on his ability to
articulate the audience's feelings, the ideas they can't quite articulate
themselves—has isolated him from the audience, made him unreachable, has isolated him, it seems, even from the Band. They
seem to disappear behind him, as if they were still his backup band.
The Band play modestly behind Dylan, and they're mostly outside
the frame—although the camera does catch Robbie Robertson, the
obvious leader on every other number in the film, shooting wary
glances at Dylan, watching him, trying to follow. And looking at the
film now, we can read another story in the songs Dylan performs at
Winterland—an old blues by the Reverend Gary Davis, and two
yearning, prayerlike compositions of his own, "Forever Young" and
"I Shall Be Released." We can read in them the story of Dylan's next
public incarnation, as an evangelical Christian.

This method of isolating a face, a performance, a moment of
identity that implies a story, that embodies the experience that created it, is a natural technique for documentary: since real stories can't
always be filmed in progress, and often can't even be identified as
stories until they're over, documentary filmmakers inevitably tell
many of their stories retrospectively. This technique—which depends on establishing the audience's perception of a *gap* between
the person or image we're watching on the screen and what the
person once was, what the image once meant—in Scorsese obviously goes beyond the demands of documentary: he builds these
gaps into his fiction films as well.

In his next feature, *Raging Bull* (which he once referred to as "a
documentary with actors"), he creates a narrative gap even more
radical than *New York, New York*'s: when the camera again picks up
La Motta, years after the end of his boxing career, he's so totally
transformed that it takes us a while to recognize him. And in *The*

King of Comedy, Scorsese has taken the next step, showing us *only* the transformation, the re-created image, the final state of identity that's self-defining and self-parodic. The only references to the pasts of the characters are glancing and allusive, as in a documentary: Rupert Pupkin's childhood is somewhere in the shadows of his climactic monologue, like the stories of the Band and Dylan and Woodstock in the music of *The Last Waltz*; Jerry Langford's story is present on screen only in a brief pan across the photos on his mantelpiece—like the home movies of the boy Steven Prince which punctuate Prince's sordid, disturbing monologue in Scorsese's documentary profile *American Boy*.

With *The King of Comedy*, Scorsese completes what he began in *New York, New York*, moves beyond elliptical, discontinuous narrative to a form that isn't really narrative at all, but a kind of still life. The gap between a character's, or a culture's, past and its frozen, definitive identity in the present doesn't exist anymore, because Scorsese has stopped representing the movement of the past on screen, has eliminated the process of becoming: now the gap is between the film and the audience, between our own memories and associations and the fixed objects of contemplation on the screen.

When Scorsese cast Jerry Lewis, he already had the actor framed: "Lewis brought to *The King of Comedy* a fuller entertainment, show-business character than a real talk-show host like Johnny Carson, who was considered for the part. He's been an actor, a director of some note, a stand-up comic, a comedian in skits, part of an act, the Dean Martin–Jerry Lewis act . . . he's the epitome of the Las Vegas entertainer. He's a philanthropist, with a national image as that [as host of the Muscular Dystrophy Foundation's annual fund-raising telethon]—a national image as a man who's a philanthropist who, pushed far enough, could go over the deep end on television, right in front of you. That tension, I think, is real in him. In his telethon, that's part of the thing that gets the money, therefore it has to be pushed—and he can act it, but I think it's real. At a certain point, you get so tired you let all your guard down, and you just let it be seen, what you are, how you're feeling at the moment. . . . And that alone is amazing, that tension: the way he turns, the way he looks, the way he glances at people. . . ."

None of this background is actually represented in the film, but it's all supposed to be there somehow, incarnated in Jerry Lewis. He *is* the most interesting thing in the movie: his scenes are like pieces of a documentary on Jerry Lewis—which is, perhaps, the film Scorsese really wanted to make. But it's De Niro as Rupert Pupkin whose face holds the screen for most of *The King of Comedy*, right up to the final image, and it's a face with no history, nothing to document: the gap we'd have to cross to find Pupkin's story is nearly infinite, like the long, bare corridor we see him standing at the end of, fixed before a photo of the audience.

If there's a story to be read in the frozen features of *The King of Comedy*, it's a story of exhaustion: the exhaustion of its creator translated into a vision of a whole culture's exhaustion. The key scenes in this story are *New York, New York* and *The Last Waltz*. *New York, New York* was Scorsese's try for a masterpiece, a work he kept putting more and more into in the attempt to overwhelm the audience—and it didn't play. He speaks of it now as "a big lesson." "It's a good movie, I just think it's a little meandering at times. All the scenes have to be there in order to tell the story fully, but I wish we'd found ways to combine two or three scenes and make one scene. That's the trick, that was the thing to do. But that's the way we learned."

He learned to tell his stories within tighter structures, yes, but he also learned to put less of himself in. And he learned to abandon the exploratory attitude and style of the earlier films in favor of a style that brutally appropriates faces and images for a preconceived end. One of many fascinating things in *American Boy* is Scorsese's unusually honest portrait of himself as director: we see him prodding his subject to tell this or that story; we see him, at one point, wearily motioning the camera off himself, directing it back to Prince; and we even see him, at the end, cajoling his subject into two extra takes of the final anecdote, forcing Prince to tell the story just as he told it to Scorsese before the filming, so it ends with just the words the director wants. We end, in *American Boy*, with an identity that's rock-hard and totally ambiguous in its origins: a "Steven Prince" who's created himself, or been created as product by his culture and his times, or been created by the director. There's no telling, and Scorsese and, for that matter, Prince probably don't know, either.

It's the sort of question that *New York, New York* struggled with, groping, improvising, exploring its way toward answers that weren't, finally, fully coherent. *The Last Waltz*, which attempts to create a final image for a restless, improvising, exploratory period in history, and for a music which had tried to weave every popular tradition into one overwhelming sound, is also Scorsese's final image of the large, inclusive, energetic spirit that failed him in *New York, New York*. It's the Band's farewell to their diminished audience, in a culture that's simply worn out from the effort of making itself up as it goes along, exhausted with its own experiments.

The Band are tired after all the years on the road, too tired to keep knocking themselves out for an audience that doesn't respond the same way anymore. They're tired and disappointed, and so's the culture, and so's Scorsese, but the recognition that it's all over seems to energize everyone: this is it, no more road beyond this, there's no sense holding back. The Band and Scorsese built a frame for their final image, carefully—but once they've placed themselves inside, they just let it rip. The music is alive, and very moving; so is the filmmaking. Scorsese holds to the frame and provides the Band with its defining image; since their essence is movement, the frame, to be true to its subjects, has to keep moving with them—and when it moves, it defines the filmmaker's identity as well.

In *The Last Waltz* Scorsese is too busy being himself to worry about the origins of identity, the source of images. But from then on, the question takes on some urgency, since the films have gradually closed in on themselves, like La Motta huddling in a corner of the ring, protecting himself from his opponent's blows; they've stopped providing the images of process or development that might explain where the rocklike identities come from. *Raging Bull* gives us a little—at least the "bull" La Motta gets to snort and stomp around a bit within the ropes—but *The King of Comedy* yields nothing, just characters defined by a culture grown so dense, so overpowering, that the very idea of development seems ludicrous. It's all imitation, repetition, and Scorsese is content—or perhaps feels doomed—to imitate the flat, plain style of Hollywood's overpowering tradition. "It *plays,*" Scorsese says of his latest film. "It plays with an audience." But what audience is it? The same audience that rejected the explorations of *New York, New York*? The same audience that laughs at Rupert Pupkin's jokes?

If we try to read Scorsese's story from the temporary end point of *The King of Comedy*, we'd have to read it as a story of fatigue, disillusionment, and finally disgust with the culture for which he produces images. We could choose, as his defining image, his own brief scene in the picture, playing the director of *The Jerry Langford Show* who records the static, blurry video image of Pupkin that goes out to America. Or we could choose to define Scorsese by his peaks, like *The Last Waltz*, and choose an image like that of the Band's Levon Helm beating furiously, ecstatically, on his drums while he sings, with unaccountable exuberance, "Why do the best things always disappear?"—an image of Scorsese's work that hasn't lost its meaning yet, that resonates across the gap.

Sight and Sound, Summer 1983

Brian De Palma

Brian De Palma, like all good surrealists, is happier with knives and razors than with guns. He uses the intimate weapons of our nightmares—the ones that require the killer to stalk his victim, to close in, to feel, finally, the warmth of the victim's blood on his own hands—with poetic force. They hover, they fly, they gleam like wedding rings. The instruments of death so dominate De Palma's films that they become, like Buñuel's razor, important structural elements in the works. The structure of *Blow Out*, for instance, is the narrowing circle of the garrote. And De Palma's new gangster movie, *Scarface*, is as distant, as impersonal, as linear as a gunshot—which is, perhaps, why it seems such a strange movie for him to have made.

With *Scarface*, De Palma is taking his shot at simplicity: telling a "classic" story straight through, with no split screens or 360-degree pans, no dream sequences, no elaborate lyrical set pieces, and up to a point he succeeds. This is an efficient gangster picture, a good, nasty entertainment. It's probably a conscious departure: his previous film, *Blow Out*, is in every sense a closed circle, the completion and perfection of all his work. It's no wonder that he's followed the complex, personal *Blow Out* with this distanced and straightforward narrative—the problem is, De Palma has no simplicity in him. Oliver Stone's script for *Scarface* is a fairly schematic updating of the Hawks and Hecht original, a rise-and-fall story with a few contemporary twists—Tony Camonte, the Italian immigrant who makes his fortune in bootleg liquor, becomes Tony Montana, a Cuban exile who strikes it rich dealing cocaine—and De Palma serves it well. Almost *too* well. He carries his Hollywood-style impersonality so far that it creates a kind of tension, an unease that transcends the predictable, classic line of the scenario. The movie seems to give off a sinister, mechanical buzz, like a chain saw.

De Palma has certainly made audiences uneasy before, but never in quite this way. The most unnerving sequences in *Carrie*, *The Fury*, *Dressed to Kill*, and *Blow Out* depend for their effect on the presence of a helpless, sensitive observer: every crime has its witness, and every nightmare, of course, has its dreamer. Every film has its viewer, too, and De Palma's distancing techniques—like the slow motion he uses for the deaths of Carrie Snodgress in *The Fury* and Nancy Allen in *Blow Out*, both sympathetic characters killed in full view of people who love them—paradoxically increase our identification with the watching characters by making us more aware of ourselves as spectators.

But *Scarface*'s violence is shot realistically, even in the film's most shocking (by now infamous) scene, in which Tony Montana, double-crossed by a couple of South American drug dealers, is forced to watch his friend dismembered with a chain saw in the bathroom of a squalid Miami hotel. De Palma directs the scene for maximum shock, emphasizing the brutal confinement of the space, the shudder that runs through the killer's body when the chain saw starts up, the spray of blood on Montana's face and clothes, and the constant, echoing, nerve-destroying noise; but here the shock isn't deepened by Montana's reaction. When we see Montana's face, we see some fear and a lot of rage, but no grief; when he gets his revenge on the killer, a couple of minutes later, it's just a swift, casual shooting on the street, a long shot in bright sunlight. This is alienated, businesslike horror: a gruesome murder that's little more than a gratuitous display of power—a killer's proud performance—and a revenge that's only a balancing of the books.

It's an impressive performance by the director, too, in a manner that he sustains throughout the picture. Nothing else in *Scarface* approaches the savagery of this early scene, but the chilling tone of emotional neutrality persists. *Scarface* could, perhaps, be read as a nightmare of freewheeling, American-style capitalism—except there's no dreamer here, no one to register the appalling images, to give them their true emotional weight. We never get any closer to Tony Montana than we do in his first scene—his face held in close-up, the camera moving around him, catching every angle of his face as he tries to lie his way past the immigration officials. When De Palma pulls back from his protagonist, he pulls back for good. Tony's hard cunning is all we need to see; the rest is violence.

In a sense, *Scarface* is De Palma's first fully American movie: just as he once flooded lurid little horror numbers like *Carrie* and *The Fury* with elegant poetic effects, here he works against the grain of this big, respectable production by telling his story in the mean, harsh, disreputable style of a B-movie exposé—the sort of work a Phil Karlson might have done in the fifties, complete with stock-footage prologue explaining the background of the "shocking" social problem. This certainly isn't homage—De Palma is, of his generation of American filmmakers, by far the least reverent of the Hollywood past—but something closer to parody. It's De Palma's imitation of a Hollywood hack, performed with such ferocity that it seems to strip the style bare.

The film is all surfaces, and none of them shine: De Palma seems to have turned the Florida sunlight into a kind of cold fluorescence. But this rigorous superficiality gives the film a real, though perilous, coherence. The style combines with other elements of the work—Montana's machismo; the notorious overuse of the four-letter word for sexual intercourse; the presence of all that bright, white, neutral-looking powder that provides its user with the illusion of mastery; the zombielike remoteness of Montana's blond wife—to produce a film that's essentially a bitter dirty joke about the limits of capitalist ambition: you grow, you expand, you become, as a businessman, something hard and unyielding; and yet you can't get in very far, you keep butting up against the harder surfaces of the culture. (Even in a purely geographical sense, Montana hasn't penetrated very deeply in American society—just the few hundred miles from Cuba to Florida.) The film's brightness and its willful opacity define its distance both from the original *Scarface*, whose rich nocturnal images carry the sense of dark secrets discovered, and from De Palma's earlier work, which at its best seems to be breaking right through into our dreams: everything in this *Scarface* seems to be happening in the open, as if there were no crimes left so horrible that they need to be hidden.

In the end, Tony Montana, high on cocaine and shooting it out with a Bolivian hit squad, seems to explode, firing his bazookalike machine gun into the heart of his own mansion. The surfaces crumble, the vast central hall fills with smoke and blood, bodies and debris, as if Montana's shell—his body, his property—were destroying itself from within, a hard object finally burst from all that's been put into it. Montana's death, in smoky slow motion, the same dying gestures seen from several angles, is shot like the death of Childress, the corporate monster with the dead arm who blows up at the end of *The Fury*, destroyed by the gaze of Gillian, that film's sensitive observer. *Scarface*'s protagonist seems to have been destroyed by the cold fury of the camera itself, whose greed for bright things has, after nearly three hours, reached the point of surfeit—the point at which it's alienated enough from its own objects that it's capable, at last, of destroying them.

De Palma himself is walking a fine line between alienation and identification in *Scarface*. As a hired director, he has to deliver the goods—a huge load of blood, sex, coke, noise, vulgarity, big cars, and enough social background to set off Al Pacino's star performance. It's an assignment that puts him in the position of having to identify with his protagonist, who's carrying the same kind of serious weight. Yet the scenario is critical, even contemptuous, of Montana, and he's not the sort of character that De Palma has been sympathetic toward in his past work.

His solution is, in a sense, a variant of the helpless-observer motif of his other films: he uses his own distance from the material as a means of identifying himself with his alienated, inhuman hero, conceives both his own activity and Tony Montana's as exercises in consumption which become, in the end, acts of self-consumption. De Palma's approach is detached, intellectual, and a little scary—like his teenage telekinetics, the privileged killers of his earlier work, he is practicing a kind of violence of the mind, the revenge of the observer turning his or her gaze *against* the object, willing its destruction from a point beyond horror and beyond despair. De Palma

has always been shocking, has always skirted the edges of exploitation, but with a redeeming self-consciousness; the shock of *Scarface*, compared to his previous films, is that the director seems not
to want to distinguish it at all from its genre.

Neither *Carrie* nor *The Fury* has a plot that would distinguish it
from the general run of horror exploitation pictures—*Carrie*'s is
crude and serviceable, *The Fury*'s crude and nearly nonsensical—
but the films are powerful and terrifying in a way that exploitation
films never are. The horror in *Carrie* and *The Fury* has an insinuat-
ing, sensuous quality that's like an extreme form of adolescent self-
consciousness, an awareness of both emotions and physical
sensations that's exhilarating, fragmented, painfully sharp. The
young heroine of *The Fury* is desperate to understand her powers
and desperately afraid of them: when she's having one of her visions, she makes whoever is near her bleed, as if her mind were
gripping the world too hard.

Both films generate horror from nightmarish exaggerations of
the experience of adolescence: the feeling that your impulses have
gone out of control, that even your own body is alien, perhaps
hostile; the powerful sense of isolation, of exclusion from the secrets
of the great, organized, social world; the yearning for connection
that sometimes takes the form of furtive, inexpressible love, the kind
of love that waits and watches, storing images of its object in the
mind. In *The Fury*, De Palma's vision of teenage love is stylized and
almost comically pure. Gillian feels attracted to a boy she's never
met, whom she knows only through her visions, and tracks down
the young psychic because she thinks he's the only one who could
possibly understand her. There isn't a horror effect in either picture
that isn't based on some characteristic of the adolescent consciousness. In this sense, De Palma is a true exploitation filmmaker: he
doesn't merely represent his teenage "target audience" on screen,
just to have victims whom his viewers can identify with—he exploits
his audience in a more intimate and more serious way, using their
fears, their locked-in desires, and their potent fantasies as the substance and the unifying sensibility of the films.

Both pictures are variations on the theme of the sensitive loner,
but *Carrie* keeps everything linked to its satiric view of an American
high school, while the more purely oneiric *The Fury* seems to be

floating somewhere above our heads, like the boy psychic Robin in his final scenes. It takes the petty, local betrayals of *Carrie* beyond high school into the vast, dark world outside, where a gifted kid isn't just a joke, but is a valuable commodity, a weapon to be wielded by an obscure "company." Although it's not at all explicit, *The Fury* is in some sense an allegory of co-opted genius. Gillian's piercing talents are a burden to her in her conventional high school; when she moves to an institute for psychic research, where she's treated as an individual and surrounded by sympathetic mentors, her powers begin to develop into something controllable and even pleasurable—it's nearly a parody of the university experience, the delirious rush of freedom, ease, and intellectual power that gives bright kids the feeling of being home at last. But her visions of Robin, who has recently been in the same position, are disquieting, a look at her own future that's like a nightmare of being recruited by a corporation: Robin has been kidnapped by the "company" (the CIA or something like it), which seems to be honing him as an instrument, shaving away the edges of his character—his moral sense, his love for his father, his ability to enjoy his own extraordinary vision—until, by the time Gillian and his father catch up with him, he's no more than a hard, gleaming blade of malice.

The rich suggestiveness of *The Fury* isn't inherent in its story; it comes out of the disproportionate visual and emotional intensity of the horror scenes. The movie is as determined to shock as any exploitation picture (and as indifferent to narrative logic), but the horror set pieces are so scrupulously designed, building on each other with echoing motifs, that they have an obsessional quality more suggestive of surrealist dream research than of B-movie market research.

Having done a high-speed car chase early in the film, De Palma uses an out-of-control car to kill Hester, Gillian's sympathetic teacher at the institute. Hester's head smashes a windshield, the glass motif recalling both the scene in which Gillian causes another teacher to bleed and her blood to stain a glass table, and Gillian's visions of Robin crashing through a window in his attempt to escape from the institute. Later on, Robin sends a carnival ride full of Arab tourists (who remind him of the terrorists in the opening scene, who he believes have killed his father) spinning out of control; one of the cars detaches itself and shatters the plate-glass window of a restaurant. Near the end, he finishes off the woman who—on Childress's orders—has become his lover, by lifting her in the air (telekinetically) and whirling her faster and faster until her body is drained of blood. The exsanguination is also a step in a formal progression of blood scenes: from the trifling nosebleed that Gillian induces in one of her high school classmates, to the teacher's blood gushing on the breakfast table, to this—and beyond, to the explosive end of Childress. *The Fury*'s narrative is delirious, out of control, but its horror is rigorous, with the unexpected formal correspondence of a collage.

As the director of *Carrie* and *The Fury*, films he didn't write, De Palma seems to be discovering his themes through his technique: staging scenes of remote-control violence requires, on the technical level, some consideration of the dialectics of distance and intimacy, of action and reaction, an awareness of the camera's role as both a passive recorder of images and an active instrument of shock. His next two big-budget films, *Dressed to Kill* and *Blow Out*, both scripted by De Palma, make these considerations explicit by transforming the telekinetics, the sensitive human recording devices of the earlier films, into the technological whiz kids played by Keith Gordon in *Dressed to Kill* and John Travolta in *Blow Out*. These two pictures, like *Carrie* and *The Fury*, are a linked pair—the second is, again, darker, more dreamlike, more convoluted as narrative, and more despairing.

Dressed to Kill is, appropriately, something of a technical exercise itself: an essay on the tracking shot, framed by a pair of dreams. Its major sequences are all variations on the idea of surveillance, and they all turn out to be elaborate little jokes on the audience's belief that it has been "following" the action; in this flashy, shameless thriller of sexual anxiety, the audience is always taken from behind.

The most brilliant sequence, a museum pickup/chase scene involving victim-to-be Kate Miller (Angie Dickinson) and an attractive stranger, alternates, to the accelerating rhythm of Kate's clicking heels, close-ups of Kate with subjective tracks from her point of view as she wanders through the mazelike galleries, the stranger occasionally popping into view from behind a partition. The suspense of the sequence—since there are no shots from *his* point of view—is in our confusion about where the characters are in relation to each other, and our uncertainty (perhaps Kate Miller's as well) about who's following whom. Just when the chase appears over and Kate is leaving the museum, the stranger pops up again, dangling her lost glove from the window of a cab, and as Kate moves gratefully toward him, a blonde in a black coat, whose presence hasn't been signaled at all, passes behind her and picks up her other discarded glove.

A later sequence, a subway chase involving Liz Blake (Nancy Allen), the hooker who's the only witness to Kate's murder, is shot in a more objective style. We've seen the killer following her, sometimes from her point of view and sometimes not, and the camera tracks from angles that couldn't possibly be her pursuer's, such as from outside the windows of the speeding train. But again it keeps us in the dark about just where her pursuer *is,* and again it produces multiple surprises at the end: the killer suddenly appears behind Liz, and Kate Miller's son turns up out of nowhere, behind the killer. There are many more instances of this sort of trickery, in which we are encouraged to follow the camera's tracks, to read the action "correctly" in terms of conventional film grammar, only to find that we have assumed too much and left ourselves wide open to attack from somewhere else.

De Palma is so confident in this picture, and so determined to show us the errors of our perceptions, that he can repeat an effect and fool us the second time, too. In the opening sequence, we're startled first when an apparently subjective track into the Millers' bathroom and a shot of a man shaving lead us to believe that whatever threatens the showering Kate Miller will come from in front of her, until she's grabbed abruptly from behind; and second, when the assault turns out to have been a dream. And then he does it again in the final sequence, which begins with the lunatic Elliott's escape from the hospital, a scene shot so expressionistically that we know this *must* be a dream, then proceeds to a recapitulation of the opening scene (this time with Liz Blake in the shower) which builds suspense so skillfully that we doubt, then forget, that we're in a dream—despite the scene's resemblance to the earlier one, and despite the presence in nearly every shot of a brilliant, sourceless point of light in the middle of the frame (an echo of Kate Miller's gleaming wedding ring in the first dream), sometimes reflecting on a doorknob or a razor, sometimes shining inexplicably from outside the window. And yet again—this time with sleight-of-hand cutting, a mirror, and a pair of shoes—he convinces us that we know just where the killer is, and produces him from behind.

This relentless demonstration that we shouldn't trust what we see is reinforced by this film's observer figure, the teenage scientist Peter Miller (who, by all accounts, is a near version of the director's adolescent self), whose amateur surveillance efforts—bugging, a stop-motion camera set up outside Elliott's office—not only don't lead him to the truth, but lead to a misconstruction of reality that nearly gets Liz killed, in a scene that makes Peter an appalled spectator on the other side of a barred window. The worst doesn't happen here; De Palma saves that for Jack Terry, the grown-up whiz kid who's the hero of his next film. *Dressed to Kill* is an elegant conjuring trick, but it's just a warm-up for the darker magic of *Blow Out*.

It's easy to believe in De Palma's reported teenage fascination with technology: his meanings, in an individual film, are most often an extension of his technical means; and his body of work, up to *Blow Out*, has an unusually systematic progression, like a series of experiments. He treats both his own previous works and the works of others (especially Hitchcock's) as research to be built upon, suggestive hypotheses to be tested and then surpassed. *Blow Out* looks like a conscious summation of De Palma's themes and techniques.

He draws his principal collaborators—actors John Travolta, Nancy Allen, John Lithgow, and Dennis Franz, cinematographer Vilmos Zsigmond, editor Paul Hirsch, composer Pino Donaggio— from his earlier films; lays out his full array of technical tricks—360- degree pans, elaborate tracking shots, split screens, slow motion; deploys all his usual themes and visual motifs—surveillance, political and sexual paranoia, doomed love, the helpless observer, blood, and breaking glass; places at its center his autobiographical character, the technology whiz. He introduces the subject of filmmaking itself (and even includes a parody of his own work); takes another crack (after the failure of the too slavishly imitative *Obsession*) at capturing the dreamlike romantic horror of *Vertigo*. And he places it all in the narrative context of an assassination conspiracy plot that draws elements from the John Kennedy assassination, Ted Kennedy's Chappaquiddick scandal, the Watergate coverup, and urban mass murderers such as New York's Son of Sam and San Francisco's Zebra killer, all the most powerful images of violence and corruption from the past twenty years of American history, and in the visual context of a scrupulously maintained color scheme of red, white, and blue. What De Palma was working toward all along, it seems, was this thrillerized autobiography of an American film-maker.

The presence of an adult, rather than a teenager, at the center of the film is the key to *Blow Out*'s form and to its meaning. *Carrie* and *The Fury* were about people experiencing events with a first-time intensity, and were structured as series of shocks, progressions from innocence to cruel knowledge; the shocks are muted here, and deeper, and the structure is circular, because *Blow Out*'s subject is the horror of repetition, the adult experience of having seen and heard it all before, events playing and replaying in our minds in an endless loop. The film means to have this effect on the viewer's memory, to send us circling back into the past at every point, both the past outside the film—*The Fury* and *Dressed to Kill*, *Vertigo* and *Blowup*, the Kennedy assassination and Watergate, even the revolutionary history of America (the action takes place in Philadelphia during a historical celebration called Liberty Day)—and the past within the film as well. *Blow Out* ends where it began, in a screening room, and with the same piece of film, a shower murder from the trashy slasher movie *Coed Frenzy*; the sounds we hear in the film's key scenes—gunshots, footsteps, breaking glass, thunderous fire-works—are the same taped sounds that Jack Terry is collecting and labeling in the credit sequence; and Jack's pursuit of the killer of a presidential candidate ends in a reenactment of the central trauma of his life, a botched surveillance operation that causes his confeder-ate's death. Visually, the film is all circles: Jack's spinning reels of tape; the killer's garrote.

Jack Terry's story describes an arc from detachment to involve-ment and back again—back to something far beyond detachment, an anesthetized professionalism. His art as a movie sound recordist allows him a certain distance: not only can he pick up sounds from far away, he picks them up dissociated from the images they will accompany on the screen. But when he hears, and records, the blowout that killed Governor McRyan, he begins to close the gap: by playing the tape again and again; by becoming involved with Sally, the other witness; and finally by attempting to put sound and image together. He makes a flip book out of a series of cut-out magazine photos of the crash, then animates the sequence, then synchronizes his tape to the animation—all the while neglecting his work on *Coed Frenzy*—and these scenes reach back, exhilaratingly, into the history of film: this jaded exploitation filmmaker is recovering an earlier, more vital self, rediscovering a reason for his art, reinventing a cinema of crude materials and passionate technique.

In the end, when Terry's newfound joy in his technique has failed him and left Sally dead in his arms, he sits on a bench and listens to her last words on tape, then the tape spins on its reels in Jack's editing room when no one's there, as if it's circling on its own, and in the screening room her recorded scream is coming from the mouth of the girl shrinking from the looming knife in *Coed Frenzy*, De Palma's camera gliding around the figure of Jack watching and listening, saying "good scream" over and over as the film plays again, until he puts his hands to his head and covers his ears.

It's a purely harrowing scene, De Palma's greatest shock, a confessional moment rendered with an objectivity that keeps us suspended between distance and identification. We know, as De Palma does, where this horror comes from, the despair that overtakes us as we watch ourselves, technicians, cut the deepest pain out of ourselves and turn it into product, into images of violence whose triviality is surreally disproportionate to their traumatic sources. What we don't know, as De Palma doesn't, is whether this communal replay of private nightmares, the American movie, is invigorating or numbing—or, like the drugs Montana deals, somehow both at once. De Palma's assumption of the identity of a Hollywood pro in *Scarface* is his way of exploring the last implication of the sick joke at the end of *Blow Out*, plunging himself at last into the cold heart of the American screen.

Sight and Sound, Spring 1984

Chris Marker

Trying to remember Chris Marker's *Sans Soleil* after seeing it for the first time, a viewer might recall nothing but how he feels at the end—dazed and excited, overwhelmed by a smooth, rapid flow of images and ideas. Or he might recall only vivid, random moments: the face of an African woman and a porcelain cat with one paw raised; an emu on the Île de France and sleeping passengers on a Japanese train; a carnival in Guinea-Bissau and a volcano erupting in Iceland. And if, as an *aide-mémoire,* he has taken notes as the film unrolled, his impressions will be more concrete, but perhaps more confused. Did he really manage to take in, during the first ten minutes of the film, an epigraph from Eliot's "Ash Wednesday," a shot of three children on a road in Iceland in 1965, a short sequence on a train in Hokkaido, shots of women on the Bissagos Islands off West Africa, a prayer for the soul of a lost cat in an animal cemetery outside Tokyo, a dog on a deserted beach, a bar in a rundown district of Tokyo? How did he assimilate, at the same time, the lyrical, aphoristic commentary—in the form of letters from a traveler we never see, read by a woman we don't see, either—and how did he get his bearings in this no-man's-land of documentary images and oblique fiction? Finally, recalling the vertiginous speed of the film's transitions, he suspects that his notes are incomplete, inaccurate, a distorted memory. He'd have to see the film again.

The creation of the need, and the desire, to see things again is part of the method of *Sans Soleil*; and also, perhaps, its real subject.

What Marker means to communicate to us is the solitude of the film editor at his machinery, his reverie over the footage he's shot (or that has been sent to him by friends), the scenes he watches over and over again. He wants to explain why he returns to Japan, the subject of his 1965 film *The Koumiko Mystery*; why the images of the emu, the porcelain cat (called *maniki neko*), the children in Iceland won't go away, why they keep bobbing up in the course of *Sans Soleil*; how it's possible to see *Vertigo* nineteen times; how images are replayed as memories, as obsessions, and as the troubled dreams of travelers.

This film has so many showpieces of montage, under such imaginative and varied pretexts—a visit to San Francisco intercut with scenes from *Vertigo*; a deserted island in the Atlantic where the narrator "can't believe the images that crop up," shots of Tokyo crowds mixed with the lush Impressionist landscapes of the Île de France; an imaginary science-fiction movie in which images of poverty and desolation are linked by the consciousness of an investigator from the year 4001; a sequence on a Tokyo train in which the sleeping faces of commuters are cut with television images of samurai films, horror movies, erotic entertainment, all attributed to these exhausted travelers as their dreams—so much virtuosity, in fact, that *Sans Soleil* risks being seen as no more than an exercise in the art of editing, a highly conscious miming of the involuntary processes of memory.

In a sense, it *is* that. But there's something else in Marker's work, something which distances him even from his own models, like Dziga Vertov and Eisenstein. It's in those qualities that aren't easily transcribed as notes: not simply the juxtaposition of shots but the rhythms of their juxtaposition. The sequences in which disparate times and places are made to correspond have the speed and urgency of passionate argument. Other scenes, like a Tokyo festival with dancers whose hands seem to be telling a story we don't quite understand, are rapt and quiet, as if the editor and commentator were simply transfixed. *Sans Soleil* is an editor's film, worthy of the Russian masters, but its undulating rhythms—rushing forward, stopping to gaze, following, corresponding across great distances, returning to the same places—are those of a melancholy, obsessed lover.

This tone isn't so difficult to identify, but its source—the real object of this love—is more elusive. In Marker's earlier film about Japan, the object was a face, the face of Koumiko Muraoka picked out of the crowd at the 1964 Tokyo Olympics. The filmmaker follows her, interrogates her in the crowded streets and the department stores, photographs her in a revolving bar high above Tokyo, the city moving in a slow circle behind her, as if she were merely the focal point of an investigation of Japanese culture. But in the last section of *The Koumiko Mystery*, the focus shifts. The filmmaker has gone back to Paris, having left Koumiko a short questionnaire—he receives her answers on tape. The noises of Tokyo, the bits of radio transmission which have interrupted the soundtrack, have dropped away, leaving only the taped voice of Koumiko to evoke Japan for the distant interrogator.

Visually, the mix is as before: a combination of crowd shots with and without Koumiko, images (ads, samurai films) picked up from Japanese TV, footage of exotic ceremonies and a variety of close-ups, often stills, of Koumiko's face. What has changed is the relationship between the soundtrack and the images: Marker has exchanged the you-are-there documentary illusion he started with—the clipped, present-tense narration ("Koumiko Muraoka, secretary, more than twenty years old, less than thirty . . ."), the on-camera interviews—for a tone of retrospection, past-tense narration. The illusion in this last section is that what we see is what Marker is seeing as he listens to Koumiko's tape, the images summoned by her voice and the memory of her face, as if time and distance have turned a job of reporting, the investigation of a culture, into something more intimate and novelistic—the story of a relationship. Koumiko is never made to represent Japan, but she seems, in these passages, to replace it.

The shift from the present tense of documentary to the past tense of reverie isn't just a formal experiment in the relationship of sound and image. It's not playful, like the passage in *Letter from Siberia* in which a single montage of village life is played three times with three different narrations (Communist, capitalist, and "objective"). In *Koumiko* the effect is haunting, because it embodies the chronic melancholy of the traveler, who's always leaving places and people behind, places which, from a distance, cannot be fully imagined

distinct from the consciousness of those who remain. (How can
Marker run a sequence of the Tokyo monorail on his moviola without thinking of Koumiko? How can he hear her voice without a
picture of the Ginza owl flashing through his mind?) The traveler,
better than anyone else, knows that isolation from others means not
seeing the same things every day.

We're aware, in the last section of *The Koumiko Mystery*, of the
distance Koumiko's disembodied voice has had to travel to find a
listener, as she says: "Always, every day, every night, every morning,
always things are happening, all sorts of things. . . . It's like a wave
of the sea: when the earth trembles, even if it's from some accident
far away, the wave advances, little by little, until it reaches me."
We're aware, as she makes these comments about history which
might almost have been scripted by Marker himself (but weren't), as
we watch the traveling shot from the front of the monorail train
which might almost be what Koumiko is seeing while she speaks
(but, of course, isn't), that *The Koumiko Mystery* has become, in
Marker's editing room, the record of a conversation whose intricacy
is the reflection of a passion for intimacy—like the coded messages
prisoners bang out on the pipes, hoping the sounds will reach each
other's cells.

When the unseen protagonist of *Sans Soleil*, the man with the
movie camera, returns to Japan, he finds much of what *The Koumiko
Mystery* found: the Shinbashi locomotive, the Ginza owl, the Dream-
land amusement park, Western-looking mannequins in the stores,
the same right-wing orator holding forth at the same downtown
square, and shop windows filled with *maniki neko,* the cat that
salutes. "Everything interested him," says the female narrator, telling
his story. He felt, she says, "joys he had never felt upon returning to
a home," and the shots keep tumbling out, as if someone were
rummaging in a box full of jumbled photos, looking for a special
picture, looking faster as he gets near the bottom. Koumiko isn't
there. Is her face what he's looking for? There's no reason, really, to
believe that it is, yet her absence seems to alter Marker's vision of
Tokyo: his images, without her face as a focal point, look shallower
(more "Oriental," perhaps), with no foreground and background,
no perspective, no point of rest, and there are *more* of them. And
this time, treating his own history without a Koumiko as intermedi-

ary, he invents a correspondence between the man who films (he names him Sandor Krasna) and the distant woman who, receiving his messages, is made to see the world through his eyes. This time around, without Koumiko, Japan seems more complex, less assimilable. In a sense, *Sans Soleil* is *The Koumiko Mystery* remade as *The Marker Mystery*.

In conventional documentaries, the filmmaker is primarily a reporter, answering a questionnaire: How do people live in Siberia? Is Castro's revolution working? How does Israel survive? Marker's earlier films, like *Letter from Siberia* (1957), *Description of a Struggle* (1960), and *Cuba Si!* (1961), may not have given conventional answers, but they remained within the framework of the understood questions. *Koumiko*, while it plays with this style of reportage only to abandon it, fools us for a while but finally reveals itself: the question, all along, was not What is Japan like? but Who is Koumiko? But *Sans Soleil* seems, rather, to be generating its own questions in the audience, like: Where are we now? Is this a film about Japan? About Guinea-Bissau? Why does he bring up the children in Iceland, *here*? Was there a project? Or several? Why *Vertigo*? Why the emu?

These stupid questions (which are also the sort we might ask of a bad, incoherent film), strangely, help pull us along through the movie: we keep following the subject, feeling that it's almost in our grasp—if only the speeding images would slow down a bit, if only those passages that look and sound like summations would allow us to linger before they rush us on to new information, new syntheses. And the stupid questions turn out to be the right ones. *Sans Soleil* is the diary of a return, a return which induces—naturally—retrospection, reverie, the need to account for the distance traveled in coming back: a review of notes from other places, beginning with three children in Iceland in 1965 (the year after *Koumiko* was shot).

These notes—the odd shots saved from Marker's own travels, supplemented by footage sent by friends—are, like all notes, taken spontaneously, for their own sake, or perhaps for the sake of a vague sense that they might someday fit a pattern. Returning to Tokyo, Marker seems to feel as Koumiko did sixteen years earlier when she complained that her head was full of "things, things, things—all mixed up, without any order"—and he must feel that way again when he's back home editing his footage, reviewing his notes, the cans of film all mixed up, as he tries to analyze and recreate that feeling, with no tape from Tokyo to listen to, just Marker the editor asking questions of Marker the photographer: Why do these shots exist? Where are we now?

This is the way I imagine Marker working on *Sans Soleil*. His method invites this sort of attempt to evoke him: it's both profoundly personal and utterly detached: the films have a distinctive voice, but it's the voice of a ghost whispering in your ear. The far-flung documentary images of *Sans Soleil* are assembled as an autobiography—the film has no subject except the consciousness, the memory of the man who shot it—yet Marker attributes this consciousness to the invented "Sandor Krasna," removes it from himself to a yet more spectral entity. And then he adds further layers of mediation: "Krasna" himself is often made to attribute his thoughts to others (as, for instance, when he imagines the alien time traveler from 4001 commenting on the twentieth century); and the entire narration is read by another invention, the nameless woman receiving Krasna's letters.

Marker has always had a fondness for complication, subterfuge, disguise: even his name is a pseudonym. For *Si J'Avais Quatre Dromadaires* (1966), a feature-length assembly of still photos taken all over the world between 1955 and 1965, he invented a commentary for three voices, a photographer and two friends. In *Le Fond de l'Air Est Rouge* (1978), a four-hour history of the years 1967–1970 composed of newsreel footage and fragments edited out of Marker's earlier films, he submerges his own voice almost entirely. (In his introduction to the published text, Marker confesses to having "abused" his function as commentator in earlier films, and says that his aim here is "for once . . . to return to the spectator, through montage, 'his' commentary, that is to say his power"—as an extension, perhaps, of the *cinéma vérité* method of his 1963 documentary on Paris, *Le Joli Mai*, although in that film Marker reserved for himself as commentator the first and the last words.)

In his 1982 book *Le Dépays*, a photo-and-text record of the same trip to Japan which provided the material for *Sans Soleil*, Marker writes his impressions, not in the first person but in the second—because, he finally admits, he wants "to establish a distance between the one who, from September 1979 to January 1981, took these photos of Japan, and the one who is writing in Paris in February 1982. . . . One changes, one is never the same, it's necessary to address oneself in the second person for all one's life." Most of Marker's works are, like *Sans Soleil*, mixtures of documentary and invention, intimacy and distance, self-revelation and disguise, but the self-alienation tendency he explains in *Le Dépays* is perhaps best examined in its most extreme forms: in Marker's only wholly fictional film, the "photo-novel" *La Jetée* (1962; released 1964), and in *The Train Rolls On* (1970), a documentary from the seven-year period in which Marker signed none of his work, functioning as an anonymous member of the film-making collective called SLON.

La Jetée is an elegant and elaborate fiction. Turning to completely imaginary material, he decided to go all the way—not socialist realism, but the real artifice of Borges or Hitchcock. It's a science fiction story, told entirely in still photographs, which begins with a short sequence in which a young boy sees the face of a woman and witnesses a man's murder on the jetty of Orly Airport. The story then leaps forward to Paris after a nuclear war: the survivors live underground and some of them, including the now grown-up witness of the opening sequence, have become subjects of time-travel experiments, attempts to raid the past and the future for sustenance. On his travels into the past, the hero meets and falls in love with the woman whose face he'd seen at Orly. Finally, attempting to escape from the experimenters, he finds himself back on the jetty, running toward the woman from the past, but followed by an agent from the underground. Just before he is killed, he realizes that "the moment he had witnessed as a child, which had never stopped obsessing him, was the moment of his own death."

The film's brevity (twenty-nine minutes), its circular structure, and the solemn, high-literary tone of the narration evoke the metaphysical fables of Borges, the dry, conservative Buenos Aires librarian who seems to generate his hermetic fictions entirely out of the experience of reading and writing literature, for whom the past, the present, and the future are bound *exactly* like the pages of a book— not the likeliest model for a well-traveled leftist filmmaker, Marker the foreign correspondent. But the spirit of Borges's fiction isn't so alien to the man who edits the footage and comments on it—Marker at home, in a dark room with a moviola, like Borges's "Funes the Memorious," who remembers everything as he sits in his sunless shack—or to the man who includes in his published scripts the texts of commentaries for "imaginary films" called *America Dreams* ("Thus America dreams. The prisoner in his prison, the traveler in his photos . . . the man in his memories") and *Soy Mexico*, documentaries existing only in the mind, whose commentaries precede not just the editing, but even the shooting of the film.

In 1962, when he shot *La Jetée*, Marker wasn't traveling. He was in his home city of Paris: in that year, he also shot (with Pierre Lhomme) and edited *Le Joli Mai*, a documentary portrait of the city. This is one of his most straightforward films, composed primarily of on-camera interviews and coverage of current events, but it's also a film whose commentary (sparing though it is) seems to be reaching toward fiction, a more fantastic framework, an alien perspective on familiar landscapes. *Le Joli Mai*'s first half assumes a detached, lofty vantage point—this section is called "A Prayer from the Eiffel Tower"—and its second-half narration imagines a city haunted by "the return of Fantômas," the mysterious criminal of Louis Feuillade's silent serials, here transformed into a metaphor for Parisians' fears and uncertainties near the end of the Algerian war. And at the end of *Le Joli Mai*, Marker shows us a prison in the heart of Paris, and his commentary asks us to imagine a prisoner who has had no part in the daily life that the film has chronicled, and asks us, finally, to assume the prisoner's perspective upon his release, as he looks into the faces of ordinary Parisians and sees only their tense unhappiness, the features of another kind of prisoner.

La Jetée—whose vision of Paris after the apocalypse begins with a shot of the Eiffel Tower and then descends to an underground prison—seems almost a pendant to *Le Joli Mai*, part of the same attempt to achieve a perspective on a moment of transition between a traumatic past and an unforeseeable future. Again, it's a prisoner's perspective, an eerie evocation of a solitude filled only by images from the past. In *La Jetée*, the imagination looks like an escape, a means of survival; but the experimenters can't seem to find the imaginative roads to the future, and the past turns out to be a plan that has already been fulfilled. The images from the jetty (a setting which implies flight, though we never actually see a shot of a plane taking off) have a different meaning the second time the hero sees them: after his long return journey of the imagination, the scene he witnessed as a child and experienced only as a shock finally comes back to him with all the details filled in (the faces of the murderer and the victim). He has closed the circle, taken full possession of the obsessive image from his past—but it's just as if he'd committed a slow suicide in his cell.

The movie's ambivalence about the value of imagination is, I think, a reflection of Marker's mixed feelings about creating imaginative fiction on film. Stuck in his home city at a moment in history too unsettled and contradictory to be seen clearly, and having decided that fiction (and science fiction, at that) was the right response, Marker seems to have discovered that fiction filmmaking can be a process of deepening isolation—the solitude of the scriptwriter repeated as the solitude of the editor. It's a departure from his documentaries, in which he skips the scripting stage and goes straight to the shooting, and also from his "imaginary films" like *America Dreams*, for which he writes the script but leaves out the shooting and the editing.

If, as I've suggested, Marker's documentaries are a kind of interrogation, a correspondence between the man who films—spontaneously—and the man who edits—analytically, reflectively—then what correspondence can take place in a scripted film like *La Jetée*, whose shooting is following a plan? What he does, in his editing room, is reduce the filmed footage to stills, in the attempt to return the story to the moment of its conception (but with all the details filled in), to return it to the writer who, in solitude, imagined it. He gives it back, not as a moving picture, but as a truly imaginary film: a storyboard. By eliminating movement, the illusion of immediacy, Marker makes a film in which the present seems not to exist. The power of *La Jetée* is that he makes us feel the full poignancy of its absence.

Perhaps the reason why Marker didn't repeat *La Jetée*'s experiment in fiction was that it was too successful: creating a film entirely out of his imagination seems to have brought him close to the weary detachment of the film's lonely artisan, Hitchcock, the master storyboarder who often claimed that his interest in a film was exhausted in the planning, before the shooting began. *Vertigo* is clearly an important film for Marker, but its significance, as *Sans Soleil* illustrates, is that of a powerful memory, not a model of the filmmaker's activity. We can see something closer to Marker's true model—a favorite myth—in the SLON documentary *The Train Rolls On*, a film which isn't his solitary creation, but the product of a collective. It's not difficult, though, to imagine Marker's part in this short profile of the Soviet filmmaker Alexander Medvedkin: the beginning, a montage of stock footage (the October Revolution, cavalrymen, Lenin's funeral) and stills (Eisenstein, Dziga Vertov and his brother Mikhail Kaufman, the futurist art of El Lissitzky), is a reverent but graceful evocation of the period, and it has Marker's stamp on it. The early years of the revolution are imagined here as a kind of golden age for both society and the arts, and a time, besides, when film was the most important art because it served as the witness, the record of social change. "First, the eye," says the voice-over commentary. "Then the cinema, which prints the look."

After this lyrical prologue, Medvedkin, now an old man, tells his story about the cinema train he took through Russia in 1932. We see, as he tells it, stills of railroad cars equipped with editing machines, a lab, and a projection room—everything needed to shoot films, develop them, edit them, and project them, all on the run. Medvedkin and his crew filmed farmers at work, showed the footage to the people they'd filmed, and led discussions on the efficacy of their methods; they did the same in factories. "The cinema," says Medvedkin, "could be a great and forceful weapon, reconstructing not just factories, but the world." It's hard to imagine a more stirring image for revolutionary filmmakers, a train that travels everywhere, filming and changing the world as it goes—a filmmaking process that's nearly immediate, the distance between shooting and editing reduced to almost nothing. In a final romantic burst, the narrator links Medvedkin's train to "everything that's advancing and moving— history, the cinema. . . . The biggest mistake one could make would be to believe that it had come to a halt."

Medvedkin's train, Marker's ideal, may have been rolling in the fervent, hopeful days of the late sixties and early seventies, but from the evidence of *Sans Soleil*, it seems to have stopped before it reached the eighties. "Tokyo is a city crisscrossed by trains," Marker tells us, but the trains we see are vehicles of dreams: the passengers file in from underground shopping malls, and the train's smooth movement lulls them into a sleep filled with samurai and ghosts and beautiful women from TV ads. (The narrator imagines "a single film made of the dreams of people on trains.") When the ride is over, and the crowds spill up from underground into the January light, they seem to have acquired an otherworldly beauty—whether because they've been refreshed by their images or because they have, at last, been released from them is impossible to say.

But the images Marker sees when he dreams at his moviola are of those things that were "advancing and moving" years earlier, like the revolution in Guinea-Bissau, but have since been arrested. The one that keeps returning is the face of an African woman whose eyes meet the gaze of his camera for exactly one twenty-fourth of a second, the duration of a single frame of film. Or he sees again the "image of happiness" he began with, the blond Icelandic children on the road, who have "grafted themselves into" a sequence from Tokyo showing a Shinto blessing on the debris left after a celebration, a blessing which is "a ceremony for everything that's been left behind." The last time he sees the blond children, he holds the shot for its full duration, including the bit he'd edited out earlier, when the image starts to tremble, the camera blown by the wind. And this time, he follows that shot with a friend's footage of the volcanic eruption that wiped out the town in Iceland five years after: it is, he says, like watching the destruction of his memories.

Marker's return to Tokyo in *Sans Soleil*, like the time traveler's return to the jetty, produces a more detailed image, one which includes everything that has passed in between. He finds, again, the huge advertisements, the mannequins, the statuary, the flood of TV imagery, but he also finds local festivals and a wide variety of commemorative celebrations: for lost cats; for the war dead; for broken dolls. He finds a letter from a princess of the Heian period who speaks of the "contemplation of the tiniest things . . . things that quicken the heart," and a man with a video synthesizer who plays with the traumatic images of history (the Second World War, Vietnam), distorting them into abstract, colorful shapes, "drawing profiles of what's gone." Japan, this time, seems one huge festival of commemoration, a precise reflection of the mood of the traveler who's left so many places, people, political movements, and past selves behind, but kept bits of them on film, notes which have lost their immediacy, things which have stopped moving but inspire in him the desire to reanimate them at the editing table—the only way available to him to commemorate the things that have quickened his heart.

When the traveler sits, at the end of the film, before Hayao Yamaneko's video synthesizer (an EMS Spectre) and watches the images of *Sans Soleil* in vivid outline, lingering on a beautiful distortion of the African woman's fleeting look, as the woman on the soundtrack wonders "Will there be a last letter?" he seems to have arrived at another alien perspective, as if the accelerating, circular movement of self-interrogation had finally spun him off into orbit—and from this distance (as if from the year 4001), his own images, rendered in the crude, liquid beauty of synthesized video, look like the cave paintings of animals in Lascaux, still pictures that are moving because we sense the movement of the mind and the hand that made them, in commemoration.

This isn't, perhaps, what Marker had in mind in the early seventies: this movement isn't the steady, effective rolling of Medvedkin's train, but a high-speed, crisscrossing motion, trains and planes zipping frantically through the world and leaving, the first time, only traces of their motion, afterimages on the retina when we close our eyes. In *Sans Soleil*—if we return to it a second time—the lines resolve themselves into an image, just visible across the distance of time and fiction, a ghostly face.

Sight and Sound, Autumn 1984

Bill Forsyth

Watching a movie by the Scottish writer and director Bill Forsyth is a little like listening to a long anecdote told by someone whose mind is far away. The narrative keeps wandering off the track, but the digressions are odd enough to keep our attention and even to surprise us into laughing—sporadically and uncertainly at first, then more steadily, until we are brought up short by the punch line we nearly forgot was coming. The end of the story is always a letdown, neither as interesting nor as funny as the circuitous route we've taken to get there. The storyteller has drawn us into his mind's peculiar terrain and allowed us to wander happily, wondering where we are, not wanting to be let off at any of the usual stops. Forsyth's movies have a dreamy, distracted air, a surface modesty, and none of the usual jokes. They mimic the style of a befuddled storyteller so uncannily that we may not catch on right away to their daring and originality: these comedies want us to laugh in the wrong places.

Forsyth's new picture, *Comfort and Joy*, is his riskiest and most ambitious work—a comedy about depression, loneliness, ice cream, and the radio. Its hero, Alan Bird (Bill Paterson), is a Glasgow radio personality known to the public as Dicky Bird. His morning drive-time show dispenses music and cheerful patter, along with the grim necessities of time, traffic, and weather, in a smooth, easy-to-swallow mixture for shut-ins and groggy commuters. Sitting in his studio with his headset on, swiveling in his chair, surrounded by other people (engineers, newsreaders, the traffic girl)—all isolated, like him, in windowed booths—Dicky Bird gives a masterfully orchestrated performance of soothing inanities. He makes jokes about the 6:00 A.M. newsreader falling asleep at his console, invites his listeners to enter a contest whose prize is a day's use of the station manager's American Express card, creates characters out of the station's personnel ("Ah, here comes the lovely Ann!"). His show conjures up the illusion of a workday paradise, a family of charming creatures who converse in the trilling tones of commercial jingles—and it's an illusion that Alan Bird probably couldn't create so well if he didn't half believe in it. The comic premise of *Comfort and Joy* is that Bird's half-belief will, for a few days, be fully and sternly tested. At the beginning of the film his girlfriend of four years, the lovely (but slightly crazy) Maddy, interrupts a peaceful evening at home by announcing that she's having a couple of friends over to move out her things. She walks out of his life, leaving him stranded in an apartment suddenly barer and lonelier than Dicky Bird's studio.

Forsyth knows that you don't have to be deep to be depressed, and he dignifies his hero's personal tragedy with a few bleak, piercing scenes: Bird standing in a light snowfall watching Maddy's van pull away; wandering disconsolately through the empty apartment, pouring himself a drink, avoiding the bedroom as long as he can; dreaming of Maddy's return every time he falls asleep, and waking up, every time, alone. But Forsyth also knows that the attempt to escape depression, to change your life (once, of course, someone has already changed it for you), can be deeply funny. Alan Bird, a man who by both temperament and profession is light, amiable, and easygoing, decides to become more serious: maybe he'll do a documentary on the "real" Glasgow, the violence and industrial squalor he's glossed over every morning on the air, which he seems to be seeing now for the first time, as if the city reflected his own gloomy state of mind. The basic situation here is close to that of Preston Sturges's *Sullivan's Travels*, in which a successful Hollywood director of musicals and light comedies decides to make a "worthy" picture (to be called *O Brother, Where Art Thou?*), and goes out on the road disguised as a hobo to see at first hand the lives of the poor and the dispossessed. The vehicle that Bird finds for his new seriousness is the opportunity to serve as the mediator in a territorial battle between two rival ice-cream operations—the sleek, powerful Mr. McCool and the renegade Mr. Bunny.

Once the ironies of the narrative are in place, we can laugh wherever we like, and Forsyth plays Bird's mission for maximum absurdity. "Mr. Bunny does not play by the rules," exclaims Mr. McCool (who is, it turns out, a rather elegant Italian gentleman). "Mr. Bunny is a rogue elephant." On his morning show Dicky Bird begs his listeners' indulgence while he gets "a teensy bit serious" and relays a message on the air from Mr. McCool to Mr. Bunny. His descent into the ominous nocturnal world of the Glasgow ice-cream wars cheers him with new purpose and new metaphors: "My life," he explains to his friends and his alarmed boss, "was the wrong flavor."

The flavor of *Comfort and Joy* is strange and rich, but not completely unfamiliar to those who have sampled Forsyth's humor in *That Sinking Feeling, Gregory's Girl*, and *Local Hero*. His movies are filled with people who feel that they're in the wrong place and yearn (with varying degrees of urgency) for someplace else. The Glasgow youths in *That Sinking Feeling* decide that crime—that is, pinching a load of bathroom fixtures—is the remedy for the boredom and poverty of unemployment; the teenage boys in *Gregory's Girl* lurch timidly into the world of romantic love, a couple of them desperate enough to get out on the highway and start thumbing their way to Caracas, where women, they've heard, outnumber men eight to one; *Local Hero*'s hotshot young oil executive winds up wanting to trade places with the innkeeper of the Scottish coastal village that he's been sent from Houston to buy out. After four movies, this starts to look like a theme—unobtrusive, but persistent enough to give Forsyth's pictures a distinctive rhythm, a pace unlike anything we're used to in screen comedy. It's not the lickety-split timing of farce or the accelerating gags of silent slapstick or the steady, metronomic rationing of jokes in situation comedy but the languid, daydreaming tempo of a Sunday drive.

The films are funny because Forsyth seems to be following his dreamers at just the right distance, watching them swerve and meander but keeping his own eye on the road. What amuses him is the way our fantasies foul up our relationship to the place we're in, the way they put us at odds with mundane things—the time, the traffic, the weather. He loves adolescents like Gregory, because they're so profoundly out of it, as if they didn't fully inhabit even their own bodies. For Gregory, going about the little business of life, such as getting himself off to school, is a fantastic adventure. He rolls out of bed, beats aimlessly (but vigorously) on his drum set for a minute or two, wanders downstairs with an electric toothbrush whirring in his mouth, lays it down, still running, to buzz and travel erratically across the kitchen counter as he fixes his breakfast; and then, finally out and on his way, shirttail flapping as he lopes across the highway, he somehow manages to put himself in the path of the only car for miles around. Gregory's mind is always miles away, which makes him silly but gives him a kind of comic grace. To be "not all there" is a real gift if "there" is Glasgow, or high school. Forsyth also confers this gift, for a while, on Mac, the young businessman of *Local Hero*, whose stay in the village of Ferness begins as an assignment and ends up a blissful holiday. His suits and ties give way to floppy pullovers, he stops carrying his attaché case on the beach, he lets the shaving go for a few days. He even leaves his beeper watch, which tells him that it's meeting time in Houston, on a rock, and never misses it.

Gregory's Girl is probably Forsyth's funniest movie, and *Local Hero* (which, in the end, returns the reluctant Mac to Houston) is his most satisfying, the smoothest blend of irony and reverie. *Comfort and Joy* shares those films' desultory rhythms and out-of-place humor, but, perhaps because its hero is older and apparently settled in his life, there seems to be more at stake here—real violence, real depression, an even greater yearning for escape. Forsyth is trying to stretch his delicate comic vision to its limit, and he nearly brings off something very difficult: a comedy that delights us and disturbs us at the same time. For the first time in his work Forsyth has a mixture of elements so volatile that they demand a resolution, a punch line, and he can't quite deliver a satisfactory one. Sturges, facing a similar problem in *Sullivan's Travels* but blessed with a brash, aggressive style, just went ahead and belted out a stupid one: Sullivan learns that his mindless, frothy movies are worth more to America's unfortunates than his beloved social-problem picture ever could be. *Comfort and Joy*'s gentler, fablelike resolution completes the ironic curve of the story, using the radio and Bird's lightweight charm to effect the end of the ice-cream wars. It's graceful and clever, but too simple, too self-consciously charming; it brings Forsyth perilously close to endorsing the fun-conquers-all moral of *Sullivan's Travels*.

Forsyth seems more comfortable in the film's very last scene—just a coda, really—and he tosses off a lovely riff that leaves us half believing in the value of the commercial daydream that Dicky Bird provides for his audience. Sitting at his mike on Christmas Day, with no company at the station except an engineer who brings him a tiny piece of cake, Bird spins out the illusion of a joyous Christmas party ("Don't you feel too sorry for us!") and promises his listeners a day of nothing but music and jokes—no time, no traffic, no weather reports. His radio show in this last scene takes on a beauty as unearthly and as unexpected as Glasgow's in the streetlit evenings through which Bird has chased down Mr. Bunny vans. It has the beauty, too, of an apt and resonant metaphor for the art of Bill Forsyth's comedies, these diverting, original anecdotes that are both daydreams themselves and sympathetic reports on the daydreamers. Forsyth's movies always end by telling us, from someplace far away, that the traffic on the way to wherever we'd rather be is moving slowly, but the weather is good and there's all the time in the world.

The Atlantic, November 1984

François Truffaut

François Truffaut, who died last October, at the age of fifty-two, was first a critic and then a filmmaker. As a filmmaker, he was at his best in historical films, like *Jules and Jim*, *The Wild Child*, and *The Story of Adèle H.* As a critic, he did his most passionate writing in obituaries for directors he loved. A tone of retrospection, of elegy, came easily to him. The period films are made poignant by his wholly distinctive editing style: rapid, fleeting, episodic, a series of intense moments that often appear to have been cut off prematurely, before we can surrender to the illusion of their dramatic immediacy—vignettes linked only by matter-of-fact narrations whose effect is strangely melancholy, interpreting and mediating, and thus reminding us that the lives we're watching are long over. These pictures are moving in the way discovered letters and journals are, intimate and remote in equal measure: we follow the traces of once vital passions. In his writings on film, Truffaut was always looking for such traces in the work of his favorite directors, scanning even the most apparently opaque Hollywood surfaces for the features of the artists behind them. (This is the essence of the *"auteur* theory," which Truffaut championed in *Cahiers du Cinéma* in the fifties.) What interested him was the personality of the filmmaker, and his criticism often reads like a peculiar form of biography—as if every director's body of work were the journal of a life, as if every individual movie were a letter addressed to him. Truffaut's articles, and especially his obituaries, express a profound desire for identification with their

80

subjects, coupled with an ironic awareness that they can be no more than sympathetic commentaries, voice-overs.

In the course of his erratic career, Truffaut left elements of autobiography, signs of himself, everywhere, and in a variety of forms. His works include the explicitly autobiographical Antoine Doinel series of films (*The 400 Blows*, the "Antoine and Colette" episode of *Love at Twenty*, *Stolen Kisses*, *Bed and Board*, and *Love on the Run*); three movies (*The Wild Child*, *Day for Night*, and *The Green Room*) in which he played an important character himself, and others in which he did Hitchcocklike cameos; a memorable appearance as a UFO expert in Spielberg's *Close Encounters of the Third Kind*; innumerable interviews; a large handful of graceful, very personal prefaces, mostly to editions of his own screenplays and to the work of his mentor, the critic André Bazin; the text of his extensive conversations with Alfred Hitchcock, known here as *Hitchcock/Truffaut*; and his own selection of his critical writings from the mid-fifties through the mid-seventies, *The Films in My Life*. Truffaut clearly wanted members of his audience to be able to evoke him as they watched his films—for him this direct contact between the filmmaker and the moviegoer was the essence, the real experience, of the movies. He once characterized the films of Jean Renoir, the director he most admired, as "conversations," and the body of Renoir's work as "thirty-five natural and alive films, modest and sincere, as simple as saying hello."

Truffaut's descriptions of his own early moviegoing, in the forties, are lyrical and finely detailed, almost reverent, with a kind of awe at the feelings these movies stirred in him. In his introduction to one of Bazin's collections, Truffaut wrote about the first movie he could remember seeing, Abel Gance's *Paradis Perdu*: "The coincidence between the situation of the characters in the film and that of the spectators was such that the entire audience wept, hundreds of handkerchiefs piercing the darkness with little points of white. Never again was I to feel such an emotional unanimity in response to a film." The movies were for Truffaut what the radiant femme fatale Catherine was for Jules and Jim, what Lieutenant Pinson was for Adèle Hugo, what water and sunlight were for Victor, the wild boy of Aveyron—the first great experience, the one that seems to embody all the world's secrets, the moment to which our imaginations are ceaselessly returning. Truffaut's idea of cinema was of a sacred, magical instrument that transmitted to him, across great distances, the voices of great men; and too frequently, both in his criticism and—more damagingly—in his films, he made the mistake of believing that the greatness of cinema could be found in the properties of the instrument itself rather than in the quality of the voice or the magnitude of the emotional response. When he grilled Hitchcock for fifty hours on the secrets of his technique, when he tried his hand at his own "Hitchcock films" (*The Bride Wore Black* and *Mississippi Mermaid*), and when, at the end of his career, he began to turn out smooth and utterly impersonal exercises in classical style, like *The Last Metro* and *The Woman Next Door*, Truffaut was perhaps conducting experiments on the source of the cinema's grace—hoping, with a seminarian's uneasy faith, that it could be found in perfectly imitated forms, precise invocations.

His youthful passion for moviegoing may have dwindled, over time, to a mythic notion of "cinema," but Truffaut's best movies were also triumphant vindications of that passion—proof that a full and sympathetic response to movies, or literature, can be the means to a complex understanding of experience. The exhilarating early scenes of *Jules and Jim*, in which the two young intellectuals of 1912 argue about literature, experiment with love, and discover Catherine, their feminine ideal, are the work of an artist who knows that exuberance, that playful and profound rapture. What makes the movie so unsettling is that Truffaut also knows (just two years after *The 400 Blows* and the rest of the first crop of New Wave films had seemed to reinvent the rules of the game for cinema) the fading of that spirit, the messy accumulation of experience that blurs the clear outline of the ideal. The movie's buoyant, helter-skelter rhythms stop abruptly with the outbreak of the First World War, and from then on the narrative proceeds by way of long leaps in time, the characters losing sight of each other for gaps of weeks, even months; and every time we pick them up again we read their faces closely (Why does Jules look so wan and small, swaddled in his bulky sweater? Why has Catherine's mouth set that way?) to fill in the gaps, to figure out how these people got so tired from living up to their younger selves. The beauty, the real wisdom, of *Jules and Jim* is that the disillusionment of its characters—their painfully protracted awareness of failure—doesn't diminish the value of their moral experiment.

If you see *Jules and Jim* at the right age—in college—you may feel the way Truffaut did when he saw *Paradise Perdu* as a child, overwhelmed by the possibilities of movies, or the way he felt later on while watching Renoir's films, as if he were engaged in a lively, intimate conversation; what we hear in *Jules and Jim*, though, isn't a master's voice but that of a brilliant and generous student. Perhaps better than any other filmmaker, Truffaut conveys the thrill of *learning,* and the wide range of emotion in *Jules and Jim* reflects the range of its director's long apprenticeship in the movies: from his childhood discovery of their power, to the more articulate appreciation of the young critic, to the anxious joy of making movies of his own, of hearing for the first time that mysterious language spoken in his own voice. This excitement, strangely, doesn't come across so forcefully in the autobiographical Antoine Doinel pictures that followed *The 400 Blows*, or in his movies about movies, like the Hitchcock pastiches and *Day for Night*. Maybe he needed the distance of history to be able to express himself freely; maybe he worked best when the very making of the movie was a process of learning, when he could immerse himself in the effort of understanding and re-creating a past age. Or maybe Truffaut, with his double perspective of filmmaker and critic, the iconoclastic New Wave pioneer and the reverent *auteur* theorist (who gave the heading "The Big Secret" to his writings on directors who began in the silent era), brought to his historical films his deepest and most complex sense of himself: that his own passions, his most spirited inventions, would someday—like those of his characters and of his cinematic masters—be things of the past, objects of study.

Truffaut's habit of retrospection, the melancholy that invaded *Jules and Jim*, was more pronounced in his later films, as he became (in technical terms, at least) less the adventurous student and more the confident master. The madness of Adèle Hugo, the heroine of Truffaut's last masterpiece, is kin to the romantic folly of Jules and Jim, but the style of the film is hermetic, perfectly controlled: the love affair that is Adèle's obsession is over before the story begins, and *The Story of Adèle H.*, with sympathy and irony, traces her attempt to turn her passion into a myth, to immortalize herself as her father, Victor Hugo, immortalized her drowned sister, Léopoldine. "Despite my youth," she says, in voice-over, as we watch the beautiful nineteen-year-old Isabelle Adjani writing in her journal, "I sometimes feel I am in the autumn of my life." Near the end, as she glides through the streets of Barbados in a long, dark cloak, Adèle seems truly disembodied, and the narrator, over a still photograph of her grave, tells us that she spent the last forty years of her life in a clinic, writing her journals in a secret language.

In his final appearance on the screen, Truffaut played the lead in the morbid, unpleasant *The Green Room*. His character, Julien Davenne, is a man obsessed with preserving the memory of his dead wife and of all his compatriots killed in the First World War; he works for a newspaper no one reads anymore, and is a genius at obituaries. Davenne's behavior is outrageous, but we can't read any irony in Truffaut's face or hear it in the voice of the film. And in the movies that followed *The Green Room* the author's voice isn't audible at all—as if he had finally drowned in the imperious language of his masters. The sight of Truffaut, as Davenne, yearning for a reunion with his beloved dead is unnerving: it's an extension of the ideas in *Adèle H.*, and it's consistent—as an extreme consequence— with some of the traces of personality he scattered through his work. But a portrait of the artist based on this image would be a distortion—a death mask, more obituary than true biography. *Jules and Jim*, for all its elegiac consciousness of youthful spirits' eventual exhaustion, taught a generation of movie lovers and moviemakers that the process was more important than the end, that the give-and-take vitality of conversation was everything—that the giddy, briefly magical convergence of Jules and Jim and Catherine mattered more than Jules's ultimate solitude. Everything converged for Truffaut in the middle of his career as a director with *The Wild Child*, his most beautiful film and his fullest revelation of himself.

The Wild Child, set in 1798, is based on the writings of Jean Itard, a French doctor who tried to educate a "wild boy" found in the forest of Aveyron. Truffaut cast himself as Itard, and the scientist's earnest, rational eighteenth-century spirit dominates the film, as if it had taken possession of the director: the movie is lucid and serenely paced, composed primarily of medium and long shots in elegant, plain black-and-white, the narrative thread provided by Truffaut's voice-over reading of Itard's precisely worded observations of his humane experiments with the wild boy. The only "effect" is an archaic one: the repeated use of an iris—a device that isolates a detail in a kind of cameo within an otherwise darkened frame—as a transition between scenes. (In order to avoid the impersonal look of effects created in the laboratory, Truffaut's cinematographer, Nestor Almendros, actually searched for, and found, an iris that had been used in the silent era. "The iris of the silent film," Almendros has written, "had the quality, now lost, of a handmade thing.") The homage to the early days of movies isn't arbitrary: this film about an experiment in education, the attempt to teach an inarticulate boy to speak, is suffused with Truffaut's radiant love for the movies' beginnings, when everything was being done for the first time, when the language was learned.

The movie, filmed eight years after *Jules and Jim* and eight years before *The Green Room*, has a miraculous kind of balance: between freedom and control, originality and homage, the discovery of new experience and the contemplation of the past—between the boy Victor's mysterious ecstasy as he opens his mouth to drink in the falling rain and the supremely rational pleasure of Itard as he stands by the window and records the progress of the lessons, his journal bathed in the clear light of the eighteenth century. In this film, Truffaut gives us an image of himself as both master and student, the image that contains all we need to know of him. The story of *The Wild Child* is just an episode artfully isolated from the lives of Itard and the wild boy: the film doesn't tell us how Victor came to be abandoned in the forest (the truth was never known), and it doesn't tell us, either, that Victor lived almost thirty years longer without ever coming close to mastering verbal communication. At the end, when Victor returns to Itard's house after a brief attempt at escape, Truffaut just irises out on the wild boy's youthful, intelligent, troubled face suspended within the surrounding blackness of the frame as he ascends the stairs.

The New Yorker, December 31, 1984

Satyajit Ray

The movies of the Indian director Satyajit Ray tell stories the way faces and houses and landscapes do. Ray's narrative methods are like the time-lapse photography that's sometimes used in nature films, showing us almost imperceptible processes like growth and erosion as a sequence of images captured at precisely metered intervals and then projected at normal speed: the changes that in life we would notice only after the fact in Ray's films seem to happen before our eyes. Ray's new film (his twenty-fifth) is *The Home and the World*, an intimate epic set in Bengal in the early twentieth century, when nationalist movements were gathering force and ancient traditions were beginning to lose their strength. The director first planned to film Rabindranath Tagore's novel thirty years ago, and the movie he has now made seems to link all the stages of his career in one elegant and continuous motion—to arrange in sequence three decades of images of characters wandering through the familiar rooms of their homes and along the intricate roads of the world, looking for a place in themselves where the two dissimilar geographies might coincide.

Like *Charulata*, an earlier Ray adaptation of a Tagore story, *The Home and the World* is about a triangle that's as much philosophical as it is romantic. Nikhil, a rich, liberal landowner (played by Victor Banerjee, best known to Western audiences for his splendid Dr. Aziz in *A Passage to India*), encourages his wife, Bimala, to come out from behind the screen of purdah—the traditional seclusion of the

Indian wife—and enter the world. The first person she meets is his old friend Sandip, now the leader of the *swadeshi* movement to boycott foreign goods. She is attracted by the radical's ideas and his forceful personality, which seem to her more worldly than her husband's sensitive, ambivalent temperament. Sandip manipulates her easily, both for his cause and for himself, and Nikhil can only watch as his wife grows further away from him and the tenuous political harmony of Bengal is disrupted.

Although Ray makes an occasional gesture toward reproducing the novel's multiple-narrator technique—a few brief scenes in which the three main characters express their thoughts in voice-over—for the most part he tells the story straightforwardly. The meanings emerge, as always in his films, from looks and gestures and the movement of people within spaces that are rigorously defined—emotionally as well as physically.

In the first part of the film Ray explores the geography of Nikhil's mansion, where most of the action takes place, and we always know exactly where we are—in the sitting room, in the *zenana* (the apartments where women in purdah spend their days), in the corridor between the *zenana* and the outer apartments, or in the couple's bedroom, which opens onto that corridor. Little events keep accumulating in these rooms, in a leisurely, apparently aimless way, until at some point we realize that the spaces have been charged with all the sparks of awareness we've seen in the characters' faces.

In the later scenes Ray hardly needs dialogue to tell us what the characters are feeling, because the house is radiant with associations. We're always aware that the sitting room, where the wife and the revolutionary meet, is a kind of neutral territory, neither Sandip's world nor fully Bimala's; every scene in the *zenana* carries the memory of Nikhil's early attempts to educate his wife and the disapproving glances of his conservative, widowed sister-in-law. The corridor between the inner and outer apartments seems to vibrate, throughout the film, from the force of the early scene in which Bimala takes her first steps out of the *zenana*—her pace momentously slow, fear and pride mixed in her eyes. And the scenes in the bedroom—reserved but intimate early on, chilly and tense later—build to a moving sequence of reconciliation followed abruptly by separation, and a final scene in which the world appears for the first time from the perspective of the house: a tableau framed, with heartbreaking plainness and clarity, by the bedroom window. The last act of this tragedy is played out according to a kind of moral choreography in which every entrance and exit is thrilling, significant, in which even the most delicate movements expand to fill the room, the screen, the mind.

The Home and the World isn't one of Ray's masterpieces; for all its grace, it can't always get out from under the philosophical weight of Tagore's original. But it's a fully characteristic example of the director's narrative means, and of the complicated effect his films have on Western audiences—often puzzling us with their cultural remoteness yet seducing us with their extreme emotional accessibility. In a Ray film we don't know the names of the trees but we seem to know the most intimate thoughts of the people strolling among them; we couldn't say, perhaps, what a rupee is worth, but we're able to measure the weight of every transaction—the exact value of what's been bought and the spiritual price that's been paid.

These films make sense, even to Western viewers, because the director gives each character a dense, detailed history, and because Ray's storytelling has a history too—a continuity with Western forms of narrative. The Apu trilogy—*Pather Panchali*, *Aparajito*, and *The World of Apu*—is the cinema's purest *Bildungsroman* (the nineteenth-century novel form that tells the story of a young man's education in the ways of the world). Many other films have used the classic plot elements—the provincial boyhood, the adolescent schooling, the move to the city, the poverty and the idealism of the beginning writer, the first love. But the pace of Ray's trilogy is distinctive and surprisingly apt: a reflective unfolding of action and consequence which seems novelistic without being self-consciously literary. The long stretches without dialogue, the many scenes of people just walking around (especially in the last and richest film of the trilogy, *The World of Apu*), frame the story's action in an almost discursive way. Like the passages of analysis in a George Eliot novel, they give us images of both the expectation before an event and the reflection after it, images that complete the human significance of the action: Apu's slow walk across the railway after a series of dispiriting job interviews; his buoyant crossing of the same tracks after receiving a letter from his absent wife, as he anticipates seeing her again; his wandering in the forest after her death, his face in close-up, so that the leaves around him seem to pass by in a blur.

That blur reappears in the opening sequence of Ray's superb *Days and Nights in the Forest*, made eleven years later. This time it's a Bengal forest seen from a speeding car whose occupants, four well-off, Western-educated young men from Calcutta, are on their way to a holiday in the country. The men are laughing, bantering, in weekend spirits, but the flowing, indistinct shots of the forest are vaguely melancholy. Though the patterns are lovely, they aren't clear, because the car (whose driver, Ashim, is played by Soumitra Chatterjee, the Apu of the trilogy's final film) is going too fast: they suggest the passengers' murky awareness of the world and therefore of themselves. Once the men arrive at their rural guesthouse, the film adopts a strolling rhythm, a pace at which the individual features of things can be made out and patterns become more lucid and more complex. Real characters begin to emerge from a forest of types, and new people—two vacationing Calcutta women, the reserved, ironic Aparna and her brother's young widow—are added to the initial four. The forest itself, while losing none of its density, takes on a shining clarity, each leaf catching the light as a mirror would. *Days and Nights in the Forest* is about the gradual reawakening of sensibility, of attentiveness to the world, and it builds to a series of small, piercing revelations in which the characters seem to be moving, hesitantly, toward one another from behind their screens.

There's a slow, beautiful scene near the end, in which Aparna discloses to Ashim the suffering that is the source of her cool, protective irony. The distance between them varies, and they never do quite touch, but they have at least remained still long enough to get a good look at each other. Ray's composition includes a huge, solitary tree, whose leaves and intricate bark become by the end of the scene as familiar and memorable as a beloved face.

In his three decades of moviemaking Satyajit Ray has slowly revealed more and more of his own face to the audience. From the stark, neorealist beginnings of *Pather Panchali* and *Aparajito* Ray's work has grown to include elaborate dissections of the Hindu aristocracy (*The Music Room, Devi*), ferociously pointed contemporary morality plays about Calcutta's commercial middle class (*Company Limited, The Middleman*), and even lighthearted detective stories for children (*The Golden Fortress, The Elephant God*). Over the years he has assumed more and more of the diverse tasks of filmmaking: since his seventh movie, *Two Daughters*, he has composed his own scores, and he now operates the camera as well. As far as it is possible in this complex art, Ray's films are the expression of a single sensibility—one that combines what V. S. Naipaul has called the "passionate introspection" of Anglo-Bengali culture with the probing attentiveness to experience of the nineteenth-century European novel. Just as the young men from Calcutta are vaguely disturbed by the ancient Bengali customs they come upon during their days and nights in the forest, audiences in this country may be jarred, and moved, by the "Western" characteristics of Ray's art, by our uneasy recognition of a moral and aesthetic territory that was once a more prominent feature of our own cultural geography. His work has the qualities—the patient analysis of character, the scrupulous and sympathetic way of understanding the world—that our own art seems, at times, to have simply speeded past.

The Atlantic, April 1985

John Huston

In 1950, James Agee wrote of John Huston: "In his life, his dealings and his work as an artist he operates largely by instinct, unencumbered by much reflectiveness or abstract thinking, or any serious self-doubt." And thirty-five years later, Huston doesn't seem to have changed a bit: he's still working on gall and intuition, trusting his wits, his actors, and what Agee called "the peculiar kind of well-earned luck which Heaven reserves for the intuitive and the intrepid." He has made thirty movies since 1950—including a big-budget musical, a couple of Westerns, a handful of thrillers, *The Bible*, *Moby Dick*, a biography of Freud, an Arthur Miller original, and adaptations of Stephen Crane, Carson McCullers, Tennessee Williams, Flannery O'Connor, Malcolm Lowry, and Kipling—and his luck, in individual films, has frequently deserted him, unpredictably: his failures range from heroic near-misses on ambitious projects (*Moby Dick*, *Under the Volcano*) to unabashedly "commercial" pictures sabotaged by indifference and laziness (*Annie*, *The Mackintosh Man*). But his gambler's mix of heedlessness, ego, and fatalism has made him, uniquely among major American directors, just about impervious to failure: he has had far more flops than hits, and he has still made nearly a film a year for over forty years. "The calendar takes care of everything," says his daughter Anjelica in *Prizzi's Honor*, and her eyes move toward the camera as she says it.

Prizzi's Honor is, like every good Huston picture, unlikely, miraculous: a quirky, deadpan Mafia comedy, perversely cast and staged with such confident disregard for period detail that we're never quite sure whether the story is set in the 1950s or the 1980s or some time in between. Jack Nicholson, of all people, plays Charley Partanna, the underboss and enforcer of the Brooklyn Prizzi family, a good soldier who's shrewd in the ways of "the environment" but in little else; when he falls in love with Irene Walker, a freelance contract killer played by Kathleen Turner, his awestruck slowness of response is sort of endearing—but it's the same dullness that allows him to kill unquestioningly for the Prizzis.

Whatever inspired Huston to cast the quick-witted Nicholson as this gaping, smitten thug, the gamble pays off beautifully. Nicholson has been telling interviewers that he didn't get *Prizzi's Honor* at all when he first read it and never felt comfortable with his role, but put his "not understanding the material together with the character's dumbness into a kind of dynamic on how to play him." Enough of the actor's natural intelligence comes through—despite a padded upper lip, a thick Brooklyn accent, and the nauseating yellow sports jacket he wears in his first big romantic scene—to keep Charley Partanna from becoming just a violent clown and the film from crossing the line between ironic fable and crude cartoon. And Nicholson's performance seems to give the movie its distinctive and satisfying rhythm: his watchful but slightly stupefied air and his languidly timed double takes at every outrageous turn of the plot have the effect of slowing the narrative to a majestically easy pace. As Charley tries to figure out what's hitting him, we, and Huston, take a little extra time to savor the jokes.

Huston, of course, couldn't possibly have known that this apparent miscasting would serve his picture so well, couldn't have counted on the transformation of his leading actor's confusion into a real and vivid quality of the character. As he has done so many times before, he just played a hunch. Agee's description of the performance of Alfonso Bedoya, the nonprofessional whom Huston cast as the grinning, volatile bandit Gold Hat in *The Treasure of the Sierra Madre*, gives an early look at the director's method: "It worked because this inadequate actor was trying so hard, was so unsure of what he was doing and was so painfully confused and angered by Huston's cryptic passivity. These several kinds of strain and uncertainty, sprung against the context of the story, made a living image of the almost unactable, real thing; and that had been Huston's hunch."

The casting of Nicholson in *Prizzi's Honor* is a similar kind of good Huston hunch, and the product of one or more kinds of shrewdness. Aesthetically, Huston might have seen that Nicholson's customary heavy-lidded cunning and sly, drawling speech patterns could, with a little exaggeration, pass for the mannerisms of a stupid man; financially, he surely knew that Nicholson's name in the credits would help get this eccentric project off the ground. And personally, he may have hoped that the presence of Nicholson, the longtime companion of Anjelica Huston, would somehow make it easier for him to coax the performance he needed out of his daughter.

Playing Maerose Prizzi, Charley's ex-lover and the granddaughter of Don Corrado, the head of the Prizzi family, Anjelica Huston has the role that's the heart of the picture, the real *Huston* part. Although John Huston himself, by virtue of his age, his crafty intelligence, and his proficiency at acting alarming patriarchs, could certainly have taken the role of Don Corrado, the character really isn't the kind of natural extension of Huston's personality that his roles in *Chinatown* and *Winter Kills* (adapted, like *Prizzi's Honor*, from a Richard Condon novel) seemed to be: robust, high-rolling tycoons whose dominance (and unscrupulousness) is the product of gigantic and varied appetites. Don Corrado—played wonderfully by William Hickey in the film—is greedy and playfully devious, but he's a small man, shriveled meanly in the corners of the deep red, throne-like chairs in his Brooklyn home, and the size of his appetites is precisely expressed by the plate of little cookies that's the centerpiece of a key scene between him and Maerose: he offers her one, with a dirty but not very insistent gleam in his eye, and when she declines he nibbles it delicately himself.

Maerose, the black sheep of the Prizzis, is more Huston's speed. She's imperious and impulsive: her banishment from the family was the consequence of her having "dishonored" Charley with a wild, vengeful fling with another man in Mexico, and when Charley visits her apartment, for the first time in years, she startles him by saying, "Let's do it. Right here on the oriental." Although she is as cunning and unforgiving as the rest of the Prizzis, the wounds that Maerose schemes to avenge are large matters of personal pride, not petty financial embarrassments: she wants to make her father suffer for exiling her, and she wants Charley back. When Charley asks Maerose's advice about Irene Walker, after he discovers that his new love has been stealing from the Prizzis' casino in Las Vegas ("Do I ice her? Do I marry her?") and Maerose responds with her line about the calendar taking care of everything, we can tell by the look in her eyes that she plans to take care of a few things all by herself.

In the end, Maerose has her triumph, and Anjelica Huston's face is the last image in the movie before the credits roll. John Huston seems to have chosen his daughter to stand in for him this time, to represent onscreen the family traits: a combination of philosophical fatalism—the let's-see-what-happens passivity which has sometimes made Huston's actors very uncomfortable—and a steely determination to get exactly what one wants.

Huston's statements about his own working methods often suggest an improvisational (or what Mailer, who developed some of his own eccentric theory and practice of movies from reflections on *The Maltese Falcon*, might call "existential") approach to filmmaking. He told Agee, "In pictures, if you do it right, *the thing happens, right there on the screen,*" and he wrote in his 1980 autobiography, *An Open Book*, "It is best to shoot chronologically. In this way you can benefit by accidents, and you don't paint yourself into corners." And his heterogeneous, almost random choice of material ("I read without discipline," he has said) tends to confirm that impression. (His taste—good enough to attract him to Melville, Crane, Carson McCullers, and Flannery O'Connor, bad enough to drag him down into Romain Gary, Arthur Miller, and John Milius—is as erratic as that of America's other great freestyle director, Robert Altman.) He has certainly never been a meticulous planner, much less a believer in story boards, but—with the exception of the loose, goofy *Beat the Devil*—he doesn't just make it up as he goes along. In fact, it's hard to think of an American director who is more concerned with the architecture of scripts, or with the precise reproduction of literary effects on the screen. Like the character his daughter plays in *Prizzi's Honor*, John Huston isn't such a fatalist that he doesn't believe in making a good plot.

Huston began his career, after all, in the Hollywood studio system, and despite his reputation as a maverick, he seems not to have found the old system especially confining. His moviemaking values, then and now, aren't really so different from those of a shrewd producer or a studio boss: strong story, swift, efficient shooting, and performances charged with the volatile immediacy of star power. He just takes all the elements a little further, enforcing the traditional Hollywood aesthetic by pushing it to the extreme, so that the picture won't go dead on the screen: not just strong stories, then, but overstuffed, baroque ones or established classics; shooting concentrated to a form of daredevil shorthand, with few multiple takes and fewer master shots; and a conception of acting based on accidental revelations, an attempt to trap the startling aliveness that gives stars like Bogart or Nicholson a heightened reality.

This last quality is what has often made Huston seem inspired, even radical. His films with Bogart are an extraordinary series of explorations of a personality, a surprisingly varied set of discoveries about the features of a rather ordinary face: the grin that looks cool and vaguely menacing in *The Maltese Falcon* is avid, psychotic in *The Treasure of the Sierra Madre*, then bizarrely romantic in *The African Queen*, and finally rather innocent and bemused in the international babel of *Beat the Devil*. Huston's search for those elusive, "unactable" qualities that transcend the role has also made him appear, at times, merely quixotic and wrongheaded. He hoped, clearly, that Audie Murphy's stature as a war hero would lend resonance to his performance as the young soldier in *The Red Badge of Courage*. But Murphy's limitations as an actor defeated him; and Huston's eagerness to direct Marilyn Monroe in *The Misfits*, in a role obviously designed to reveal some version of her "true" self, must have blinded him to the defects of the pompous, overexplicit script. Like all Hollywood filmmakers, though, Huston's primary concern has always been story; he may have looked like a rebel in the 1940s simply because he wasn't satisfied with the illusions of reality that conventional pictures settled for. He worked out a way to make *his* tall tales grittier and more spontaneous-looking—the better to put them over on us.

Prizzi's Honor, like *The Maltese Falcon*, is an ideal Huston story: an intricate, layered fable in which fate disguises itself as a series of outrageous accidents, a plot which is just one damn thing after another until it all winds up, somehow, at a predetermined end. It's a dark, gleaming engine, full of schemes, catastrophes, sudden revelations, and unforeseen consequences, and dense with conflicting motives and interests. And like *The Maltese Falcon, Prizzi's Honor* has at its center an edgy romance that is resolved, finally, in a lightning burst of pragmatism, a shrewd act performed with the shocking speed of instinct. Everything we need to know about how this plot will turn out is in the quick tableaux which open the picture, showing Charley's youth from his birth, with his father and Don Corrado looking on, to his initiation into the crime family, mingling his blood with the old don's as he swears to uphold Prizzi honor.

Huston never quite lets us forget that the Prizzi organization is a closed system, the kind of self-perpetuating principle that always wins out over individual desires, or that Charley's romance with Irene is just a little grit in the smoothly functioning machinery, easily ground away—but the furious complications keep us distracted from the inexorability built into the conception. He achieves this effect, in part, with a concentrated visual and narrative plan that keeps us *inside* most of the time, within the Prizzis' homes and offices, and avoids the light-and-dark contrasts which defined the difference between the underworld and the world outside in the *Godfather* films. The Prizzis' universe is lit normally and there's nothing in the film to compare it to, and before long even Don Corrado, who shows a surprising flexibility on questions of Prizzi honor, looks nearly reasonable. And that allows Huston to spring his characteristic joke: all the activity, the characters' elaborate calculations of cause and effect, is just lively, meaningless diversion, and the apparent flexibility of the Prizzi code means only that it's a very *smart* system. As always in Huston, the gamblers have a good run, but the house wins. The bird is a fake. The gold does blow away.

In his autobiography, Huston claims not to be aware of any favorite themes in his movies. Unreflective even now, in his seventies, he also denies awareness of a personal style; in fact, he refuses to admit anything that would impose a pattern on his life or his work. But he is certainly drawn to stories of failure (he acknowledges, grudgingly, that "success stories, per se, are not really of much interest to me"): sometimes extravagant, as in *Moby Dick, The Treasure of the Sierra Madre*, and *The Man Who Would Be King*;

sometimes small, personal, and pathetic, as in *Fat City* and *Under the Volcano*; and sometimes, as in his first picture and his latest, small but intricately ironic.

The movies of the first group show Huston at his most expansive, with wide vistas of seas and mountains and deserts, empty except for a handful of figures and a cosmic laugh. The second kind of story is a trouble area for him: he clearly believes in the material—perhaps too much. These tales of inevitable decline are straightforward almost to the point of abstraction, as if the truth of Billy Tully's or the Consul's fate were so self-evident that it need only be presented. Despite their spare beauties, these movies are more relentless than dramatic. And the films that (as of now) frame this long career are the best, richest Hustons of all: between *The Maltese Falcon* and *Prizzi's Honor*, the full range of his work is visible, and in more than a temporal sense. The immense good humor of these two works, their evident delight in both complication and ironic resolution, is more revealing of Huston than his autobiography is. (When people say "My life is an open book," what they mean is they're not going to tell you any more about themselves than you already know.)

In these movies, the contradictions in Huston's style and in his vision are precisely balanced: they're like lessons in Hollywood moviemaking, without illusions but without despair. The system (the Knights of Malta, the Prizzi family, the classical script) prevails, as it was designed to, but the individuals in it can have an exhilarating ride on the twisting, accident-strewn paths along the way, gambling with their lives and filling their roles with the unpredictable and unsustainable energy of risky acting, caught at the moment it bursts the frame—and persisting, as images do, beyond the running out of the movie's time.

John Huston knows all about that kind of persistence, the indelible joys of transitory moments. When he's on a roll, as he is in *Prizzi's Honor*, as he was over forty years ago in *The Maltese Falcon*, everything appears to take care of itself and the calendar hardly matters. The style is constant and, unself-consciously, timeless: *The Maltese Falcon* is as fresh and fast as any contemporary picture, *Prizzi's Honor* as grandly and confidently crafted as a studio movie of the forties. At the climax of *Prizzi's Honor*, Huston does some-

thing a little uncharacteristic of his traditionally clean, straightforward technique—he slows the movement of the film's final murder
almost to a stop, suspends each instant of what would in real time
be an uncommonly swift action. He doesn't really need to freeze the
moment in order to heighten it; the scene would be shocking
enough on its own. It's a bit arbitrary, but it seems wholly appropriate that Huston, as usual, went ahead and said, "Let's do it"—
allowing himself perhaps to savor his success at the moviemaker's
game of making time stand still. For the moment, John Huston
seems to have beaten the odds.

Sight and Sound, Autumn 1985

Paolo and Vittorio Taviani

The Sicilian landscapes of Paolo and Vittorio Taviani's new film, *Kaos*, are timeless and alienating all at once, like the surface of the moon. Everything in them—the abrupt outcroppings of rock, the ruins of ancient buildings, the walls that seem stacks of jagged stone, the brusque alternation of lush groves and bleak fields—looks as if it once belonged to something else, to a terrain we might recognize if all the broken pieces came back together. It's a movie of pieces too, an anthology of four self-contained narratives based on stories by Luigi Pirandello, made by a pair of brothers who collaborate by directing alternate scenes. The tales are linked only by swooping aerial shots from the point of view of a raven flying over the countryside and by an epilogue that shows Pirandello's return, after many years, to his native Sicily, the source of his stories. But *Kaos* has a remarkable unity of style and vision. By the end of the film, when Pirandello meets the ghost of his mother, who tells him to "learn to see things with the eyes of those who see them no more" and who then recounts a shimmering childhood memory of her own, it feels as if all the broken bits of narrative, of history, of individual experience, had joined up again, had become at last a single story.

This is a mythic, romantic effect, a feeling that only the most conscious art, or the most innocent, can evoke. The Tavianis, who are both in their fifties, are experienced filmmakers and longtime Marxists. They have arrived at their current simplicity through years of experimenting with styles and ideas: documentaries in the fifties,

Godardian political dramas in the sixties and early seventies, and the rich blend of fable and argument that they have been refining since their first international success, *Padre Padrone* (1977). No Taviani film earlier than the 1974 *Allonsanfan* has been distributed in the United States, but that film (released here only this year) provided hints of the more uncompromising aesthetic program that preceded their current manner. *Allonsanfan*, telling the story of a group of failed nineteenth-century revolutionaries who called themselves the "sublime brothers," consistently sacrificed its historical drama to stark, schematic compositions and long passages of political debate. The 1980 film *The Meadow*, a lugubrious contemporary morality play, seemed a partial regression to that overly cerebral mode, and it didn't find much of an audience. The Tavianis' best movies— *Padre Padrone, The Night of the Shooting Stars* (1983), and *Kaos*— don't abandon history or ideas but turn them into vital, even stirring, narratives.

Padre Padrone is based on the autobiography of the Sardinian linguist Gavino Ledda, who was raised among shepherds, illiterate and virtually alone until the age of twenty. It's set in an island landscape as harsh and barren as Sicily's, and in an even wilder, more primitive society. Sardinia looks like no more than an *idea* of a place to live, a blank slate that is humanized by tremendous efforts of will, or not at all—and the Tavianis, like their protagonist, make the effort. We can feel their determination to shake this world to life. The movie is deliberately jarring, both visually and aurally, with human figures isolated in extreme long shots or paired in intimate, claustrophobic compositions, and with a sound track whose long silences are pierced by cries (human or animal), sudden music, sounds whose sources can't always be identified. The Tavianis adapted Ledda's book very freely, adding a variety of distancing techniques and touches of the fantastic (at one point we even hear the thoughts of the sheep) to his straightforward narrative. Ledda's story is about his progress from inarticulateness to communication, and the Tavianis seem to have conceived of the task of adaptation as a vigorous, emphatic conversation with the author.

The difficult beauties of *Padre Padrone* are generated mostly by its intellectual rigor. The Tavianis don't presume to get too close to Ledda or to his frighteningly ignorant father, who is determined to block his son's passage from the isolated sheepfold to the articulate world outside. They schematize the story, but with such precision and force that the movie's argument turns into a kind of poetry. In an early scene, when Gavino is six, his father—who has just torn him out of the classroom and put him to work on his own, tending sheep—shows him how to identify the sounds of his lonely post. It's night, and the boy hears nothing until his father says, "The oak," and the camera pans from a close-up of the child's ear through the darkness to an ancient, rustling tree, and our ears fill with the sound of what we're seeing. Later, when Gavino is miserably alone with his father's sheep, he hears a garish, sprightly music—a full band on the sound track, but really just a young man with an accordion walking down the road. Gavino trades two sheep for the instrument, which sounds bleating and disharmonious until he learns, through trial and error, to arrange the notes in song. When Gavino finally leaves home to join the army, at first he can't interpret the sounds of the town where he's posted; when he returns, knowing Italian as well as his native Sardinian dialect, his father sees him listening to a symphony on the radio and goes into a murderous rage—his son is being transported, gone for good, and the father would rather see him dead than forever outside the fold.

Gavino Ledda's experience, transformed by the ferocious attack of the Tavianis' style, becomes a kind of myth of the varieties of human articulation, of language and music—the sounds that take us far from home and return us changed, individual, mysteriously complicated. Education in *Padre Padrone* is inseparable from the pain and joy of exile, of being thrust into the world. When the Tavianis, six years later, transformed their own memories into *The Night of the Shooting Stars*, the story of a group of refugees from San Martino, a Tuscan village, at the end of the Second World War, their style had mellowed but the theme remained constant: the villagers, forced by German occupiers and homegrown Fascists to leave their homes, become different people on the road, seeing fantastic things, performing heroic deeds, learning the unfamiliar world. The directors' technique is no less conscious and no less diverse than it was in *Padre Padrone*, but the tone is softer, more lyrical—perhaps because the movie assumes, partially, the innocence of a tale told to a

child, and perhaps because the Tuscan countryside, scarred by the
war, has the poignance of a landscape only recently ruined, not
blasted from the beginning of time like Sardinia's.

The experiences the villagers of San Martino have are large-scale,
made larger yet by the epic distortions of the narrator, who was a girl
of six at the time and is now a grown woman recounting the fabulous events to her own child. The emotional responses they evoke,
both in the characters and in the audience, are extreme: exhilaration
and deep sorrow, following one another so swiftly and unpredictably that they seem a single feeling. The Tavianis are by no means
innocents, but they do remember the undifferentiated wonder with
which children respond to experience, and they respect it enough to
acknowledge that even the worst things—the horrors of war—can
produce a kind of rapture if we've never seen them before.

The people of San Martino, escaping by night, listen in darkness
to the sounds of the village exploding, their way of life disappearing,
and throw away their keys to homes that no longer exist. Along the
way several of the men change their names, becoming "Achilles" or
"Owl" or "Requiem," to join a resistance group and fight a brutal,
almost comically impassioned battle against the Fascists in a wheat
field. The grand events seem to give the smaller, more ordinary
incidents an extra charge, a fuller resonance. Near the end, after the
convulsive struggle in the wheat field, the leader of the expedition,
an old man named Galvano, for the first time sleeps with a woman
he fell in love with forty years earlier, now a very proper grandmother on the road without her family; it's like a reward after a
wearying and anxious odyssey, and we know it's something that
wouldn't have happened otherwise, in the steady life of the village.
This small miracle occurs in another village on the eve of the feast
of San Lorenzo, the night of the shooting stars—the night, the
narrator tells us, when all wishes are granted. The old couple wake
the morning after to a larger miracle, the arrival of the liberating
American troops. Everyone starts, exultantly, the return journey to
San Martino, but Galvano, a little dazed, shaken by all that has
happened, isn't ready to go—he wants to sit awhile in the square of
this other village, in this sunny, refreshing rain, and let all he has
seen and heard and felt soak into his skin.

Omero Antonutti, who plays Galvano (and also the terrifying

father in *Padre Padrone*), reappears as Pirandello at the end of *Kaos*, coming home to Girgenti, Sicily, after years of seeing his birthplace only in his mind—of reinventing it, from a distance, in the stories we've been watching. The actor's face is the first of many echoes in this great, daring sequence: when Antonutti turns up after four tales told with almost baffling simplicity and elegance, he seems to return us to the complex sensibility of the earlier Taviani films. He's a spirit leading us from the bright, clear, folkloric world back to our home territory of doubt, dim memories, and overburdened consciousness.

Pirandello, exhausted by the rigors of his life in Rome, has slept all the way to Girgenti, and when the train arrives—sounding at first like the wind howling through the peasant graveyard at the end of the last tale—he's rudely awakened and virtually hurled from his compartment, as abruptly as a baby being born. He's disoriented, and so are we. He has to place himself again in the land he came from, and he looks blank, uncomfortable, estranged—just as the real Gavino Ledda looked when the Tavianis brought him onscreen for the conclusion of *Padre Padrone*. (Pirandello and Ledda have more than a look and a narrative function in common: each wrote a doctoral thesis on the dialect of his native island.) And we have to place ourselves in a different relation to the stories we've seen, to consider them, perhaps, as not just shapely individual anecdotes about a village madwoman, a moonstruck husband, a greedy land-owner, and wily peasants but the dreams of a great modernist writer as he travels through the world.

Once Pirandello appears, the movie begins to transform itself in our minds. The story of the madwoman who is obsessed with her two sons in America, who haven't written her in fourteen years, becomes a parable of distance and memory. The tale of the young husband who goes mad whenever the moon is full seems now to have something to do with alienation, the individual mysteries that abruptly separate us from our surroundings. The landlord's enor-mous broken jar in the third story suggests an image of a divided world, a classical harmony disrupted. The final tale, about an outlaw community fighting to have its own cemetery, appears to propose a bleak remedy for disharmony—a reunion with the earth, the land made home by the presence of the dead. The stories are still, of course, primarily what they seemed at first to be: plain but ingeniously constructed fictions. The Tavianis mean only to estrange us a little from our initial responses, to make us see the stories fresh, through the eyes and the divided consciousness—half traditional, half modern—of their author.

Kaos is a brilliantly structured work, but the beauty of its imagery transcends the conscious sophistication of the Tavianis' design. In Pirandello's conversation with his mother's ghost we can identify the filmmakers' characteristic ideas. The dead woman tells her son the story of a childhood adventure, a journey in a fishing boat with a red sail to visit her father, a political exile on Malta—it's a tale her son has heard a hundred times before but has never succeeded in transforming into one of his own stories. Recalling her feelings on the trip, she speaks of her "uneasiness about so many new things." She says, "That's what exile meant: new things to be gazed at"—and we hear in her voice the vertiginous, disorienting sensation of fresh experience, the distinctive tone of the Tavianis.

This time, though, the voice is unearthly, emanating from some privileged territory outside of time and consciousness, where the world is magically whole again and the moon has rejoined the earth. It's a mythic territory, carved out of the Marxist romance of the return to an original, more integral human state, the healing of the divisions and alienations of modern history. When Pirandello's mother tells of stopping on the way to Malta at a deserted island with massive inclines of gleaming white pumice, when we see her and her brothers and sisters scramble up the soft slopes of volcanic ash and tumble down them, ecstatically, into the sea, the image is so moving and so mysteriously lovely that we believe for a moment that the Tavianis' art has found a truly magical source, a place where the ancient and the modern speak to each other, not as parents and rebellious children but as brothers. In *Kaos*, Paolo and Vittorio Taviani have created one of those rare sequences, and rarer movies, that make film seem a language we've never really understood before.

The Atlantic, November 1985

The Brothers Quay

They bill themselves as the Brothers Quay, which has an archaic and faintly ridiculous ring, as if they were a vaudeville comedy act or a family of acrobats. Photographs of Timothy and Stephen Quay, who are identical twins, look like trick shots from the early days of cinema, products of the cheap camera magic that makes a single actor double and allows him, before our eyes, to talk to himself. In interviews the comments of one brother are never distinguished from those of the other: they speak as if with one voice.

The Quays, born in Philadelphia, have lived and worked together for all of their forty years, most recently in London, where since 1978 they have absorbed themselves in the absurd and intricate form of play known as puppet animation—that naively mechanistic genre of film art that preserves, a frame at a time, the memories of a childish delight in small effigies of ourselves, our wonder when at a human touch the dolls begin to move, and our vague horror as we watch their manipulated forms reflect and parody the actions of our own bodies.

Puppet animation is, as the Quays themselves admit, a freakish, marginal art: it can be as trivial as the singing, dancing raisins of American television advertising, or as ponderously symbolic as some of the Eastern European political allegories that turn up with alarming frequency on film-festival programs. But the Quays' puppets seem, like the mysterious twins who make them, to have found in their own marginality an eerier and more suggestive kind of life, a shadowy, feverish half-existence in which their movements are like the choreography of dreams. These puppets have the quality, unique in the genre, of appearing to be aware of their secondhand status, conscious that they're the crude doubles of beings once or still alive. And the films—with their sinuous camera movements through rooms full of dust and clutter and dirty glass, the interiors of a playhouse decrepit from overuse—are informed by the philosophical melancholy of their creators, whose art is perhaps the product of an endless and unresolvable obsession, who make puppets perhaps because each of them has spent every day of his life looking at and talking to a moving, three-dimensional, terrifyingly exact copy of himself.

There is, of course, something fanciful about the notion that the Quays' art is a complex ritual of twinhood. It makes the Quays out to be characters in a Romantic horror story—artists haunted by their creations, men looking over their shoulders for the doubles they know (or imagine) are following them, denizens of the unsettling mirror worlds of Hoffmann and Kafka, Poe and Borges. If we see them this way, it's because the films themselves encourage us to. Just as there are dreams so intense, so cryptic, that they hold our imagination for days, even years, the Quays' short movies have the power of the truly uncanny: we sense, without knowing why, that there's something *necessary* in their mastery of this arcane craft, that they're not so much telling stories with puppets as they are searching for the human ghosts in their wood-and-cloth machines. The intimacy of the Quays' relation to their dolls is creepy. Watching these films, we feel like Hoffmann characters ourselves, enchanted into an uneasy self-consciousness by arts so overwhelming that they verge on the demonic. We seem, somehow, to have been twinned—dancers mesmerized by the strange reflections of our own movements in the mirror beyond the barre.

The metaphysical theater of the Brothers Quay—whose work until now has been visible only on British television, in European film festivals, and in a film series called *Alchemists of the Surreal*, which has toured English art cinemas since last fall—has taken its show on the road in the United States this year, on a characteristically small scale. In January the United States Film Festival in Utah showed a program of four Quay films: *Leoš Janáček: Intimate Excur-*

sions (which runs for twenty-seven minutes), *The Cabinet of Jan Švankmajer* (fourteen minutes), *Little Songs of the Chief Officer of Hunar Louse, or This Unnameable Little Broom* (eleven minutes), and *Street of Crocodiles* (twenty minutes), their most recent film, and their first in 35mm. This same program has had a week's run at New York's Film Forum, and a slightly different selection was screened at the San Francisco Film Festival. There's talk of taking the program on tour to other cities and of showing one or more of the films on public television, but nothing is definite. Right now these films are obscure, sneaking in and out of theaters furtively, which seems oddly appropriate: they're such unlikely objects, and flash past our eyes so quickly, that they leave us dazed, unsure whether we've really seen their images or merely hallucinated them.

Even at their most straightforward, as in the Janáček film, the Quays are disorienting. The brothers, along with their longtime collaborator, the producer Keith Griffiths, have often worked in the portrait-of-the-artist genre, partly because television is always eager to supply funds for such "educational" films: they've also done a biography of the Belgian playwright Michel de Ghelderode, which was mostly documentary, and the jazzy, hilarious puppet film *Igor— The Paris Years Chez Pleyel*, about Stravinsky, with Jean Cocteau (who at one point appears in a tutu, dancing to a pianola score of *Petrushka*) and Vladimir Mayakovsky (whose body is an origami nightmare of revolutionary posters) hovering at the edges.

But the Quays' biographical films are like no one else's. In *Janáček*, as in the Stravinsky film, the artist-doll is a startlingly poignant composite—a puppet's three-dimensional body supporting a cutout photograph, slightly oversized, of the great man's head. This technique isn't simply a way of avoiding caricature. Janáček's head, monochromatic and 2-D, has the shocking gravity of many old photos: it's the visual equivalent of the ghostly scraps of the composer's diaries and correspondence that are read to us in voice-over. ("When someone speaks to me, I listen to the tonal modulations in their voice, more than to what they are actually saying. . . . I can feel or rather hear my hidden sorrow.") The tenuous relationship between head and body makes the Quays' Janáček seem, poetically, all mind, and as animated tableaux of the composer's work pass before us, we can't help feeling that we're seeing and hearing this music the way Janáček must have dreamed it. This illusion, almost too fragile to sustain, derives its force and beauty from the rhythms of the Quays' camera, moving in mysterious concord with the stately tempos of the music itself. The camera circles the extraordinary sets—a forest of leafless trees, Janáček's bare room, a deserted gymnasium with grillwork windows, a prison, a ruined church—catching glimpses of spindly, insectlike puppet figures through the trees and the bars of windows, images as fugitive as those that appear and disappear, flickering in the mind's eye, as we listen to a piece of music. At Janáček's death all the phantoms of the composer's imagination—the frail puppets from his works, including *Diary of One Who Vanished*, *The Cunning Little Vixen*, and *The Makropulos Case*, among others—gather around him for a moment in the forest, which has moved, somehow, into his stark room, the trunks' dark vertical forms merging with the shadows of the windows' grilles, echoing the cathedral's pillars and the prison's bars, filling the space around his fading features with a tangle of lines, like a passionately scribbled score. The delicate calligraphy of a musician's mind has never been represented more beautifully.

The Cabinet of Jan Švankmajer and *This Unnameable Little Broom* (as its impossible title is usually abbreviated) are, though brilliant, perhaps the Quays' most difficult and off-putting films. These two shorts are harder-edged and less lyrical than the Janáček film, and depend more heavily on the Eastern European puppet-film tradition: there's a hint of didacticism in them, even though we're never quite sure what we're meant to be learning. The Švankmajer film is in fact a tribute to a Czech animator whose work has influenced the Quays. It's structured as a series of little lessons in perception, taught by a puppet with an open book for hair, to a doll with a hollowed-out head, in finely detailed settings that evoke the style of encyclopedia illustration (as well as, at various points, Ernst, de Chirico, and the mannerist painter Arcimboldo). For the viewer, the movie is a short course in the principles of animation, conducted as if the art of Švankmajer and the Quays were a lost discipline of the Renaissance, an ancient form of anatomical drawing.

This Unnameable Little Broom, which is, according to the filmmakers, a portion of "a largely disguised reduction of the *Epic of Gilgamesh*," is a swift, savage, and largely baffling movie about a tricycle-riding monster who traps a strange winged creature in his lair. The camera whips back and forth in slashing, aggressive gestures, and the effect is stunning, but the battle is abrupt and not quite satisfying. We have no context for what we're seeing—the film is actually a fragment, a single episode from a planned full version of *Gilgamesh*—so the whole encounter, inventively choreographed as it is, seems too starkly mythic.

But *Street of Crocodiles*, the Quays' very free adaptation of Bruno Schulz's dreamlike memoir of Poland between the wars, is a fully articulated vision. Schulz's hallucinatory prose, which renders the world as a fantastic construction whose laws seem always on the tantalizing verge of our understanding, is perfect for the Quays. Schulz writes, in the voice of his narrator's deranged father:

> Figures in a waxwork museum . . . must not be treated lightly. . . . Can you imagine the pain, the dull imprisoned suffering, hewn into the matter of that dummy which does not know why it must be what it is, why it must remain in that forcibly imposed form which is no more than a parody? . . . You give a head of canvas and oakum an expression of anger and leave it with it, with the convulsion, the tension enclosed once and for all, with a blind fury for which there is no outlet. . . .
>
> Have you heard at night the terrible howling of these wax figures, shut in the fair-booths; the pitiful chorus of those forms of wood or porcelain, banging their fists against the walls of their prisons?

The Quays, clearly, have heard these sounds. The puppet hero of *Street of Crocodiles*—who, as we learn in a black-and-white live-action prologue, is part of an elaborate contraption locked away in a provincial museum—looks around him in something like terror when the thread connecting him to his unseen manipulator is snipped, and then, with a haunted, stricken stare, begins to explore. His environment is ominous, a decaying city inside a box, with an inscrutable system of threads and pulleys running along the ground, screws that pull free of floorboards and dance in the dust, shop windows full of blank mannequins and mechanical monkeys beating their cymbals furiously when a light shines on them, and dolls rotating shoulders whose joints are disturbingly exposed. Everything in this world seems to hint at obscure connections—the screws' threads are somehow related to the wires from which the hero has been disengaged, and also to the filaments of the light bulbs in the shops—and everything is a reflection of the weathered materials of which this abandoned puppet is made. It's no wonder he looks anxious as he wanders timidly through this labyrinth of wood and glass, no wonder the camera seems to be skulking with him, moving carefully, as if afraid of what it will find around the next corner. The Quays' *Street of Crocodiles* is a puppet film that, in its self-consciousness, transcends itself. It's about the chill of discovering, through play, what we're made of—about gazing on an aging world and seeing our own fragile anatomies reflected there.

The Atlantic, June 1987

Stanley Kubrick

A new movie by Stanley Kubrick is something big, like a manned space mission. In the time it takes him to make a picture—he has done five in the last twenty-three years—you could get to Jupiter. The long gestation period between the idea and its fulfillment creates an agonizing, not very pleasant kind of suspense, an anxious, slow-motion tedium of anticipation in which the tiniest events (or rumors of events) are magnified absurdly, until they are swollen with meaning. And when the great creation is, at last, delivered, it has become—partly through Kubrick's labor and partly through our own imaginative projections—as daunting and inscrutable as a monolith, a great black object that doesn't take the light.

It's no wonder that critics often approach a new Kubrick film with an almost childlike timidity: ever since *2001*, which was greeted rather rudely on its initial New York release in 1968, they've been worried that they're not quite *evolved* enough to penetrate the mysteries of Kubrick's higher consciousness. His idiosyncrasies are so confident, so authoritative, his methods are so deliberate, it seems inconceivable that the weird stuff he has been putting up on the screen could be the reflection of simple confusion rather than the product of a highly sophisticated aesthetic and intellectual system. Now Kubrick's "Vietnam movie," *Full Metal Jacket*, has arrived, in an atmosphere of muted awe—though no one seems quite sure what it *is*. It's one of the strangest war movies ever made, at once so hysterical and so austere that it suggests an unnatural coupling of

111

Sam Fuller and Robert Bresson. In a sense, it's the picture he has been working up to all these years: The Big Dead One.

Kubrick is certainly no stranger to war. It has been the subject of two of his most successful films, *Paths of Glory* and *Dr. Strangelove*, and two others—*Spartacus* and *Barry Lyndon*—have featured battle sequences: with *Full Metal Jacket*, that accounts for half the movies he has made in the last thirty years. What's surprising about his new film is not its subject, but the specificity of the material. Gustav Hasford's novel *The Short-Timers*, from which *Full Metal Jacket* is adapted (by Kubrick, Michael Herr—author of *Dispatches* and the voice-over narration in *Apocalypse Now*—and Hasford), has very particular settings: the Marine training camp at Parris Island, South Carolina, and then Vietnam in 1968, around the time of the Tet offensive. The action of the novel could only have happened in these places, at that time, and we all know it—and the historical nature of the material is a formal constraint that Kubrick has deliberately avoided for virtually his entire career. He favors vague futures and remote, explicitly imaginary pasts, and locations that can't be pinned down too precisely, that are neither here nor there. His movies, with their artificial, eerily pristine look, are self-consciously timeless and, in essence, placeless, too: adrift in space, where time bends back on itself. The massive, symmetrical compositions of *2001* and *The Shining*, blindingly lighted and sparsely detailed, look as though they were filmed on location in eternity.

On the face of it, Hasford's gritty and idiomatic novel (which was based on his own experiences as a Marine in Vietnam) seems an unlikely candidate for Kubrick's characteristic spatial and temporal abstractions. It's difficult to imagine that even an artist as strong-willed as Kubrick could dare to transform this story, this war that is still so fresh in our memories, into something "timeless," a slide show of generalities about human aggression. But that is exactly what he tries to do: with some success in the film's harrowing first half, which records the Marines' stateside basic training, and with disastrous consequences thereafter, when the action shifts to Vietnam.

Military training is, by its very nature, something fixed and uniform and repetitive, an endless, numbing loop of drills and chants, and on Parris Island Kubrick truly seems at home. He is much more

reluctant to leave this highly structured environment than the novelist was: Hasford devotes a mere thirty pages (out of the book's 180)
to the training camp, and Kubrick spends nearly half the movie on
it. The barracks are as vast and antiseptic-looking as the kitchen of
the Overlook Hotel, as menacingly self-contained as the huge uter-
ine cabin of *2001*'s spacecraft. It is immediately clear that a large part
of what attracted Kubrick to Hasford's novel was its vision of the
Marine Corps as an alternate universe, a shadow world with its own
laws and language.

Kubrick's Parris Island (recreated, of course, on English sound-
stages and countryside) is a science-fiction landscape, suggesting
variously a laboratory, a giant incubator, and an operating theater:
the movie opens with a montage of recruits having their heads
shaved, as if they were being prepared for surgery on their brains.
For the next forty-five minutes, Kubrick takes us through the whole
operation, in grisly, clinical detail—a process by which all traces of
civilization are ground away and human impulses are reduced to a
pure, murderous animal essence. "You're not even human fucking
beings," the recruits' drill sergeant (Lee Ermey) tells them, in their
first encounter. And he announces his intentions: "You will be a
weapon." At Parris Island, these young men are meant to die as
themselves and be born again as killing machines, helpless and
forlorn as that ax-wielding cosmic puppet Jack Torrance: psy-
chopaths of glory.

On its own terms, this long training-camp sequence is remarkable—a rigorous, concentrated, brilliantly sustained assault on the
sensibilities. Kubrick gives us very little conversation among the
recruits, and almost no information, visual or otherwise, to enable us
to distinguish one from another. The only recruits to stand out at all
are the narrator, Private Joker (Matthew Modine), who does John
Wayne imitations and is occasionally allowed to register a thoughtful
look, and fat Private Pyle (Vincent D'Onofrio), named (like all the
others, by the sergeant) after the bumbling hero of a Marine TV
comedy of the sixties, because he is the stupidest and most physically inept of the bunch.

The recruits' experience is rendered almost entirely in static,
repetitive scenes of the demonic Sergeant Hartman screaming abuse
("You're so ugly you could be a modern art masterpiece") and of the

recruits running grueling endurance courses, sprinkled with a few Monty Python–like drill routines in which the Marines trot in step while chanting inane military doggerel ("I love working for Uncle Sam/It lets me know just who I am"). It's all ritual, incantation, and furious grimacing by pale, shaven-headed men in skivvies—a real theater-of-cruelty spectacle, presented with a single-mindedness that's startling in a big-budget studio movie. This is not exactly a new mode for Kubrick, and the themes it serves—dehumanization, the blurring of individual differences, the devolution of personality to something brutish and fundamental—are among his most character-istic. But he has never let us know just who (he thinks) we are with such relentless savagery of attack. It is not only Hartman who seems to relish the violent stripping of the recruits' identities: we sense, too, the director's satisfaction with the grim efficiency of his work, and with the awful and, in his eyes, inevitable power of its outcome.

Visually, Kubrick's misanthropic argument is flawless, hermetic as an airlock. The compositions are so stark, so minimalist, that they could be, well, modern art masterpieces—white skivvies on white flesh against shining white walls and floors, all bathed in bland fluorescence or the milky light of almost-sunny days. The look of the film, at this point, is as bare and basic as Kubrick wants us to believe his message is: it's the look of the laboratory, of truths painstakingly arrived at by the scrupulous exclusion of contingency, the systematic elimination of all variables. In aesthetic terms, Kubrick's approach in the Parris Island segments seems radical: philosophically, though, it's retrograde. His thought is nineteenth-century, positivist, the kind of pseudoscience that classifies human behavior by observable (and prejudicial) physical traits—the size and shape of the head, say.

Kubrick reportedly cast this film by remote control: American actors auditioned by way of videotapes sent to the director in England. The actor's physical presence was not required, the blurred definition of the video image deemed sufficient to establish types. Most of the actors playing the recruits seem to have been chosen for their dull, all-American similarity. They are lean and wiry and their features are regular—the same type as the astronauts (both frozen and unfrozen) in *2001*. Against this uniform human background (the control group, in experimental terms) the anomaly, carefully isolated visually, is fat Pyle, cast by Kubrick both against credibility—this appalling specimen would hardly have passed a Marine physical—and against the novel's description of the character as a "skinny redneck."

In Hasford's book, where the horrors of both training and war are disturbingly casual, Pyle is nothing special, just a simple-minded country boy who goes crazy in the pressured environment of the camp. Transplanted to Kubrick's world, where nothing is casual, Pyle has become a swollen, overstuffed metaphor, a great white whale of meaning. The blubbery Pyle Kubrick puts before our eyes is explicitly infantile: we are meant to see in him a symbol of what the Marine Corps is giving birth to. In some sense, Pyle—who gradually becomes Hartman's most perfect creation, a being who identifies himself, totally and unthinkingly, with his rifle—is an overprogrammed machine that runs amok and turns on its creator, as HAL did. But Kubrick, by casting an actor who suggests an overgrown baby, pushes his interpretation of Pyle's breakdown beyond the realm of the mechanical, into the biological.

The violent resolution of Kubrick's Parris Island experiment is a confrontation between Hartman and Pyle (with Joker, as always, observing), and takes place in a gleaming lavatory with exposed toilets—a set he treats with an odd reverence, as if it were a shrine to the body and its most basic, undeniable demands, the ultimate metaphor for the human condition. (In the novel, this scene is set in the squad bay where the recruits sleep. The change of location is certainly Kubrick's idea. Several of the key scenes in *The Shining*, including Jack Torrance's long encounter with his murderous predecessor/alter ego Grady, took place in lavatories, too.) It's a place where human beings are equalized by their needs, where our physical nature, in Kubrick's view, gives the lie to our myths of individuality, of unique identity—where, in *Full Metal Jacket*, the creator and the creation, the father Hartman and the baby Pyle, achieve the absolute equality of dead matter, brains and guts smeared on the chamber's walls like illegible graffiti.

It may be significant that the door to this room is labeled, military-style, "Head"—because the head, Kubrick's head, is where this movie is really taking place. The most fascinating thing about *Full Metal Jacket* is that for the first time in years Kubrick has a story that forces him to engage, on some level, an external, verifiable reality:

he has to "get into the shit," as Hasford's Marines refer to going into battle. And he can't do it. As a longtime expatriate, Kubrick undoubtedly finds it difficult to identify with the native country he has rejected. But shooting the entire film, both the "American" and the "Vietnamese" segments, close to home in England suggests something in Kubrick that goes beyond the desire to maintain an aesthetic, ironic distance: the willful perversity of this decision seems the symptom of a deeper confusion.

In *Platoon*, Oliver Stone kept telling us, "I was there"; Kubrick goes to extraordinary lengths to tell us that *he* wasn't. His Vietnam looks, very self-consciously, like the bombed-out European landscapes of World War II movies (the climactic scenes set in Hué were shot in south London). The formal distance he imposes on the material is, like his refusal to sympathize with his characters, the habit of a lifetime: these qualities even serve him well in the Parris Island segment, where a cold, dehumanizing institutional ferocity is the subject. But when he gets to "Vietnam," his methods seem worse than inappropriate: they're evasive. It's unseemly of him to dissociate himself, in this haughty, aestheticized way, from what America did in Southeast Asia. He wants us to know he's clean, and in doing so wipes out his Marines' personalities as thoroughly as the drill sergeant does. We can almost feel him scrubbing harder and harder to get the damned spots out, and there is something very sad about the effort.

Oliver Stone's autobiographical narration in *Platoon* expressed the idea that Americans in Vietnam were really at war with themselves, and that is perhaps the only sense in which Stanley Kubrick can be said to be "in" Vietnam: if *Full Metal Jacket* is about anything, it is about an artist at war with himself. For years, Kubrick has been elaborating the idea that what we think of as human identity is an empty concept, that the very notion of an essential self is a sham. It must have been a great relief to him to move from the rock-hard American star personality of Kirk Douglas in *Spartacus* (that picture, Kubrick's last in the United States, was also produced by its star) to the chameleon virtuosity of Peter Sellers in his next two pictures. As the playwright Clare Quilty in *Lolita*, Sellers assumed a variety of accents and disguises in the course of his demonic surveillance of Humbert and Lolita. In *Dr. Strangelove*, Kubrick had Sellers play three different characters—a British air force officer, the American president, and the high-Teutonic Dr. S.—and surrounded him with American actors, each locked into a single cartoonish role.

The Americans in *Strangelove* seem to illustrate what Kubrick thinks of people with solid, highly defined identities: they are absurd and dangerous and totally artificial. In a kind of extension of the Quilty role in *Lolita*, Kubrick uses Sellers's extreme changeability, his capacity for emptying out his own personality and filling it with an infinite variety of others, as a reproach to the forceful styles of George C. Scott, Sterling Hayden, and Slim Pickens. The only reason for Sellers to be playing three roles is to celebrate the principle of violent mutability upon which his acting is based. In a sense, Kubrick's entire career since then—both the material circumstances of his move from America to England and his developing "philosophy" of personality—may be attributable to the difference between Kirk Douglas and Peter Sellers.

His next two films after *Strangelove* explored imaginary future worlds in which human beings are blank, featureless, floating in a void, and the liveliest personality belongs to an artificial intelligence (*2001*); and in which even our strongest impulses are subject to manipulation by technology, processes that turn our malleable natures from evil to good and back again with the ease of changing channels by remote control (*A Clockwork Orange*). And Barry Lyndon, played by a colorless Ryan O'Neal, was Kubrick's characteristically abstract and extreme version of a classic picaresque hero: an alienated, unprincipled character who thinks nothing of changing his name, his appearance, his speech patterns, his very identity to facilitate his progress through the world. (Every picaresque hero is a man without qualities, whose facility in immersing himself in radically different environments is a reflection of the most profound detachment.) Kubrick had, at this point, developed a cinema in which only three kinds of people exist: ones with no personality at all; ones with *over*determined personalities—caricatures—who are invariably gross and vicious; and (the most interesting category) those whose "personalities" consist of a succession of assumed identities. Each of these types, of course, is a variation on a single idea: that identity is form without content.

What made these films so infuriating (even at their most impressive) was their air of superiority: the spectacle of Kubrick systematically dismantling the integrity of his characters' selves while asserting, with his overbearing technical mastery and formal control, the awesome force of his own personality. But *The Shining*, his messy, hall-of-mirrors horror movie, hinted at a slightly less assured, more ambivalent attitude. For the first time since *Spartacus*, twenty years earlier, Kubrick allowed a big star—an American, at that—a place in his meticulously ordered world. The way he used Jack Nicholson is, in a sense, predictable. As Jack Torrance becomes madder and more deadly, the actor gradually hardens into a wicked caricature of himself—"Jack Nicholson" trapped in a tight corridor of quotation marks, literally frozen in place, a statue with permanently arched eyebrows. Torrance, though, is also in some sense Kubrick as he sees himself in the mirror—an obsessive, isolated artist-figure who is more at home with the phantoms of his imagination than he is with real human beings, who is imprisoned by a sense of his own timelessness, who asserts his one small truth ("All work and no play makes Jack a dull boy") doggedly, endlessly.

It is impossible to know how consciously *The Shining* is a derisive self-portrait of the artist, but something about either the story or the star, or both, seems to have spooked Kubrick. We sense a slackening of his iron control here, an inability to resolve all the thematic and visual associations into an airtight formal scheme. As the picture careens from one room and one idea to another and another, helter-skelter, we sense a tremor of fear, a bit of vertigo from Kubrick's lofty overlook. It is as if, while editing the film, he had begun to shine to the implications of his notions of identity, as if he suspected that what he had done to his American star—rendered him static, immutable—might be the image of what he had done to himself. The final incoherence of *The Shining* is, for Kubrick, an act of self-alienation—which in this case may also be a form of self-protection.

"Talking to dead people is not a healthy habit for a living person to cultivate and lately I have been talking to dead people quite a lot," says Hasford's narrator in *The Short-Timers*. That statement is nowhere to be found in *Full Metal Jacket*, which seems strange: surely these words should be resonant for the man who made *The Shining*.

But *Full Metal Jacket* shows Kubrick once again approaching and then pulling back from the exploration of his own identity. He doesn't have to love working for, or on, Uncle Sam—but shouldn't it tell him something about who he is? Inadvertently, it does. Kubrick's camera, helplessly expressive, is as fascinated by the awful Sergeant Hartman as it was by Torrance in *The Shining*. Kubrick must be aware that Hartman is, among other things, a monstrous parody of a godlike, autocratic director, and that basic training is a nightmare image of actors rehearsing their roles. The overtly theatrical intensity of these scenes, combined with a flicker of recognition in Kubrick's treatment of Hartman, suggests a (near) acknowledgment by the artist that his fancy ideas about the essence of human nature are, in fact, ideas about acting. Carried to its conclusion, this would be scary self-knowledge indeed. It would mean that for much of his artistic life Kubrick has been guilty of the same brutal subjugation of nature that the military practices in its training courses and that the United States inflicted on Vietnam, and for the same reasons—sheer "American" arrogance and desire for control. And Hartman's death, in these terms, would be the director's suicide, a bizarre ritual disembowelment of himself.

As it turns out, though, Kubrick only appears to fall on his sword in shame: he fakes it, for effect. The rhetoric of the film is that the sergeant's death, occurring halfway through, marks a turning point. Kubrick has given him such prominence that his absence in the second half of the movie actually defines (and thus distorts) the meaning of the Marines' experience in Vietnam. In retrospect, we see Hartman's orderly, authoritarian world as somehow preferable to living "in the shit" of a war without rules, without form. It's certainly aesthetically preferable, since the Vietnamese half of the film, to be effective, would need some emotional center, a few characters who haven't been dehumanized, whose deaths we would feel as loss—but Kubrick can't identify with the grunts. He is still with Hartman, trying to direct from a vast distance, from beyond the grave. His perfect compositions look increasingly irrelevant, unreal; his Vietnam looks more and more like a landscape of the mind; his control is remote control, like a stateside general's. His failures of nerve, of sympathy, of self-knowledge hauntingly embody his coun-

try's failures in the Southeast Asian war: against his obvious intentions, this movie brands Stanley Kubrick as an all-American filmmaker, naive and trapped as an astronaut. How far into space will
he have to go before he meets himself again?

Sight and Sound, Autumn 1987

Philip Kaufman

For long stretches of Philip Kaufman's *The Unbearable Lightness of Being*, we seem to be looking at nothing but the eyes of lovers: gazing at each other as they lie in bed, searching for signs of infidelity; watching themselves in mirrors as they make love, mediating their intimacy with another—imagined—perspective, seeing themselves as a voyeur or an artist might; staring at rooms left empty by a vanished other and trying to gauge the finality of the departure; scanning the face of a lover who has reappeared out of nowhere and trying to judge the permanence of the return; looking through the lens of a camera at the history that changes lives, as if their eyes had become everyone's and everyone's theirs, as if the act of fixing and printing a moment of vision were the most complex kind of personal intercourse, a way of restoring a shattered relationship with the world; or alternating glances at each other with concentration on the road ahead, their vision blurred by the rain on the windscreen and interrupted by the rhythm of the wipers (regular as a metronome or a pulse), but shared, for a few seconds, with each other and with us, in the film's, and their, last image, before everything dissolves into a whiteness that hurts our eyes.

After nearly three hours of Kaufman's film, we sit staring at a white rectangle as if at the blank page at the end of a novel we've stayed up all night to read, and try to gather all we've taken in into that space, to project on the blank screen our own most personal

121

imagery. Our impulse, on finishing a work we love, is to hold on to it for a while, and we strengthen our hold by means of unconscious, benign distortion of what the author has put before us—bending his point of view a few degrees until it becomes ours, freezing a handful of moments from the temporal flow of the narrative and merging them with our memories as if they were part of our own experience. The white screen at the end of the *The Unbearable Lightness of Being* might stand for the moment when Philip Kaufman read the final words of Milan Kundera's novel and, not wanting to let it go, gave himself over to the reverie that became this film.

Kaufman's movie is an extraordinary adaptation of a difficult book. Just how remarkable it is may not be fully apparent on a single viewing, when readers of the novel may be distracted by what looks like Kaufman's simplification of the material and also by the peculiarly *American* tone of his treatment—which is unmistakable despite the European locations and omnipresent Czech accents, the all-European cast, the Janáček music on the soundtrack, and the participation of Pierre Guffroy as production designer, Sven Nykvist as cinematographer and Jean-Claude Carrière as Kaufman's collaborator on the screenplay. This adaptation has a kind of fidelity to its source that's different from what we're used to: it's faithful to the novel as it exists in the mind of a reader, rather than to the novel considered as some sort of autonomous entity, or to a notion of the author's intent.

In interviews, Kaufman has said that the novel's most interesting character is Kundera himself, the discursive, digressive narrator who keeps interrupting the telling of his fairly simple story with long meditations on Nietzsche, Beethoven, Parmenides, kitsch, the history of Europe, the relationship between the body and the soul, and the very art of narration, and who makes clear that the story he relates in this fragmented way is just one part of his thought process, an instrument of speculation. "It would be senseless," Kundera says at one point, "for the author to try to convince the reader that his characters once actually lived"; in his new book, *The Art of the Novel*, he repeatedly defines characters as "experimental selves."

Without Kundera's voice, the novel would be immeasurably diminished; paradoxically, Kaufman's elimination of it doesn't weaken the film. Kaufman seems to understand instinctively that it would be senseless for him to try to convince the audience that his film represents the mind of Milan Kundera; senseless for him to pretend that the film's characters are merely notional, speculative, since what we're watching are living, breathing actors on the screen; senseless for him to imagine the characters as someone else's experimental selves—even if such an act of projection were possible, it would drastically limit the filmmaker's ability to define his own relation to the characters, which is all that matters. The movie's most interesting character is Philip Kaufman.

Kundera's novel is overtly, determinedly self-reflective. Kaufman's presence in the movie is only implicit, but no less pervasive: instead of introducing himself as a character, he simply makes self-reflection the dominant theme of the work. The staggering variety of looks the characters give each other and the world outside, with each of the film's innumerable close-ups seeming to register a fresh emotional nuance of these people's shifting, exploratory relationships, is, in a sense, a record of the filmmaker's own explorations—the gaze he levels at the text and the experience it represents, his attempts to penetrate, with the lens of a camera, an alien consciousness, a history that can't be his.

We never stop being aware that this movie is an American artist's effort to understand a profoundly European sense of life, because the film is at every moment reminding us of the heartbreaking distances that separate people's imaginations, of the enormous difficulty of seeing the world through another's eyes. The air of erotic melancholy that hangs over Kaufman's film is a reflection of the distances that persist even in the most intimate relationships, of the imperfections of all our projections. There's a section of Kundera's novel called "Words Misunderstood"; Kaufman's movie is about images misunderstood.

At one point, the film's heroine, the innocent Tereza (Juliette Binoche), is horrified to discover that photographs she has taken of the Russian invasion of Prague are being used by the Communist authorities to identify those who resisted the tanks: as her pictures are flashed before her, moments of her own experience, her eyes begin to blur and the images lose their definition. The sequence ends with an ominous close-up of the lens of the slide projector, its single eye beaming a blinding light. It's a shocking perversion of the powers of vision, and a metaphor, somehow, for the small personal betrayals that have made Tereza's marriage to the philandering Tomas (Daniel Day-Lewis) into a series of agonies for her. (She sees his acts of infidelity nightly in her dreams.) At this crucial point, about halfway through the film, we begin to sense how wide and how deep Kaufman's ambitions are: he has conceived his *Unbearable Lightness of Being* as an epic of cognition.

The story, reduced to its outlines, would seem too fragile to support that sort of undertaking. Tomas, a talented young neurosurgeon at a Prague hospital and an inveterate womanizer, meets an earnest country girl named Tereza who becomes, much to his surprise, the first women ever to spend an entire night in his bed—he wakes up to find her hand tightly gripping his. They marry, but Tomas continues to see other women: his favorite, and longest-running, mistress is an artist named Sabina (Lena Olin), with whom he has a playful, ironic relationship defined by a fetish (a bowler hat) and an urge to watch themselves in mirrors when they make love.

After the Russian invasion in 1968, first Sabina and then Tomas and Tereza leave Czechoslovakia and settle in Switzerland, where they live, for a while, with the wary freedom of exiles until, one by one, they leave: Sabina flees to America when her earnest lover Franz (Derek de Lint) leaves his wife and announces his intention to move in with her; Tereza can't sell her photographs of Czechoslovakia and can't photograph what would sell (nudes and plants), so she returns to Prague; Tomas, the last one left, misses his wife and follows her back. Tomas can't get his old job back, because he had once, almost as a lark, written an article using Oedipus' blindness as a metaphor for totalitarianism; rather than recant, he works as a window cleaner, which gives him fresh opportunities for adultery.

Tereza, more tormented than ever by his unfaithfulness, tries to revenge herself on him (or perhaps simply to understand him) with a one-night stand of her own—but then fears that her affair was set up, engineered by authorities watching her with hidden cameras. They move again, this time to the country, where their beloved dog dies, but they feel happier together, free of scrutiny, closer. After a blissful night of drinking, dancing, and making love in a country inn, their truck crashes on a slick road. Sabina gets a letter in California informing her of their deaths.

It sounds like little more than a soap opera with some political overtones, or, at best, one of those old-fashioned romances in which the lovers are "swept up in the tides of history" or some such. In the novel, Kundera's philosophical digressions and his fragmented, nonchronological narration keep us from getting that gooey *Zhivago* feeling. But Kaufman tells the story straight, from beginning to end, flirting with the Hollywood-love-story grand manner, almost daring us to find his film banal or sentimental. He makes us realize, though, that this is the way the story has rearranged itself in our heads after reading the novel—and also that its very plainness is a large part of what makes it so moving. Kaufman's directness in this respect links him to Tomas, the no-nonsense seducer who simply gazes at women and commands, "Take off your clothes": he examines them and makes love to them at the same time. That, in a way, is what Kaufman does to Kundera's novel—he strips it so he can know and love it better.

But that's not his only mode of knowing. Sabina is one of his experimental selves, too. Her restlessness and her uninhibited sense of play are qualities that Kaufman has demonstrated, not just here, but throughout his career. His films have been unusually diverse, each one radically different from the others and stylistically eclectic in itself. *The Great Northfield, Minnesota Raid* (1972) is an atmospheric, unsentimental Western in which Jesse James is portrayed as, of all things, a religious fanatic. *The White Dawn* (1974), about a trio of New England whalers marooned among the Eskimos, is a historical film shot almost as a documentary: the loose narrative seems far less important than the anthropological investigation of the Eskimos' society. His 1978 remake of *Invasion of the Body Snatchers* is a surprisingly funny and lyrical science-fiction satire, in which the target of the conformity-inducing pods is the freethinking, anything-goes culture of San Francisco. *The Wanderers* (1979) is a rambunctious comedy about Bronx gangs in the early sixties, and a much more serious movie than it initially appears: in its slapdash way, it actually tires to capture and define a key moment of cultural change. And *The Right Stuff*, his 1983 adaptation of the Tom Wolfe book about test pilots and astronauts, is a three-hour all-American jamboree, a movie that mixes styles and tones so promiscuously that it seems, finally, to express everything that is most beautiful, most heroic, and most irredeemably stupid about American life, all at once.

Sabina is this movie's primary wanderer: as an artist and as a woman, she shuns permanence with an instinctive horror. In Prague, her paintings are elegant, suggestive abstractions with an ominous sexuality reminiscent of Georgia O'Keeffe. In Geneva, her art is constructed of daggerlike shards of mirrors: her apartment/ studio is like an Expressionist changing room, in which a visitor, undressing, is constantly surrounded by splintery images of himself. In California, Sabina spray-paints seascapes for elderly buyers: the paintings are blandly serene, as if the sea (as in Baudelaire) has become her mirror but she doesn't quite see herself in it.

Her sex scenes with Tomas are, thanks to the mirrors (she has one in Prague, too), dazzlingly complex, and all the more erotic for their formal complexity. The relationship of their bodies to each other keeps shifting in the frame, in unexpected configurations, and their (and our) angles of vision do, too. Nothing is fixed—or heavy, in Kundera's terms—and their lovemaking sequences come to seem perhaps the movie's purest expression of the delights of irony: the exhilaration of seeing oneself, and others, always from a bit of a distance, of being able to observe, with amused dispassion, the infinite patterns our parts can arrange themselves in. When, on Sabina's last night in Geneva, Tomas visits her in a hotel room and they lie in bed together looking directly into each other's faces— without benefit of mirrors for the only time in the movie—it's one of the saddest moments in *The Unbearable Lightness of Being*. A terrible weight seems to have settled on them. Looking straight into each other's eyes, their self-reflective irony has deserted them. Their frank gazes have the desperate, commemorative urgency of last looks: they reflect nothing but the sudden, startling desire to fix a final image of something precious about to disappear forever.

In that scene, Tomas and Sabina find themselves looking at each other, for one surprised moment, in the way that Tereza *always* sees the world, and from that point on, Tereza's way of seeing begins to dominate the film. There's a brief scene in which the shift is made explicit. After Tereza has left Geneva, Tomas sits in their empty apartment and stares at a small potted cactus, a bleak little object that Tereza had spent hours contemplating, because a Swiss magazine editor suggested that this was the sort of photograph he might be interested in. Tereza has looked at this absurd thing with growing misery, unable to photograph it, unable, we feel, even to *see* it—an object that, like everything in Geneva, she is incapable of discovering her relation to, a sight she feels not the slightest impulse to commemorate.

As Tomas sits before the cactus, he—and we—are invaded by Tereza's vision, her frustration and despair at gazing always, in her exile, at things that remain so stubbornly outside her, things she can never truly feel are hers. As if possessed by Tereza's spirit, Tomas, too, goes back, and the film takes on a more somber tone. At first, we miss Sabina mightily: the sequences that follow Tomas's return to Prague (and precede the final, pastoral section) are the shakiest passages in the film. Even Kaufman seems a little dispirited: deprived of the occasions to exercise his visual inventiveness that Sabina's scenes provided him, his moviemaking briefly loses a bit of its zest. But Tereza's worldview does finally take hold, because Kaufman has prepared us for it—it has always been one of the possible visions proposed by the movie—and because Tereza, too, is clearly an aspect of himself.

In the first section of the film, before the invasion, Tereza, though charmingly played by Binoche, is nearly as puzzling to us as she is to Tomas. She's unformed, compared to the other characters, and her simplicity and possessiveness seem out of place in the liberated atmosphere of Dubček-era Prague: she's an outsider among the sophisticates, an intent but slightly baffled observer. The exuberance of these early sequences suggests that this period in Czech history is, for Kaufman, the easiest part of the story to represent—a time when his characters live, in a sense, as Americans do, heedlessly and optimistically. He doesn't *need* to assume Tereza's perspective until the tanks roll in and he has to call on something that will take him far beyond the frame of his own experience.

The invasion sequence is Tereza's first big moment, and Kaufman does it full justice. It's a wrenching montage of stock footage and stills, mostly in black and white, intercut with shots of Tomas and Tereza rushing through the crowds (all shot as if they, too, were part of the grainy file film), as Tereza snaps more and more pictures: finally, almost all of what we're seeing is imagery her camera has caught. Kaufman's treatment of the invasion is actually fuller and more emotionally intense than Kundera's, for a good reason: Kundera needs to distance himself from this pivotal event in his life, to gain perspective on it; Kaufman, who has experienced the invasion only through documentary footage, newspaper photos, and Kundera, needs to get closer.

And that's why Tereza becomes more important to Kaufman as the film goes on, why he treats her with greater tenderness than her creator does. Kundera sees her fierce attachment to home, her heavier passions, as weakness, and in doing so seems to be conducting an argument with himself—against whatever impulses he might feel to return to his native country. To Kaufman, however, she is the mystery that must be penetrated for him to make this film: the most rooted of the characters, the least "American" in spirit. And in the invasion sequence, we feel the excitement of his discovery of what connects him to her. Her picture-taking brings everything into focus. He understands, because he's such an emotional image-maker himself, her impulse to fix moments on film as a way of making sense of her own life: her need to possess these images and her need to possess Tomas are essentially the same urge—an urge that can't be so unlike what impelled Philip Kaufman to put this book on film.

Between the invasion and Tomas's return to Prague, Tereza's point of view gathers force. In that section of the film, there's an extraordinary sequence in which Tereza and Sabina take turns photographing each other in the nude in Sabina's mirror-crammed studio. This is the scene in which the movie's experiments in vision come together, the give-and-take of the two women's examinations of each other complicated by the implicit presence of Tomas: looking at each other unclothed, each is aware that she is seeing what Tomas has also seen. By the end of this superbly choreographed play of visions, some miraculous unity seems to have been achieved, a resolution of Tomas's and Sabina's and Tereza's points of view into a single, undifferentiated image of happiness as the two women lie naked and laughing on the floor. (This is, surely, just as Tomas would imagine it.) But that image is erased immediately by the arrival of Franz, which precipitates Sabina's flight from Geneva and thus begins the process of sending the characters again on their separate roads.

It's no wonder that Tereza's possessive spirit holds sway in the second half of the film. The moment of harmony dissolved so quickly, and nothing like it occurs again until the very end, during Tomas and Tereza's night at the inn and their drive home. Through the artifice of Kaufman's editing, Sabina seems to be present, too. The scene in which she receives the news of their deaths comes halfway through the dancing, so the rest of Tomas and Tereza's story might almost be happening in her imagination. Tomas turns to Tereza and says, "I'm thinking how happy I am," in the moment before the screen—their view of the road—begins to go white, another harmonious vision vanishing too soon. But in this movie Philip Kaufman has made such a vision appear before our eyes twice, with Tereza onscreen both times, as if her dogged, heavy, loving spirit had led him to it once and then again, just as she led Tomas back to Prague. She's the filmmaker's guide both because she's the farthest from him and because she's the nearest. She seems to have made him believe that the taking of images—the impulse to hold on to what we love—is the highest form of reading the world, and the truest guarantee of eternal return.

Sight and Sound, Summer 1988

Mike Leigh

The films of the English director Mike Leigh, whose *Life Is Sweet* was one of last year's best pictures, are fresh, imaginative, and sensationally well acted comedies about the ordinary trials of contemporary life. Between his first feature, *Bleak Moments* (1971), and his second, *High Hopes* (1989), all his films were done for British television, and none of them have ever been shown on American television or released theatrically here. There's a Leigh retrospective currently making the rounds of museums and film archives in the United States: it began in Chicago, moved on to San Francisco, and is now getting under way in Boston (at the Museum of Fine Arts); in the second week of April, it comes to the Museum of Modern Art in New York; stops in Washington, D.C., Los Angeles, Cleveland, Houston, and Minneapolis (and perhaps other cities) will follow. The show, which includes almost everything Leigh has made, is a revelation. Individually, the films are (mostly) terrific; they're small-scale, beautifully textured explorations of the dense weave of everyday relationships, and the humor is all based on the absurd intensity of the characters' interactions with family members, coworkers, and neighbors. Taken together, the movies are even more affecting. Leigh's world of drab furnishings, behavioral minutiae, mundane crises, social awkwardness, and flat-out silliness turns out to be a startlingly coherent and suggestive vision of experience. His way of seeing seeps into you, and it doesn't go away after you've left the theater.

130

When you step outside, everything looks clearer; your senses have been refreshed, sharpened.

From the beginning, Leigh has developed his scripts in collaboration with his actors. He starts not with a plot but with a group of characters: the actors rehearse and improvise in character for weeks or months, and the story emerges from their workshop sessions. The final form of the movie, though, is determined by Leigh. When the cameras roll, the actors aren't improvising anymore—the dialogue is scripted and the story is fixed. (Until the late eighties, the authorial credit on Leigh's films read "Devised and Directed by Mike Leigh." He switched to the more conventional "Written and Directed" largely, it seems, because interviewers tended to concentrate on his method of filmmaking rather than on the results.) But even when the shape of the movie is set, it's not the usual dramatic shape. The story never proceeds in a straight line toward an inevitable conclusion. The halting, unpredictable rhythms of improvisation remain in the scripted scenes; comic digressions interrupt the flow of the action; the focus of the story keeps shifting—from one character to another, from the workplace to the home, from major crises to the little business of life. The elliptical, apparently casual approach to structure in Leigh's movies can take some getting used to: if the films weren't so funny, their meandering narratives might make audiences very restless.

On the evidence of the retrospective, this loose-limbed technique was something Leigh had to get used to, as well. *Bleak Moments* is actually a bit of a chore to sit through: it's all blank looks and uncomfortable silences, and it doles out its laughs and its revelations of character rather sparingly. In the TV films of the middle and late seventies, Leigh seems intent on using his style to create something snappier and more entertaining. The eccentricities of his characters become more outlandish, the conflicts between them become more extreme and more explosive. In *Nuts in May* (1976), he focuses on a middle-class couple on a camping holiday. The husband, Keith (Roger Sloman), is a pompous know-it-all who has a rigidly organized approach to life. For him, there's one right way of doing everything—pitching a tent, taking pictures, touring the countryside—and his sweet, meek wife, Candice Marie (Alison Steadman), gamely tries to keep up with his exhaustingly detailed agenda. They sing folk songs in the open air, and clearly think of themselves as wholesome, down-to-earth people. But in this natural setting, their profound unnaturalness is thrown into high relief. They're totally unequipped to deal with the vagaries of the weather or with the presence of other campers. *Everything* offends Keith's sense of propriety; Candice Marie is slightly more tolerant, but she stands by her husband in the petty disputes he gets into. The small shocks to Keith's tightly sealed system take their toll; by the end of the picture, he's lashing out at everybody like a threatened animal. *Nuts in May* occasionally feels like an overextended series of revue sketches. But they're good sketches, superbly performed, and the comedy makes a point. Its theme is also the basis of Leigh's filmmaking method: the movie is about the cost of maintaining a worldview that doesn't allow for the accidental, the unexpected. And the relationship of Keith and Candice Marie is the beginning of Leigh's explorations of the comic mysteries of marriage: the intricate patterns of adjustment and accommodation that permit radically different people to live together in tenuous peace. The good marriages in his movies have the easy rapport—the delight in timing and anticipation—of veteran comedy teams. In the bad marriages, the partners seem like actors who can't get their styles to mesh—or who have simply been playing the same scenes for too long.

The seventies films lean heavily on the sort of cultural collision that takes place on the campsite battleground of *Nuts in May*. The protagonists of *Abigail's Party* (1977) and *Who's Who* (1979) are, like Keith, savagely uptight middle-class characters who struggle unsuccessfully to keep the unruliness of the rest of the world at bay. Beverly (Alison Steadman again), the heroine of *Abigail's Party*, turns a simple cocktail party for her neighbors into a frenzied social nightmare. She's trying so hard to impress her guests with her taste and graciousness that she won't let them alone: she tells them when to eat, when to drink, when to get up and dance, and she keeps the conversation rolling by quizzing them, with an inane smile, on embarrassingly intimate subjects. Alan (Richard Kane), the main character in *Who's Who*, is a middle-aged clerk in a London brokerage firm who puts on the airs of an aristocrat. At home he struts around in an ascot and a double-breasted blazer, and he spends his spare time collecting form letters and autographed photos from the famous and the highborn: television presenters, Tory politicians, peers of the realm. These are comedies about self-delusion, about people who have, in a sense, miscast themselves in their own lives: Beverly and Alan have got themselves locked into roles that haven't emerged from their particular histories and don't suit their real circumstances, and the effort of maintaining these personas is killing, desperate work.

In these pictures, you can sense Leigh's attempt to define himself and his art against the traditional forms. Characters like Keith and Beverly and Alan might almost represent the futility of trying to mold oneself to the inflexible outlines of received images, familiar roles. The fun Leigh has at the expense of these characters is surprisingly affectionate, though, and the spirit of the films is exuberant and playful. The seventies pictures work off the contrast between willfully overdetermined characters and those whose sense of themselves is more tentative and ambiguous, and the result is an unusually inclusive comic perspective. The movies are designed to make us laugh, but they keep bursting their boundaries. With each successive film, the craziness on the screen seems to become richer, more resonant. By the time of *Grown Ups* (1980) and *Home Sweet Home* (1982)—two of the funniest films in the series—Leigh's unique style of realist cabaret is so fluent and expressive that the contrasts he sets up don't feel jarring at all: the wild variation in people's responses to experience seems perfectly natural.

The Leigh retrospective is a celebration of the art of acting, and a celebration, too, of the inconceivable complexity of human behavior. There isn't a film in the series that doesn't show us something new and specific about how people deal with the mess of their lives. Leigh's method is always the same, but the movies are all different from each other: every experience has its own contours, as distinctive as the lines of a fingerprint. *The Short & Curlies* (1987) is a lovely trifle: a hilarious twenty-minute-long romantic comedy about the courtship of a goofy compulsive joker and a rather sullen drugstore salesgirl who changes her hairdo more frequently than she changes her expression. In *Four Days in July* (1984), Leigh takes us into the homes of two Belfast families, one Catholic and one Protestant; the film's gentle, low-key humor has an undercurrent of melancholy, and by the end we feel the political tragedy of Northern Ireland in our bones, with a vivid and unshakable immediacy.

To my mind, the film that best embodies the range of Mike Leigh's generous, democratic art is *Meantime* (1983), about a working-class family in which all the men—a father and two sons—are unemployed. The politics of *Meantime*, like those of *Four Days in July*, are felt rather than stated. The family's edginess and hair-trigger irritability as they squeeze past each other in the cramped rooms of their housing-estate flat tells us a lot about their frustration, and so does the way they snipe at their middle-class suburban relatives. A visit to the mother's well-off sister (Marion Bailey) is like torture for them: the unemployed father glowers and says little; the older son, Mark (Phil Daniels), delivers a stream of rude, sarcastic commentary; the mother takes out her anger on the younger son, Colin (Tim Roth), who is retarded. The film is quick-witted and bracingly unsentimental. Colin is often the butt of Mark's bitter humor, and Leigh doesn't try to wring pathos out of their one-sided exchanges, or to turn Mark into a villain: we see where his mean remarks come from, and we understand that there's no real malice in them—what they express above all is a fierce intelligence that has nothing to apply itself to. The characters in *Meantime* live dreary, restricted lives, but the movie, miraculously, isn't grim or tedious. Leigh keeps us aware of the persistent vitality of people who don't have anything constructive to do: he makes us feel the energy surging underneath the characters' enforced indolence, and it's a complicated energy. The domestic tensions, the class resentments, and the unexpressed love that run through every scene in *Meantime* are as powerful—and, sometimes, as difficult to sort out—as the delicate emotions in a Chekhov play. The movie could be seen as an up-to-date example of the Angry Young Man school of British drama, but that would be too narrow a definition. The feelings and ideas and flickering moods evoked by *Meantime* transcend simple anger. Leigh shuns dramatic conventions for the best possible reason: he wants to avoid the nailed-down meanings that they produce. The body of his work is evidence that filmmakers can still reveal the world to us, if they're willing to look at it with an unprejudiced eye. Mike Leigh's retrospective is the most exciting and heartening movie event to come to America in a long time.

The New Yorker, February 24, 1992

Part Three

MOVIES

BARBAROSA

Fred Schepisi's *Barbarosa* looks like a Western, but at heart it's a ghost story. It opens with a magnificent desert landscape, a composition of rocks, mesas, sky, and open land that looks hard-edged and immutable—and then it begins to change. The light keeps shifting—the background darkens, then the foreground, the middle ground lights up like a radiant stripe across the screen, then it's all reversed, and a shadow seems to darken boulders one at a time, in abrupt, unpredictable jumps—changing in ways we can't quite follow, or fix into a pattern. This mysterious landscape is seen several times more in the course of the film, and the narrative never places the characters in it. But in *Barbarosa* the Western landscape is a haunted house: we know the mythic characters are there, whether we see them or not. There's a moment early in the film when Barbarosa seems to pop up out of nowhere, as if he's ridden up out of the ground; and there's a moment later on when he seems to disappear into thin air as he's running through a forest. *Barbarosa* is full of wandering, of sudden departures and unexpected returns, movements that seem as capricious as the light on the desert—but all within a fixed frame, a sharply limited physical and psychological geography; the film is all repetitions, variations, echoes.

The fixed frame here is a story of exile, a story whose details emerge gradually, one small bit at a time. Barbarosa (Willie Nelson) has been a fugitive from his own family for thirty years, driven from the Zavala home on his wedding night by his father-in-law, Don

Braulio (Gilbert Roland). He's condemned to circle around his own wife and daughter, darting through Braulio's defenses for two furtive visits a year, spending the rest of his time eluding and, reluctantly, killing the young Zavala men who are sent out to kill him. Karl (Gary Busey), the farm boy whom Barbarosa picks up along the way, is on the run from his in-laws, too: he killed his sister's husband in a fight. Karl, clearly, is an image of the young Barbarosa—he sees his future in the old outlaw, and Barbarosa sees his past in him. They tell their stories to each other as they ride through the ghostly landscapes, and as they sit by the fire at the camps they make in the ruined adobe shells of abandoned homes.

Karl's story is a simple one, but Barbarosa's is complex, full of history—a story that's lost its innocence. When Braulio tells it to a room full of Zavala boys—boys whom he will some day send out, one by one, in search of Barbarosa—the legend comes out in one smooth piece, polished by years of telling and retelling, too perfect for us to trust it very much. And the children seem to know their responses by heart, like a litany: Braulio may tell them this story every night, sitting in his windowless, cavelike room spinning the image of a mythic Barbarosa out of thin air. But on the night we hear the story, the living Barbarosa is elsewhere in the house, visiting his wife, and Karl, his eventual successor, is watching and listening at Braulio's door.

This may be *Barbarosa*'s strangest scene: it's an important bit of exposition, but it comes halfway through the movie and its staging is stylized almost to the point of parody (the flickering light and cavernous decor; the hushed, automatonlike responses of the children; the squawking raven at Braulio's side). But it's a crucial scene, a graphic illustration of how superfluous the real Barbarosa has become. He's in the house, within Braulio's reach, but the old Don is unaware of his presence, totally possessed by the mythical Barbarosa that he's created. Barbarosa isn't onscreen at all while Braulio tells his story, yet he's present, defined completely by the elements of his myth: Braulio, its author; the Zavala boys, its audience; and Karl, its future incarnation. As the scene goes on, the bizarre ghost-story atmosphere seems more and more appropriate. The living man who's known as "Barbarosa" (we never do learn his real name) doesn't exist here, doesn't need to—he's been disembodied.

Barbarosa isn't the first of Schepisi's heroes to suffer this fate. The seminary teachers in his first film, *The Devil's Playground*, have spent their lives trying to forget their bodies—to "transcend" them—and some of them, a little horrified, realize that they've succeeded. Their aim is to become pure spirit, and that's what they're teaching their students, too: one seminarian boasts of being so alienated from his body that he no longer feels discomfort or pain, and in his attempt to prove it by swimming in a freezing creek, he dies—the ultimate transcendence. What's moving about *The Devil's Playground* is that its characters *know*, or are in the process of finding out, that their goal is a kind of death—the denial of their sexual urges makes them feel a little unreal to themselves, almost spectral.

The hero of *The Chant of Jimmie Blacksmith* feels unreal, too. As an aborigine in a white society, he's invisible to his masters. When, in frustration, he murders the white family that he can't be a part of, he *makes* himself visible, forces the society to acknowledge his existence. But his social existence is still just an image in the minds of his oppressors: he's now a legend, a symbol—the murderous, ungrateful black. And, of course, he's forfeited everything with his crime; from the moment he commits his first murder, he's a dead man. All of Schepisi's films are ghost stories: they're about people who exist for others only as spirits, myths, abstractions, people who have died to the world in advance of their physical deaths—and who continue to live in some strange, painful middle ground, homeless, neither here nor there.

Barbarosa, though, doesn't have the grim intensity of the earlier films. Barbarosa's the oldest of Schepisi's protagonists, the one who's lived with his situation the longest, and he's gone past anguish to a kind of resignation: even when night puts him in a melancholy, reflective mood, his words of wisdom are "What can't be remedied must be endured." What Barbarosa has to endure is the living out of the legend created by Braulio's obsession, a myth that he knows can't be changed or destroyed but only manipulated a bit, played with. The pain is there, but after thirty years Barbarosa isn't a tormented or an angry spirit—he's rather a wistful, prankish one. The tragic force of the earlier films is present only in Karl's story: he's younger, his wounds are fresher, and he's not at all used to being the object of another man's obsessive vengeance. When he arrives back home after months of wandering with Barbarosa and is forced to kill Herman Pahmeyer (the vengeful father of the man he killed), his violence isn't cathartic: Karl doesn't *want* to kill Pahmeyer, and the act doesn't change anything, anyway—Karl's father is already dead, and he loses his only sister not long after. Karl feels no triumph, and we share his feeling of emptiness. It's the way Barbarosa must have felt after killing his first Zavala: Karl shouts "No!" before shooting Pahmeyer—just as we've heard Barbarosa do before killing one of his would-be assassins. This is Schepisi's characteristic method, building his film with a gradual accumulation of details, repetitions, allusions, toward a climax which illuminates the film's concerns without fully resolving them.

Those details and allusions are more densely layered in *Barbarosa* than ever before—so densely, in fact, that it's just about impossible to sort out all the repetitions and variations in the film's visual and narrative motifs. They just merge into a single, omnipresent entity, a kind of persistent echo like the swelling chants of "Barbarosa" that occur at several points in the course of the film. The allusions are hypnotic, like a rhyme scheme, and they all have to do with death (a cantina that looks like a burial mound; Barbarosa rising from his grave as Karl is burying him; Barbarosa cauterizing a wound, smoke rising from his body as he applies the burning stick, a shot later recalled by an aerial view of his cremation) or with the gradual convergence of Karl's identity and Barbarosa's (the marks on the cheek that each receives in his first scene—Karl's from a thorn, Barbarosa's from a Zavala bullet; Karl's early chance encounter with Eduardo, ultimately Barbarosa's killer; the shouts of "No!" before killing). The first time Barbarosa and Karl appear in the same frame, they're bending over a dead Zavala.

The extraordinarily dense texture produces interesting effects, unexpected ones. One thing it *doesn't* produce is a symbolic structure: the repetitions and variations don't "work out" to a coherent statement about myth, or identity, or anything else. Schepisi and his screenwriter William Witliff (who also wrote *Raggedy Man*) aren't even very interested in exploring the truth or falsity of the myth: Barbarosa's isn't a heroic myth, one that the man himself must be measured against and found worthy or unworthy; and by the end of the film we *still* don't have a full, reliable account of the incident that caused the rift between Braulio and Barbarosa, the origin of the legend. Schepisi's real subject is less abstract, but more elusive, more mysterious. *Barbarosa* is about how it feels to live inside a myth, to be a character in someone else's story—how it *feels* to be turned into a ghost. The myth is always there, but only as the landscape the characters ride through, the fixed frame, the house they haunt. And the repetition of motifs is what creates this effect of enclosure: the narrative moves easily, loosely, from one incident to the next, ranging over a vast and various landscape, but it keeps coming back to the same themes, the same locations, wandering and then returning home. The landscape becomes *familiar.* By the last third of the film, the visual and narrative associations have piled up to such an extent that every scene is charged with a kind of inevitability; everything, by that point, feels to the viewer like remembered experience.

So we know before Karl does that he's going to assume Barbarosa's myth after the outlaw's death. We've already seen him become a part of the myth, the "gringo child" who rides with Barbarosa; we've seen him begin to fall in love with the outlaw's daughter; we've seen him shoot a gun exactly as Barbarosa's taught him; we've seen him grow a wispy, reddish beard; we've seen him lose his own home, his own family; we've seen him ride with Barbarosa through a desert so bright, so dazzling, that both riders become, for a moment, transparent. We know, too, that Barbarosa the man has been dead to the Zavala family for thirty years: Karl's just another body to fill the myth, a slight shift in the light on the landscape. And Schepisi has created a vision of the West in which death and loss are the constant background, and memory's as tangible as the rocks—the ruined adobes, the half-buried bodies sticking up out of the sand. When Karl rides into Braulio's courtyard, whirls his horse around, and disappears back into the night, he's become the tangible memory of Barbarosa—just as Barbarosa, for better than half his life, had been the memory of himself.

And just as *Barbarosa*—unlike most Westerns, which reach back into the past or the history of the genre for their emotional resonance—creates its own past, its own memories within the viewer. *Barbarosa* is too original, too self-sufficient, to be judged as a Western. It is, rather, the latest of Fred Schepisi's fables about the oppressions and losses that turn men into ghosts.

Film Quarterly, Winter 1982–83

THE PURPLE ROSE OF CAIRO

Woody Allen makes jokes about God the way other comedians make jokes about their wives. In his new movie, God is either Fred Astaire, whose voice—singing "Heaven, I'm in Heaven," the opening line of "Cheek to Cheek"—is both the first and the last voice we hear, or the unseen pair of hack writers who concocted a movie called *The Purple Rose of Cairo*, the sort of thirties comedy in which Broadway sophisticates mix *very* dry martinis before rushing out to catch the floor show at the Copa and the innocent hero, Tom Baxter, exclaims, "To think that only yesterday I was in an Egyptian tomb and now here I am on the verge of a madcap Manhattan weekend!"

This glittering black-and-white world—within the full-color world of the Woody Allen movie called *The Purple Rose of Cairo*—is Allen's sweetest and funniest version of the afterlife, his greatest God joke ever, because it's really awfully silly, full of spirits so blithe they verge on idiocy, and the creator's grip isn't quite as firm as it seems to be: one of these debonair beings, the gallant, open-faced archaeologist chap from the Egyptian tomb, steps right off the screen in a New Jersey movie house and carries off a young woman from the audience. He's an angel escaped from the choir, a virgin sprung.

This impossible event throws the Depression-era Jersey town into an uproar, as planeloads of Hollywood types, including the alarmed producer Raoul Hirsch, descend on the little theater—and transports the lucky woman from the audience, a timid, dreamy housewife named Cecilia, into a state of blissful romantic confusion. It's a more familiar sort of miracle to us, and to Woody Allen: no stranger than the magic-lantern apparitions of *A Midsummer Night's Sex Comedy*, the infinite transformations of Leonard Zelig, or the magical bedroom farce of "The Kugelmass Episode," whose unfortunate hero shuttles back and forth between his dreary life in New York and a passionate affair with Emma Bovary, and winds up trapped in a book called *Remedial Spanish*. In *The Purple Rose of Cairo* (both Allen's film and Raoul Hirsch's), people just materialize—here one minute, there the next, and everything in between has been edited out.

To think: Tom Baxter was in this swanky apartment just a blink of the eye ago, and now he's at the Copacabana; Cecilia, kissing Tom in an abandoned amusement park, was at home with her brutish husband the last time we looked; the actor who "created" Tom, Gil Shepherd, last seen at a Hollywood party, is suddenly bumping into Cecilia in New Jersey. In the world of a movie, where we never have to see the distance traveled from one place to another, the impulsive leap from the screen into the audience almost makes sense, and it's easy to see why the editing of a conventional Hollywood picture would, to a lifelong New Yorker like Woody Allen, seem an attribute of heaven: imagine getting where you want to go without having to search for a cab, stew in midtown traffic, or expose yourself to the rigors of the subway. The big-screen miracle is a pair of lovers having a madcap Manhattan weekend without budging, locked in an embrace in the center of the frame as a bright-lights montage—El Morocco, the 21 Club—whirls by behind them.

The magic-carpet style of filmmaking, with scene after scene of characters who seem to have dropped into place right out of the sky, isn't wholly new to Woody Allen. He's always been fond of jumping from one spot to another, from his first movies, which were constructed in chunks of autonomous shtick, archipelagoes of skits, to later and more unified arrangements of bits, like *Annie Hall* and *Zelig*; his restlessness is less arbitrary, more artful now, but he's still reluctant to show the connecting material, the hard traveling of narrative—the progress of the characters from one comic or dramatic moment to the next.

One of the reasons why Allen's last movie, *Broadway Danny*

Rose, goes a little flat from time to time is that it's mostly about a journey, a car trip from New Jersey to Manhattan, and the story has a tendency to stall. It's a road movie made by a man who isn't really interested in how things move. (And the people in *The Purple Rose of Cairo*, living through the Depression in a town whose plant has closed, gamble and hustle and fantasize in movie houses because they can't believe in progress, either.) What *is* new about *Purple Rose* is the effortless way it glides over the gaps, a combination of airiness and intricacy so graceful that we barely notice the steps and little jumps, but see only a smooth dance routine—and all achieved within the frame of the story, without the benefit of the kinds of intervention which have served Woody Allen so well in the past: the voice-over monologue, the mock-documentary narration, even his own presence as an actor.

Here, Woody Allen speaks through his story and through his actors, and the acting is inspired. The cast of the movie within the movie, which includes John Wood, Edward Herrmann, Deborah Rush, Zoe Caldwell, and Van Johnson, are a hilarious formal-dress ensemble, lounging and complaining in their penthouse set as they wait for Tom Baxter to return from his foray into the outside world, all of them vapid and cheerful and dazed, as if the thin air up there on screen had made them light-headed. Jeff Daniels, looking a little goofy under Tom Baxter's pith helmet but wholesomely dashing in Gil Shepherd's Hollywood threads, gives a finely shaded and very funny performance, shuttling easily between the perfect innocence of the movie hero and the more calculated boyishness of the career-wise young actor (who's hoping to play a real hero, Charles Lindbergh, and become a star). And Mia Farrow's Cecilia is a wonderful creation, a woman who always seems to be looking *up*—at her looming husband, at the tall, noble frame of Tom or Gil, and, constantly, at the huge figures on the screen. As Farrow plays her, Cecilia is enraptured and distracted (she's always dropping plates full of food), but her vivid imagination is a kind of survival skill: her life makes no sense, and her immersion in the blunt, madcap clarity of the movies gives her a peculiar strength.

Everything in this movie makes heavenly sense. Woody doesn't have to materialize on screen to pull everything together—he remains above it all, pulling lines and characters and situations out of thin air and dropping them back to earth with flawless aim. In *The Purple Rose of Cairo*, the creator's absence is the subtlest, slyest joke of all: we're forced to *imagine* Woody Allen, and the picture we get is of a small man in top hat, white tie, and glasses, who moves, like Fred Astaire, in mysterious ways.

Sight and Sound, Summer 1985

BLUE VELVET

When David Lynch, the director of *Eraserhead, The Elephant Man, Dune,* and the new *Blue Velvet,* wants to share his bad dreams with us, he doesn't fool around. *Blue Velvet* is horrifying in ways that genre horror movies never are. If in an ordinary movie a gunk-spewing alien or a masked slasher appears on the screen, we know how to distance ourselves from our fears—by hiding our eyes, or clutching a companion's arm, or simply giggling at the conventions. None of those responses, though, protect us from the unease that images like these produce: a man having a seizure as he waters the lawn on a sunny day, the green hose gnarling around a branch just before he falls; a bruised, naked woman stumbling out of the suburban darkness to embrace the teenage hero, as his demure girlfriend looks on; Dennis Hopper, as an obscene, bug-eyed sadist, planting a messy kiss on the boy's lips and then reciting, in a sinister whisper, the words of the Roy Orbison song that goes "In dreams, you are mine—*all* of the time." This is real nightmare stuff, inexplicable and thus inescapable: we don't know where it's coming from, so we don't know which way to run.

The small logging town of Lumberton, where *Blue Velvet* is set, is a bland American community, as ominous as only places that consider themselves truly safe can be. The streets are so nearly silent that no one notices the persistent, enveloping resonance, the echo, perhaps, of buzzing chainsaws; and because there's no need for much lighting, and the trees are healthy and full, Lumberton by night

149

is voluptuously shadowed, its sidewalks, overhung with branches, like tunnels into a sensuous dark. Every image and every sound in *Blue Velvet* tells us that the ordinary is teeming with unspeakable, innumerable dangers—and some viewers will probably decide, halfway through, that the only safe place is outside the theater altogether, far, far away from the hellish Our Town that David Lynch calls home.

Part, but not all, of what makes *Blue Velvet* so unsettling is that Lynch's nightmare has a sort of irregular, homemade quality, as if it had been cooked up with familiar but not entirely wholesome ingredients—a fresh apple pie with a couple of worms poking through the crust. Lynch tells his story in the form of a boy's detective novel, the kind of tale in which an earnest young fellow happens on a mystery and resolves, on his own, to "get to the bottom of it": in its blunt expository scenes, *Blue Velvet* has the gee-whiz tone of young-adult thrillers, but the bottom of this mystery is *really* the bottom, a long, steep fall away. Lynch's hero, nineteen-year-old Jeffrey Beaumont (Kyle MacLachlan), gets involved in his adventure when he finds a severed human ear in a vacant lot; the police, for some reason, figure that this discovery has something to do with a nightclub singer named Dorothy Vallens (Isabella Rossellini), and Jeffrey wants to know more. While she sings "Blue Velvet" under a ghastly blue spotlight in a Lumberton dive called the Slow Club, he hides in a closet in her apartment, then spies on her through the louvered door when she comes home. It's a kinky stakeout, disturbingly intimate from the moment she walks in the door: Jeffrey's gaze, and the camera's, remain fixed on her as she rips off her wig, strips to black bra and panties, and walks wearily down the long, murky corridor to her bright bathroom.

This hushed sequence has a powerful grip: by this point, Jeffrey's boy-sleuth curiosity has turned into a more intense form of scrutiny, an eroticized alertness to sensual detail. Once Lynch has us watching this way with Jeffrey, really appalling things start to happen, and images seem to enter our minds in a liquid, dreamlike slow motion, one drop of perception at a time, till we're saturated, dazed with experience. What Jeffrey sees from here on is a lurid vision of the adult world, all corruption and cruelty and brutal, scary sex, magnified and made vivid by the shock to his innocence, but a little blurred, too. This stuff is coming at him (and us) out of the blue; and without a context, some link to convention or ordinary experience, nothing can be absolutely clear. When Jeffrey, still lurking in Dorothy's closet, watches her being abused, verbally and physically, by a deranged gangster named Frank (Hopper), the sick little scene is indelible because what Lynch makes us privy to is both too much and not enough. The ugly emotions of the scene come through with overwhelming force, yet we're not quite sure what's at stake in Frank and Dorothy's relationship, and the visual style keeps us off base. From his vantage behind the slats, Jeffrey is right on top of the grotesque couple, but Lynch uses a distorting lens that makes them look farther away and slightly foreshortened—mean and pathetic figures. The lighting and decor are just as disorienting: both Frank and Dorothy have luminously pale flesh, bathed in harsh fluorescence, but neither their clothing nor the apartment's low-to-the-ground, mud-colored 1950s furniture seems to take the light at all. Everything is clear—punishingly direct—yet all the while we're straining to see more.

In passages like these, Lynch achieves a kind of radiant seediness. The drama that's played out before Jeffrey's innocent, greedy eyes is all the more riveting for being a bit tacky: Lynch has even borrowed, artfully, the look of late-fifties nudie movies, with their variable lighting, their peekaboo camera placements, their arsenal of low techniques that keep us gazing avidly, neither sated nor frustrated. *Blue Velvet* is all revealing and concealing, its shutters opening and closing so rapidly we're driven half mad with excitement. That is to say, it's a real movie, the first one in a long time that turns the viewer's passivity into furious cognitive activity. Every image, even those that seem most shockingly new, teases us with a hint of familiarity, a glimpse of some frayed connection to home. Just as every dream has a thread of reality—corrupted but recognizable bits of remembered life—that keeps us believing in it, *Blue Velvet* maintains a constant, tantalizing hum in the background, a subliminal music like pop melodies dimly recalled. If Lynch's mystery has a key, it's the song "Blue Velvet" itself, or rather the kind of song it is: a trashy romantic ballad that can insinuate itself into the mind and get tangled with deeper, more potent impressions. What we hear in the background of *Blue Velvet*, what we struggle to identify, is Lynch's own warped oldies album of innocence and experience.

Even the roughest, potentially most alienating elements of *Blue Velvet*—the abrupt shifts of tone, the awkward dialogue, the primitive, almost childlike elisions in plot and character development—work for Lynch here, as they didn't in the failed science-fiction spectacle of *Dune*, because they're all his: his dream associations, picked up from the flotsam of 1950s and 1960s pop culture, and carried along on a relentless undertow of obsession, a somnambulist's rhythm. *Eraserhead*, which was also based on an original script by Lynch (and which also had Frederick Elmes as its cinematographer), had a similar pull, but even that movie, more overtly hallucinatory, was less disturbing than this. It was a midnight movie in more ways than one—so claustrophobic, so unmistakably interior, so dark, that it could only have taken place in the small hours of the morning. The more expansive *Blue Velvet*, alternating the 1950s and the 1980s, bland sunlight and rich obscurity, teenage innocence and ripe adult corruption, is practically a new genre: the demented matinee.

One measure of how seductive this particular nightmare is is the astonishing quality of the performances. Actors in dream movies often have a glazed, puppetlike demeanor. (The most extreme example is Werner Herzog's *Heart of Glass*, in which the performers reportedly played their scenes under hypnosis; the most effective use is probably in Buñuel's *Belle de Jour*, where Catherine Deneuve's beauty is as icily perfect as a doll's.) Lynch's actors are not only brilliantly cast—they actually behave as if they're tuned in to the director's bizarre frequency. Rossellini, her face a battered memory of her mother, Ingrid Bergman, is exotic and vulnerable; MacLachlan, who looks a lot like Lynch himself, manages a very tricky mixture of Boy Scout rectitude and teen-age prurience; Laura Dern, an all-American girl, gives a delicate, ironic twist to her most naively idealistic sentiments, and turns her pleasant face into a rubbery, poetic cartoon of grief when she's confronted with the world's ugliness; and Hopper and Dean Stockwell, the two most alarming of the movie's villains, are sensationally evil, a pair of 1950s child stars gone to seed, whose faces are like maps of three decades' pop-culture insanities. This disparate crew have all found their way into

Lynch's intensely imagined American landscape. There's no point in denying that in some corner of our minds—next to the jukebox, maybe—this is our hometown, too.

The Nation, October 18, 1986

THE COLOR OF MONEY

The first voice we hear in *The Color of Money* isn't an actor's but the director's. Over a montage of images from the mysterious, self-contained world of pool—gleaming cues, blue chalk, green felt, a white ball rolling slowly across the table and colored balls dropping into pockets—Martin Scorsese reads a short explanation of what the games we're going to watch are all about:

> Nine-ball is rotation pool. The balls are pocketed in numbered order. The only ball that *means* anything, that *wins* it, is the nine. A player can shoot eight trick shots in a row, blow the nine, and lose. On the other hand, a player can get the nine on the *break* if the balls spread right. Which is all to say that *luck* plays a part in nine-ball. But for some players, luck it*self* is a *skill* . . . or an art.

This game, Scorsese wants us to know, isn't the same one that Paul Newman, as Fast Eddie Felson, played against Jackie Gleason's Minnesota Fats in the 1961 Robert Rossen film *The Hustler*: then, the game was straight pool, in which the players called their shots and luck had nothing to do with it. "Straight pool's *pool,*" says the older Fast Eddie in *The Color of Money*. "A guy had to be a surgeon to get over. It was all finesse. Now everything's nine-ball because it's fast." Like a pro, Eddie tries to adapt to this flashier, less personally rewarding way of playing the game. And maybe, by reading himself that little introductory voice-over on nine-ball, Scorsese is telling us

154

that he's adapting, too, to a kind of moviemaking that doesn't allow him to call all his own shots anymore. *The Color of Money* is fast and absorbing and often thrillingly well made, but there's something impure about it: it's a streamlined, best-sellerish replay of Scorsese's work in the 1970s, from *Mean Streets* through *Raging Bull*. He's making all the old moves, investing just enough conviction in them to get over, and working that way, he's bound to run out of luck. In *The Color of Money*, Fast Marty dazzles us over and over again—then leaves the nine ball on the table.

Scorsese and his screenwriter, Richard Price, set everything up beautifully, but they can't win, because there's an irresolvable problem built into the story. (They bear full responsibility, since almost nothing of the late Walter Tevis's quiet, reflective novel survives in their adaptation.) At the end of *The Hustler*, cocky, talented Fast Eddie finally defeated his nemesis, Minnesota Fats, and walked away from big-time pool forever rather than pay off the oily, satanic gambler played by George C. Scott. When we first see Eddie in *The Color of Money*, twenty-five years later, he doesn't look as if he has any regrets. He's almost shockingly dapper, having made a small fortune selling liquor and providing financial backing for young pool hustlers. He has, in fact, taken on the identity of the Scott character in the earlier film: a stake-horse, jaded and prosperous. When he spots a brilliant but not very worldly young player named Vincent (Tom Cruise)—who loves pool so much he wants to keep playing even after his opponent runs out of money—Eddie smells a good thing and takes Vincent, along with his tough-cookie girlfriend Carmen (Mary Elizabeth Mastrantonio), out on the road. The rhetoric of the movie is that Vincent reminds the older man of himself in his hotshot days, and that while he's educating his protégé in a variety of scams, all the corrupt and lucrative tricks of the pool-hustling trade, Eddie is slowly rediscovering his own love of the game. What this scenario ignores is Eddie's relationship to an art whose rules have changed. Price and Scorsese present their hero's return to competitive pool as a triumph of Eddie's true nature over a cynical and self-protective obsession with money. To do that, they have to keep their distance from Eddie's feelings—what it means to him to devote his talents and ego to *nine-ball,* a debased form of the subtle and elegant art he practiced in his games with Fats.

Eddie's disparaging comments about nine-ball ("This ain't pool. . . . This is like handball. . . . It's like cribbage or something. . . . What the hell, checkers sells more than chess I guess") come before he's really started playing again, at a point at which they could be interpreted as no more than envious digs at Vincent's generation of hustlers. It's just one-upmanship, which is all *The Color of Money* turns out to be about, anyway. Scorsese and Price know this turf almost too well: *Mean Streets, Raging Bull*, and Price's novels *The Wanderers, Ladies' Man*, and *The Breaks* are among the classics of street smarts, filled with the intricate strategies of barroom competition, the fine points of macho codes. Price's dialogue is so pungent and Scorsese's direction, with its trademark combination of languorous, caressing camera moves (the cinematographer is Michael Ballhaus) and edgily precise cutting, is so atmospheric that the movie can ride on sheer savvy for a good stretch. For the first two-thirds of the film, we're given a pretty exciting tour of the pool subculture, in a series of set pieces that provide both quick lessons in hustling technique and flashes of insight into the mixed motives and desires of the players. It's very knowing about pride and fear, resentment and humiliation, ambition and greed—all the gut elements of male competitiveness, the stuff that's churning beneath the surface when the balls are on the table.

Fascinating as all of this is, the movie's command of hustling lore and male psychology seems finally a bit smug and show-offy, its cynicism too glib. After a wonderful scene in which Eddie, his guard down because he's so desperate to prove he can match his pupil's skills, allows himself to be hustled by a chubby, sweet-faced black kid in jeans, the picture goes dead. At the very point where we need to see the characters deepen and develop, Scorsese and Price freeze them in place, and the final scenes, at an Atlantic City nine-ball tournament where both Eddie and Vincent are entered, are an elaborate but mechanical working out of the petty tensions that have built up. The climax of *The Color of Money* is just a pissing contest: as Eddie and Vincent stalk each other, Scorsese's camera circling them both, we realize there's nothing much at stake here except who's got the bigger stick, and it's tough to care. Maybe it's to the filmmakers' credit that they don't actually answer the question, but it's disheartening to think that it's the only one they know how to ask.

Richard Price, for all his gifts, may not know more than this: his last novel, *The Breaks*, had structural problems nearly identical to *The Color of Money*'s. And Tom Cruise, whose charmless manchild showboating is just barely more palatable here than it was in the appalling *Top Gun*, surely doesn't. Price's writing, like Vincent's pool shooting, is wizardly but thin, all samurai flourishes and nervy chatter. Newman knows more: his performance, an old-pro turn that effortlessly tops his earlier work in *The Hustler*, gives the movie its only emotional weight. He lets his aging face (decorated with a sharpie's mustache) do most of his work for him, and his trim body (pricily dressed) does the rest. His brisk, confident movements—the way he enters a poolroom, sizing up the talent in a couple of discreet glances, the way he turns around on a barstool, slowly, as if taking only the most casual notice of the action on the green tables behind him—tell us everything about how Eddie Felson has protected himself from his twenty-five-year-old disappointment, and the flickering alternation of cunning and boyish vulnerability in his eyes tells us why.

Throughout, the camera lingers on Newman's features, documentary-style, as if Scorsese recognized something there, a quality he can't quite locate anywhere else in the material of this movie. What Newman seems to have—even when he's just counting his money—is an urgent, vital drive, not just to prove himself, but to *justify* himself. He has, that is, the kind of intensity that charged every frame of *Mean Streets* and *Taxi Driver* and *The Last Waltz* and, for all their flaws, *New York, New York* and *Raging Bull*, too. At his best, Scorsese still has the emotional transparency, the unembarrassed need to express himself, that he once had—but he's fighting it back. In the wake of his own disappointments—the box-office failure of *The King of Comedy* and the inability to get funding for his pet project, *The Last Temptation of Christ*—Scorsese has been trying hard to adjust to a filmmaking climate that's no longer conducive to his very personal approach. He's trying to be a pro, to prove himself with prodigious, empty displays of technique like last year's *After Hours*, with good-soldier assignments like an episode of *Amazing*

Stories (which *was* the best half hour of that show's first season), and now with this big, expensive commercial picture. His relative detachment from his recent material has certainly loosened up his style, which was becoming tense and oppressive in *The King of Comedy*, but *The Color of Money* suggests that Scorsese might be outsmarting himself: he seems to have nearly convinced himself that craft and flash, all his various kinds of smarts, are enough, that just being able to play the game makes an artist a "winner." In a way, it's a relief that he doesn't quite bring this movie off. This shouldn't be his game: it's like cribbage, or something.

The Nation, October 25, 1986

SID AND NANCY

For its first hour, before it spirals downward into the junkie tragedy of the Sex Pistols' Sid Vicious and the girlfriend he loved and (probably) killed, Alex Cox's *Sid and Nancy* is a kind of *Hard Day's Night* in hell—a rare try at capturing some real rock-and-roll madness on screen. Watching Vicious and Johnny Rotten (played by Gary Oldman and Drew Schofield), the stars of England's most notorious—and best—punk band, smash the windshield of a Rolls-Royce, brain members of the audience with their instruments, pitch darts at each other in a pub, and throw up in elegant restaurants and hotel suites isn't *quite* the same as seeing the Fab Four, mop-tops bobbing, scamper cheerfully around London with squealing fans in pursuit, but still—different styles of hysteria for different times. In 1964 the Beatles' buoyant music, shaggy hair, and cheeky, throwaway wit were liberating, a happy anarchy. By 1977, when Sid Vicious joined the Sex Pistols as their bass guitarist (replacing Glen Matlock), something stronger was clearly required to get our attention. Johnny Rotten, ranting like an inspired subway crazy, kicked off "Anarchy in the U.K.," the group's first single, by announcing, "I am an Antichrist," against a musical background so fast and so shatteringly loud it sounded as if the band were playing in a suicidal rage, attacking themselves with their own instruments. If the Beatles' music seemed to go directly to some pleasure center in the brain, the Sex Pistols' was like a pure jolt to the central nervous system, and the effects weren't all that different. What both bands aimed for, and

159

achieved, was maximum immediacy, the one quality common to all great rock and roll; the music wouldn't be so exhilarating if it cared about being timeless.

The trouble with most movies about rock is that film tends to memorialize its subjects. The Beatles movies, intended as quick, unfussy exploitations of a hot new act, are nostalgia items now, and the Beatles' performances are the occasions not of screaming ecstasy but of contemplation, through the filter of everything that has changed. We watch *A Hard Day's Night* knowing that this clear, open music would become, under the influence of psychedelics, more complex and inward; that bitter personal and financial differences would blow the band apart; that John would be shot dead in New York City. In D.A. Pennebaker's 1967 documentary of Bob Dylan, *Don't Look Back*, which has just been released on videocassette, the young Dylan's anger—even when it took the form of cruel, condescending wit—looks remarkably innocent and straightforward compared with his sour posturing in the late 1970s and the 1980s. Elvis, in his countless awful movies, looks pathetic and trapped to us now, because we know that he would never stop wasting his huge talent. One of the best rock movies, Michael Lindsay-Hogg's documentary *Let It Be*, which showed the Beatles bickering and sulking their way through one of their final recording sessions (and finally saying the hell with it and playing a loose, impromptu concert from the roof of their studio), was already a memorial on the day it was released, in 1970: by then the group had split for good. And the finest rock-and-roll film of all, Martin Scorsese's *The Last Waltz*, was actually designed as a commemoration— an elaborately staged farewell concert by the Band, who play ferociously and do look back. Playing as if there's no tomorrow, with the possibility that everything's going to fly apart, is crucial to rock and roll. At its most thrilling, it's a scary, tenuous, abandoned art. The threat of dissolution gives live rock its charge, but actual dissolution—which movies, by fixing the ephemeral sounds and images forever, inevitably remind us of—makes everything poignant, elegiac. It complicates the original, heedless excitement of the senses with something reflective and diffuse. Every art loses some vitality, and perhaps even some meaning, when it turns into history, and the most immediate have the most to lose.

The Sex Pistols, who lasted only long enough to make one album, have plenty to lose on film. No group was ever faster, rawer, or more reckless, and they screamed "No future" as if they really meant it. The existing movies of the band don't even constitute a proper memorial. Lech Kowalski's documentary *D.O.A.* had a lot of footage from the group's chaotic U.S. tour, their last performances together, but both the images and the sound were pitifully amateurish (as was the filmmaker's attempt to explain the sociology of punk). A later film, Julian Temple's *The Great Rock 'n' Roll Swindle*, was apparently meant as a satirical postmortem on the group, but the movie has never been distributed in the United States. This absence of commemoration, of visual spurs to nostalgia, is oddly appropriate to what the Sex Pistols were all about. They were built not to last but to shock and stimulate and stir things up and then pass, like a hurricane or a furious three-minute song. So it's almost a folly to attempt a historical, dramatic reconstruction of their era, even for a devotee like Cox, whose 1984 science-fiction comedy *Repo Man* is about the closest that movies have come to true punk style. Yet *Sid and Nancy* succeeds, because Cox is very canny about what the form allows him to do and what it doesn't. Working with actors and a script (cowritten with Abbe Wool), at nearly a decade's distance from the events, gives Cox a kind of freedom he wouldn't have had if he'd filmed the Sex Pistols' story as it was happening in 1977. He can't give us the band's original, electrifying performances (their music is re-created in the film by Matlock, with Oldman and Schofield imitating Vicious and Rotten—passably—on the vocals), but the artifice also means that if he's careful, he can avoid the death-mask pathos that has invaded rock documentaries over the years.

And Cox is extremely careful. His direction of *Sid and Nancy* is rather muted—it's a far less idiosyncratic movie than *Repo Man*, his aggressively weird take on L.A. car culture. Although the sound track of his first film featured some of the hardest-core West Coast bands (like the Circle Jerks) and the lead actor (Emilio Estevez) wore a single earring, it wasn't music or fashion that made the film so authentically punk. *Repo Man*'s punk quality came from its combination of dreary landscapes and hopped-up characters, its jagged, unpredictable editing rhythms, and its distinctive mood of offhand nihilism. It was a movie in which everything was disposable—cars, jobs, lives—and it proceeded as if every few minutes the director were crumpling up his last set of ideas and throwing them away, and then picking up something new from all the junk out there on the street. Cox seems to have known, instinctively, that the nearest cinematic equivalent to the punk-rock aesthetic is B movies, which are trashy and assaultive, hilarious and scary, and not at all fussy about technique. (The Ramones, America's cheerful, mock-moronic counterpart to the Pistols, once recorded a song based on *The Texas Chainsaw Massacre*.) *Repo Man*, with its random shocks, its erratic bursts of obscene humor, and the presence, in a key role, of scuz-movie icon Harry Dean Stanton, had the attitude that more ambitious punk movies lacked. Next to it, a picture like *Rude Boy*, Jack Hazan and David Mingay's semidocumentary about the very political punk band the Clash, looked all wrong. Cox's—and the Sex Pistols'—brand of punk has no ambitions, no revolutionary project: it's just a chain saw with a deafening buzz, shredding stuff that isn't worth anything anyway.

Sid and Nancy is constructed of short, torn-off scenes, but it sticks to the point and it's economical. Sid, a weedy, dim-looking working-class kid, joins the Sex Pistols and meets Nancy Spungen (played by Chloe Webb), a brash, peroxided American groupie who turns him on to heroin. He gets famous, more for his attitude than for his talent—he can't play a lick, but he looks great, sneering and spitting at the audience and pounding spastically at his bass guitar as if he were just too *angry* to keep the beat. (In the film the group's manager, Malcolm McLaren, played by David Hayman, sees Sid as a kind of found art: "Sidney's more than a mere bass player. He's a fabulous disaster! He's a symbol! A metaphor! He embodies the dementia of a nihilistic generation.") The band breaks up at the end of its U.S. tour, and Sid and Nancy, still hooked on heroin and each other, move into a squalid little room in New York City's Chelsea Hotel, where art and self-destruction are enshrined together, where there's a genius barfing or nodding out in every room. Sid's just an image, not an artist; his attempt at a solo career (managed by Nancy) is a dismal flop, and all they have to do is drugs. In October 1978, barely a year after the Sex Pistols' breakup, Nancy is found dead in their room, apparently stabbed by Sid, perhaps in a suicide pact he failed to complete. In any event, he finishes himself off with an overdose a few months later.

Cox just lays it all out, simply enough to do justice to Sid and Nancy's painful story, but not so starkly that he flattens out or falsifies the energy of punk. As *Repo Man* showed, he's a director who understands recklessness, disposability, the euphoria of not giving a damn. He doesn't have to explain punk, because it's running in his veins. Cox's unforced sympathy for his subject enables him to bring off the very tricky evolution of the film's tone, from the spirited, rudely funny spectacle of the Sex Pistols thrashing about England and America in the final throes of their career, to Sid and Nancy's grim, intimate dissolution. He doesn't turn the doomed couple into metaphors—he keeps them specific, and certainly doesn't underestimate either Sid's stupidity or Nancy's psychotic self-destructiveness—but he makes their excruciating slide into oblivion seem continuous with the self-consuming nature of the Sex Pistols' music, an extension (and perversion) of punk's hell-bent aesthetic. Sid, pathetically, lives the brief remainder of his life after the band's breakup as a drugged, slow-witted parody of his public image. He looks as if he were playing back the short, intense history of his fame to his own sluggish rhythms, and the story of Sid and Nancy, in the second half of the film, is like the Sex Pistols' "Pretty Vacant" slowed from 45 rpm to a torpid 33⅓: the song lasts a little longer, but at that speed there's no point, and it ends anyway. Cox makes us see Sid's end as punk's cruel joke on a dumb kid, and the ironies cut the pathos. *Sid and Nancy* can't quite help being a kind of memorial to Sid Vicious and Nancy Spungen and the Sex Pistols, who all flamed out fast, but it is, for once, an elegy in the spirit of its subjects: pitiless, sardonic, and shockingly funny. In Cox's densely detailed compositions and Oldman and Webb's eerily empathetic performances there's a vitality that gives the lie to the dreamy pop-culture nostalgia of most rock movies. When the actors, improvising their climactic dance of death in the Chelsea Hotel, hurl each other back and forth across the room, wanting to end it and not wanting to, being themselves and acting something out, the camera following every unexpected move, it's as terrifying and ecstatic as anything the Sex Pistols ever did. Cox and his actors know when to turn their amps up all the way, and *Sid and Nancy*, without wanting to be a classic, lingers in the mind like a piercing blast of feedback.

The Nation, November 1, 1986

THE STEPFATHER

"What I sell," says Jerry Blake (Terry O'Quinn), the murderous realtor who's the central figure of *The Stepfather*, "is the American Dream"—and he's his own best customer. The expression on his face when he sits down to his first Thanksgiving dinner with his new wife (Shelley Hack) and teenage stepdaughter (Jill Schoelen) is reverent, awed: "Everything looks absolutely perfect," he pronounces, and his pleasure in the family tableau he's constructed for himself is so profound that actually eating the meal seems sacrilegious. Jerry's not a consumer, he's an artist, self-consumed. When it comes to family life, he accepts no substitutes—it's perfection or nothing. At the slightest hint of a flaw in the picture, he gets depressed, then slashes the canvas and starts all over. You might say Jerry's a believer in serial monogamy; he's also a serial killer.

As played by O'Quinn, Jerry Blake is a self-made parody of a TV father: "It's like having Ward Cleaver as a dad," his rebellious stepdaughter complains. This bland, benign-looking guy—solid but wiry, like a utility infielder on the high school baseball team—is the most convincing psycho in recent movies. Although the character is essentially a sick joke, O'Quinn, screenwriter Donald E. Westlake, and director Joseph Ruben *(Dreamscape)* get a lot more out of it than laughs and screams. The conception of Jerry as a man without an identity—who marries into families in order to pursue a perfect middle-class happiness and then slaughters them when, inevitably, they "disappoint" him—is an unusually suggestive one for this kind

165

of low-budget thriller and, in its uninsistent way, the movie has an echoing, haunted quality even in its most gruesomely funny scenes. Westlake, who's a veteran writer of crime fiction, knows his genre well enough to understand how it can, sometimes, transcend itself. It's an abstract, stylized form; and a great murderer, one whose actions are imagined as horrifyingly precise expressions of the most familiar motives, can be a fabulous metaphoric figure, radiating meaning like a perfect conceit in a sonnet. A character like Jerry Blake is terrifying not because he's out of control, the way the faceless, demonic slashers of *Friday the 13th*–type movies are, but because his control is so absolute, so uncompromising. In the best thrillers, the murderer's rage is just too rigorous for his victims: it has the knifelike clarity of an unanswerable argument.

The writers and filmmakers who have been most effective at drawing us into the obsessively orderly premises of the psycho's sensibility—Hitchcock and Patricia Highsmith, for example—often seem creepily single-minded themselves: their works, at their most ingenious, function like torture chambers, no-exit rooms filled with machinery so fathomlessly intricate that it renders us helpless. Westlake and Ruben have enough of that demented-inventor quality to make *The Stepfather* a more than efficient shocker within the genre's own terms, but the satiric spin they put on the conventions keeps throwing us outside the tight little world of the thriller. Even at the height of the horror, Ruben cuts into Jerry's maniacal pursuit of his intended victims with sly but unmistakable movie references—images lifted from *Psycho* and *The Birds*, some delirious De Palma–like tracking—and the jokey self-consciousness works for him (as it does for De Palma) as a strange kind of sanity. What makes Jerry a psychotic, after all, is that he has no sense of context, and therefore no sense of humor. His vision of bourgeois tranquillity, conceived with a child's self-sufficiency in front of the television, has simply never adjusted itself to adult realities. He doesn't see forms as forms, as structures outside those of his own mind: to him, a beautiful, empty house necessarily implies a flawless family to occupy it. That these spotless premises might be filled with screaming, reckless kids and irritable parents, a group of human beings leading ordinarily reckless lives, wouldn't strike him as funny at all: it would be reason enough for murder. The filmmakers' good-humored awareness of the form they're rattling around in is their defense against the jerry-built aesthetic of genre purity. Unlike their hero, they never delude themselves into thinking they've made a permanent home for themselves.

Very modestly, *The Stepfather* is a brilliant subversion of the way family has turned into ideology in 1980s America: it's the renters' revenge on the homeowners. The biggest joke in Westlake's screenplay is that the nature of Jerry's psychosis actually seems to protect him from discovery. He's got the values and mannerisms of a regular American dad down so perfectly that almost no one—not his neighbors, not even his wives—notices the superhuman strain of his performance, how the awkward, gee-whiz boyishness is contradicted by the cold vacancy of his eyes. His civic-booster optimism doesn't strike anyone as inane, and the studied, robotic stiffness of his gestures can be chalked up to simple middle-class tension: it signifies that he's taking his responsibilities as head of a household pretty darn seriously. At one point, his stepdaughter surprises him in his basement workshop while he's throwing a frighteningly ugly tantrum—he seems not just angry, but possessed—and, composing himself with magical alacrity, he comes up with a hilariously glib family-man excuse for bad behavior: "We all have to let off some steam. You know how it is." (He's just another nuclear-family reactor.) Everybody in the movie—except the stepdaughter, whose hostility to Jerry is easily dismissed as anger at the loss of her real father—acknowledges, implicitly, that Jerry's stranglehold on domestic stability is nothing out of the ordinary. It's only good sense, the community of homeowners seems to feel, to hold on tight to what you've got in times like these: Jerry kills everyone close to him just to keep them from getting away from him.

The irony, of course, is that what Jerry Blake is holding on to so tenaciously isn't really his own, anyway: he's only a *step*father, a replacement husband—a beneficiary, in fact, of life's instabilities, of the very unpredictability that, in other contexts, inspires his murderous frenzies. He moves into these families the way an actor moves into a cherished classical role, determined to "make it his own." Real actors know that there will be other roles, and that others have played, or will play, theirs: only a lunatic thinks his performance will wipe out all memories of everything before and all possibilities of anything after. In aspiring to make his every turn onstage into something timeless, *The Stepfather*'s hero condemns himself to endless, self-canceling repetition: he's trapped in reruns. Terry O'Quinn is certainly a real actor, and his performance as Jerry is sensational. He changes so quickly and so subtly that we can barely keep up with him. He's the model tenant for this kind of character, and his volatile but lucid portrayal exposes Jerry's bogus control with an oddly moving precision. *The Stepfather* isn't the first good psycho thriller, and it won't be the last, but the filmmakers have, with cunning self-awareness, renewed the lease on the genre. Realty: what a concept.

The Nation, May 30, 1987

THE UNTOUCHABLES

There are no shocks in *The Untouchables* to match the ones Brian De Palma has given us in his previous movies, none of those hallucinatory, cruelly extended moments of terror like the prom sequence in *Carrie*, the elevator murder in *Dressed to Kill*, the exploding of John Cassavetes at the end of *The Fury*, the chain-saw bloodbath in *Scarface*, and just about everything in his perilously sustained paranoid masterpiece *Blow Out*. The shock of *The Untouchables* is what a clean, uncomplicated—and successful—piece of Hollywood entertainment De Palma has made. After a career of funky counterculture comedies, messed-up commercial projects, and bloody, poetic, audacious thrillers, the bad boy seems finally to be going straight, with a vengeance.

The Untouchables, which tells the familiar story of how Treasury agent Eliot Ness brought Al Capone to justice in the corrupt, frontier-town atmosphere of 1930s Chicago, has pretty much everything we'd expect it to have: old cars, Tommy guns, stakeouts and raids, bad cops, cynical wisdom spoken in Irish accents and florid threats spoken in Italian ones, courtroom drama, swift killings, men in vests and shoulder holsters plotting strategy. This is genre-movie making on a grand scale, with luxurious production values and broadly conceived, vastly enjoyable movie-star acting by Robert De Niro (as Capone) and Sean Connery (as the oldest member of Ness's team, an honest Irish cop who tutors the Treasury agent in the ruthless ways of Prohibition-era Chicago). Working from a spare, functional

169

script by the playwright David Mamet, De Palma delivers the goods, and even throws in an extra case or two of his own special brew: a steady undercurrent of dark unease and several of his eye-popping, dizzyingly complex passages of action choreography. The virtuosity of these sequences—like the scenes in which a pair of killers stalk Connery from window ledges and fire escapes as he potters around his apartment, or Ness (Kevin Costner) pursues the skull-faced hit man Frank Nitti (Billy Drago) on the staircases and roof of the courthouse, or Ness shoots it out with a bunch of Capone's gunmen on the steps of a cavernous train station—is almost more than the movie can contain. De Palma's technique in the violent set pieces is more meticulous, more elaborate, than it really needs to be for this simple gangster picture: tantalizingly, it hints at a sensibility that goes far beyond the limits of the genre.

But only hints. The weird thing about *The Untouchables* is that De Palma has clearly regained the power and confidence that seemed to have deserted him after *Blow Out*, six years ago—his direction here is nothing less than sensational—yet his passionate inventiveness and distinctive sense of menace never quite take over the movie. He's near the top of his form, but his originality seems a fugitive, mystery ingredient in *The Untouchables*, something this plain concoction's been spiked with to give it a little kick. If you believe, as many do, that De Palma's style in *Carrie, The Fury, Dressed to Kill*, and *Blow Out* is self-indulgent, overbearing, and inhuman, then this movie will probably look like a sign of maturity, maybe even the best work he's ever done. But if you think—as I do—that those films, far from being flashy exercises in cold-blooded technique, are brilliant essays in the physical and spiritual geography of betrayal, you're likely to come out of *The Untouchables* feeling slightly puzzled, both at the real pleasures it gives and the deeper ones it doesn't.

The beauty of De Palma's more personal films is the way they mask their passion in genre trashiness, sadistic jokes, and self-conscious technical expertise. The telekinetic themes of *Carrie* and *The Fury* and the surveillance motifs of *Dressed to Kill* and *Blow Out* may look like conventions, but they're not. They're the disguises that this artist's consciousness takes, devices both of self-protection and self-expression—metaphors for the extreme and intricate watchfulness

that comes out of a profound sense of the world's treachery. ↓
De Palma's technical mastery emerges from this obsessive, near-
paranoid attentiveness to danger, too. His best sequences, like the
museum chase in *Dressed to Kill* and the climactic audio-surveillance
scene in *Blow Out*, are all explorations of the geometry of spaces
turned sinister—feverish, whirling attempts to get all the points
plotted exactly before they close in and strangle us. And when,
having held us so long in the belief (felt, not stated, in the camera
moves and the cutting) that our heightened attention will somehow
stave off disaster, De Palma finally springs the horror on us, it's
especially piercing. We watch and watch and then we have to turn
away. His technique is flashy, but it isn't cheap; his vision is pessimistic, but, surprisingly, more melancholy than cynical.

In *The Untouchables*, De Palma unleashes his strangely moving
sense of perceptual dread in the big violent scenes, and he gets the
effects he wants. Actually, the picture comes closest to achieving
some kind of emotional depth in its showiest and most overdetermined moments. (Costner's performance, likable but a little dull
elsewhere, seems to deepen in those scenes, too.) But the emotions
are transient, because Mamet's script doesn't give them a coherent
context. Although formally *The Untouchables* is an exceptionally
straightforward old-Hollywood narrative, Mamet's just a bit too hip,
too ironic to pin himself down to a classic gangster-movie tone. The
movie isn't sentimental and street-tragic the way the Warner Brothers pictures of the 1930s were (De Niro's Capone, though funny and
charismatic, is clearly a monster, and his henchmen are grotesque).
It comes nearer to the other available convention—the righteous,
heroic, government-authorized mode of FBI movies—but Mamet
clearly isn't comfortable with that, either. He keeps us aware
throughout that the law Ness and his men are enforcing, Prohibition,
is a stupid one, and, at various points, suggests that the battle against
Capone is a game, a play, a ritual. It's scrupulous of him to acknowledge this, and also too easy: it separates the audience's (contemporary) consciousness from the characters'. Whatever suspicions the
Untouchables may have about the value of their mission, the moral
ambiguity never seems to affect their behavior as characters, to have
any dramatic consequences. Mamet tries, halfheartedly, to reestablish the mythic verities of good versus evil by portraying Ness as a

family man bent on protecting the innocent, decent middle-class
home from the indiscriminate fury of the gangs. But he can't quite
put over that old-movie corn, either—he keeps snickering about
what a boy scout Ness is, and obviously relishes stripping him of his
scruples in the course of the picture. And the domestic scenes in the
Ness household are completely outside De Palma's range: they have
a saccharine quality that could either be failed sentiment or failed
parody.

Mamet's script provides a solid movie-action framework for the
material without supplying a fully satisfying attitude toward it. His
treatment is neither simple enough to be purely rousing nor complex enough to be disturbing; this evasiveness keeps *The Untouchables* from being a classic. A lot of the time, it feels like one anyway.
De Palma's sinuous camerawork (the film was shot by Stephen H.
Burum), his obsessive detailing of spatial relationships, and the
sinister beauty he imparts to nearly every composition are hypnotic.
In individual sequences, his visual sense is so powerful that it seems
to override the incoherence of the basic conception; we find ourselves responding to characters' emotions as if they'd been set up
dramatically, when they really haven't been. For the two very swift
hours of *The Untouchables*, De Palma comes awfully close to making us think with our eyes alone.

If there were any justice in American movies, an artist like De
Palma wouldn't have to pour his ideas into conventional genre
pieces that could probably get along perfectly well without them.
There's something almost touching about the intensity of the work
in this picture. On his first raid, Ness tries to rally the compromised
Chicago cops with the cry "Let's do some good," and that seems to
have been De Palma's attitude going into this big studio project.
Ness is ridiculed for his enthusiasm, and the raid is a disaster, but his
stance is honorable. (The line that, early on, defines Capone—"I'm
responding to the will of the people"—is a much more Hollywood
sentiment.) De Palma is determined to be an entertainer here, and
he goes about it without the hired-gun cynicism of, say, Scorsese in
The Color of Money, or the total suspension of critical intelligence
that appears to have afflicted Coppola in *Peggy Sue Got Married* and
Gardens of Stone. Thanks to him, the picture is phenomenally enjoyable despite its flaws, and doesn't make us feel condescended to or

cruelly used. Big-budget moviemaking is one of those dirty jobs (like police work or bootlegging) that somebody's usually more than willing to do, and not many directors in recent years have done it as excitingly as De Palma has in *The Untouchables*. He's proved he can do some good, and more, for a straight Hollywood product. That's fine—as long as he only has to prove it once. This picture is his movie-industry merit badge: if we're lucky, he'll find a way to twist it into a deadly weapon next time out.

The Nation, June 27, 1987

HOUSEKEEPING

The Scottish director Bill Forsyth makes movies for dawdlers and daydreamers—people who stare out the window at nothing at all and turn away, hours later, with strange, dazed smiles on their faces, delighted by whatever mixture of memory, fancy, and dogs crossing the street has just unreeled inside their head. His films—especially the last two, *Local Hero* and *Comfort and Joy*—are about the varieties of imaginative escape, the drifting gaze of those who don't feel too strongly connected to their time and their place. *Housekeeping*, his fifth movie, is in many ways an apparent departure: it isn't primarily a comedy, not a bit of it was shot in Scotland, and it's adapted from someone else's material, a 1981 novel by an American writer, Marilynne Robinson. His screenplay is almost slavishly faithful to Robinson's poetic, very literary book, which is based on her own idiosyncratic childhood and adolescence in 1950s Idaho; yet Forsyth doesn't wholly submerge his own personality. He moves right into Robinson's world and makes himself comfortable there, throwing open windows and dozing in sagging armchairs until the spirit of this unfamiliar place has seeped into him. You'd never know he's just passing through.

Robinson's novel is a moody, fragile thing—the kind of episodic memoir of youth whose effect depends almost entirely on the emotional qualities of its narrator's voice. It's the story of a pair of sisters growing up in a small Western town called Fingerbone, and most of the plot gets told in the first three sentences:

174

My name is Ruth. I grew up with my younger sister, Lucille, under the care of my grandmother, Mrs. Sylvia Foster, and when she died, of her sisters-in-law, Misses Lily and Nona Foster, and when they fled, of her daughter, Mrs. Sylvia Fisher. Through all these generations of elders we lived in one house, my grandmother's house, built for her by her husband, Edmund Foster, an employee of the railroad, who escaped this world years before I entered it.

The few other facts we need to know—that Edmund Foster died in a train that plunged off the bridge over Fingerbone's lake and that the girls' mother, Helen, drove her car into the same lake on the day she brought her children to their grandmother's house—are rattled off before the first chapter's over, and the rest of the book is detail, texture, reflection, and the slow unfolding of memory. The novel is about transience and fragility, the difficulty of holding on to people and things, and, true to its theme, it doesn't offer much for a film-maker to hold on to, either. It seems always on the verge of slipping away, like the girls' restless, distracted Aunt Sylvie (Christine Lahti), who keeps disappearing on long walks and knows the times of all the trains by heart. Forsyth's approach to this determinedly elusive material seems the only one possible—although not many other directors would have thought of it, and fewer still could have carried it off. He follows the book's wayward, tentative rhythms, the bobbing motion of its becalmed narrative and gently unsettled characters; he allows himself to drift along with Robinson.

And no one making movies today drifts as gracefully as Bill Forsyth does. He seems transfixed by the mountains and lakes and forests of the Northwest landscape, like a railroad traveler who finds himself suddenly moved by places he's never seen before. This feeling is the subject of his best movie, *Local Hero*, in which a young Houston oil executive, sent to negotiate with the people of an obscure Scottish village where his company wants to put a refinery, discovers that he's powerfully attracted to the villagers' way of life. After a few days there, he offers to exchange his life for that of the man he's been negotiating with. For Forsyth, Robinson's novel may be that kind of enchanted place, isolated and distant and apparently timeless, somewhere for the overburdened mind to wander. The virtue of this material for him is that despite the American setting and the all-female cast of characters, the story has a free-floating, abstract quality, as if, like the ramshackle house the girls grow up in, it were somehow outside of history, a safe haven from the obligation to be specific—to be, in any sense, defined by social experience. Robinson's world is, for all its melancholy, peculiarly idyllic: an adolescent's dream of retreat from everything in life that threatens to become too hard and fixed and would therefore be too painful to lose. She imagines a state of permanent indeterminateness, a universe presided over by dotty aunts rather than by parents, teachers, or lovers, and presents it as the state of nature, transcending time, sex, everything. It's easy to see why Forsyth, spotting this place from the train, would want to get off there. For someone of his temperament, it's accommodatingly vague and indifferent—no questions asked, a transient's paradise.

He finds his way around, in part, by superimposing his own map of memories, emotional connections, and hoarded images onto Robinson's. Shy, gawky Ruth (Sara Walker) inhabits roughly the same territory as the moonstruck teenager played by Gordon John Sinclair in Forsyth's *Gregory's Girl*. The scenery has the mysterious placidity of the Scottish coast in *Local Hero*, and the house itself evokes a sense of piercing isolation in the midst of familiar clutter— just as the studio from which the deejay in *Comfort and Joy* broadcasts his morning monologue creates an overpowering feeling of loneliness. Forsyth seems, at times, to be drawing on images and moods from movies other than his own, the films he's never been able to get out of his head: the Northwest landscape, the stray dogs in Fingerbone's desolate streets, the disquieting textures of ice in winter and mud in spring, and the languid, gliding rhythms of the direction often suggest Robert Altman's dreamlike Western *McCabe and Mrs. Miller* (an acknowledged favorite of Forsyth's); the deliberate pace of the narrative, the close attention to domestic detail, and the yearning for trains sometimes call to mind *Pather Panchali*, Satyajit Ray's great film about childhood. And Forsyth seizes greedily on every one of the opportunities Robinson's novel gives him for his special brand of offhand visual comedy: a scene in which Sylvie and Ruth steal a boat from under a fisherman's appalled gaze, while pretending they don't know it's anybody's property, is much funnier than it is in the novel; and the long sequence in which the house is flooded is filled with wonderful, tossed-off bits of comic business.

Forsyth doesn't quite make *Housekeeping* his own—it's Marilynne Robinson's, and he knows it—but he's produced a superbly empathetic reading of it, a reverie on the novel's themes. Without departing from its spirit, the movie is actually an improvement on the book. Forsyth's fluid, relaxed style is, weirdly, more expressive of the story's motifs of transience and flux than Robinson's carefully worked, often painfully elaborate literary prose is. The beauty of her imagery sometimes seems to be fighting its way through a thicket of stiff, almost archaic diction: "What twinges, what aches I felt, what gathering toward fecundity, what novel and inevitable rhythms, were the work of my strenuous imagining." The book's about a kind of freedom, yet the writing is oddly constricted; it never says the hell with it and just plays hooky, as the characters do. In Forsyth's movie, Robinson's images—the bridge, the inviting lake, the enveloping chaos of the house—come to us unobstructed, clarified by their passage through the filmmaker's consciousness. Their loveliness is direct and unforced, so we can wander among them as Forsyth does, discovering our own resonances, finding the connections to the private movies inside our heads.

The casting of Christine Lahti as Sylvie is perfect. Like Peter Riegert and Denis Lawson in *Local Hero*, and Bill Paterson in *Comfort and Joy*, Lahti is a low-key character actor with skill and charm enough for leading roles. Forsyth is about the only director around who gives actors like these such important parts—something else he may have picked up from Altman—and in each case his risky, intuitive casting decision has paid off. Lahti, a tall, friendly-looking woman who moves in long, loose strides, gives Sylvie a full-bodied warmth that the character desperately needs. On the page, this childlike, half-mad drifter occasionally seems too mysterious and ethereal, and at other times verges on the cliché of the lovable eccentric. Lahti's performance is confident and unfussy: She plays Sylvie as a hopeless dreamer who always appears to herself utterly practical and down-to-earth. Her every bizarre action is carried out with startling briskness, as if it were the most natural thing in the world, and Lahti, without obvious effort, keeps pulling off delicately timed miracles of reading and gesture: the way Sylvie muses, genuinely puzzled, about why she doesn't read books anymore; the cracked insouciance of her morning greeting to the girls as she stands knee-deep in water in the flooded house; how she bounds from tie to tie across the railroad bridge, just a shade too quickly for perfect safety. In the movie's gorgeous final image, she walks for a second time across the bridge, into the darkness, this time followed by young Ruth, who has discovered her affinity with her aunt's strange sense of freedom. The novel *Housekeeping* is about that fragile rapport of sympathetic dreamers. The movie *Housekeeping*, with Forsyth and Lahti making all the right connections, actually embodies it.

The Nation, January 16, 1988

WHO FRAMED ROGER RABBIT

Robert Zemeckis's *Who Framed Roger Rabbit*, a manic comedy in which animated cartoon characters interact with live actors, is an amazing feat of entertainment engineering. It's like a Disneyland ride, or one of those special-process World's Fair movies designed to give us the illusion that we're falling through the sky without a parachute or riding a gigantic tidal wave or getting thrown six counties by a tornado. Sure we're impressed—also pretty relieved when the experience is over. Now we know how *that* feels, we tell ourselves (as we try to breathe normally again). So now, thanks to Zemeckis and a small army of animators and special-effects artists, we know what it feels like to live in a world where drawings of bunnies, babies, and talking taxicabs have as much reality as human beings. This is "movie magic" at its most elaborate and most daunting: like a Vegas magician's colossal finale (making an elephant disappear from the stage, or something), it inspires awe rather than simple delight.

In *Roger Rabbit*, which is set in Los Angeles in 1947, Zemeckis and his team mean to pay homage to the Hollywood animation of the thirties and forties. Just about every popular cartoon character of that era, from Betty Boop to Dumbo, does a walk-on (or fly-on), and the movie's frenetic, gag-a-minute pace is clearly inspired by the great Warner Bros. comedy shorts that "starred" Bugs Bunny, Daffy Duck, and, later, the Road Runner and Wile E. Coyote. But *Roger Rabbit* doesn't have the right spirit. The best animators—the *funni-*

est ones, like Tex Avery and Chuck Jones—weren't big-deal magicians at all. Their effects were more like the tricks that close-up magicians do with cards and coins: small marvels of lightness and dexterity timed to follow each other so quickly and so smoothly that they seem effortless. Zemeckis does his best to keep things moving in *Roger Rabbit*—to give us the illusion of crazy, daredevil invention—but he can't quite disguise what a massive, backbreaking strain it is to try to make all these complex interactive effects both convincing and wildly funny. Studio animators like Jones and Avery worked with a handful of gagmen and artists, and cranked out six- or seven-minute comedies at the rate of one every five weeks. Poor Zemeckis needed to marshal the forces of dozens of animators (supervised by Richard Williams), a huge live-action crew, and a few more dozens of special-effects technicians, and to produce out of all this mobilized wizardry a relentlessly zany feature-length movie. (The film runs a hundred and three minutes.) This is about as likely to succeed as Wile E. Coyote's tortuously ingenious attempts to trap the Road Runner: he rigs up ever more elaborate devices for, say, launching a boulder to squash his speedy prey, but the big rock always lands on the coyote, and the Road Runner beep-beeps on by.

Zemeckis directs as if he suspected that he's going to get squashed. The movie begins with an animated short featuring a pair of original characters: Baby Herman, a placidly destructive infant, and the floppy, oversized, neurotic Roger Rabbit, a comic victim, who is stretched out of shape, bounced off walls, and pulverized by kitchen appliances as he zips around trying to contain the havoc the baby creates. As in many cartoons, the character who expends the most energy—the coyote, Elmer chasing Bugs, Sylvester chasing Tweety, Tom chasing Jerry, Daffy Duck doing anything—is the butt of all the jokes. In cartoons, the tiny, quiet, clever creatures always frustrate the strenuous efforts of the bigger ones, and the Baby Herman short is true to the classic form. It's also not very good. The cartoon is the movie in miniature: it's technically scrupulous and respectful of its sources, but it has a frantic, anxious, self-destructive quality that throws the timing off. In its desperation to please, this cartoon is as screwed up and out of control as its nervous second banana Roger, who, after a climactic gag in which he's flattened by a refrigerator, walks off the "set" jabbering to the (human) director that he'll try harder, do better, do *anything* that's asked of him. (We'd like to ask him to shut up.) The whole movie's like that: it keeps shoving itself in our faces, promising and pleading and contorting itself into different shapes, trying to dazzle us so that we don't see what it really is—one of the big, greedy, ungainly animals whose efforts always come to grief.

Who Framed Roger Rabbit is a folly; what's more, it's a trivial one. The script, by Jeffrey Price and Peter Seaman (based very loosely on a novel by Gary K. Wolf), is a painstaking elaboration of a fairly witty conceit: that cartoon characters, called Toons here, are ordinary contract players in the already skewed universe of the old studio system. This wouldn't be a bad idea for a short subject. In 1940, it *was* a short subject: Friz Freleng's *You Ought to Be in Pictures*, in which Daffy Duck and Porky Pig negotiate with the real, live head of Warners' animation department, Leon Schlesinger. Price and Seaman have pumped up the notion by placing the Toons in a conventional forties mystery plot, featuring a seedy, hard-drinking private eye played by Bob Hoskins (when the novelty of seeing Bugs Bunny and the hippos from *Fantasia* strolling around the back lot begins to flag, the filmmakers can fall back on genre parody), and by giving the Toons' situation a hint of social significance. The Toons are presented here as an exploited minority who live in a kind of ghetto (called Toontown), and provide the entertainment at a place known as the Ink and Paint Club, where only human beings are served. The plot links the discrimination against the lovable Toons with various dastardly schemes to corrupt the innocence and (supposedly) idyllic charm of L.A. in the forties. Formally, all the elements come together, but the net effect is a little oppressive: Do the moviemakers *have* to turn their slight, clever notion into a metaphor for racial integration just to get us to buy it?

Maybe they do. After all, Zemeckis and company aren't exactly tapping into a common fantasy, fulfilling the audience's secret dreams. It's likely that very few moviegoers even in those innocent forties ever imagined themselves having a drink with Bugs and Daffy, or yearned to see their favorite actors and their favorite cartoon characters become great pals. (The rare previous attempts to combine animation and live action—Gene Kelly dancing with the cute mouse Jerry in *Anchors Aweigh*, for instance—are obviously just stunts, and not very satisfying.) Part of this movie's problem is that it has to work awfully hard to convince us that its miscegenation of forms is something we *should* desire.

All there is to *Who Framed Roger Rabbit*, really, is an illusion of lunacy, a nostalgia for zaniness: technology and elaborate plot mechanics laboring mightily to evoke an aura of freedom and uninhibited joy. It asks us, in its sentimental all-star ending, to believe in the values of a happier, more spontaneous age, yet there's hardly a spontaneous moment in the movie. There are bits that work wonderfully: Roger's sireny wife, Jessica, a Toon with a curvy human form (and with the speaking voice of Kathleen Turner and the singing voice of Amy Irving), is a funny character; Hoskins is heroically unself-conscious under the circumstances, and gives a subtly stylized, amusing performance; Christopher Lloyd provides a spark of maniacal delight in his portrayal of the villainous Judge Doom. And the effects are ambitious and are impeccably executed. But Zemeckis doesn't seem like a happy filmmaker here: his work isn't nearly as fresh and inventive as it was in *Used Cars* and *Back to the Future* (both of which he wrote, with Bob Gale). He's trapped in a huge machine whose ingenious parts might easily have been supplied by the Acme Corporation, the source of the coyote's fiendish but ineffectual contraptions. Actually, the parts are courtesy of Disney's Touchstone Pictures, Steven Spielberg's Amblin Entertainment, and George Lucas's special-effects division, Industrial Light & Magic. With these three giant magic factories breathing down a director's neck, he's not going to be a relaxed guy: this is hardly a situation in which the anarchic spirit of the best forties animation is likely to flourish. Chuck Jones once said, "These cartoons were never made for children. Nor were they made for adults. They were made for *me*." If Zemeckis had said anything like that while he was making *Who Framed Roger Rabbit*, someone would probably have dropped a refrigerator on his head.

The New Yorker, July 11, 1988

BOYFRIENDS AND GIRLFRIENDS

Eric Rohmer's latest movie, *Boyfriends and Girlfriends* (*L'Ami de Mon Amie*), could hardly be more insubstantial. It's a light romantic comedy in which four completely unremarkable young people—two women, two men—reshuffle their affections so that, after the usual misunderstandings, hesitations, and temporary disappointments, each winds up with the "right" partner in the end. And nearly all the action takes place in the most banal setting imaginable: a modern community in the suburbs of Paris—Cergy-Pontoise, a self-contained development of high-rise housing, sleek office buildings, pristine recreational areas, and cozy, overdesigned clusters of shops and cafés. Cergy-Pontoise isn't a futuristic horror. It's a parody of a town, a calculated and slightly ridiculous attempt to create a happy, secure community out of nothing at all, but the people who live there don't mind: they look very content as they stroll, in bright, crisp sports clothes, through the spotless town square, or windsurf on the lake amid the splashing and the jagged laughter of children. The town is a middle-class playground, perfectly ahistorical: it suggests neither the heavy, weary Old World nor an especially brave new one. Rohmer didn't invent Cergy-Pontoise—it actually exists—but the place has the wispy, unreal quality of an abstraction, one of those literary never-never lands designed to allow young lovers to find each other. It's a bland utopia, a bourgeois Forest of Arden.

Boyfriends and Girlfriends is fluff of a rarefied order. The movie is so rigorous and elegant and extreme that it seems, finally, to be about its own weightlessness—not so much a thin romantic comedy as a comic meditation on the thinness of romance. It's a French intellectual's beach-party movie: fluff degree zero. Yet, for all its formality and self-consciousness, the film isn't lifeless. It's artificial without being oppressive—a graceful, friendly abstraction. Like all of Rohmer's movies, *Boyfriends and Girlfriends* unfolds slowly. The characters walk around, chat about this and that, tease each other a little, argue amiably, eat a couple of meals, bump into each other on street corners; as we watch their aimless daily routines we're wondering just who these people are and what, if anything, is going to happen. The beauty of Rohmer's best films is that his characters seem to be wondering the same thing: they're in a state of expectancy, waiting for some half-imagined significance to emerge from their everyday selves, and trying to decide whether there's anything they can do to speed the process along. They, and we, discover that in Rohmer's world meaning takes its sweet time and turns up in unexpected forms. *Boyfriends and Girlfriends* is essentially the same leisurely comedy of self-knowledge that Rohmer has been making for nearly twenty years—since *My Night at Maud's*—but this time he treats his themes with a frivolous, casual, almost dismissive air. The young lovers of Cergy-Pontoise aren't as introspective or as driven as Rohmer's usual protagonists, and they suffer only minor spiritual agonies in the course of selecting their mates. Blanche (Emmanuelle Chaulet), a direct, uncomplicated girl who lacks confidence and blushes when she has to tell a lie, develops a crush on a passive lady-killer named Alexandre (François-Eric Gendron); her best friend, Léa (Sophie Renoir), who's willful and a bit devious, lives with a good-natured windsurfing enthusiast named Fabien (Eric Viellard). By the end of the movie, Blanche has paired off with Fabien, and Léa with Alexandre, and not for any very profound reasons: Blanche and Fabien simply feel comfortable together, and Léa and Alexandre enjoy each other's little games. The women have a few stabs of guilt about poaching on each other's territory, but their qualms don't seriously threaten the suburban idyll. The final arrangement of things seems so natural, so effortlessly right, that no one's inclined to complain or feel betrayed. The lovers shrug and accept their happiness.

The cheerful superficiality of *Boyfriends and Girlfriends*—its relative lack of moral tension and emotional complexity—is a bit of a surprise, especially since this film concludes the six-part cycle of Comedies and Proverbs, which Rohmer began, in 1980, with *The Aviator's Wife.* If we were expecting some great summing-up, a true resolution, this movie isn't it. The real climax of the series turns out to have been the fifth film, called *Summer* in this country. Its original title, *Le Rayon Vert*, means "The Green Ray," and refers to a rare visual phenomenon that, according to Jules Verne, occurs the instant after the sun has dropped below the horizon. In this amazing film, which followed the two weakest and most contrived of the Comedies and Proverbs, *Pauline at the Beach* and *Full Moon in Paris*, Rohmer relaxed his customary iron control over the narrative: the movie was made in an on-the-run documentary style, in 16mm and with direct sound, and the dialogue, usually chiseled and epigrammatic in his movies, was largely improvised by the actors. It's as if Rohmer knew that the time had come for him to subject himself to the kinds of uncertainties and anxieties that he had always been content merely to observe. In *Summer* he's exploring, a little nervously, hoping that something will emerge from the mess of daily improvisations, wondering if anything will *happen* as he follows his restless heroine from one French vacation to another. Of all Rohmer's films, this one comes closest to being a self-portrait. Delphine (Marie Rivière) is a slim, dark, delicate-featured depressive. Since breaking up with her boyfriend, she has become cautious, conservative, almost pathologically wary. Her response to everything is refusal: she's a vegetarian, she flees from men who approach her, she won't even admit, after two years, that her love affair is over. Rohmer, whose art is based on refusal—he quietly declines to indulge in the ordinary, vulgar pleasures that movies provide so easily—understands her very well. The movie has the tentative, irresolute rhythm of its heroine's search for a place where she can feel at ease on her long French summer holiday. This woman is comically, absurdly, infuriatingly incapable of enjoying herself: she goes somewhere, gets disgusted with it, returns to Paris, takes off for someplace new, and is unhappy everywhere. Her idea of vacation reading is *The Idiot.* She drives us crazy, but she's in real pain, the mundane, annoying, debilitating kind that won't go away yet isn't spectacular enough to win much sympathy—like a migraine. When relief

comes, it's sudden, arbitrary, a stroke of luck or grace. While Delphine is waiting for a train in Biarritz to take her back to Paris after
another vacation fiasco, she decides, impulsively, to tag along with
a pleasant young man on his way to the coastal town of Saint-Jean-
de-Luz. She surprises herself, and us, with her boldness: after all her
self-imposed restrictions, this act has the force of a reckless break
with her old self, or perhaps a return to a freer, more spontaneous
relationship to experience. In Saint-Jean-de-Luz, she's rewarded:
watching the sun go down, she sees the green ray, which, according
to Verne, enables its viewer to "see clearly into his own heart and the
hearts of others." She cries "Yes!" and clutches her gentle companion. This is one of the purest moments of happiness in recent
movies: we feel that Rohmer, along with his heroine, has finally
found a way to release himself, to be at ease with the accidents, the
scary contingencies, of the natural world.

   Summer is a great film. *Boyfriends and Girlfriends* isn't, and isn't
meant to be. It's the afterglow of the green ray: though the film was
fully scripted by Rohmer, its mood is relaxed, blissfully inconse-
quential. His suburban characters are too young and too protected
to have suffered much or to have developed very complex responses
to experience, and they live in an inglorious environment of commercial artifice, but Rohmer finds real beauty in both the people and
the setting. He takes pleasure in the cleanness and brightness of this
world, in the contented buzz of shoppers and office workers and
Sunday picnickers, in the forthright way his characters pursue their
comforts. This is, of course, an intellectual's dream of simplicity and
unself-consciousness; there's no condescension in it, though. Rohmer even allows himself to indulge in some of the conventions of
popular French comedy. (Not that the movie is likely to be confused
with abject crowd-pleasers of the *Cousin, Cousine* variety.) In a way,
this picture is a perfect conclusion to the Comedies and Proverbs
series. Its ease is unexpected, a green bolt from the blue: as Rohmer
has often suggested, the end of our self-explorations is something
we didn't know we had been waiting for. *Boyfriends and Girlfriends*
looks accidental, but its lovely insubstantiality is hard-won.

The New Yorker, July 25, 1988

ALICE

In *Alice* the Czech animator Jan Švankmajer plays with objects the way Lewis Carroll played with words, and creates out of Carroll's Wonderland a world of more ambiguous, more unsettling nonsense. Švankmajer, who animates household items and worn-looking dolls, makes nonsense physical, palpable, and thus gives Alice's adventures in illogic an undertone of menace. Things that won't behave normally are scarier than words that won't, and when those things are the material of our ordinary lives, the stuff we manipulate happily every day, the favorite toys we surround ourselves with for comfort, the effect is chilling, claustrophobic. When objects start moving from the places we've assigned them on our shelves and in our cupboards, when they rebel against the order our minds have imposed, their freedom may at first seem magical, but it quickly turns sinister: What's to stop these newly animated things from turning on us, crowding us out completely? When the figures of our imagination "take on a life of their own," we're somehow con-fined—as helpless as dreamers who can't wake up or madmen backed into corners and flailing at phantoms. At the beginning of the movie, we hear a young girl's voice recite, "Now you will see a film made for children, perhaps. But you must close your eyes. Other-wise, you won't see anything." *Alice* is a film for children of a certain kind, for the quiet, solitary ones who spend hours in conversation with their dolls; who invest the smallest cast-off objects with secret significance; who on being interrupted at play react with blurred shock, flashing at the intruder the wary, glazed look of a suddenly awakened cat. It's a film for a child whose play will, over the years, perhaps turn into a lonely, obsessive craftsmanship—of the sort that animators have.

Švankmajer's Alice, played by a big-eyed little girl named Kristýna Kohoutová, begins to dream in a darkening room where she's alone with her possessions: stuffed animals, dolls in bright frocks, a tea set, playing cards, half-eaten sweets, and plenty of that mysterious, unidentifiable bric-a-brac that only a kid could find and only a kid would save. There's a strange hush in this cluttered domain, the aura of a child's fatigue in the aftermath of furious play. Everything shows the effects of hard use: the toys lie around in odd postures of exhaustion, like casualties on a battlefield. This room is evidence of the fervor and heedless energy of the girl's imagination. From the moment when her stuffed White Rabbit begins to stir, dresses himself in a red coat and hat, pulls a big pair of scissors from a coffinlike drawer in the bottom of his display case, and smashes the glass and escapes, we sense a kind of frenzy in Alice's dream images: her fantasy universe is one of violence, confinement, and obsessive repetition. Švankmajer, while following the outline of Carroll's story, mostly keeps the action indoors: his Wonderland, the landscape of Alice's imagination, is a domestic maze of doors, drawers (the "rabbit-hole" this Alice falls into is the shallow drawer of an old wooden table), stairs, hallways, cabinets, shelves, and, inside the house, smaller houses—dollhouses, with their own configuration of doors and windows, their own minutely ordered rooms. And in this world—the half-familiar, half-obscure territory of the shut-in child, susceptible to the mystery of inaccessible corners, suspecting that great secrets (good or evil) are hidden in the places she can't reach—everything has a heightened, shockingly vivid physical presence. Every floorboard groans and every door creaks loudly when it's opened and every object seems to clatter resoundingly against every other. Even the puppets keep reminding us of what they're made of. When the Mad Hatter, a wooden marionette with an open back, drinks his tea, we see the liquid dribbling out of his hollow body; the White Rabbit has a pocket watch sewn into his tatty fur, so whenever he checks the time (as he does frequently) sawdust spills out of him and he has to close himself up with a safety pin; the

Caterpillar, a woolen sock with a pair of glass eyes and a set of chattering false teeth, delivers his message to Alice and then, alarmingly, darns over his own eyes as he settles down to sleep. These sequences are small miracles of stop-motion animation, and more than that. Švankmajer's attention to the resilient properties of these shabby, Old World materials has the effect of making Alice, the only human being in this world, look disturbingly fragile.

This Alice—who isn't at all the cheeky, commonsensical little girl we find in Carroll but simply a curious and rather apprehensive observer—actually seems sturdier when, for a few sequences, she turns into a doll. (She has, of course, drunk the liquid that makes her small.) In one particularly eerie and imaginative scene, the doll-Alice grows to full size while remaining a doll, and we can see the real Alice trapped inside, her eyes peering out through a mannequin's hollow sockets (an image that recalls Georges Franju's great lyrical horror film *Eyes Without a Face*). Alice punching her way out of this lifelike shell is perhaps the key image of the movie. The girl seems to have liberated herself, to have refused the status of an object, to have *grown* in some real way—an imago emerged from its cocoon—and she has managed it with a burst of violence, of the physical force that (rather than words) is the means by which this pent-up child expresses herself. But her actions don't release her from the dream labyrinth, this airless studio of absurdities. There are still more rooms to enter and escape from; more fierce creatures animated from dead matter; more shocks and indignities—including a mock trial in which this Czech Alice, who (unlike her English original) has found no freedom in language, is asked to read a prepared statement condemning herself while the objects clank and squeal in the jury box.

Švankmajer clearly brings a pessimistic, absurdist, Eastern European sensibility to bear on Carroll's material. A self-described "militant Surrealist," he has been making short films, mostly puppet animation, since 1964—sometimes with the financial support of his government, sometimes not. *Alice*, his first feature, is a Swiss-German-English coproduction. The executive producer for Britain's Film Four, Keith Griffiths, is also the producer of the Švankmajer-influenced animated films of the Brothers Quay (*Street of Crocodiles*). Švankmajer's work has a stubborn, unyielding quality that the

Quays' (for instance) doesn't. All puppet animators practice their art in a kind of feverish isolation, in small rooms where tiny figures are nudged repeatedly into infinitesimal movements; such artists operate like mad children. Švankmajer, perhaps because of the added loneliness of trying to create his painstaking magic in a closed society, seems to have become a little rigid. In *Alice* he sticks to a rhythm of repeated motifs which is for the most part convincingly dreamlike but is sometimes schematic and wearying. The sparse dialogue, spoken in voice-over, is always punctuated with the same shot of the little girl's mouth intoning "said Alice" or "said the White Rabbit" or whatever, and the device is annoying. The sequences—mostly in the second half of the film—that depend on repetition to create a sense of accelerating absurdity, such as the Mad Hatter's tea party, can seem interminable. (In any event, watching animation is more exhausting than watching live action, and Švankmajer, almost defiantly, doesn't use any music, which might have helped to move us along more smoothly.) The filmmaker's obsessions, like his child heroine's, may have been locked up in his head for too long—he seems to know how easily they could escape from his control, and keeps too tight a grip on them. But this is an extraordinary piece of work: a brilliantly inventive demonstration of the animator's art and a piercing, original vision of the child's imaginative landscape—a movie that manages to be large and small at the same time.

The New Yorker, August 8, 1988

MARRIED TO THE MOB

Jonathan Demme's *Married to the Mob* is a crazy comedy about normalcy. Its heroine, Angela (Michelle Pfeiffer), is married to an up-and-coming suburban gangster, and she doesn't feel good about her life; she's avid for ordinariness. Unlike the other mob wives, she finds it a little unsettling that the living room of her expensive Long Island house is piled high with hot appliances (in unopened boxes); that her son is relieving the neighborhood kids of their allowances by running a three-card-monte game in the backyard; that when her husband (Alec Baldwin), a handsome hit man known as Frank the Cucumber, can't find his gun their son knows exactly where it is. Frank thinks it's "a swell house," and he's proud of the boy for conning twelve bucks out of his little pals. "Everything we own fell off a truck!" Angela screams. "Everything has blood on it!" When she mentions divorce, he just laughs and laughs: he can't believe how naive she is. The other wives sense something peculiar about Angela, but they can't imagine that anyone might actually be dissatisfied with the consumer wonderland they all live in, or uneasy about the nature of the family business; to them she's just a bitch. And after her husband is murdered these fierce women view Angela with even greater suspicion. Unattached, this gorgeous young woman is a threat to their most prized possessions, their men. Their condolences to the widow are delivered with menacing undertones: "We are your friends, Angela, whether you like it or not." She flees this nightmare parody of middle-class comfort with a righteous urgency,

191

giving all her tainted worldly goods—virtually the entire contents of her house—to Goodwill Industries, and moving herself and her reluctant kid into a cramped, peeling, tub-in-kitchen apartment on the Lower East Side. The funniest thing about all this is that Angela—a tough suburban cookie with a sinus-clearing Long Island accent, a mop of savagely permed dark hair, a face whose muscles are taut from ferocious gum-chewing, and the killer walk of a woman who has been wearing pants a size too small and heels an inch too high since about the sixth grade—really is an angel. Her hoop earrings are as big as halos.

Although the script, by Barry Strugatz and Mark R. Burns, is fairly conventional, it's not hard to figure out what must have attracted Jonathan Demme to this material. While zipping through the plot's screwball convolutions—Angela is being pursued by her late husband's boss and murderer, Tony (the Tiger) Russo (Dean Stockwell), who's got the hots for her, they are both being stalked by Tony's insanely jealous wife, Connie (Mercedes Ruehl), the Feds are after the lot of them, and Angela is falling in love with a goofy young FBI agent (Matthew Modine) who's tailing her—Demme takes the opportunity to indulge in his own low-key brand of cultural anthropology. It obviously tickles him to juxtapose the crass opulence of "family" life on Long Island (and in Miami Beach, where the story has its climax) with the multiethnic funk of the Lower East Side, and to make grubby Rivington Street the locus of the movie's values, the place where Angela can feel *normal*. He's right on the verge of seeming too cool, too hip, too culturally correct, but he's saved by a kind of natural innocence that is perhaps the same thing as a filmmaker's curiosity. When Demme shows us a mob hangout called the King's Roost, a restaurant whose garish fake-medieval facade looks about the size of the Babylonian set for *Intolerance*, and an ornate love chamber in the Fantasia Motel (where Frank, arriving for a rendezvous with Tony the Tiger's mistress, meets his end), we don't sense any superiority in his attitude toward these bad-taste monuments. He seems amazed by them—thrilled by their brazenness, delighted at how fully their extravagant design expresses the outsized personalities of the characters who move through them, awed at the discovery of a culture in which such structures are the landscape of ordinary life. Even in the cartoonish world of *Married to the Mob* Demme is happy simply to observe, without imposing himself on the material. Of the major American directors, he's the least erratic, the most consistently good company, because he has interests rather than obsessions.

Demme, who makes documentaries and music videos as well as fiction films (*Citizens Band, Melvin and Howard, Something Wild*), is great at providing incidental pleasures, the weird, heterogeneous stuff that American culture is so abundant in. As usual in his pictures, the music is terrific. David Byrne's original score suggests an inspired parody of spaghetti-Western music, and there are a couple of dozen songs by a diverse bunch of performers, including New Order, Sinéad O'Connor, Tom Tom Club, Chris Isaak, Brian Eno, Ziggy Marley, the Feelies, a samba band called Pé-De-Boi (who are seen performing in a dance-club sequence), and Rosemary Clooney (who sings "Mambo Italiano" over the opening credits). One of the film's music supervisors, Gary Goetzman, plays the small role of the pianist at the King's Roost, who gives Tony the Tiger some impromptu theme music when the mob boss walks in: "Hey, it's Tony the Tiger, he's the *paisan* the sun always shines on." (This is a piano player who knows how not to get shot.) Demme pauses in the middle of a surveillance scene to allow his FBI-agent hero to harmonize with some street singers (the group True Image), and then lingers for a minute on a sidewalk performer who calls himself Mr. Spoons. And the casting is superbly eccentric. Tiny roles are filled by such distinctive actors as Charles Napier, Joan Cusack, Trey Wilson, Tracey Walter, Al Lewis, and David Johansen (playing a priest); strange, memorable faces seem to be popping out at us all the time. Dean Stockwell makes Tony the Tiger a wonderfully demented villain, a middle-class thug who loves to sing burger-chain jingles; who after practically raping Angela in her yard on the day of her husband's funeral smiles sweetly to himself, as if he had truly conquered her heart; and who lives in mortal fear of his wife, who has vowed to hunt him down "like an animal" if she discovers that he has been unfaithful. Mercedes Ruehl makes us believe it. Her Connie is overpowering, implacable, horrifyingly funny. When she shouts "You can call me a ball-buster, but it's just the way I am!" Ruehl fills us with pity, terror, and glee.

The major pleasure of *Married to the Mob*, though, is Michelle

Pfeiffer. What resonance this comedy has comes directly out of her classic, fine-featured American beauty; even with that hair, that wardrobe, that walk, that accent, she manages to suggest an unkillable innocence, a spirit that refuses to be coarsened. She gives an extraordinary performance: she makes both Angela's toughness and her goodness believable, funny, and touching. Her vulgarity and her almost ethereal delicacy seem indistinguishable—which makes her a perfect embodiment of what Jonathan Demme's movies are all about.

If the movie feels a little thinner than Demme's very best work, it's partly because Modine's character is underwritten, so the romantic resolution of the fairy tale isn't fully satisfying; we don't quite know what it means for Angela to have wound up with this gawky, sweet-natured junior G-man. As gangster comedies go, *Married to the Mob* doesn't have the satiric kick of *Prizzi's Honor* or the wild lyricism of *Shoot the Piano Player*. It's just a smart, genial entertainment that gives us plenty to look at and listen to. It comes as close to being a normal Hollywood movie as anything Demme has made—yet it's not like anything else around right now. If only all American movies were as ordinary as this one.

The New Yorker, August 22, 1988

THE THIN BLUE LINE

Errol Morris's documentaries have a luxuriant weirdness, a deep unfamiliarity. In his first two films—*Gates of Heaven* (1978), a report on pet cemeteries in California, and *Vernon, Florida* (1981), a loosely assembled collection of tales from a small Southern town, told by rambling coots and half-demented good old boys—his choice of material and his fondness for lingering on the cracked discourse of his interview subjects identified him as a true connoisseur of native eccentricity, a hoarder of oddball Americana. His new movie, *The Thin Blue Line*, shows that he's more than an inspired believe-it-or-not artist. Telling the story of a 1976 cop-killing in Dallas, and detailing the process by which a man who is almost certainly innocent was convicted and sentenced to death for the crime (with the likely killer as the prosecution's star witness), Morris burrows into a nightmarish realm of duplicity, faulty perception, and bottomless ambiguity. The movie is both detached and fanatically intense. Its materials have the heterogeneity, the heedless comprehensiveness, of documents in a dossier: there are interviews with the principals, close-ups of key words and paragraphs from the newspaper accounts, courtroom sketches, maps, family-album snapshots of the suspects, diagrams of the crime scene and of the entry and exit wounds in the victim's body, and a series of eerie reenactments of witnesses' different versions of the murder and the events that led up to it. But this stuff isn't organized in ways that we're used to. *The Thin Blue Line* doesn't have the structure either of *60 Minutes*–style investigative journalism or of detective fiction, though it borrows elements from both; its form is circular, spiraling, its obsessive, repetitive visual motifs echoed in Philip Glass's hauntingly monotonous score. This is documentary as epistemological thriller; Morris seems to want to bring us to the point at which our apprehension of the real world reaches the pitch of paranoia—to induce in us the state of mind of a detective whose scrutiny of the evidence, whose search for the connections between stubbornly isolated facts, has begun to take on the feverish clarity of hallucination.

The movie is a trancelike, almost lyrical rendering of a small, messy murder case—the kind of story that's usually found only in local newspapers and, sensationalized, in true-detective magazines—and it's as hypnotic as *Vertigo*. Although Morris himself doesn't appear in *The Thin Blue Line*, he is the film's true detective, the investigator whose insomniac consciousness keeps reshuffling the evidence, generating ambiguous images of the crime from the contradictory testimony of witnesses, swerving constantly between words and pictures, between facts and hypotheses. He came upon the story by accident. In 1985, Morris was interviewing prisoners in a Texas penitentiary for a documentary on Dr. James P. Grigson, a Dallas psychiatrist who is known as Dr. Death, because his expert testimony in capital cases virtually guarantees that the defendant will be sentenced to death. One of the filmmaker's interview subjects was a man named Randall Adams, who claimed to have been wrongly convicted of a policeman's murder. Morris did some digging into the records of the case and the trial, became convinced that Adams was innocent, and wound up on a long detour from the Dr. Death movie; the question of how Randall Adams could have landed in jail for something he probably didn't do took over the filmmaker's mind. Undoubtedly, the urgent, compulsive quality of *The Thin Blue Line* is, at least in part, a consequence of the film's unusual origin. The subject seems to have seized Morris's imagination unexpectedly—in much the same way that another Dallas murder, the Kennedy assassination, has drawn people, almost against their will, into its labyrinth of half-truths and contradictions, closed files and intimations of conspiracy.

Officer Robert Wood was killed on a cold night in November 1976. He and his partner had stopped a car in a bad section of town just to tell the driver to turn his headlights on; when Wood reached the window on the driver's side, he was shot, several times, by the man at the wheel. Since the crime was apparently so senseless, and since the only known witness, Wood's partner, wasn't very observant (the movie suggests that she may have violated procedure by remaining seated in the patrol car, drinking a milkshake, while Wood approached the killer's car), the Dallas police had no leads and hardly any clues. A month later, they questioned sixteen-year-old David Harris, who had been bragging to his buddies in the small town of Vidor that he had killed a Dallas cop. He admitted to the police that he had been in the car that Wood pulled over, but claimed that the person who had done the shooting was Randall Adams, a hitchhiker he had picked up earlier that day. After interrogating Adams—who insisted that the teenager had dropped him off at his motel a couple of hours before the time of the murder, and who refused to sign a confession—the police decided that they would believe Harris, despite what might have seemed fairly strong circumstantial evidence pointing to him as the killer: both the murder weapon and the car had been stolen by Harris in Vidor; since he knew that the car was stolen, he would have had far more reason than Adams to panic at being stopped by a patrol car; he had a substantial criminal record, and was facing charges in Vidor at the time he gave his evidence, whereas Adams had no record at all and no history of violence. So why, the movie asks, was Adams prosecuted, much less convicted and sentenced to death?

Morris's answers, or suggestions of answers, are complex, and whirl by us at such speed that we're barely able to keep up. We register one fact, and then another comes at us, then another and another, until, finally, we seem to be taking it all in on an almost subliminal level—our attention is so intensely focused that everything resonates, everything connects, with a logic we have stopped even trying to articulate. In showing us the lies, the fears, the social pressures, the cultural influences, the unwarranted assumptions, the ulterior motives, the stubbornness, and the plain confusion that combined to produce the case against Randall Adams, Morris—who has a degree in philosophy, and who once worked as a private detective—seems to be investigating not just this squalid murder but the very nature of untruth. It's hard to think of another movie (let

alone another documentary) that has such a richly developed sense
of the *texture* of falsehood, that picks out so many of the strands
that, woven together, blind us. The Dallas police, their anger stirred
and their pride challenged by the murder of one of their own,
needed to arrest someone: if they believed Harris, they had a crime
with a witness; if they believed Adams, then Harris was alone in the
car, and they had nothing. The district attorney, Douglas Mulder,
who had never lost a capital case, needed a conviction and a death
sentence: Harris, as a juvenile, couldn't be tried for first-degree
murder; Adams, who was twenty-seven, could. At the trial, the victim's partner, who was feeling the heat of a departmental investigation of her conduct on the night of the killing and therefore may
have been especially eager to cooperate, changed her testimony
from her original report: having initially said that there was only one
person in the car, she now claimed to have seen two; the driver was
now described as having had bushy shoulder-length hair (like
Adams), rather than short hair and a fur-collared jacket (like Harris).
The judge, the son of an FBI agent, was a man with a passion for law
enforcement; he admits that he "welled up" during the DA's emotional closing argument about "the thin blue line" of police risking
their lives to protect society. One of the prosecution's chief witnesses, sprung on the defense at the last moment, was a woman
named Emily Miller, who "used to watch all the detective shows on
TV" and loved to make herself useful to the authorities—particularly
in this case, since there was a twenty-one-thousand-dollar reward
involved, and her daughter had just been arrested for a felony. (The
charges were quietly dropped.)

Morris sucks us into the process by which a man, Randall Adams,
becomes a kind of fictional character in a story whose momentum
seems unstoppable. Adams, labeled a "drifter" by the police and the
press (although he had been holding down a decent job ever since
he arrived in Dallas, two months before the murder), is, when we
see him interviewed in prison, a wan, ghostly, soft-spoken man. He's
much thinner than the mustached hippie we've seen in newspaper
photos from the time of his arrest, and he has a flat, weary voice.
Although Adams isn't on Death Row anymore—in a complicated
legal maneuver, the State of Texas commuted his sentence to life
imprisonment in 1977 (after the Supreme Court struck down his

death penalty), so that it wouldn't have to give him a new trial—he looks and sounds like someone on the verge of disappearing. He seems barely real, a shadowy image animated only sporadically by glints of bitter humor. The recreations of the murder and the events surrounding it have a stronger presence than Adams himself. Even when these scenes are representing accounts that are probably false, they're compelling. We watch the same actions occur over and over again, with slight but significant variations, on the same dark stretch of road—a setting that Morris endows with an unearthly vividness, composed of the piercing beams of headlights, silhouetted figures, flashes of gunfire, the revolving red light on top of the police car, and rich, enveloping nighttime blackness—and we think, against all reason, that one more detail, a different angle of vision, will suddenly reveal the truth, that these reconstructions somehow have the power to take us to the heart of things. Once David Harris had told his story, Randall Adams's life was obliterated, to be replaced by an endless series of constructions and reconstructions of a single moment (a moment at which he was most likely asleep in his motel room). It's as if time had simply stopped for him the instant the image of him shooting Robert Wood lodged in the minds of the Dallas police, and he had been condemned to live the rest of his life exclusively in the minds of others: cops, judges, juries, lawyers, newspaper readers, Errol Morris, audiences watching this movie— all of us, for our various reasons, rehearsing that terrible moment, with the figure of Randall Adams flickering in and out of the picture.

Adams's fate is worthy of a Borges hero, one of those melancholy spirits trapped in infinite loops of metaphysical treachery. It's no small feat for Morris to have made a documentary that evokes this kind of existential unease in its audience. There are times, though, when things get all muddy and confused, and that's not because reality is, you know, hopelessly ambiguous; it's because the filmmaker's style is too fancy and elliptical, or because he just hasn't bothered to give us information we need. The legal proceedings, in particular, are almost never entirely lucid. The flowering absurdity of Adams's experiences with the courts wouldn't lose its horror if Morris troubled to explain a few crucial points of law. But this is a powerful and thrillingly strange movie, and Morris's occasional excess of artiness shouldn't be taken as an indication of indifference to the reality of Randall Adams's plight. In fact, the filmmaker himself uncovered several pieces of new evidence, testified in Adams's behalf at hearings on motions for retrial, and coaxed a near-confession out of David Harris, which we hear, on tape, in the movie's final scene. (Harris has since, in a recent interview with a newspaper reporter, come even closer to an outright admission of guilt. He's on Death Row for another murder, and Adams is still petitioning for a new trial.) Morris, who clearly has a very sophisticated understanding of the relationship between art and reality, did a thorough, painstaking investigation in the real world, and then did something different on film: he turned the case into a kind of tabloid poetry, a meditation on uncertainty and the fascination of violence. If we quibble every now and then with his presentation of the facts, it's his own fault; *The Thin Blue Line* makes us all obsessed detectives.

The New Yorker, September 5, 1988

(Author's note: On March 1, 1989, the Texas Court of Criminal Appeals overturned the conviction of Randall Adams. He was released from prison shortly thereafter, and the Dallas District Attorney's Office announced that it didn't intend to try the case again.)

DEAD RINGERS

David Cronenberg's *Dead Ringers* is a psychological drama that feels like a horror movie. It tells a lurid story with chilling, clinical austerity. We come out clammy, shaken, a little numb, as if from a particularly upsetting visit to the doctor: Cronenberg palpates us all over, probes us with latex gloves, and then won't tell us what we've got. *Dead Ringers* is about identical twins, Beverly and Elliot Mantle (both played by Jeremy Irons), who become gynecologists and run a very successful fertility clinic together. Although their personalities are distinct—Beverly is introspective and scholarly, Elliot is outgoing and rather callous—they have shared everything about their lives since childhood: they live together, practice medicine together, and sleep with the same women. They have an almost mystical sense of their emotional and physical bond: in Beverly's dreams, he and his brother are joined like Siamese twins; Elliot says, "Whatever is in his bloodstream goes directly into mine." The Mantle twins are a worst-case version of the possibilities of human intimacy, a frighteningly self-contained domestic unit. And the Mantles' world becomes more bizarre and hermetic and off-putting as the story progresses; by the end, when the doctors have retreated together into the muffled, remote consciousness of drug addicts, we have nothing to watch except the twins stumbling morosely through overlit, debris-filled rooms. The world outside barely exists for them, or for us—as if the doctors, having fed off the world like vampires, had finally drained it dry. *Dead Ringers* is a horrible story about a freakish case, and it probably shouldn't get to us. But somehow it does.

Cronenberg, most of whose previous work has been in the horror genre (*The Brood*, *Videodrome*, *The Dead Zone*, and the 1986 incarnation of *The Fly*), has always been attracted to repellent material, and he knows what to do with it, how to keep us transfixed by things we'd rather turn away from. The secret of horror movies is subtext—metaphors that attack like viruses and produce a fever of associations in our minds. (Cronenberg's first feature was called *They Came from Within*.) The character played by Jeff Goldblum in *The Fly*, suffering the degenerative effects of having had his genetic material scrambled with a fly's, seems by the end of the film to be dying of a randomly metastasizing suggestiveness: his condition first evokes the false euphoria of the drug addict, then the middle-of-the-night terror of the cancer patient, and, finally, the hopelessness and need of the AIDS victim. That movie's most powerful scenes are the ones in which Goldblum looks in his mirror and examines what's happening to him. There are few scenes in movies more unbearable than the one in which he staggers away from the mirror, sits on the edge of the tub, and says to himself, "Am I dying?" He's more alone right then than any of Bergman's island neurotics discovering that God has abandoned them in the universe; we're never more isolated than we are at the moment when symptoms appear, when the body first reveals to us its treachery, in the sealed-off cell of a bathroom. This is subtext with a vengeance. It's an overdose: it turns us in on ourselves.

Dead Ringers is a relentless, excruciating elaboration of the mirror-gazing motif in *The Fly*. The Mantles look at the world and see only each other; they're dying of self-reflection, a genetically enforced insularity, a narcissism they're helpless to transcend. There's a weird innocence about their relationship to reality. We see them first as children, discussing the mysteries of sex in a detached, solemn way and then approaching a neighborhood girl with a blunt proposition; they might almost be applying for a research grant. (She turns them down, none too gently.) In medical school, they distinguish themselves by inventing a sinister-looking surgical instrument, the Mantle Retractor. This alarming tool becomes, in the course of the movie, a kind of metaphor for the way the twins probe and manipulate the world: they have a profoundly alienated, mechanical perspective, even as fertility specialists examining women's bodies to facilitate the creation of life. When, late in the movie, Bev withdraws into barbiturate-induced reverie, he comforts himself by fondling a gold-plated model of the Retractor; at the height of his madness, he has a special set of grotesquely primitive obstetric instruments made up and actually attempts to use them on an anesthetized woman. In one sense, this movie is an unsettling satiric confirmation of patients' fears about arrogant, egotistical doctors— our suspicion that we aren't quite real for them, that while we're being examined or operated on our bodies might as well be inert matter, anatomical dolls. When, in one gruesomely comic scene, a helpless patient complains to Bev that he's hurting her, and he simply carries on with the procedure, berating her furiously ("*This* hurts? It couldn't possibly hurt"), it's everyone's nightmare of being at the mercy of a sadistic doctor.

At this point, the twins' attitude toward the world—in the form of the women who pass through their clinic—is purely delusional. Wielding the Retractor, Bev claims, "There's nothing wrong with the instrument. It's the body. The woman's body was all wrong." He says, "The patients are getting strange. . . . Their insides are deformed." He's clearly out of his mind now, but this insanity is only a late, rampant stage of a lifelong disease—the manifestation of the twins' congenital inability to connect to anything or anyone but each other. Their insensitivity to their patients and the need to mediate with technology their experience of women are extensions of the eerily clinical tone of the childhood attempt at seduction.

The movie has a powerful erotic subtext, which may be the most disturbing thing about it. When we first see the twins as adults— after the brief sequences of childhood and medical school—they seem to approach sex as one of the perks of their gynecological practice. It's part of the child's game they're playing with the world. They select a likely woman from among their patients and each sleeps with her in turn, as if they were consulting on a diagnosis; she never has to know that she's making love to two different men. The woman who breaks the pattern is an actress named Claire Niveau (Geneviève Bujold). Beverly examines her, Elliot—impersonating his brother—goes to bed with her first, but Beverly begins to fall in love with her and to want to keep her for himself. Initially, this seems positive, the expression of one twin's impulse to establish some sort of real emotional link to the world outside. Of course, the attempt is doomed, and not just because Elliot is jealous. The nature of the attraction between Claire and Beverly is, from the very beginning, more than a little perverse. He seems to be drawn to her at least in part because she's a biological anomaly: she has a uterus with three chambers, and in his eyes that makes her unique. (During one examination, he jokes with her about "beauty contests for the insides of bodies.") She's attracted to him, in a masochistic way, because he's a witness to the inadequacy of her body; her triple-chambered uterus makes her incapable of bearing children, and she hates herself for her incapacity. The first time she and Bev make love, he ties her to the bed with surgical tubing and clamps; this is an *extremely* kinky doctor-patient relationship. Bev desperately wants to be in love with her, but nothing in his experience has prepared him for it. When they're separated, by Claire's commitment to shoot a film on location, he goes through a traumatic withdrawal: he can't bear to tear himself away from her. Catastrophically, he calls her at her hotel and a man answers the phone. It's only her assistant (who is, besides, obviously gay), but Bev, as possessive as an infant, is convinced that she has betrayed him; he vents his fury on the assistant by reciting detailed instructions about how to give Claire a gynecological examination. (This is the same plot device that triggers the hero's downfall in *The Fly*: in each case, a self-absorbed, inexperienced lover is driven to self-destruction by the mere suggestion that his beloved could be unfaithful to him.)

Once Beverly has begun his downward slide, his horrified retreat from his one tentative foray into the world of other people, Jeremy Irons has to carry the movie. His performance needs to be a technical tour de force, and it is; but it's more than that. Irons complicates this movie's already intricate resonances by allowing himself to be buffoonishly pathetic: bulging eyes and limp, boneless gestures make him a nightmarish cartoon of decadence. His face seems to be aging into one of those disquieting masks of ruined beauty, like Dirk Bogarde's or Gig Young's, and his skin has a ghastly pallor: the Mantle twins, cocooned in their apartment, look as if they'd never seen the sun—almost as if they'd never been born.

Cronenberg's concentration is extraordinary. Even when nothing seems to be happening, *Dead Ringers* has a scarily focused intensity that keeps us watching. The script, by the director and Norman Snider, is very loosely based on a bad novel called *Twins*, by Bari Wood and Jack Geasland, which was itself inspired by the real-life story of the Marcus twins, New York gynecologists who were found dead together in an East Side apartment in 1975. The script is an improvement both on the novel and on reality. It's a model of construction, a complex and perfectly balanced instrument of unease. Everything works with everything else, and everything penetrates until it hurts. The movie is beautifully thought out in visual terms, too. The medical scenes are dimly lit, the surgeons wear blood-red gowns, and we can never quite make out what's going on. But the twins' apartment—their womb—is garishly bright, starkly furnished; there we see every detail, as if we were looking through one of those uncomfortable optical devices that doctors use when they want to see deep inside us. As always, Cronenberg's work gleams with intelligence, and goes as far as it can go. Yet there's something suspect about his imagination. In *Dead Ringers* the *Weekly World News* material and the subtexts of sexual perversity and biological paranoia are deployed with an almost unnatural cunning: Cronenberg hits our sensitive spots with a disturbingly practiced touch. This movie about narcissism keeps turning further and further inward—the twins' story is one of helpless regression—and it makes us do the same. By the time it's over, we feel as if we, too, were huddled in a mirror world, hemmed in by images of our own fears and inadequacies, and sensing our vulnerability to everything outside the smooth circle of reflection. Cronenberg stirs up emotions that are so threatening, so overpowering, that we can respond only by withdrawing—by alienating ourselves in any way we can. He shines a bright, cold light on inoperable terrors inside us and then leaves us staring, with blurred incomprehension, at the instruments in his clinic's pristine cabinets.

The New Yorker, October 3, 1988

DO THE RIGHT THING

In his first scene in *Do the Right Thing*, Spike Lee wears a Chicago Bulls jersey with a big "23" on it—Michael Jordan's number. Mookie, the character Lee plays, is no superstar: he's an ordinary young man who lives with his sister in a Bedford-Stuyvesant apartment, works—just hard enough to hang on to his job—at the pizzeria at the end of his block, and gets along pretty well with everybody. Amiable Mookie as the divinely inspired Jordan—who plays basketball so brilliantly that it sometimes looks as if he didn't need his teammates at all—is a bit of a joke. It's Spike Lee who's the one-man team here: he's also the writer, the producer, and the director of *Do the Right Thing*, and, as the most prominent black director in the American movie industry, he probably feels as if he were sprinting downcourt with no one to pass to and about five hundred towering white guys between him and the basket. Lee has all the moves. Since graduating from NYU's film school, in 1983, he has managed to get off three improbable shots, all lofted over the outstretched arms of the movie establishment—three movies, made and distributed, about black experience in America. The first, the buoyant and imaginative sex comedy *She's Gotta Have It*, seemed to come out of nowhere: made independently, speedily, and on the cheap, it just streaked past all the obstacles, scored big commercially, and earned Lee the chance, almost unprecedented for a black filmmaker, to make entirely personal movies with major-studio backing. On the evidence of *Do the Right Thing*, Lee is all too conscious of

206

both the responsibility and the power of his position. (Later in the movie, Mookie changes into a Dodgers shirt with Jackie Robinson's number on it.) He seems willing to do anything—to take on huge themes and assume the burden of carrying them both in front of and behind the camera. He just won't accept being ignored. He turns himself into the whole show, acting like Superman because he refuses, absolutely, to be an Invisible Man.

In *Do the Right Thing* this apparently fearless young moviemaker has, in Hollywood terms, cut to the chase. His two previous films (or three if we count—and we should—his splendid hour-long NYU thesis film, *Joe's Bed-Stuy Barbershop: We Cut Heads*) tried to dramatize what American movies weren't showing us about the real lives of black people in this grueling, reactionary decade; to find, if possible, a visual style specific to that experience, not borrowed from Hollywood or Europe; and to make it all so funny and vivid that everyone would have to pay attention. That's more than enough ambition to sustain a filmmaker through an entire career, but Spike Lee's no ordinary artist. Eager to keep things moving, to force the tempo of the game, he has decided to go for it right now, to catch us off guard—again—by rushing head on at the biggest, most dauntingly complex subject imaginable: racism itself. Who's to stop him? He's got the talent, the passion, the crew, the cast, and the money. But he stops himself: the gigantic theme ultimately exposes his weaknesses, overshadows his strengths. In the end, he takes what looks like a big risk, goes for the killer shot, and blows it.

By now, everyone must know that *Do the Right Thing* is about racial tensions in a black neighborhood on a punishingly hot day; that the focus of the action is the pizzeria where Mookie works, Sal's Famous, which is apparently the last white-owned business on the block (there's a Korean market across the street); and that the movie's climax is a full-scale riot sparked by a monstrous act of police brutality. The film's tortured message has been debated in the pages of the *Times* and *Newsweek* and the *Village Voice*, and on *Nightline* and *Oprah*; the movie has become, by virtue of both its explosive subject and its rather slippery point of view, a real cultural event, and if you haven't seen it yet you might almost feel that you no longer need to. Despite the interpretative deluge in the media, you *do* need to see it for yourself. It's a very unusual movie experience—two hours of bombardment with New York–style stimuli. You feel your senses alternately sharpened and dulled, as on a sweltering midsummer day, when the sights and sounds of the city are dazzlingly clear individually yet somehow unassimilable as a whole, overwhelming, brain-fogging, oppressive. Lee is nimble-witted, and he's always on the offensive; he stays in your face until you're too exhausted to resist. You have to watch your reactions closely or he'll speed right past you, get you to nod assent to an argument you haven't fully realized he was making. Most American movies just want to knock you senseless immediately and get it over with; *Do the Right Thing* tries to wear you down, and its strategies are fascinating.

In form, *Do the Right Thing* is a multicharacter, portrait-of-a-community movie. When this sort of picture is done skillfully, it can be exhilarating: Renoir's *The Crime of Monsieur Lange*, Altman's *McCabe & Mrs. Miller*, and Scorsese's *Mean Streets* come to mind. The pleasure of community movies is their open-endedness, the (relative) freedom they allow us to observe the particulars of relationships in small, self-contained social units; they seem unusually responsive to the ambiguity and variety of experience. For long stretches, Lee's movie is enjoyable in this way. Characters are introduced, and while we wait to find out what they'll have to do with each other we can take in an abundance of atmospheric details—the lack of air conditioning in the apartments, the way the sunlight looks sort of hopeful at the beginning of the day and then turns mean, the street wardrobe of T-shirts, bicycle shorts, and pristine Nikes—and listen to the casual speech of the neighborhood's residents, learn to hear in its varied rhythms how people who have lived too close for too long express their irritation and their affection. As we get our bearings, the movie has an easy, colloquial vivacity, and a sensational look. The superb cinematographer Ernest Dickerson (who has worked on all Lee's movies) gives the images a daring, Hawaiian-shirt glare: if the light were just a touch brighter, the colors a shade bolder, we'd have to turn away, but Dickerson somehow makes these clashing sensations seem harmonious. Lee's script seems to be trying to do something similar, but, despite its ingenuity, it doesn't succeed. As the long, sticky day goes on and the exchanges between the characters get edgier, nastier, more elaborately insulting, we begin to feel something ominous creeping in, which at the time we may take to be our realization that racial violence is inevitable, but which later on we may identify as our intuition of a different kind of disharmony—the jarring incongruity of Lee's "open" manner and his open-and-shut argument.

When the smoke clears—from the screen and from the insides of our heads—there are only two characters who really matter in *Do the Right Thing*: Mookie and his boss, Sal (Danny Aiello), who go one-on-one at the end. The rest of the characters are there to represent something or to move the plot along. There's an old drunk known as Da Mayor (Ossie Davis), who gets no respect from the younger people on the block but retains a certain wobbly dignity, and the sharp-tongued, independent-minded Mother Sister (Ruby Dee); they stand for the older generation, whose cynical, "realistic" attitude toward living in a white society may have kept them from finding ways out of their poverty but may also have helped keep them alive. The next generation is represented by a trio of middle-aged gents who sit on the corner in kitchen chairs and provide, for anyone who wants to listen (only themselves, as it turns out), a running commentary on everything from neighborhood events to the melting of the polar ice caps. They're completely useless—their major occupations are drinking beer, boasting about sex, and coming up with new ways of calling each other "fool"—but their confident, vigorous inanity is very winning. Lee lets their routines run a little longer than they need to, just because the three actors (Paul Benjamin, Frankie Faison, and the wonderful Robin Harris, who plays the one called Sweet Dick Willie) get such sizzling comic rhythms going; these are the movie's loosest scenes. As examples of younger women, Lee supplies a responsible one, Mookie's sister Jade (played by Lee's sister Joie Lee), and a wilder one, his girlfriend Tina (Rosie Perez), who also gets to stand for unwed mothers and Hispanics. The young men consist of three mad-prophet figures: Smiley (Roger Guenveur Smith), a stuttering weirdo, who hawks photos of Martin Luther King and Malcolm X shaking hands; Radio Raheem (Bill Nunn), a rap fan, who walks the streets with a mammoth boom box (it takes twenty D batteries), playing Public Enemy's "Fight the Power" over and over; and Buggin' Out (Giancarlo Esposito), a loudmouthed "political" type, who wants to boycott Sal's because the pictures on its "Wall of Fame" are all of Italians. The whites are Sal's sons: Pino (the overbearing John Turturro), who's a virulent racist, and Vito (Richard Edson), who isn't. (Vito just looks passive and dim, actually.)

The thinness of the characterization isn't a big problem for the first hour or so, while the tone is still mostly light and comic. Lee is showing us types, but at least he gives us a lot of different ones (Hollywood movies rarely seem aware of any diversity in the black community), and their encounters are often funny. It's only later, when the whole crowded movie reduces itself to the symbolic confrontation between Mookie and Sal, that his approach lets the audience down. At its most basic, Lee's intention in *Do the Right Thing* is to demonstrate how in the context of a racially polarized society the slow accumulation of small irritations—the heat, some casual slights, bits of anger left over from old injuries, the constant mild abrasions of different cultural perspectives rubbing against each other—can swell to something huge and ugly and lethal. It's a solid idea for a movie—to show us the everyday texture of racial misunderstanding. But Lee wants to go further, to prove the inevitability of race conflict in America, and he can't do it, because no filmmaker could: movies aren't very good at proving things. The obvious inspiration for the story is the appalling incident in Howard Beach, Queens, in 1986: three young black men, stranded by car trouble in that very white neighborhood, were attacked outside a pizzeria by a bunch of youths armed with baseball bats; one of the victims, Michael Griffith, ran in front of a car while trying to escape and was killed. From this tragic event Lee has retained the charged iconography—the pizza parlor and the baseball bat—and changed everything else, with a view to making its significance larger, more general. He wants to create an event that can't be explained away as an isolated incident. And he's not about to let us believe that racism comes only in the form of teenage thugs.

So in *Do the Right Thing* it isn't Sal's vicious son who precipitates the violence but Sal himself—a man who, despite a fairly limited imagination, isn't an obvious racist. For most of the movie, Sal is a sympathetic figure: he's proud of the place he owns and proud of having fed the people of the neighborhood for twenty-five years, and he won't listen to Pino's suggestion that he sell the pizzeria and get out of Bed-Stuy. ("I've never had no trouble with these people," Sal says.) But in the end he becomes the enemy, and Mookie—the most easygoing and most rounded of the young black characters—becomes his adversary. By pitching his battle between the two most likable characters in the piece, Lee makes room in his story for the big statement: that in this society blacks and whites, even the best of us, are ultimately going to find ourselves on opposite sides. It's like a political rationalization of his aesthetic practice: eventually, everyone reverts to type. The final conflict begins at the very end of this long, hot day, as Mookie and Sal are trying to close the pizzeria for the night. They stay open a few minutes longer to serve slices to a group of neighborhood kids, and in walk Buggin' Out and Radio Raheem; Buggin' Out starts yelling at Sal again about the absence of black faces on the wall, and Raheem's radio, turned up to earsplitting volume, is playing "Fight the Power" (which is also the movie's theme song). After the day he's had, Sal can't take it anymore, and goes berserk; he launches into a tirade, during which the word "nigger" slips out, smashes Raheem's radio with a bat, and a fight breaks out. When half a dozen cops (all but one of them white) arrive, they go straight for Raheem, and subdue this large, strong-looking man with a choke hold, which kills him. The cops drive away, and the neighborhood people are all gathered outside Sal's, stunned by the tragedy. Mookie, who has been standing next to his boss, crosses the street to join his neighbors, picks up a garbage can, hurls it through the pizzeria's window, and the riot begins. Sal's is destroyed, as retribution for the death of Raheem.

In part, this powerful climax—and it *is* powerful—seems to come from Lee's sense, as a filmmaker, that he needs a conflagration at the end, a visually and emotionally compelling release for the steam that has been building up throughout the film. His model is clearly the Scorsese of *Mean Streets* and *Taxi Driver*, but in Scorsese's films the final bursts of violence are generated entirely from within, from the complex internal dynamics of the communities and individuals we've been watching. Lee's climax only seems to have that sort of terrible inevitability. In order to believe it, and to find the characters' behavior in these disturbing scenes wholly comprehensible, we have to accept a proposition that's external to the terms of the movie, an abstract notion of the kind that no movie can truly demonstrate: that we're all bigots under the skin. Lee prepares us for this with a sequence in which various characters—Italian, Korean, Hispanic, and black (Mookie)—shout racial and ethnic slurs directly into the camera. Sal's exasperation with Buggin' Out and Raheem, after he has spent twelve hours standing next to pizza ovens on a ninety-eight-degree day, doesn't seem a particularly racist response—until he says "nigger." (Being driven out of your mind by blaring rap music doesn't have to have anything to do with race. At that volume, Def Leppard or Philip Glass would have the same effect.) Raheem certainly doesn't deserve his fate, but without that inflammatory racial epithet Lee would have a tough time convincing any audience that Sal deserves his.

Does Lee really believe that, as he says in his published production diary, "sooner or later it comes out"—that any white person, pushed hard enough, will betray his contempt for blacks? Does he believe, for that matter, the tired notion that anger brings out people's *true* feelings? And does he also think that lashing out at Sal because he's white and owns a business and is therefore a representative of the racist power structure of the American economy is a legitimate image of "fighting the power"? If you can buy all these axioms smuggled in from outside the lively and particular world this movie creates, then *Do the Right Thing* is the great movie that so many reviewers have claimed it is. But if you think—as I do—that not every individual is a racist, that angry words are no more revealing than any other kind, and that trashing a small business is a woefully imprecise image of fighting the power, then you have to conclude that Spike Lee has taken a wild shot and missed the target. He ends his movie with a pair of apparently contradictory quotations—one from Dr. King, advocating peaceful change, and one from Malcolm, advocating violence (in self-defense). The juxtaposition suggests an admission that he doesn't know all the answers, but the movie, perhaps inadvertently, gives the lie to this confession of ambivalence. The imagery of the riot overwhelms the more incidental truths about human relations in the rest of the film, and Lee pays the price of all the little feints and evasions necessary to give his movie a socko ending: the half-truths add up, too. By the end, when Sal and Mookie are standing toe to toe in front of the burned-out shell of the pizzeria, and Mookie accepts his back wages, and more, from his employer, Lee actually seems to be saying that although Sal may not be the worst oppressor around, *someone's* got to pay; the implicit message to the small businessman is "Too bad it had to be you, but what did you expect?" I think audiences, black and white, have the right to expect something more thoughtful than this from one of our best young filmmakers.

The "power" isn't guys like Sal, even though they benefit, modestly, from the biases of the economic system; they're just guilty by association, responsible for the deaths of young blacks like Raheem only in the most theoretical, distanced way. Although Lee must know this, he's clearly willing to sacrifice some political clarity for the sake of movie-style power. In order to make himself heard, he has chosen to adopt the belligerent, in-your-face mode of discourse that has been the characteristic voice of New York City in the Koch years. Spike Lee's movie isn't likely to cause riots (as some freaked-out commentators have suggested), but it winds up bullying the audience—shouting at us rather than speaking to us. It is, both at its best and at its worst, very much a movie of these times.

The New Yorker, July 24, 1989

CARNIVAL OF SOULS

When people compare movies with dreams, they're usually talking about the terrifying, irrational power that projected images can have, or about the helplessness and solitude we sometimes feel as we're pulled along in the dark. The only way in which most of this summer's movies are like dreams is that it's so hard to remember them. We may, upon leaving the theater, have a vague sense that something has been nibbling at our consciousness; but, whatever it was, it didn't linger. (If I were pressed to account for my whereabouts on a given date in August 1989, I'd have to think twice before claiming I was at the movies watching *Cookie* or *Shirley Valentine* or *The Abyss* or *The Little Thief*; even hypnosis might not prove that I had actually seen any of them.) Among the movies in current release, one of the very few that stay in the mind is Herk Harvey's *Carnival of Souls*. This bleak, unnerving low-budget horror picture was made in 1961 and released (mostly to drive-ins, on a double bill with something called *The Devil's Messenger*) in 1962, and hasn't had a theatrical run in New York until now. It's one of those movies that turn up on television at two in the morning, for people who prefer to take their bad dreams in the form of lurid, cheesy shockers interrupted by commercials. In the twenty-seven years since it was first dumped into theaters, this picture has never quite gone away. Even when its only life was as flickering, jumpy images on a small screen, it wouldn't stay dead. It's a real hour-of-the-wolf movie: it wakes you up and keeps you up.

214

The movie begins with an accident: a car with three young people inside plunges off a bridge into a river in Kansas. The townspeople gather to search for the bodies, alive or dead. Long after they've given up hope of finding survivors, a blond woman, Mary Henry (Candace Hilligoss), emerges from the water; she can't remember how she got out of the car. Soon after that—it's apparently just a day or two later—we see her pounding away at an enormous pipe organ. Despite her trauma, she seems to want to get on with her life: she's due to begin work as a church organist in Utah, and she's determined to arrive on time. On the long drive to Utah, Mary starts seeing things: the face of a pale, unsmiling man appears at the window of her moving car; a bit later, he seems to be standing in the middle of the deserted highway. For the rest of the movie, this ghastly guy won't leave her alone: wherever she goes, he turns up, watching her. Adding to the spookiness is a huge abandoned building at the edge of the Great Salt Lake: without quite knowing why, the young woman finds herself drawn to this looming edifice, a failed resort with a cavernous ballroom. She's afraid she's going crazy. We suspect that what's going on is a good deal direr than that.

The supernatural answer proves to be the correct one—no surprise. But *Carnival of Souls* isn't a conventional ghost story. Although it's obvious that Mary Henry is sort of *different*—not fully engaged in life, let's say—the manner of her not-quite-being is unusual. She seems to flicker in and out of existence. In the movie's most original scenes, Harvey disengages his heroine from her surroundings for several minutes at a time. At one point, Mary goes into a cubicle in a department store to try on a dress, and when she comes out she can't hear anything—worse, no one (except the audience) can hear or see her. It's a terrifying sequence, an unbearably direct expression of the world's indifference. (Imagine *Topper* directed by Ingmar Bergman.) After a while, she snaps out of it, but her relationship to everyday life remains fragile, tentative. She's more alone than any other horror-movie heroine you've ever seen. Her living quarters, in a boardinghouse, are as drab and featureless as Janet Leigh's motel room in *Psycho*. She's a kind of existential transient: her life fades in and out, as if she were watching it on an old TV with unpredictable reception.

Carnival of Souls, which was made, in black-and-white, for

about $30,000, by a bunch of industrial filmmakers based in Law-
rence, Kansas, uses its cheapness expressively. The performances
are variable, the settings are stark, the sound recording is erratic, and
somehow it all works. The movie keeps going dead and then coming back to life. Some of the picture's stiffness, especially in the
dialogue scenes, is clearly not intentional, but some of it is: Harvey
(who has never made another feature) pulls us through the movie
by alternating scenes of everyday life with visions of death, and
daring us to locate ourselves; in the flat, neither-here-nor-there landscape of *Carnival of Souls*, we're never entirely sure where we are.
George Romero has claimed this picture as an inspiration for *Night
of the Living Dead*; the shockingly avid ghouls of his movie are
obviously descended from the dead who dance in the ruined ballroom at the climax of Harvey's film. And David Lynch must have
seen it, too. Now that this inspired oddity has been resurrected with
a brand-new 35mm print, we may regret not seeing it in the small
hours, alone in front of the tube. But, no matter how many people
are in the theater or what time of day it is, *Carnival of Souls* has the
power to detach you from your surroundings and put you in the
middle of its own distinctive nowhere. For eighty-eight minutes,
you're immersed in it; and when you come up, the world looks
stranger.

The New Yorker, September 4, 1989

CASUALTIES OF WAR

For American moviemakers, as, perhaps, for most Americans, the war in Vietnam has signified an almost unimaginable chaos: a moral swamp, a jungle of ambiguity, an acid-rock inferno, a purple haze in which nothing can be seen clearly. To watch the war on the nightly news in the late sixties was to experience it as a nightmare or a bad trip—there was never enough context to allow us to interpret the horrors before our eyes—and that, for the most part, is the Vietnam the movies have given back to us: the war that took place inside our stunned minds, the one that wasn't so much about Vietnam as about *us*.

Looking at *Apocalypse Now* or *The Deer Hunter* or *Full Metal Jacket*, you'd think that the real obscenity wasn't that a small country was invaded by America, but that America's consciousness was invaded by what it most feared: doubt, self-consciousness, the everyday awareness of mortality. Even Oliver Stone's *Platoon*, less solipsistic than the others, fell back on the egregious notion that the primary conflict was within the souls of Americans.

Brian De Palma's *Casualties of War* transcends the chaos. De Palma isn't interested in expressing his shock at the treacherousness of the world: he's known about that for quite some time. *Casualties of War* is the strongest, the simplest, and the most painful of all the Vietnam movies because it isn't about how terrible it is not to understand what's going on around us—it's about the agony of seeing terrible things too clearly. The screenplay, by the playwright David

Rabe (*The Basic Training of Pavlo Hummel, Streamers*), is based on an incident reported by Daniel Lang in *The New Yorker* in 1969: the rape and murder of a young Vietnamese woman by the members of a U.S. Army patrol.

What makes the story extraordinary is that we see it through the eyes of the one member of the five-man patrol who refused to participate (and later brought charges against his comrades), an ordinary Midwesterner named Eriksson (Michael J. Fox), who can't believe the evil that's taking place in front of him. The leader of the squad, Meserve (Sean Penn), a tough soldier nearing the end of his tour of duty, is the organizer of the kidnapping: the movie shows us the factors that have driven him to this—the sudden death of a close friend, the denial of a pass, and the constant, corrosive unease of living in a treacherous landscape, never knowing where the enemy might be coming from. De Palma, as we might expect, does full justice to the dangerous unpredictability of this environment, but he isn't dazed by it. His vision has a bracing clarity: he never allows us to suspend our moral judgment, to believe, even for a moment, that disorientation excuses everything.

De Palma doesn't treat Vietnam as if it were a remote, totally alien place, the great exception to all we've learned. It's a landscape he knows well, the ferocious and intricately threatening world for which his thrillers have provided such potent metaphors—a traumatized world, in which unspeakable crimes are played out before helpless witnesses, then replayed endlessly in their dreams. Doubt, self-consciousness, and mortality invaded him a long, long time ago. Acknowledging them isn't an issue for De Palma anymore: living with them is.

In a sense, he has been making films about Vietnam his whole life, using a painstaking exploration of thriller technique as a way of dealing with his fear and outrage. (His thrillers and horror movies have always made audiences more uncomfortable than even the most graphic slasher pictures, perhaps because we sense something more urgent and serious in his images than a simple desire to shock.) In *Casualties of War*, he seems to have arrived, finally, at the terrifying source of his sensibility; and his unmistakable style feels not so much simplified as purified. The suspense here is heartfelt and unendurable. It's tragic suspense.

The longest and most brilliant section of the film is its middle hour—from the brutal abduction of the young woman, Oahn (Thuy Thu Le), to her murder—and there are few passages in movies in which terror is so agonizingly sustained. Oahn has no English, but her tears and her struggles and her screams speak directly to us, the sounds of her suffering isolated from the undifferentiated din of the war. Her pain is a constant presence that can't be ignored, or taken for something else, or forgotten when it's over. It registers, with a piercing clarity, in us as it does in Eriksson. Michael J. Fox's unremarkable, sympathetic face is the ideal screen for her horror to be projected on, and his performance is quietly astonishing: the soldier's anguish is plain and eloquent.

The crime is not more awful because this decent American is seeing it, but it *feels* more awful because Eriksson's awareness provides a moral (and physical) tension that we couldn't experience so powerfully if we were simply watching a unanimous bunch of madmen. Eriksson is us, saying (as we do in any great suspense sequence), "This can't be allowed to happen." And for a few, heart-stopping moments he takes us to the verge of believing that it won't: although he feels trapped by his role as a grunt taking orders (and it's clear that the deranged Meserve wouldn't hesitate to kill him if he stepped too far out of line), he tries, after a good deal of delay and indecision, to take Oahn away from her tormentors. But there's no escape.

Finally, Oahn is killed by the squad in the midst of a hectic skirmish with the enemy, and Eriksson, fighting for his own life, can't save her. De Palma's staging of this climactic sequence, which takes place on a set of railway tracks on the side of a hill, is both a formally stunning bit of action filmmaking and the embodiment of the movie's rigorous morality. All hell is breaking loose, everything's happening at once, yet, in the middle of the chaos, our attention remains—passionately, almost obsessively—on Oahn, who's always somewhere in the frame and always in focus. The fate of this Vietnamese woman is all that matters; she's running toward us along the straight, clear lines of the tracks as she dies.

Sight and Sound, Winter 1989–90

BLACK RAIN

Shohei Imamura's extraordinary *Black Rain* begins on August 6, 1945, in Hiroshima, about three minutes before the bomb fell. A clock reads 8:12; four or five shots later, we see it blown clear off the wall. In this movie in which so much is altered by a single moment, a split-second flash, what changes most radically seems to be time itself—or, at least, our sense of it. The abruptness with which we're plunged into the inferno of the devastated city is shocking, and so is the transition, just minutes afterward, to a tranquil-looking country scene and a very different kind of story. Suddenly, it's 1950, and the people we last saw making their way through the wreckage of Hiroshima—a young woman, Yasuko (Yoshiko Tanaka), and her aunt and uncle, who are her guardians—now live in a remote village and are preoccupied with a traditional problem of Japanese movie families: arranging a marriage. We're in a conventional domestic drama, with a stately, unhurried pace. But we can't settle into this familiar form; it's far less reassuring than it should be.

The leisurely rural existence of Yasuko, now twenty-five, and her guardians is restful in only the most superficial ways: both the uncle, Shigematsu Shizuma (Kazuo Kitamura), and the aunt, Shigeko (Etsuko Ichihara), suffer from radiation sickness and have been ordered not to work too hard. What in any other context we might experience as the serene rhythm of contemplation is in *Black Rain* the enforced ease of the desperately ill—a false peace, life put on permanent hold. And the attempt to find a husband for Yasuko has a strangely detached, almost hypothetical quality, a sense of something willed but only half believed: the family feels that if a marriage can be arranged, despite the local gossip that the young woman, too, was contaminated by the blast, then the rumors will have been disproved and the image of a future created. No one really knows what effect the bomb had on Yasuko: she was a few miles outside the city at the time of the explosion, but she was exposed to the "black rain" (a mixture of precipitation and radioactive ash) that followed it. Her guardians' marriage scenario is a hopeful fiction—a story that posits a Yasuko who is unambiguously and forever well, and a myth in which the family reenters the swift, directed flow of real time.

The members of this odd, slow-motion household, which the uncle describes as "a community bound by the bomb," live in a perpetual state of suspension, a constant twilight. Their survival is too tenuous to give them much joy; it's more like a wary, static persistence. They're watching themselves, and each other, all the time—monitoring their bodies and spirits, looking for symptoms, signs, reasons to hope or despair. Watching them, we feel suspended, too, unsure how to respond; we've never seen a family drama quite like this. Imamura demands that these characters be observed from a distance; he keeps us keenly aware of their estrangement from themselves. What interests him about them isn't simply their knowledge that they're going to die sooner or later; it's their peculiar relationship to ordinary life. They've been contaminated by uncertainty, and every gesture they make, every word they speak, is halting, self-conscious, tentative. They don't know what kind of story they're in, and Imamura spreads their doubt to us.

The novel, by Masuji Ibuse, from which *Black Rain* has been adapted is an established classic of postwar Japanese fiction, but Imamura makes the material his own. Ibuse uses the diaries of *hibakusha* (bomb survivors) to create a chronicle of the sights and sounds of the great catastrophe, and he's equally concerned with recording the grim medical details of radiation sickness. The event itself, as it's remembered by the witnesses, has pride of place in his narrative; the story of the Shizumas in 1950, which frames the diary excerpts, gives pathos to the scrupulously reconstructed horrors. Although it's a powerful novel, the film is a subtler and more complex work. Imamura doesn't dwell on the appalling spectacle of the bombing and its immediate aftermath. He treats it with telling poetic concision, as a series of awful tableaux (many of them taken from the book) flashing before us with the speed of memory and also with memory's painful selectivity—that cruel instinct for the most terrible and most unassimilable images. We see stiff, charred bodies, looking more like primitive dolls than like human beings, among the debris; we see a small figure—burned all over but still standing, as alien-looking as a horror-movie mutant—pleading with his brother to recognize him; we see a man screaming from his window "Where's Hiroshima? It's disappeared!" just before he falls to his death in the city's rubble. We're stunned but not overwhelmed. Imamura wants us dry-eyed and clearheaded for what follows: he has shifted the focus of the narrative to the postwar story, which is no longer a framing device or a means of intensifying an already unbearable sadness. His *Black Rain*, though it looks at times like one of Yasujiro Ozu's dignified, formal family sagas, is entirely (and blessedly) free of sentimentality. Its tone is analytical, bracingly inter-rogative; it seems to question the very reality of ordinary life, normal time. The Shizumas' existence unfolds undramatically, at the languid tempo of a dream. It's all anticipation—waiting for something to happen, and trying to sustain the illusion that their everyday lives will yield up the kind of defining moment (like Yasuko's marriage) that most of us have been led to expect. Unbelievably, Imamura has transformed this Hiroshima story into a Sartrean soap opera.

His film is also, implicitly, a reproach to the values and the style of the great Ozu, for whom he once worked as an assistant. The movies that Ozu made after the war—*Tokyo Story* is the most cele-brated, and the best—tell stories of Japanese middle-class families as if nothing very significant had happened in the forties, as if all the old beliefs in family and duty could simply be restored. His films, which are perhaps the purest representations on the screen of the culture's traditional values, are often extremely moving, but Imamura clearly has no patience with them; he's far more interested in impurity, in the more vital, even barbaric, aspects of human nature, which Ozu's lordly, fixed camera never reveals. The brilliant and original films Imamura made in the sixties and seventies— movies like *The Insect Woman* (1963), *The Pornographers* (1966),

and *Vengeance Is Mine* (1979)—seem determined to include everything the Master left out: greed, incest, and violence rule Imamura's
families (and, by implication, the society as a whole). And he developed a jagged, disorienting style to go with his corrosive vision.
Black Rain has a smoother surface than the earlier films, but it's
deceptive. Behind the calmly composed black-and-white images
there's real rage. Scenes of the family sitting around on mats alternate
with savagely funny vignettes: a shell-shocked veteran who throws
himself in front of passing buses and motorbikes, thinking they're
enemy tanks; a highly theatrical psychic who wails and chants and
carries on and then gives the Shizumas the pedestrian advice that
they can ensure Yasuko's happiness by visiting her mother's grave.
(Shigematsu mutters, "These psychics always give the same advice:
'Visit the grave.' ") And Imamura isn't keen on the idea of restoring
the old ways. In *Black Rain*, life before the bomb is represented by
three minutes of unsettling images: people in uniforms, a stray dog,
the clock. This time around, he's attacking the ethics and the aesthetics of his former boss from within: the life of the Shizumas is Ozu's
world seen in a very dark looking glass.

The most surprising thing about *Black Rain* is that it isn't depressing. It's too intelligent; every scene is drenched in irony. We
understand, by the end, that the story the Shizumas are writing for
themselves functions for them like belief in a miracle cure; it's not so
different from the aloe plants they eat, the carp blood they drink, the
prayers they sometimes recite. Imamura holds himself far enough
away from them to show us the nature and the depth of their
illusions, but he doesn't make his characters pathetic. In a way, the
Shizumas' dreamlike existence really is idyllic. It removes them from
the frantic activity of Japan's postwar industrial culture: they're ex-
empt from history, free of the obligation to share in a contaminated
notion of progress. In the movie's final shots—of Shigematsu watching an ambulance take another member of the family away, and then
of the mountains beyond the village—we feel an exalting emptiness.

The New Yorker, February 26, 1990

FOR ALL MANKIND

For All Mankind, Al Reinert's documentary about American astronauts' flights to the moon, is a great movie experience. Between December 1968 and November 1972, the Apollo space program sent twenty-four men to the moon, on nine separate missions, six of which made lunar landings, and the voyages were exhaustively recorded on film, tape, and video. From the thousands of hours of flight footage that the astronauts brought back, Reinert has made an eighty-minute film that collapses all their experiences into a single epic journey. For the soundtrack he uses recordings of their communications with the Johnson Space Center in Houston, in addition to their present-day reflections on what they saw and did; the speakers aren't identified by name, so we feel as if we were hearing one voice (with different accents). It's a simple idea that requires extraordinarily complex execution—sort of like the Apollo program itself. The movie never tries to impress us with its technique, though. It stays focused on its primary concern, which is to draw us into the shifting emotional states of the space travelers, and it makes the astronauts' feelings—and those of the people on the ground who are directing their progress, and living the journey vicariously—vivid and immediate: their curiosity, their fear, their professional detachment, their juvenile ebullience, their awe. Cannily, Reinert combines majestic visions with odd human details, and the film, for all its splendor, has a friendly, down-home quality. We feel at times as if we were in someone's rec room watching a movie of the family vacation: Our Trip to the Moon.

One of the astronauts, as his spacecraft orbits the moon, radios back to Houston, "It might sound corny, but the view is really out of this world." The movie is full of just this sort of corniness—spontaneous responses that are moving precisely because they're inadequate. When you're faced with the sight of, say, the Earth coming into view from beyond the lunar horizon, there's nothing you can say, and yet you have to say *something*: not to react would be inhuman. Reinert gives us a fair sampling of inarticulate responses—"Wow!" and "Yahoo!" and "What a ride!" and others just as primitive. But there are times—usually during periods of concentration on some technical maneuver—when the astronauts express themselves more inventively. One of them describes the feeling of getting ready for the launch as "like the big game about to start"; another, having just struggled into his bulky space suit, speaks of being "in your work clothes, ready to go to work"; cruising over the surface of the moon in their rover, the men kid each other about reckless driving; in the tense moments before the lunar module lifts off to head back to Earth, one astronaut is heard to say, "We're number one on the runway." Throughout, we're aware of the gap between where these men are and where they've come from. (One man recalls thinking, as the module is about to touch down on the moon, "This is not for real—you're back in the simulator.") We laugh at all their humor, even when it's lame, out of respect for the impulse behind it: the need to cut through the dreamlike unfamiliarity of their circumstances, to give the illusion of routine to something unprecedented, to joke away the terror of the unknown. Reinert makes the astronauts' wit seem their most heroic quality.

For All Mankind provides plenty of nonverbal humor, too—slapstick in space. As the capsule makes its way to the moon, we see unshaven men spinning and tumbling in the reduced-gravity cabin, trying to eat while their food floats away, tossing a flashlight back and forth, and watching a cassette player drift lazily between them. These sequences are scored to music that the astronauts took along with them: "Act Naturally," performed by Buck Owens; Sinatra's rendition of "Fly Me to the Moon"; and, inevitably, the theme from

2001: A Space Odyssey. The action on the moon is even giddier. The astronauts, encased in their heavy suits, bound and lurch and stumble and fall down (with unreal slowness, in soft little clouds of lunar dust); they look like unsteady toddlers in snow togs. (In a particularly hilarious scene, two astronauts supply their own background music, singing "I was strolling on the moon one day"; after their duet has ended, one of them continues to hum, ineptly but happily, as he collects rock samples.) The physical comedy is worthy of Buster Keaton—and Keaton, whose ingenuity was generated by the need to preserve himself from the unpredictability of both machines and the elements, would surely have seen these explorers as kindred spirits.

Reinert is smart to include so much comic material. Without it the movie might have been oppressively inspirational—a conventional exercise in patriotic propaganda. Or—with all those shots of objects floating languorously in the emptiness of black space, the shimmering distant views of the Earth and the moon, and the trancelike music by Brian Eno—it might have been a ponderous trip movie of the *Koyaanisqatsi* variety. From scene to scene, and almost without warning, the mood of *For All Mankind* keeps changing: from tense to childishly delighted, then to raptly contemplative. We experience the voyage, as the astronauts must have, in a state of constant surprise: every sensation is intensified, because we never know quite what to expect. (For all their training and preflight simulations, the astronauts are always coming up against things they haven't anticipated; one, recalling his first sight of the moon at close range, says, "Nothing looked right.") Reinert and his editor, Susan Korda, also make expert use of the varied textures of the visual and aural material at their disposal. Sometimes the images are spectacularly, heartbreakingly sharp (the filmmakers transferred the original 16mm footage to 35mm), sometimes they're trembly and a little vague, and sometimes they're fuzzy blowups from videotape. Each has its own kind of beauty, and the mixture keeps our eyes alert. The alternation of staticky radio transmissions with the clear, tranquil sound of the astronauts' voices in recently recorded interviews has the same sort of effect.

So when the heroes of the Apollo flights begin musing on the meaning of it all, we don't feel like groaning. We have felt, in some way, their excitement, and we understand their desire to sort out the sights and emotions that came upon them in such a dizzying rush during their missions. One of them remembers a moment on the way to the moon when he realized with regret that he wouldn't be able to hold on to all his sensations; he didn't want to let any of his images get away from him. Another recalls stepping back from himself while he collected samples from the lunar surface, and thinking that "bringing back a little bit of some kind of thought and feeling was as important as bringing another chunk of rock back." The ravishing, ethereal images of *For All Mankind* seem even lovelier in the context that Reinert has given them. We're always conscious of the men who brought them back, who carry them in their memories, and who try, in this movie, to go beyond the simple "Wow!" they felt when the unimaginable sights were before them. It's the home movie of men who can say, with only a trace of irony, "The stars are my home." (One astronaut actually says this in the film.) *For All Mankind* is an attempt to express the inexpressible. Both the filmmakers and their subjects are fully aware that they won't quite manage it; they're even a bit amused by their own presumptuousness. This is a graceful and good-humored work, and it speaks with what the Romantic poets called "the real language of men."

The New Yorker, March 26, 1990

THE COOK, THE THIEF, HIS WIFE & HER LOVER

Peter Greenaway's *The Cook, the Thief, His Wife & Her Lover* is a movie about a crude British thug whose favorite method of terrorizing people is ramming things down their throats. It begins with a scene in which the bully, Albert Spica (Michael Gambon), and his henchmen smear dog shit all over the body of a naked man and then make him eat some. Later victims are force-fed shirt and trouser buttons and pages from old books. Albert eats only haute cuisine; he and his wife, Georgina (Helen Mirren), and his low-life entourage dine every night at a posh establishment called Le Hollandais. (The name of the restaurant is a dry joke: in the dining room, there's a large painting by Frans Hals of a group of officers seated around a banquet table; the arrangement of Albert's unseemly aggregation is meant to echo and parody this composition.) He fancies himself a gourmet, but he scarfs up the exquisite dishes prepared by the chef, a Frenchman (Richard Bohringer), as if they were fast-food burgers; his instinct, apparently, is to eat with his hands and save his cutlery for threatening his dinner companions. (In one scene, he sticks a fork through a woman's cheek.) Albert's vulgarity—his lack of respect for the highest achievements of European culture—is made to seem his real sin, because this is an Art Movie, refined and terribly formal; Greenaway places the barbarian smack in the middle of his "painterly" compositions, and encourages us to see him as a steaming hunk of offal desecrating the beauty of an artist's creation.

American movies about gangsters have traditionally shown at

least some grudging admiration for their heroes' reckless vitality and huge material appetites—perhaps because our movies are fueled by similar qualities. Peter Greenaway not only lacks sympathy for his protagonist's animal nature but seems offended by it. Albert is loathsome through and through, an evil lout who just does one evil, loutish thing after another for two solid hours. As a rule, bullies aren't very interesting: their dramatic functions are simple, and their appearances are brief—they barge into scenes when a quick shock or a gruesome joke is needed to jolt the audience awake, and then are hustled off until their specialized services are required again. Greenaway's camera *lingers* on Albert, feasts on his awfulness, eats him up, and the static intensity of its regard is baffling. The movie isn't probing the character's soul; as far as the filmmaker is concerned, this beast doesn't have one. And Greenaway's relentlessness isn't an indication of passion, either; we never have the sense that he's implicating himself in the horrors he shows, acknowledging a perverse attraction to his monster. His gaze is lordly, imperial—the disdainful stare that the pukka sahib directs at a servant who has inconvenienced him.

The care that Greenaway lavishes on the structure and the imagery of his films is fantastic, obsessive. But it's all manner—obsession without an object. His previous features (*The Draughtsman's Contract*, *A Zed and Two Noughts*, *The Belly of an Architect*, and *Drowning by Numbers*) were self-consciously empty—meticulous elaborations of arid little reality-and-artifice paradoxes. Greenaway seemed to be making movies with the monotonous dedication of a hobbyist, and the products of his labors were immaculate and pointless, like ships in bottles. The pictures didn't bother much with narrative, and barely even pretended to refer to anything outside themselves. *The Cook, the Thief, His Wife & Her Lover* is no different. It gives an impression of greater consequence only because its imagery is more violent than usual and thus evokes fear and disgust—not the most enlightening emotions a movie can produce, but two more than Greenaway generally allows us to feel. The notion, suggested by several reviewers, that this movie is some kind of political allegory is absurd. Greenaway is an aesthete, and that's all he is. *The Cook, the Thief, His Wife & Her Lover* isn't about oppression, or capitalist greed, or Margaret Thatcher; it's about the superiority of its maker's sensibility. He gives us pretty pictures to look at, and they're color-coded: the dining-room scenes are red; scenes in the restaurant's kitchen are green; scenes in the parking lot are blue; and so on. And he creates a central character whose only function is to be unworthy of the high-art splendor of his surroundings. As a critique of contemporary society, this leaves quite a bit to be desired.

Greenaway has a lot more in common with his protagonist than he thinks. He obviously regards himself as a pure artist, a virtuoso—like the haughty chef in this picture—but he's really just a cultural omnivore. (He eats for taste, not for sustenance.) His manners are no better than Albert's; he chews with his mouth open—we can identify almost every piece of art that has fed his imagination. And, for the benefit of those who are too uneducated to pick up all the references and allusions, he's willing to supply them afterward: in his interviews and writings about the film Greenaway has linked himself to Hals, Jonathan Swift, the Brothers Grimm, and Jacobean dramatists. (He doesn't mention Buñuel, whom he borrows from constantly, but perhaps he doesn't want to sully himself with a comparison to a mere filmmaker.) As a conspicuous consumer, Albert has nothing on the man who invented him.

There are many ways of being a bully; physical violence is only the most direct. Greenaway doesn't seem at all averse to other forms of power-tripping, such as intellectual intimidation. His attitude toward his characters and toward his audience is one of professorial condescension. Watching this picture is like being trapped in a nightmare art-history seminar: we sit there, cowed and miserable, as the teacher spews high-toned abstractions and dares us, smirkingly, to raise a common-sense objection—we know we'll be ridiculed if we do. In Greenaway's view, what's so unspeakable about Albert has to do less with the thug's desire to hurt and humiliate people than with the way he expresses it; his *physicality* is the crime he's convicted of (and executed for). The only thing in this movie's tidy, hermetic universe which Greenaway is unable to control, or disguise with fancy brushwork, is his loathing of the body. The beatings and the killings aren't really any uglier than the eating scenes. And the depictions of sex are pointedly grotesque. In the course of the film, Georgina takes a lover, a gentle, bookish patron of Le Hollandais named Michael (Alan Howard); he is, of course, the civilized antithesis of Albert, and the affair is clearly meant to be Georgina's chance to save herself from the everyday barbarity of her marriage. But Greenaway can't bring himself to present their romance as an idyll, even though his story's structure demands it. The lovers couple in the most degrading settings—in a lavatory stall; among plucked chickens and skinned rabbits in the kitchen—and at one point we see them huddled together, naked and filthy and shivering, in a meat van where bloody animal carcasses hang.

Despite the ornateness of the design, *The Cook, the Thief, His Wife & Her Lover* has a very simple message: that nature—one's own appetites or other people's—is abominable, because it threatens the purity of the artist. I saw this picture in London a few months ago, and I didn't bother to review it when it opened in this country last month, because I assumed that American audiences wouldn't be any more interested in Greenaway's latest art-for-art's-sake exercise than they had been in his four previous ones. However, the Motion Picture Association of America did the movie the enormous favor of giving it an X rating (the distributors released it without a rating), and thus made Greenaway seem a kind of martyr, like Robert Mapplethorpe—a victim of repressive philistinism. (It must be a role he relishes.) Some prominent critics, flashing their anti-censorship credentials, proclaimed the movie a masterpiece, and a lot of filmgoers must feel compelled to buy a ticket as a protest against attempts to muzzle artistic expression. Also, because everyone knows by now that the movie features several gross-out scenes, including a climactic act of cannibalism, it is, in a sense, a perfect date movie for a certain audience—the intellectual's equivalent of a *Friday the 13th* picture. To sit through it with a worldly, unshockable air and then deliver a lengthy opinion about it is to display, irrefutably, one's liberal *cojones*. The movie is doing big business at the art houses.

You can hate *The Cook, the Thief, His Wife & Her Lover*, or even ignore it completely, without lining up alongside the MPAA and Jesse Helms. What's offensive about Greenaway's picture isn't its violence or its visceral shocks but the patrician arrogance, the smug aestheticism, the snobbishness that suffuse every frame. The film's success is a ghastly joke. Greenaway probably sees this as a vindication, a delicious irony: the vulgarians who meant to torment him have instead helped him achieve a box-office hit. He has made a movie whose object is to push us to the ground and kick art in our faces. We may not feel that it's right to take revenge on him for this rude treatment. It seems sort of abject to thank him for it, though.

The New Yorker, May 7, 1990

TOTAL RECALL

Total Recall, a $50-million science-fiction thriller, is full of relentless action and spectacular effects, and it's no fun at all. It's as heavy-spirited as its star, Arnold Schwarzenegger: imposing and implacable, like the killer robot Arnold played (or embodied) in *The Terminator*. This time, the picture itself is a terminator: when it's over, you feel as if the life had been pounded out of you, and you never want to go to the movies again.

The craziest thing about *Total Recall* is that it has an elaborate plot that is of absolutely no use to the movie. Schwarzenegger's character, Quaid, is a twenty-first-century blue-collar worker with an inexplicable desire to go to Mars; he has dreams about it. His wife (Sharon Stone) isn't keen on the idea, so he tries to satisfy his urge by dropping in at the offices of Rekall Inc., a company that implants memories of trips to faraway places. As the technicians perform the implant process, they discover that Quaid's brain has already been messed with; ultimately, he finds out that the life he thinks he remembers is purely imaginary—that his identity and all his memories are synthetic. This is a nice premise for a science-fiction story. (The script, by Ronald Shusett, Dan O'Bannon, and Gary Goldman, is based on a short story by Philip K. Dick, who was one of the most imaginative writers in the history of the genre.) But the idea, which promises intricate plot convolutions and startling perceptual flip-flops, proves to be too clever for the kind of movie that Schwarzenegger and the director, Paul Verhoeven (*RoboCop*), obviously wanted to make. Although the plot keeps twisting and turning, we stop following it before the picture

233

is half over. It's just a frame for meaty action sequences—a skeleton nestled deep inside ballooning muscles.

Verhoeven, who began his career in his native Holland, has become a specialist in comic-book visual style. His best Dutch film, *The 4th Man* (1983), had a cold elegance and a sadistic wit. He streamlined his talents for *RoboCop*; he played down the elegance and eliminated most of the wit. In *Total Recall*, the sleek, prankish filmmaker of *The 4th Man* is only a dim memory; it's as if someone in Hollywood had erased Verhoeven's former identity and rewired his mental circuits. He still composes striking images but they're crudely oppressive now, and completely impersonal: every weird angle, every close-up of a face contorted with pain, every splash of bright-red blood is an effect borrowed from horror comics. He's awfully good at staging scenes in which people scream "Arrrgggh!" as they're being impaled or dismembered. There seem to be dozens of these scenes in the movie, and formally they're impressively varied: sometimes the focal point is a grotesquely distended mouth; sometimes the composition is organized around a spurting limb; sometimes the victim screams "Urrrgggh!" To stretch his aesthetic explorations yet further, Verhoeven provides a scene in which the massive hero punches out a woman who has betrayed him.

There are probably a lot of people who keep going to Schwarzenegger pictures because they retain fond memories of *The Terminator*, which was a smart, unpretentious, and thoroughly enjoyable thriller—an ideal B movie. *The Terminator* made Arnold a star by turning all his liabilities into perverse virtues: the movie acknowledged his lumbering, robotic quality, and used it as a comic counterpoint to the snappy, quick-witted narrative. Each one of his pictures in the six years since has made it a little easier for us to forget that improbable minor triumph. *Total Recall* is so terrible that it wipes out our last, stubbornest images of the brief pleasure Schwarzenegger gave us when he played an automaton. We may even begin to believe that *The Terminator* never really happened—that it was just some kind of brain implant, a trick designed to lure us, again and again, into a dark room where a giant will knock us senseless and take our money.

The New Yorker, June 18, 1990

GREMLINS 2: THE NEW BATCH *and* DICK TRACY

The reason it's hard to enjoy most big-budget Hollywood movies—especially the ones that are released in the summertime—is that you can smell the fear in them. Filmmakers who are handed truckloads of money on the understanding that their products will generate nine-figure revenues for the studios are not likely to approach their work in a devil-may-care mood. For the most part, they're as nervous about their tasks as the drivers transporting nitroglycerin along bad South American roads in *The Wages of Fear*. The filmmakers and the studio executives may even be more anxious than those sweaty down-and-outers in their rickety trucks: the Hollywood types have more to lose—not their lives but their life-styles. No wonder the standard features of the past few years' blockbusters are perspiration, screaming, and explosions—the feel-good iconography of clenched, jittery imaginations. The joke is that these movies—made in an atmosphere of corporate caution, with every element weighed and measured and data-processed for its possible impact on the bottom line—are supposed to make us, the audience, feel happy, carefree, liberated from the stresses of our working lives. Usually, they just leave us exhausted. In the high-pressure climate of today's studio moviemaking, Joe Dante's *Gremlins 2: The New Batch*, which would be a funny movie under any circumstances, seems almost heroic. Dante and his team (which includes the screenwriter Charlie Haas and the effects supervisor Rick Baker) have made a multimillion-dollar, special-effects-crammed picture that has the loose, im-

235

provisatory feel of the great Warner Bros. cartoons of the forties and fifties. They're fearless, indefatigable gagsters. They drive their big truck with reckless abandon, not much worried that they'll hit a bump and their load will blow them sky-high, or that they'll lose control and skid off the edge of a cliff. Somehow, they've managed to see themselves not as doomed men on a deadly mission but as descendants of Wile E. Coyote, the ever-optimistic predator of Chuck Jones's Road Runner cartoons, who had hundreds of sticks of Acme dynamite go off in his face and plunged to the bottom of many a canyon, and returned after every catastrophe with another crackpot scheme for trapping his prey.

The movie begins, in fact, with a brief animated sequence in which Daffy Duck takes possession of the Warner Bros. logo from Bugs Bunny; Daffy, whose ego is as fragile as ever, feels that everyone has been making far too much of a fuss about Bugs's fiftieth birthday. This minute or two of stylish bickering is written and directed by the old coyote himself, seventy-seven-year-old Chuck Jones, and he gives the movie a lovely sendoff. *Gremlins 2* hits the ground running, and running in the right direction. The original *Gremlins*, released in 1984 (and also directed by Dante), was a gleeful and sometimes inspired horror comedy about the destruction of a peaceful small town by a horde of sharp-toothed, inventively malicious little monsters. The gremlins were like evil children—creatures with tremendous appetites, insane energy, and absolutely no inhibitions—and the joy they took in ripping apart the blandly wholesome town was irresistible. The new *Gremlins* is smarter, wilder, and more unfettered than the first one, perhaps because this time there's an even better setting for the creatures' rampaging consumption: they've been let loose in a state-of-the-art office building and mall called the Clamp Centre (after Daniel Clamp, the egotistical developer who built it). This towering steel-and-glass wedge—a monument to the runaway acquisitiveness of the eighties—and the craven go-getters who work in it offer Dante more comic possibilities than the first film's scrubbed Andy Hardy community, which never existed anywhere but in the movies (and, unfortunately, in the imagination of the actor who was our president at the time). *Gremlins 2* happily demolishes something that richly deserves demolishing.

The other big improvement over the original picture is that Dante has abandoned even the faintest suggestion that he's making a horror movie: this one's all comedy, and it openly mocks the inane monster-movie premise of the first movie's script (written by Chris Columbus). In *Gremlins*, the young hero, Billy (Zach Galligan), was presented with a cute, furry little being known as a mogwai and was told to observe these rules: never expose it to bright light; don't let it get wet; and don't feed it after midnight. What happens when the mogwai (whom Billy names Gizmo) gets wet is that it gives birth to more mogwais; fur balls pop out of its body. The newborns, if they eat after midnight, turn into gremlins, who multiply with terrifying efficiency; before long, there are legions of lizardlike nasties skittering all over in search of thrills. In both pictures Dante uses the rules purely opportunistically—to create the gremlins when they're needed and to dispose of them when his time's up—but in *Gremlins 2* he also ridicules their arbitrariness. When Billy begins to explain the behavior of mogwais and gremlins to some Clamp Centre employees, they smirk knowingly and then try to outdo each other in coming up with outré refinements of his gremlinology: What if a gremlin gets a piece of food stuck in its teeth before midnight but swallows it after? What if it has a meal on an airplane that is crossing time zones? Dante also includes a negative review of the first picture, delivered by Leonard Maltin on a show called *The Movie Police*, which appears on Clamp's cable network; and he gives us a scene in which an outraged mother drags her child from a theater showing *Gremlins 2* and complains, "This is worse than the first one." None of these self-reflexive gags have any great significance, of course; they're like the moments in Warners cartoons when Daffy and Bugs had conferences with the studio bosses or addressed the audience directly. Dante's self-consciousness never reaches the sublime level of Jones's *Duck Amuck*, in which Daffy tries to cajole his creator into giving him better roles, and the animator retaliates by placing him in increasingly incongruous settings and subjecting his form to humiliating mutations. When *Gremlins 2* makes fun of itself, it's just indulging its adolescent high spirits—letting us know that anything goes.

Dante makes his creations mutate, too, by the simple device of having them run amuck in a genetic-engineering laboratory. (This outfit, one of the less reputable tenants of the Clamp Centre, is run by a Dr. Catheter, who is played by the horror-movie veteran Christopher Lee.) After the voracious gremlins have ingested everything on the lab's menu—making cocktails of hormones and freak strains of DNA—the movie gets a whole new cast of characters: a Batgremlin, a green-haired femme fatale, a Phantom of the Opera (with a little mask on a little stick), a gremlin crossed with a spider, and, funniest of all, an articulate intellectual gremlin who speaks with the voice of Tony Randall. Even cuddly, cooing Gizmo changes his appearance in the course of the picture—not by drinking a beakerful of weird genes but by getting himself into fighting shape. He puts on a red headband, makes a longbow out of a paper clip and a rubber band, and turns into Rambo. ("I guess they pushed him too far," one of the characters speculates.) What Dante is doing is combining another principle of Warners animation—using established characters to parody familiar stories, like Daffy as Robin Hood, or Bugs and Elmer Fudd singing Wagner in *What's Opera, Doc?*—with his own manic pop-culture-in-a-blender sensibility.

By the time the gremlins have chomped and guzzled (and sung and danced) their way through the Clamp Centre's cheerless offices and boutiques, Dante and his horde of collaborators have trashed—or at least lobbed spitballs at—quite a few of the most unattractive aspects of life in these United States. When the gremlins—whose feeding-frenzy approach to the brightly packaged material delights offered by the Clamp Centre seems perfectly appropriate—gather in the building's lobby for a musical production number, the movie reaches a kind of satiric apotheosis. Like everyone else in New York (it seems), these crazed gluttons just want, as our city's official song says, to "make it there." (We're actually a bit disappointed that they never hit the streets of Manhattan, where we could watch them compete for goods and services with all the other grasping creatures at large in the city.) The climax turns the lobby into a literal melting pot, which isn't precisely what the "brain" gremlin—who wants his "ethnic group" to assimilate—had in mind. When order is restored, Clamp (played, by John Glover, as a doltish child) looks to the future: a housing project in New Jersey modeled on Billy's drawing of his hometown; some rough ideas about a line of Gizmo dolls. It's difficult to resist a blockbuster that has the nerve to poke fun at its own merchandising. The Looney Tunes spirit of *Gremlins 2* is probably best expressed by the "brain" gremlin, who, during a talk-show appearance, shoots dead one of the dopier gremlins and then muses on his action: "Fun, but in no sense civilized." If "civilized" means the overcontrolled and overbearing corporate culture represented by Clamp (whose logo is a viselike C with a squashed globe in its grip), then the low, heedless fun of *Gremlins 2* is as close as we're likely to get to subversion from within.

Warren Beatty's *Dick Tracy* is civilized with a capital C. Its comic-strip visual design—created by Richard Sylbert, photographed by Vittorio Storaro—is meticulous, pristine. Beatty has put together a first-rate cast: himself as Tracy, Al Pacino as Big Boy Caprice, Madonna as Breathless Mahoney, Glenne Headly as Tess Trueheart, and, in smaller roles, Dustin Hoffman, James Caan, Mandy Patinkin, Charles Durning, Estelle Parsons, and Dick Van Dyke. There are brand-new songs by Stephen Sondheim. It's pleasant, lovingly detailed, and eye-filling. It's everything a movie can be except interesting.

Dick Tracy isn't the kind of crass crowd-pleaser we've become accustomed to; its dullness is of a more old-fashioned variety. Everything but the film's bold, striking imagery is low-key. Beatty's performance in the title role is recessive almost to the point of perversity. In Chester Gould's comic strip, Dick Tracy always seemed like a tough, aggressive, no-nonsense guy: Beatty's Tracy is a ditherer. (This conception could be considered a witty reflection on Beatty's persona in his best roles—in *Bonnie and Clyde, McCabe & Mrs. Miller*, and *Shampoo*—but it doesn't shed any light, comic or otherwise, on this character.) And his tentativeness as an actor here is matched by the dreamy, distracted quality of his direction. Instead of drive, the picture has taste and dignity and intelligence: admirable as those characteristics may be, they're not characteristics we associate with newspaper comic strips—and particularly not with Chester Gould. Beatty's style is less "Dick Tracy" than "Classics Illustrated."

A few of the performers succeed in injecting some vulgar life into the stately proceedings. Madonna vamps entertainingly, and the script (credited to Jim Cash and Jack Epps, Jr., with the writer Bo Goldman listed as a "special consultant") provides her with plenty of ingeniously suggestive double-entendres, which she delivers like a pro. Glenne Headly, as Tracy's long-suffering girlfriend, does an expert update on the spunky-gal heroines of thirties movies. And Al Pacino, playing the Capone figure who is the hero's chief nemesis here, creates a memorable comic grotesque: a sleazy, fast-talking, ants-in-his-pants mobster who is so unself-consciously megalomaniacal that he's almost likable.

This movie, which is being released by a division of the Disney studio, bears about the same relation to *Gremlins 2* that Disney's lavish, prestige feature-length cartoons bore to Warners' speedy six-minute animated comedies back in the days when the Dick Tracy strip was at its peak. Beatty's movie has that years-in-the-making feel to it, and we can sense in it the endless committee meetings of executives and writers and ace technicians and marketing specialists and lawyers and financial planners and God knows who else, all getting together to cook up a foolproof Hollywood product. The film is scrupulously inoffensive, designed—handsomely, "classily"—to minimize the risk of corporate embarrassment. The people responsible for *Dick Tracy* have made sure that their cargo won't blow up in their faces: their vehicle, spiffy and beautifully painted, just sits there on the mountainside, parking brake on, not moving an inch.

The New Yorker, July 2, 1990

MAY FOOLS

The month in which Louis Malle's *May Fools* (*Milou en Mai*) takes place isn't just any old May. It's May 1968, when, for a few chaotic weeks, French society seemed on the verge of remaking itself—radically, comprehensively, and for good. Students were rioting: ripping up the ancient narrow streets around the Sorbonne to create barricades of paving stones; occupying buildings that represented to them the official culture of which the French are so inordinately proud; filling the air with insistent demands for the reform of the national educational system, for the fall of the conservative govern-ment of President Charles de Gaulle and Premier Georges Pom-pidou, or simply for anarchy. Seizing on the momentum of the students' protests, the unions and the parties of the left took the opportunity to bring the country's normal commercial life to a stand-still. Most of France went on strike: banks closed, deliveries stopped, trains didn't run, gas for cars was almost impossible to come by. This amazing convulsion signaled to its participants the beginning of a revolution, yet many ordinary Frenchmen—perhaps the majority—experienced it as a novel kind of entertainment: an unscheduled holiday, a few weeks of roughing it without the comforts (or the tedium) of bourgeois routine. They had the thrill, too, of feeling that great drama was unfolding around them, that the everyday reality of France was turning into the ultimate New Wave movie—heady, intense, exciting even when it wasn't quite coherent, like something by Godard. (In our terms, France in May '68 was a bizarre hybrid of the stark confrontation of the 1968 Democratic Convention and the idyllic noble-savagery of Woodstock.) When the dust cleared, de Gaulle was still in power, and France, with its usual unshakable self-confidence, went on about its business.

The characters in *May Fools* are far removed from the stirring street theater of May '68, but like everyone else in France, they're affected by it nonetheless. All the action in this film takes place in and around a rather shabby estate somewhere in the countryside: a big, musty old house stuffed with antiques of dubious value and surrounded by land that was once a vineyard and is now just land. The lord of this spacious and useless property is Milou (Michel Piccoli), a genial man in his sixties. He has the look of someone for whom life has always been serenely uncomplicated. Under his extremely casual supervision, the family's fortunes have run downhill, but his relatives don't bother him much; they're scattered all over, escapees from the rural boredom that suits Milou so well, and they're glad to let him take care of his aged mother, the rambling house, and the unproductive land. Contentedly free from scrutiny, Milou lives the life of a lazy country sensualist: he keeps bees, browns in the sun, and gropes the housekeeper. (When the roof needs fixing, he sells a Corot.) On the sunny May day when the story begins, his mother dies—taking her last breath while she is slumped on a bench where children's dolls sit—and Milou summons the rest of the family for the funeral and the reading of the will. As the relatives arrive, bringing cars, kids, lovers, and their own noisy personal agendas into the peaceful stasis of Milou's little world, the movie starts to take shape. There's a sense that things are about to change, both on the large scale of French society and on the infinitely smaller one of Milou's life; everything that has been allowed to bask, unchallenged, in happy inertia is going to be shaken up, forced to account for itself.

Malle and his cowriter, Jean-Claude Carrière, don't push the parallels too far. They use the upheaval of May '68 very deftly: it intrudes on their comedy like distant thunder on a sunny day, and the threatened downpour of Meaning never develops—we get a cooling shower of light ironies instead. The movie sometimes evokes Chekhov (especially *The Cherry Orchard* and *Uncle Vanya*) and sometimes the Jean Renoir of *The Rules of the Game*. (Milou's mother is played by Paulette Dubost, who, fifty-one years ago, was the flirtatious maid Lisette in Renoir's film.) But it doesn't really strive to be great. Malle and Carrière keep the tone airy and relaxed. *May Fools* just bounces along to the rhythm of its remarkable score, composed and played by the eighty-two-year-old jazz violinist Stéphane Grappelli; the movie, like the music, has a delicate, joyful swing to it.

And the revolution that is apparently in progress all over France is part of the texture. Everyone who arrives at Milou's house has been closer to the events than he has, and has something to tell him about the historic turmoil beyond the boundaries of his estate. He listens, although he isn't terribly interested in the outside world: he doesn't even own a television—only an ancient radio, which is invariably switched on by someone else. His daughter, Camille (Miou-Miou), turns up fuming about the demonstrating factory workers she had to drive through to get to the house. A savagely uptight bourgeoise, with a doctor husband and three children, she believes that what the protesters need is "a firm hand" to slap them down; speaking of her grandmother's death, she proclaims, inanely, "The revolution did her in." His brother, Georges (Michel Duchaussoy), a journalist, is a news junkie, who keeps his ears glued to the radio and talks only about politics. (He's a Gaullist, so he's nervous.) The arrival of Milou's niece, Claire (Dominique Blanc)—she's the daughter of his late sister—is delayed by the gas shortage. Late in the movie, Georges's son, a student named Pierre-Alain (Renaud Danner), drops in, having hitched a ride from Paris; he gives the family a fervent, lyrical eyewitness account of the revolution in the streets of the capital. "You can't know what's going on," he says. "It's completely new." Camille and Georges argue with him; Claire's young lover, Marie-Laure (Rozenn Le Tallec), is transported by Pierre-Alain and his tales of heroism, and becomes an instant convert to revolution (and heterosexuality). Milou doesn't look very attentive until the conversation turns to the sexual revolution. Pierre-Alain announces, "At last, people are making love for the pleasure of it," and the old satyr is all ears. He has been flirting seriously with Georges's young second wife, a hippie-ish Londoner named Lily (Harriet Walter); this is just the sort of talk he likes to hear.

The movie's central joke is that this aging, apolitical landed gentleman is in some sense an embodiment of the spirit of

May '68—not an enemy of the revolution but an unlikely comrade. (At one point, he belts out a full-throated rendition of the "Internationale.") He responds instinctively to the irresponsible, anarchic aspects of the students' revolt: he has lived his whole life with the sole purpose of remaining a child—free to take his modest pleasures where he finds them, in the open air and the cool, familiar rooms of his boyhood home. When the other members of the family, led by his greedy daughter, express their eagerness to sell the property and divide up the contents of the house, Milou throws a tantrum. "I want to die here!" he shouts. "It's my right! No one can rob me of my childhood!" His innocence could be pathetic, but it never is. Piccoli, in one of the best performances of his long career, is so vigorous and radiantly good-humored that we can't feel sorry for him; and Malle, although he treats Milou with some irony, is always unmistakably on his hero's side.

This sympathy is a large part of the picture's charm; sometimes, though, that charm feels a bit too easy. When *May Fools* is at its best, it seems to vindicate the childlike spirit of Milou and to give the youthful ardor of May '68 a poetic glow. Malle aims for, and mostly achieves, a graceful, drifting style, a mood of blissful sun-dazed inconsequence. When his touch falters, as it does in a few sequences toward the end, the movie verges on triviality: its concerns seem too small, its humor seems too cozily "Gallic," its point of view seems too mild and noncommittal. Its refusal to come to much could be taken, perhaps, as an ironic reflection of the ultimate lack of consequence of the May '68 revolt—France returned to the (slightly reformed) status quo with alarming speed and efficiency. But that's strictly an intellectual justification: the film doesn't have to blow away like dust just because the revolution did.

As determinedly minor as *May Fools* is, it's enjoyable throughout. It's all moments, lovely flashes of intelligence and observation, and some are exhilarating: a close-up tracking shot of Milou riding his bike through the overgrown fields; a scene in which, for the entertainment of a grandchild, he catches crayfish by sticking his hands in a stream and letting the creatures clamp onto his fingertips; a beautiful scene in which Milou, on the night after his mother's death, cries quietly in his bed and a small owl appears on his windowsill; a leisurely picnic on the grass, under a spreading tree, with the characters sprawled in a wide circle, and Milou announcing, a little drunkenly, "I haven't felt so young in thirty years—long live the revolution!" The gentle sort of liberation that Louis Malle proposes in *May Fools* seems, for an instant, to bridge the gap between 1938— when Milou felt young, and Renoir made his Popular Front film about the real Revolution, *La Marseillaise*, and Grappelli was hitting his stride—and 1968, and even the gap between 1968 and our not very hopeful present. In this picture we can almost hear Malle, as he strolls through his memories of that May, singing to himself "*Allons, enfants,*" very softly, a tender anthem.

The New Yorker, July 16, 1990

GHOST

Ghost sounds like a horror movie, but it's a romantic fairy tale. The scariest thing about it is its shamelessness. A young New York bank executive, Sam (Patrick Swayze), is killed, on the street, at a moment in his life when everything seems to be going his way. He and his beautiful, talented, loving girlfriend, Molly (Demi Moore), have just moved into a huge, airy loft, which they've remodeled and furnished themselves; we've seen them, in dreamy dust-and-sunlight shots, share the yuppie bliss of knocking out walls. He makes a Wall Street salary, she's a ceramics artist on the verge of recognition, and they're nice, unassuming folks: we understand that they're happy and affluent because they *deserve* to be—they haven't done anything piggy or unpleasant to get where they are. Not long before his death, Sam, a reflective sort, tells Molly, "I just don't want the bubble to burst. Whenever something good in my life happens, I'm afraid I'm gonna lose it." She reassures him: "You live a charmed life." Getting killed lets some of the air out of his tires, but people who have it all can't be expected to disappear just like that; Sam sticks around, as a spirit (and Swayze stays onscreen, as a body). He attends his funeral—thus acting out a popular daydream of the self-absorbed—and then watches Molly, who can't see or hear him, drift grief-stricken through the spiffy loft. These images of death have a soothing banality, like a greeting-card message from the world beyond.

Although Sam is dead, he has plenty to do; he's a spirit on the go. The screenwriter, Bruce Joel Rubin, and the director, Jerry Zucker, have given him the task of protecting Molly from the people who killed him. (He has learned that his death was not a random street crime, as it had appeared, but a premeditated murder, and that the information he was killed for is still in Molly's possession.) Through a reluctant psychic (Whoopi Goldberg), he tries to communicate with his girlfriend; later, an experienced ghost (Vincent Schiavelli) teaches him how to move objects and break stuff. Sam saves Molly and then twinkles off ruefully. (Even in death, he's upwardly mobile—climbing the spiritual ladder.) In this movie, death is treated as if it were merely a form of disability, one of those handicaps we've seen people struggle bravely with in TV movies—something for the individual to triumph over, with willpower, hard work, and love.

This creamy-toned fantasy certainly pushes the audience's emotional buttons; watching it, you feel like a VCR that's being programmed by experts. *Ghost* is a twentysomething hybrid of *It's a Wonderful Life* and some of the gooier, more solemn episodes of *The Twilight Zone*. It's designed to make us misty-eyed about our middle-class comforts, our loved ones, and—preeminently—ourselves. There's not a trace of wit or irony in it; if there were, the filmmakers' bubble would burst. Zucker, who co-directed *Airplane!* and *The Naked Gun*, lays on the sentiment here as uninhibitedly as he sprayed gags at us in his previous pictures. Perhaps the best example of his approach is the movie's climactic romantic image— of Molly dancing with Sam, as if he were still alive, to their favorite song, the Righteous Brothers' record of "Unchained Melody." The filmmakers have set this moment up by having the psychic allow Sam's spirit to enter her body, so he can touch Molly through her. Although it's much too late in the picture for us to expect anything interesting, our hopes, irrationally, flare up for an instant. Is Zucker about to present us with an image of Demi Moore caressing, perhaps kissing, Whoopi Goldberg? (In an earlier scene in which a ghost took possession of the psychic's body, Goldberg remained on-screen.) Not likely. The director passes up the chance for a funny, daring shot, and gives us the shining yuppie couple swaying in each other's arms instead. Some unseen power has intervened here, and it's not one of the higher ones.

The New Yorker, July 30, 1990

WILD AT HEART

Right from the start, just about everything is wrong with David Lynch's new movie, *Wild at Heart*, and the wrongness has an escalating, vertiginous quality. Every false move seems to lead to another, more disastrous than the one before. It's a road movie, a form that makes generous allowances for randomness and creative drifting, but Lynch's direction is arbitrary in an unusually aggressive way: he hops behind the wheel, floors the accelerator, and closes his eyes, like a kid on a bumper-car ride. The ride lasts two hours, and when it's over all you can do is stagger away in relief. You go to a Lynch movie, of course, prepared for some jolts and expecting to come out slightly dazed. What's dismaying about *Wild at Heart* is that its shocks have so little resonance; the weirdness here is inexpressive and trivial, even silly. This is a buzzing, hyperkinetic picture, but its wildness is all on the surface: the images are elaborately conceived, arresting, and meaningless, like tattoos.

At the Cannes Film Festival, where *Wild at Heart* won the grand prize, Lynch told the press that "the whole road-movie aspect" of the Barry Gifford novel the movie is based on didn't interest him much, and that's not surprising. He's a wizard at transforming disreputable pop genres into occasions of lyrical horror and disturbing comedy, and he's at his best (as in *Blue Velvet* and the *Twin Peaks* pilot) when the form he's violating is innocent, unencumbered by cultural significance. The road movie lost its innocence a long time ago; over the years, it has evolved (or degenerated) from cheap product for

248

drive-in double bills to one of the staple genres of art houses and film festivals. It's an exhausted genre; every fresh example of it seems to be running on the same thimbleful of notions about alienation, outlaw cool, and the junkiness of contemporary life. Road movies are now so flabby with intellectual respectability that they can barely move. (For some of its most devoted practitioners, like Jim Jarmusch and Wim Wenders, the form seems actually to be about stasis.) This genre doesn't need David Lynch; it's already too heavy with meaning. And he certainly doesn't need it; there's not enough room for his imagination, not enough hidden places for him to illuminate.

But if he doesn't care about this aspect of Gifford's story it's difficult to imagine what could have attracted him to the material, because there's nothing else in it. The novel is a slight, virtually plotless series of vignettes about a pair of lovers, no-account kids called Sailor and Lula, driving from North Carolina to Texas and stopping at ratty hotels and motels along the way. It seems to have been written as an exercise in road-movie attitude: its leading characters are hard-lovin' losers who smoke a lot and don't get to the place they set out for (California); the descriptive passages have a clipped, fake-iconic simplicity; and the dialogue, which is most of the book, veers between empty-headed inconsequentiality and "poetic" redneck aphorism. Although Sailor and Lula are an outlaw couple, their flight doesn't have a lot of urgency; they're on the run from Lula's hysterical mother, who sends in pursuit only her mild-mannered, ineffectual platonic swain, Johnnie Farragut. (Sailor, an ex-con, breaks his parole when he leaves North Carolina, but no one comes after him.) In adapting this languorous, arty trifle for the screen, Lynch seems to have realized that the story needed a tad more dramatic tension than Gifford provided—that the happiness of the runaway lovers needed to be threatened by something more potent than their own stupidity or an abstract, literary notion of fate. So he lays on the evil, twisted stuff, hoping to goose the material out of its inherent lethargy. He turns Lula's mother, Marietta, a pathetically repressed woman who's jealous of her daughter's passion, into a murderous gorgon: the movie's Marietta (Diane Ladd) offers Sailor a lewd proposition in a men's room, becomes enraged when she's rebuffed, and puts out a contract on him through a sinister friend named Marcello Santos (J. E. Freeman)—who, we later learn, helped her kill Lula's father years before. Lynch takes characters mentioned in passing in the novel, like a Honduran whom Johnnie chats with in a New Orleans bar, and transforms them into cartoons of wickedness, and throws in a few kinky villains of his own invention: a crippled dominatrix named Juana (Grace Zabriskie, who plays Laura Palmer's mother in *Twin Peaks*); an ill-defined leering psycho known as Dropshadow (the always alarming David Patrick Kelly); and a murder contractor called Mr. Reindeer (W. Morgan Sheppard), who conducts his business in an atmosphere of sordid opulence, taking orders for hits while surrounded by bare-breasted female slaves. Lynch kills off gentle Johnnie (Harry Dean Stanton, who—surely for the first time in his career—seems the most normal person on the screen). And he goes to town on the novel's chief bad guy, a white-trash hoodlum named Bobby Peru (Willem Dafoe), who turns up late in the story to give the young lovers the final push that will topple them into B-movie hell: as Lynch and Dafoe render him, this mean cracker seems to be Satan incarnate.

Lynch's screenplay does more than merely infuse *Wild at Heart* with enough menace to keep it perking: Gifford's poky Deep South odyssey is now an orgy of evil, a Halloween party where all the A-list monsters really let their hair down. The movie has plenty of graphic violence and grotesque craziness (such as Marietta's applying lipstick to her entire face and becoming a tandoori-chicken-colored demon), but their effect is negligible. No matter how flashily Lynch cuts from Sailor and Lula lolling in bed to people getting set on fire and screaming in agony or to killers looming malevolently over terrified victims, he can't escape the emptiness at the heart of the material: the lurid villainy always seems diversionary, a baroque disguise for a bland, lifeless, and overfamiliar story. He has to keep coming back to a pair of dull kids on the road from nowhere to nowhere.

Lynch stylizes the innocence of Sailor and Lula as floridly as he does the guilt of the other characters, and that doesn't help, either. He has cast a couple of very resourceful actors in the roles—Nicolas Cage and Laura Dern—but they're stranded without characters to play. He dresses up Gifford's thinly conceived lovers in kitschy drag, and gives them shockingly banal pop-culture dreams: Sailor models himself on Elvis, Lula on Marilyn. And their childlike belief in the benignness and redemptive power of the road is expressed in campy allusions to *The Wizard of Oz*: Lula's mother occasionally appears, in quick insert shots, in a Wicked Witch costume; the movie's fairy-tale ending is brought about through the special-effects intervention of the Good Witch (Sheryl Lee), who descends from the sky in what looks like a giant soap bubble. The cheesiness of the lovers' fantasies is probably meant to intensify our identification with their innocence, to heighten the contrast with the corrupt world around them, but it winds up having an altogether different effect. Their dreams are so infantile that we can't respond with anything but condescension; Sailor and Lula are just too dopey for us to care about.

Wild at Heart is a sorry spectacle. It's not pleasant to watch a brilliant filmmaker flailing around like this—especially when the horse he's whipping so furiously was dead before he got on it. The picture is one startling lapse of taste after another; we gaze in disbelief as the original error in judgment—the choice of material—metastasizes on the screen. It's a measure of Lynch's discomfort and confusion that the movie doesn't contain a single memorable image of the Southern and Southwestern landscapes; he settles for the usual parched roadside vistas and a shot of an old black guy nodding and smiling in front of a weather-beaten filling station. On the road, Lynch flops like a fish out of water.

The New Yorker, August 27, 1990

HENRY & JUNE

When Anaïs Nin met Henry Miller, in 1931, at her house on the outskirts of Paris (to which Henry had come, in the company of a friend of hers, to get a free meal), she immediately began to turn him into literature. Like everyone and everything else that passed through Nin's life, Miller became part of her diary—a voluminously detailed record of her everyday experience, which she started to write in 1914, at the age of eleven, as a kind of letter to her absent father. By the time she met Miller, the diary had taken on a life of its own, parallel to and perhaps more vivid than the events and feelings it purported to describe; by the time of her death, in 1977, it ran to thousands and thousands of pages. It's a commonplace that Nin's diary, and not the precious "poetic" fiction she also wrote, is her great achievement, the justification of her life as a writer. For her the diary (which she didn't begin to publish until the mid-sixties) seems to have been more than a chronicle, more than a literary exercise, more than a source of material for her fiction. It was the place—maybe the only place—in which she truly lived, because she experienced the world primarily in reflection, with one eye always on the mirror: the clear pool that she wanted not to dive into but to see herself in. Miller enters this strange world, the pages of Nin's diary, like a primitive giant, a mythological force of nature, a King Kong, and her delicate sensibility trembles excitedly: "He is a man whom life intoxicates, who has no need of wine, who is floating in a self-created euphoria. . . . His writing is flamboyant, torrential, cha-

252

otic, treacherous, and dangerous. . . . It is an assertion of instinct. . . . He finds joy in everything, in food, in talk, in drink. . . . He is a gentle savage who lives directed entirely by his whims, moods, his rhythms." This forty-year-old writer from Brooklyn, who had not yet published the novels that made him famous, seems to have been everything that Nin herself—a small, fragile, art-worshiping European woman living in the country with her banker husband—was not. "When I saw Henry Miller walking towards the door where I stood waiting, I closed my eyes for an instant to see him by some other inner eye," she wrote, and although she was soon to know this man intimately—they were lovers for a time, and lifelong friends and correspondents—the Henry Miller of Nin's diary is always, at least to some extent, a creature of that magnifying inner eye.

Philip Kaufman's wonderful new film, *Henry & June*, shows us Henry (played by Fred Ward) and Anaïs (Maria de Medeiros) in the first year of their acquaintance, the period of their brief, intense love affair. The screenplay, by Kaufman and his wife, Rose, is based almost entirely on Nin's version of events, parts of which Nin suppressed when the diary was first published. (The passages about her physical relationship with Miller weren't printed until several years after her death.) What's unusual about the movie is that it's the love story of two people who are making themselves, and each other, up as they go along: Miller and Nin are at once real people and products of their own imaginations—collaborators in a matched pair of literary myths. Everything that happens in *Henry & June* seems doubled, mirrored, as if it were taking place in some border territory of the mind, half material and half fantastic—somewhere, that is, between the gritty actuality of Miller's version and the embroidered introspection of Nin's. And the action unfolds in and around a city that seems both itself and a figment of itself: the Paris of the thirties, the land of the expatriate and the dreamer, where people came to breathe the air of art and beauty and to transform themselves into fabulous new beings, wandering innocently in a paradise of self-invention. For Miller and Nin, this place was a laboratory in which they experimented on themselves, partly conscious that that was what they were doing and partly believing that they were abandoning themselves to a larger, deeper external reality. Each needed what the other could give: Anaïs, who cultivated her intricate sensibility like an exotic plant in a hothouse, was fascinated by Henry's earthiness; Henry, who willed himself to live with the simplicity and immediacy of an animal, seemed to feel that he might learn something from Anaïs's more analytic and reflective approach to life. They constantly told each other what great writers they were, and the fact of their obvious differences in temperament must have made the praise sweeter and more convincing. Each was, in a sense, a mirror for the other: looking at himself through Nin's eyes, Henry found a clear image of the "Henry Miller" he was creating in his fiction; reflected in Miller, Anaïs began to define the hyperarticulated consciousness that is the central (virtually the only) character in her diary.

The movie is sympathetic—some might say too sympathetic—to these irritating, remarkably self-absorbed people. Kaufman's films (which include *The Unbearable Lightness of Being*, *The Right Stuff*, *The Wanderers*, and *The White Dawn*) have always been distinguished by their respect for exploration, in all its forms, and Miller and Nin were explorers. (And in their writing—Miller's, especially—they provided us with maps for the new territories they'd discovered.) But Kaufman also has the wit to present this odd literary/sexual love affair as a kind of parody image of relationships between men and women. Henry and Anaïs complement each other—they "grow" as individuals—through their affair, but their separate self-realizations are fueled by lies and evasions and half-truths, and the enduring result of their love is the perfection of two immense and impregnable egos. Kaufman brings out the bizarre, almost monstrous comedy of this relationship. At the frenzied height of their affair, Miller and Nin seem to be feeding on each other, tearing off chunks of each other's personality for the nourishment of their own rapidly expanding—and, of course, literary—selves. Writers coupling don't always make a pretty sight. In *Henry & June*, the voracity with which these lovers go at each other is often startlingly, grotesquely funny.

The third major character in the story is Miller's wife, June (Uma Thurman). She's the most mysterious figure here: when she first appears onscreen, she's lit like Dietrich in a Sternberg picture, and she seems to represent, as Dietrich sometimes did, a kind of demonic, annihilating sexual force. When Miller met her, in 1923, he was a wretchedly unsuccessful writer, and she was a taxi dancer who imagined herself a character out of Dostoyevski or Strindberg. Once they were married, she deceived him constantly, humiliating him by conducting affairs with both men and women. And although she encouraged him to write, she was an ambiguous muse: the money the Millers lived on, and traveled to Europe on, when Henry couldn't sell his work was provided (most likely) by June's sugar daddies, and, on top of everything else, she was witheringly critical of Henry's prose. (She apparently expected him to immortalize her as if she were one of Dostoyevski's tragic prostitutes, and became incensed when he portrayed her instead as an alluring, devious bitch.) Yet he couldn't free himself of her. When Anaïs and June met, the women fell in love. Nin wrote, "June is BEING. Nothing can control her. She is our fantasy let loose upon the world. She does what others only do in their dreams." Nin recognizes June's destruc- tiveness—the diary frequently refers to her as a death force—and she betrays her by sleeping with Henry, yet she remains powerfully attracted to this beautiful, crazy woman, and turns her into literature, too. June dominates the consciousness of both writers, even when Miller and Nin are making love, but by the end she is almost a tragic figure: Miller and Nin seem to have given each other the strength to write her out of their lives, in the most literal sense. The last we see of June in this picture is a fleeting, ghostlike image of a woman in the shadows, watching Henry and Anaïs embrace under a streetlight; when they look up, she's gone. It's like an exorcism, and, surpris- ingly, we feel pity for the vanquished demon. June seems somehow more human than Henry and Anaïs, more naked, more vulnerable. Because she isn't a writer, all she can do with her fantasies and desires is embody them in the world, and that leaves her terribly exposed. When Miller and Nin ally their rapacious imaginations against her, she's helpless: they *understand* her out of existence.

The presence of June gives perspective to the story of Henry and Anaïs, which might otherwise seem too hermetic, too fragile. Kauf- man gets miraculously intelligent performances from Ward and de Medeiros—they both manage to suggest the nearly inhuman de- tachment of writers who, even in the midst of passion, are always thinking of how they'll interpret and record their experience—but Thurman gives the picture a jolt every time she appears. The per- formance is uninhibited yet also weirdly delicate: her June is sexy, touching, and completely mad, all at once. She messes up the yin-yang symmetry of the relationship between Miller and Nin, destroys the illusion—which we're sometimes in danger of surrendering to—that this affair represents some sort of literary or sexual idyll. And she enables Kaufman to keep the movie's form from becoming too tidy. With June either onscreen or hovering in our minds like a nightmare, the material plays as rich, dark erotic farce: it's as if a character from a Strindberg chamber drama had barged into a performance of *Design for Living*.

Although the movie's surface is lucidly beautiful (the cinematographer is the superb Philippe Rousselot), and its rhythms are even, almost lulling, its tone is murderously elusive. The characters' motivations are so tangled in imagination and duplicity, and Kaufman's attitude toward the material is so complex and ambiguous, that the picture seems constantly on the verge of losing its balance. This sense of precariousness is part of what makes watching *Henry & June* so exciting, and the stimulating unease carries over into our reflections on the movie after we've left the theater: we remember it later as if it were a dream whose meaning we can't quite resolve. *Henry & June* creates a world, and Kaufman is both affectionate toward and clear-eyed about the people who live in it. Some of them are silly, like Richard Osborn (Kevin Spacey), a lawyer friend of Henry's who likes to think of himself as artistic: he's always complaining that his work, which no one has ever seen, is being plagiarized by famous writers. Spacey is hilarious in his few scenes: even when he's painted blue, to join an art students' parade through the Latin Quarter, he seems perfectly in character. And others, like Anaïs's husband, Hugo (Richard E. Grant), are pathetic: they bumble through the most complicated situations armed with nothing but vague notions and wan good intentions. The Paris of *Henry & June* isn't Miller's or Nin's but Kaufman's—a place that contains Miller and Nin and also people who are very different from them, all seen from a variety of perspectives. There are snippets of films from the period—*Un Chien Andalou, Maedchen in Uniform, The Passion of Joan of Arc*—and a sequence of Brassaï (who was a close friend of Miller's) at work, and there are scenes, too, that recall another movie vision of the intellectual adventurers of the first part of the century: Truffaut's *Jules and Jim*. For all the disparate material and angles of attack, however, the film has an extraordinary unity of mood. Even the sex scenes—for which the picture has been given the Motion Picture Association of America's new adults-only rating, NC-17—don't stand out from the whole. (These scenes are not particularly explicit, but they are powerfully erotic, in the best way: they show us what the characters are really feeling.)

The themes of this movie are close to those of *The Unbearable Lightness of Being*, and its approach to experience is similarly complex, but *Henry & June* is a less expansive work. Its strength lies in its concentration; its pleasures are intimate, like private jokes or family photographs, and its ambiguities are of a rather specialized kind—they spring from the ambiguities of the artist's existence. *Henry & June* is no more, and no less, than a comedy about the duplicity of writers—even, or perhaps especially, with respect to their own lives. Kaufman handles Henry and Anaïs more gently than they handle June: he doesn't understand them to death; he doesn't turn them into literature. It's refreshing to watch a movie that's concerned more with *enjoying* its characters, in all their contradictions, than with explaining them. Kaufman does his subjects the great favor of making them interesting rather than important, and of treating their sense of their own importance as simply an aspect of their natures. The most surprising, and liberating, thing about *Henry & June* is that it shows us Henry Miller and Anaïs Nin and Paris and the mirror world of the twentieth-century artist with an eye that neither magnifies nor diminishes them.

The New Yorker, October 8, 1990

L'ATALANTE

Jean Vigo, who died in 1934 at the age of twenty-nine, was one of the greatest artists in the history of the movies, and probably the most tantalizing. His body of work consists of a pair of short documentaries, a forty-seven-minute fiction film (*Zero for Conduct*), and one full-length feature—all told, less than three hours of finished film. The feature, *L'Atalante*, was released in Paris in September 1934 (just three weeks before Vigo's death), in a version the filmmaker had never seen: the distributor had cut the movie by almost a third, added a mediocre popular song, and then, for good measure, retitled the picture *Le Chaland Qui Passe*, after the new tune. *L'Atalante* was largely restored in 1940, but it has retained over the years the aura of something fragile and patched up, and that quality of seeming slightly damaged is perhaps what has made it for many viewers an object of special devotion: it's a movie that people see again and again, and love in ways they find difficult to explain. Now *L'Atalante* has been given another major renovation. This version, prepared by Pierre Philippe and Jean-Louis Bompoint, adds about nine minutes of footage not included in the previous reconstruction, and the restorers discovered in the archives of the British Film Institute a pristine nitrate print of a cut of the movie which obviously preceded the distributor's intervention; *L'Atalante* now looks and sounds better than ever. (The prints that have been circulating for the last fifty years are uniformly atrocious.) Thanks to Philippe and Bompoint, we can see all the lucid beauties of Boris Kaufman's cinematography, rather than have to struggle to imagine them, and hear Maurice Jaubert's lovely score without distortion; we can even make out the dialogue, which in previous prints was often just a low rumble of undifferentiated sound. But the best thing about this shiny new *L'Atalante* is that for all the restorers' diligence, the film is still messy, imperfect, defiantly incomplete. Like everything Vigo did, like his frustratingly brief career, *L'Atalante* is an unfinished product, unsuitable for framing: even in its current spruced-up condition, it's essentially a collection of inspired fragments, the sketchbook of an artist whose imagination was, and will forever remain, gloriously immature.

This movie was, in part, Vigo's attempt to "grow up" as a film-maker—to make a conventional commercial picture. His previous film, *Zero for Conduct*, about a revolt in a boys' boarding school, was a celebration of the pure freedom of children's imaginations, a stirring expression of resistance to the forces of authority and order—to anything that would impose discipline on the diverse, unruly energy of play. *Zero for Conduct* isn't constructed like an ordinary movie; Vigo evidently considered the discipline of narrative a form of repression, too, and his indifference to it has a lot to do with why *Zero for Conduct* still seems, fifty-seven years later, like one of the few truly subversive movies ever made. And the French censors—as alert to insubordination as the dwarf headmaster and the malevolent instructors who rule the world of Vigo's school-boys—banned the movie from public exhibition. For *L'Atalante*, Vigo agreed to work within the constraints of a simple and apparently innocuous story (from an original scenario by an undistinguished writer named Jean Guinée). Jean (Jean Dasté), the captain of a river barge named *L'Atalante*, marries Juliette (Dita Parlo), a girl from one of the villages on the barge's route. As the newlyweds travel down the river, Juliette becomes increasingly restless and disenchanted; she has escaped from her village, but all she's seeing of the world is riverbanks, the inside of cramped cabins, and her husband and his odd crew—a rambunctious old salt called Père Jules (Michel Simon) and a quiet cabin boy (Louis Lefèvre). Bored and impatient, she sneaks off to see the sights of Paris, but when she returns to the place where the barge was docked she discovers that Jean has shoved off without her. She wanders on the shore, he drifts downstream on the boat, and the separation makes them both miserable. Finally, they find each other again; life resumes its intended course.

The miracle of *L'Atalante* is that Vigo keeps breaking free of the story's ordained course: he's incapable of simply riding that dull, even current and making only the scheduled stops. He treats the story the way a jazz musician treats a popular song, improvising on the melody by plunging into its carefully sequenced chords and predictable rhythms and taking them apart to see what they're made of: he hits notes that we had never dreamed were there but that seem, once we've heard them, pure and essential, like pearls dredged from far beneath the smooth, lulling flow of the song. In one of the film's most sublime sequences, Jean, aching from the absence of Juliette, dives off the barge into the river because his bride once told him that you see the face of the one you love when you look under the surface of the water. Jean has tried the trick a couple of times before, jokingly and unsuccessfully, but this time—now that he is abandoned, mad with grief, reckless—he sees her: luminous in her wedding dress, and laughing with an unforced, innocent joy that looks like the sweetest of invitations, the promise of every kind of pleasure. The floating images of Juliette superimposed on Jean's desperate, searching face are reminders of some of our earlier views of her, and especially of a ghostly image of the bride in her white dress walking slowly along the top of the barge as it glides down the river at twilight: in the underwater sequence, Jean seems, at last, to be seeing his wife the way Vigo has seen her from the start—as an ordinary woman who becomes radiant when she is looked at with desire. This sequence tells us most of what we need to know about Vigo's eroticized approach to the art of moviemaking: he forgets his orders, immerses himself in the ordinary beauties of the sensual world, and summons up visions that shine with the possibilities of earthly pleasure.

The other key to Vigo is his attraction to chaos, clutter, sheer profusion—a quality that is, in a sense, just another side of his eroticism. The toys and gadgets and bric-a-brac that fill his movies are played with and caressed by the camera with such loving attention that they seem like fetishes. And there are so *many* of them—so many objects to divert us from the implacable responsibilities of living, so many beautiful distractions. Père Jules's cabin, overrun by cats and jammed with bizarre mementos that are the residue of a full and gleefully disorderly life, is the image not only of its inhabitant but also of its creator. This museum of useless things—with which, in a long and brilliantly sustained sequence, the old sailor enchants Juliette—is Vigo's world in miniature, a place where something to tickle the imagination or to stir memories or simply to gaze at in wonder is always ready to hand. And the character itself, as it is conceived by Vigo and played by the magnificently peculiar Simon, is the presiding spirit of the movie: Père Jules is a comic metaphor for the diversity of the world's riches; he is, in his demented, random way, a living encyclopedia. At one point, he gets excited, and all sorts of strange stuff bubbles out of him, with startling alacrity: Indian war whoops, bullfighting moves, snippets of songs and dances from Russia, Africa, the Orient. (He takes us around the world in about eighty seconds.) His body is covered with crudely drawn tattoos, and in one of the most welcome of the newly restored shots he amuses Juliette by making a face tattooed on his belly appear to smoke by putting a cigarette in his navel. Père Jules is, of course, a child, both splendid and monstrous, and there is, too, something profoundly childlike about the way the character is conceived: only a very innocent eye could see this crazy old drifter as the epitome of worldly experience.

Vigo may have been trying, with some part of himself, to make a "normal" movie—one conventional enough, at least, to get past the censors and into the commercial cinemas—but *L'Atalante* shows how hopelessly, wonderfully unsuited he was to popular moviemaking. His storytelling is still casual, almost perfunctory: the narrative will slow to a languorous drift, then abruptly begin chugging toward, then stop to give us a long look at some unanticipated marvel off in the distance, then lurch irritably ahead again. And his approach to composition and editing is so personal that audiences expecting an ordinary movie might become disoriented: shots are taken from unexpected angles, are held longer than usual, are juxtaposed with other shots in unprecedented ways. Vigo was helplessly original; he seems at times to be speaking a different language from other filmmakers. (On seeing Vigo's work for the first time, James Agee wrote, "It is as if he had invented the wheel.") He is the most playful and the least rigid of the great film artists; he had the liveliest eye, and perhaps the freest imagination. Everything he shows us looks mysteriously new, full of possibilities, and so encourages us to linger on it, investigate it, dream it, have our way with it.

In a sense, the restorers' work on *L'Atalante* springs from impulses like those—from the feeling, evoked at virtually every moment in Vigo's films, that there's something more for us to discover. The latest version of *L'Atalante* is new only in the sense that this movie has always seemed new; it isn't changed in any fundamental way. The footage added by Philippe and Bompoint is just extra stuff, beautiful and inessential and thus fully in keeping with the movie's expansive spirit. They've given us a few more glittery things to hoard in our imagination and fondle in our memories when life gets a little dull. In Jean Vigo's movies, greater profusion only creates stronger desire: his images seduce us with the promise of a larger, richer world and unbounded freedom to roam in it—the promise, that is, of endless stimulation, inexhaustible sensations. There can be no definitive *L'Atalante*, because the world of Vigo's films subverts the very idea of definition. This extraordinary movie will always elude our attempts to grasp it and keep it in its place: we'll never see everything in Père Jules's cabin; the image of the woman in the water disperses when we try to embrace it, then forms itself again and leads us on.

The New Yorker, November 5, 1990

THE RUSSIA HOUSE

Fred Schepisi's *The Russia House*, based on the novel by John le Carré, is an espionage thriller in which things are much, much simpler than they appear to be—a notion that all but subverts the premises of the genre. As is usual in such stories, there are important secrets up for grabs; here they're contained in a manuscript written by a top Soviet defense scientist, and this document whips the Cold Warriors of MI-6 and the CIA into a state of almost dangerous excitement. The intelligence professionals spring into action with characteristic deviousness and complexity, but the effect of their machinations is uncharacteristically ironic. Everything they do is oddly beside the point, because it's all based on a mistake about the nature of the story that's unfolding: their plotting is like an elaborate mathematical proof built on erroneous postulates, a furiously inventive jazz improvisation on the wrong chords. There's a fundamental disparity between the intelligence agencies' way of seeing the world and that of the Russian source, Yakov (Klaus Maria Brandauer). His manuscript, a passionate muddle of technical data and visionary philosophy, was never meant to be sold in the shadowy specialized markets of Whitehall and Langley; Yakov, a true innocent, thinks of his book as a message to the world, and tries to put it in the hands of a man he considers a kindred spirit—an alcoholic, saxophone-playing English publisher named Barley Blair (Sean Connery). The government agencies that wind up in possession of the manuscript are unwilling or unable to accept Yakov's declared intentions, and

263

so they set in motion a scheme that turns his attempt at direct communication with the West into something clandestine—a personal letter encrypted in the form of a spy story.

The novel, which was published last year, is a modest and graceful work. It doesn't have the Byzantine, occluded quality that made le Carré's novels about George Smiley so memorable; in *The Russia House*, the fine-tuned paranoia of the Cold War espionage game seems almost comic. The novel's narrator, a British intelligence agent, writes, "There is no such thing, we older hands like to say, as an intelligence operation that does not occasionally run to farce." The operation by the British and American intelligence wizards of this story is more than occasionally farcical; it is deeply and essentially ridiculous, a meticulously plotted exercise in absurdity. The choice of Tom Stoppard as the screenwriter to adapt this material was inspired; he's a connoisseur of both intricacy and futility, a writer who has always delighted in watching clever people get tangled up in their proudest intellectual constructions. And Schepisi is a virtuoso at making complicated action lucid—at keeping the audience alert to everything that's going on and yet not overwhelmed with information. The movie has a very tricky structure: many scenes require cutting back and forth between events in Russia, where Barley is trying to make contact with Yakov, and the spymasters monitoring his progress from listening posts in the West; and both the opening and the concluding sequences are constructed as flashbacks, with characters explaining the action in voice-overs that sometimes repeat and reinterpret things we've already seen. But the picture never feels hectic or flashy. It has an even, flowing rhythm, because Schepisi knows that suspense-movie technique is as irrelevant to this story as the tactical expertise of the intelligence services—that the thriller elements are a farcical counterpoint to the real story, in which all the thrills are emotional ones. The movie, like the book, diagrams the moves of the professional spy game while keeping our attention focused on the amateurs: Barley, Yakov, and Katya (Michelle Pfeiffer), the beautiful woman who acts as a messenger for Yakov.

Le Carré has created in Barley Blair a character who seems to stand for everything that was repressed by the cool, crafty, and thoroughly professional demeanor of George Smiley. What's extraordinary about the Smiley books is that while they never deviate from the thriller form, they are also penetrating explorations of a certain mode of Englishness: the reserve and wariness in one's approach to the world; the horror of calling attention to oneself; the cautious and precise relation to language, as if one were always sending and receiving messages in code. In all these respects, Barley Blair is utterly un-English. His publishing business, which he inherited, doesn't engage him much (his failure to show up at a Moscow book fair is the reason Yakov's manuscript gets dropped in the lap of MI-6); he loves drinking, playing jazz, and having long, loud, grandiose philosophical conversations with Russians. He's all intense, undirected passion—an amateur in every way—and it's this quality that both attracts Yakov and confounds the intelligence mandarins. The genius of le Carré's conception is that this unreliable middle-aged man isn't a bungler or a lost soul (as Graham Greene, say, might have portrayed him). Beneath the surface mess of his behavior Barley has a strong, clear sense of who he is and what he wants; and when he sees a reason to act he does so with startling skill and effectiveness—he becomes a tiger. Barley Blair is a great character, and a great role for Sean Connery. He imbues the character with a sharp, self-deprecating wit, and also with a kind of rough Celtic romanticism that takes us straight to the heart of le Carré's theme.

For all the brilliantly engineered spy-versus-spy gamesmanship in *The Russia House*, the point of the story is the possibility that the East and the West might be able, now, to learn the truth about each other by means other than the painstakingly choreographed dance of intelligence operations. The vehicles of this message are Barley and Katya, who fall in love and foul up the steps; improvising, they produce something better than what they've been given to perform. It's brave of le Carré to build his narrative on such an unsophisticated, fablelike notion; he risks seeming naive and sentimental. But his dry, precise style enables him to put this humanistic love story over on the page, and Schepisi, Stoppard, and the actors make us believe it on the screen. Connery and Pfeiffer are superbly matched, because they're both exceptionally direct, unfussy actors. There's nothing devious or self-conscious in their relation to the camera or to each other. We never have to guess what they're supposed to be feeling; it's right there, and they're not afraid to show it. Stoppard's cleverness actually enhances the effect of the big emotions; his irony is just a frame—it's pleasing in itself but always enables us to remain focused on what's inside, which is the real thing. (It's worth noting that Stoppard's taste for wordplay and Wodehouse-like farce construction isn't the product of an entirely English sensibility; he was born in Czechoslovakia.) And Schepisi knows enough not to lean on the audience. He doesn't manipulate us; he lays everything out and trusts us to recognize what's important. And we do.

Perhaps the reason *The Russia House* is such an immensely satisfying entertainment is that it appears to have been put together with care rather than mere calculation. The people who made this picture clearly know what they're doing, and, better yet, they seem to know why. Its professionalism is bracing because the enthusiasm and the generous spirit of the amateur are still in evidence. We can feel the thrill of conviction in Connery's acting: this is his richest and most affecting performance. And we feel, too, the unself-conscious awe of Schepisi and his cinematographer, Ian Baker, as they drink in the Russian scenery: they treat all these unfamiliar sights with affection, and even the grimmest-looking Stalinist architecture somehow becomes expressive. The movie isn't stingy with the sorts of pleasures it's willing to give us; there are small delights throughout. (Since Schepisi knows where the story is going, and isn't trying to kill us with suspense, he allows himself to linger on anything that interests him.) James Fox gives a subtle, elegantly detailed performance as Ned, the donnish British agent who runs the Yakov operation. And Ken Russell, who plays a rumpled British Sovietologist named Walter, is exuberantly funny; his joy at the prospect of rummaging through the mind of a Soviet defense scientist is childish, irrepressible. Together, Fox and Russell dramatize vividly one of the sly subtexts of all le Carré's works—the resemblance of British intelligence to a particularly intense university seminar. *The Russia House* is serious about important things, and it also knows how to have fun. The novel's epigraph is a quotation from the poet May Sarton:

"One must think like a hero to behave like a merely decent human being." (Barley speaks the line in the movie.) The kind of simplicity that le Carré and Schepisi and Connery aim for isn't easy to achieve, either. *The Russia House* has a heroic decency.

The New Yorker, December 31, 1990

THE VANISHING

George Sluizer's *The Vanishing* has a simple, powerful thriller hook: a beautiful young Dutch woman, Saskia (Johanna Ter Steege), vacationing in the South of France with her boyfriend, Rex (Gene Bervoets), walks into a highway rest stop to buy soda and beer and never comes back. The disappearance-while-on-holiday premise is a familiar one, from pictures like Polanski's *Frantic* and Hitchcock's two versions of *The Man Who Knew Too Much*, but *The Vanishing* doesn't feel secondhand. In this movie, the missing (presumably abducted) tourist isn't just a pretext for getting an innocent abroad mixed up in some international intrigue. Rex's search for Saskia, which takes place over several years, produces suspense of an unusually melancholy kind. He can't stand not knowing what happened to her; his ignorance of her fate is like a dark hole that suddenly opened up at his feet, and as he stares into this void its emptiness seems to mesmerize him, to freeze him in place. It's as if his life were suspended at the moment of Saskia's vanishing and couldn't be resumed unless he went back to that point on the highway where the path of their life together abruptly forked, and took her road instead, whatever the consequences. The logic of Rex's investigation—his obsession—is that he has to follow his lover, against all reason, down the deadest of dead ends. Both the hero and the plot he's trapped in have the tortuous, involuted quality of a complex sentence struggling to resolve itself into meaning, to discover its own inevitable form. And the conclusion justifies everything that has led up to it: it shows us, with terrifying clarity, the true shape of this labyrinthine construction. *The Vanishing* comes to a full stop, with a vengeance.

This fiendishly intelligent little movie is adapted from a novel called *The Golden Egg*, by the Dutch writer Tim Krabbé; he collaborated with Sluizer on the adaptation, and part of what makes it seem so distinctive is that its form is essentially, even defiantly, literary. It's a sophisticated example of the sort of hermetic intellectual mysteries that Borges is famous for, with their intricate structures of metaphors which always wind up closing in on the detective, entombing him (and the reader) in the rigid symmetry of his own mind. Krabbé shares Borges's taste for metaphysical paradox and his self-conscious obsession with formal shapeliness. Krabbé isn't nearly so bookish, though. Borges, who was blind, made his fictions entirely from the material inside the darkened chamber of his own brain—from the constant rearrangement and reclassification (he was a professional librarian) of the ideas and bits of esoteric lore he had collected there. *The Vanishing* is, in every sense, more down-to-earth: it's a literary trap, but one that catches an ordinary young couple on their way to the sunny Mediterranean, not scholars and ratiocinative geniuses who have set their course, with blinkered certitude, for unattainable realms of enlightenment. The fates of Saskia and Rex are worked out with an almost geometric precision; what makes *The Vanishing* linger in our memories, though, is the disparity between the beautiful abstraction of the plot and the naturalistic specificity of the characters and the settings. This perfect, meticulously ruled pattern seems to have been superimposed on a world that's too concrete, too real and recognizable; the movie gives us the disconcerting feeling of watching people we know through the tight mesh of a prison window.

Sluizer's direction is quiet and unemphatic, and it's sensationally effective. In the film's opening scenes, Rex and Saskia are driving south through France: they practice their French, she tells him a dream she had, and then the car runs out of gas in the middle of an unlit tunnel on the highway. Rex, callously or thoughtlessly, leaves her in the car in the dark while he goes back for fuel, and when he returns she isn't there. He finds her at the far end of the tunnel; she looks terrified and forlorn, and then her fear turns into anger at him.

The tension isn't fully resolved until they arrive at the busy rest stop, where Rex promises never to abandon her again. When the movie's over, we understand the structural and metaphoric importance of this odd beginning (it proves to be, in a sense, the whole story in miniature, and the movie's last shot is an ironic fulfillment of Saskia's dream), but even while we're seeing it, without foreknowledge of its place in the overall scheme, it has a disturbing resonance. It's hallucinatory yet familiar, because Sluizer appears to be working less from a plan than from sharp observation. Before anything else, he's concerned with evoking the emotional texture of a long drive: the riders' radical shifts in mood, from giddy volubility and intimacy to sudden, mute loneliness; the irritability that can flare up unexpectedly when people who know each other too well are in unknown territory and something goes wrong; and the embarrassment they may later feel at what they've revealed of themselves at the moment of crisis. In the fifteen or twenty minutes before Saskia vanishes, Sluizer gives us a fuller portrait of a relationship than most entire movies do. We don't realize until the end how telling even the smallest details of the couple's interaction are, but they register, with immediate force and lifelike ambiguity, as we're watching. And when the time comes to reflect on all the movie's strange and random-seeming moments, to fit them into their places in the story's larger scheme, we find that every one of them has stayed in our minds, as tangible and distinct as evidence preserved in clear envelopes. Even the sounds we hear during Rex and Saskia's last few minutes together seem to persist, echoing through the movie: the low and vaguely ominous hum of highway traffic; the ragged, bright noise of vacationers chattering; the excited voices of sportscasters reporting the Tour de France; the laughs and shouts that rip through the air irregularly, unpredictably, like bursts of static on a car radio. Sluizer is alert to stray sensations—to the surfaces of the world and the nuances of human behavior—and this documentary-style attentiveness gives the movie a vivid realism, a convincing sense of life. *The Vanishing* is about ordinary lives interrupted, hijacked out of time, and Sluizer, in his uninsistent way, does justice to the varied beauty of ordinariness; when Saskia disappears, we feel a visceral shock, as if some fundamental principle of nature had been violated.

(The vitality and effortless loveliness of Johanna Ter Steege have a lot to do with this feeling, too.)

After Rex realizes that his lover is missing, the movie's narrative style changes: the straight line of the story splits, ramifying into a complex network of side roads that seem always to bring the hero, and us, back to the same point—the place where the course of Rex's life with Saskia rudely stopped. He defines himself by that single terrible event in his past; nothing before or after Saskia's loss seems to matter much. While Rex is spinning his wheels, stuck in his obsession, the movie picks up the story of the man who abducted Saskia, a reserved, upright bourgeois named Raymond Lemorne (Bernard-Pierre Donnadieu). We know that he's somehow responsible for the crime—we saw him stalking his victim at the rest stop—but we don't know exactly what he has done or why. The movie tracks this monster through his everyday life, which is apparently placid and unexceptional (he has a teaching job, a wife, and a couple of kids), so the narrative has to keep circling back into his past in order to account for him. We get flashbacks to his preparations and rehearsals for his crime, and then to moments from his childhood and early married life. What is withheld, almost to the very end, is Lemorne's version of the abduction itself. The movie teases us with the prospect of revelation, toys with our desire to return to the place and time of the awful event. Lemorne, diabolically, is playing a similar game with Rex: he sends the young man anonymous notes that seem to promise the resolution of the mystery, the long-awaited deliverance of closure. The stories, in the end, do converge: the criminal, the investigator, the missing woman, and the audience come together to return, at last, to the scene of the crime, and the circle described by *The Vanishing* is completed. Aesthetically and intellectually, it's perfect, yet its perfection is horrible, unnatural, claustrophobic.

As chilling and perverse as this film is, it's also, surprisingly, moving: its rigor isn't alienating, and its symmetries are evocative rather than merely ingenious. *The Vanishing* is constructed with flawless elegance, but it's far less self-contained than it seems: traces of deep feeling keep escaping from the artifice, like puffs of breath into cold, thin air, and these wispy, ephemeral indications of unself-conscious life haunt us when the movie is over. This picture's impulses, like those of Brian De Palma's best thrillers, are lyrical rather than mechanical. Not many movies in the genre have the sort of suggestiveness *The Vanishing* has: the elusive but unshakable poetry of nightmare. It's a small classic.

The New Yorker, January 28, 1991

THE SILENCE OF THE LAMBS

Jonathan Demme's *The Silence of the Lambs* is artful pulp—tabloid material treated with intelligence and care and a weird kind of sensitivity. It's based on a 1988 novel, of the same title, by Thomas Harris, who specializes in dreaming up outré styles of serial murder. In Harris's 1981 thriller, *Red Dragon* (the movie version, directed by Michael Mann, was called *Manhunter*), the killer's signature is shards of mirrored glass placed in the eyes and mouth of each victim; in this one, the villain kidnaps women, kills them, and then peels off large swatches of their skin. Both novels are structured as race-against-the-clock manhunts, with FBI investigators subjecting every tiny bit of evidence to the most exhaustive forensic and psychological examination in an attempt to make sense of the murderer's apparently random pattern. Although Harris's stories draw some of their power from the vividly imagined monstrousness of the crimes, and some of their suspense from the agonizingly incremental nature of police procedure, the intensity of his work can't be fully explained by the skill with which he manipulates those standard, surefire elements of the genre. This picture—whose screenplay, by Ted Tally, is extremely faithful to the novel—is even more disturbing than its grisly subject suggests, because Harris and Demme don't allow the audience to distance itself in any of the usual ways. The movie has an unnerving intimacy; when it's over, you feel rattled and uncertain, as if you'd just received a threatening phone call.

The heroine of *The Silence of the Lambs* is an earnest FBI trainee named Clarice Starling (Jodie Foster). She's selected by the head of the bureau's behavioral-science department, Jack Crawford (Scott Glenn), to conduct an interview with Dr. Hannibal Lecter (Anthony Hopkins), a psychiatrist who is also a famous mass murderer: he liked to kill his patients and eat their organs, prepared as gourmet meals. The extra precautions his jailers take are an indication of how dangerous he is: his cell, in a high-security hospital for the criminally insane, is equipped with a shield of unbreakable Plexiglas; his keepers are forbidden to touch him, because he has been known to sink his teeth into the face of anyone who gets too close; when he has to be moved from his cell, he's provided with a straitjacket and an alarming-looking restraining mask, and is lashed to a hand truck on which he can be wheeled from one place to another. Lecter, who also appeared in *Red Dragon*, is Harris's Professor Moriarty: the mythological criminal genius, the investigator's ultimate test. He is, like Moriarty, the final problem—the evil that can't be resolved. Crawford sends Starling to see Lecter in the hope that the psychiatrist's twisted expertise can somehow be used to help the bureau catch the flayer-killer, known popularly as Buffalo Bill. (Starling thinks her assignment is in service of a long-term research project; Crawford doesn't tell her his real purpose right away.) The first face-to-face meeting of Starling and Lecter sets the tone for the movie. He stares at her, through the Plexiglas, with the piercing concentration of a predator. We sense that he's probing her, searching for her weak spots, taking her measure with a psychiatrist's practiced eye. The gleam in that eye, however, is clearly not professional; the burning-bright look he trains on his subject is openly malicious—an inhuman combination of avidity and clinical detachment. And Starling doesn't flinch. We know she's spooked, but she's too proud to avert her eyes from his scrutiny, and her strength seems to take Lecter by surprise; it piques his interest, makes him want to know more. Starling, without quite understanding what she's doing, turns Lecter's curiosity to her advantage: in the course of the film, their conversations turn into edgy, complex transactions in which she reveals pieces of her inner life—her fears, her memories—in return for Lecter's hints on how to find Buffalo Bill.

Starling and Lecter have only four scenes together, but their relationship dominates the movie. Hopkins plays the monster with fine cold relish. He's in superb control of his effects; although Lecter's madness is relentless, absolute, Hopkins keeps it from becoming monotonous. He gives it shadings—variations in intensity, flashes of macabre wit, and even, at one point, a suggestion of simple human feeling. When Starling comes out with an especially painful memory from her childhood—one that seems to account for her moral core, which is what Lecter finds so fascinating about her—he says, quietly, "Thank you, Clarice," and looks as if he meant it. (Five minutes later, his teeth are tearing into the flesh of one of his guards.) Lecter is conceived as the incarnation of something totally alien, beyond our understanding: he can only be played in a stylized way, and Hopkins, with compact gestures and elegantly sardonic readings, gives the character a mesmeric animal stillness, the terrifying opacity of a cobra.

The impact of this performance is heightened by its contrast with everything surrounding it: the scrupulous realism of Demme's style, the mundane details of police procedure, and, in particular, the emotional transparence of the heroine. What's really original about Harris's treatment of the police-procedural form is the way he portrays the investigators: his cops aren't the remote, can-do authority figures we know from TV action shows—those reassuring guardians of the social order—but people whose relationship to their job is ambivalent, conflicted. For Will Graham, the hero of *Red Dragon*, the process of investigation is a kind of mental torture, and the social authority he represents is no comfort to him. He catches serial killers by forcing himself to see the world through their eyes, by reproducing their madness in himself; he's uncannily receptive, like an impressionable child. Graham's imagination has a frighteningly anarchic quality: there's no mechanism for repressing even the most unassimilable, unbearable images and feelings. (He's the detective-story equivalent of the tormented, reluctant clairvoyants of horror fiction like *The Dead Zone* and *The Fury*.) Starling's empathic faculties aren't freakishly overdeveloped, as Graham's are. Her vulnerability derives from her youth, her eagerness to learn, and her need to find out who she is. She's a student, and the goal of her education is to acquire the armor of police technique and manner. But she isn't quite there yet. She has to confront the horrors of Lecter and Buffalo Bill without any way of knowing whether she's adequately protected, physically or psychologically.

The fragility of Harris's cops—the suggestion that they're always, in some sense, operating in the dark, in a zone where it's nearly impossible for them to orient themselves—gives his work a distinctively unsettling resonance, an emotional realism that makes us feel as exposed as Graham or Starling. In *The Silence of the Lambs*, the panic that is ordinarily repressed by the certainties of forensic technique and institutional identity isn't fully mastered, and so the detective's progress toward the resolution of the mystery takes on a strangely ambiguous quality. Most thrillers of this sort have a straight-ahead kind of suspense: the detective can't wait to get his hands on the killer, and bulls forward implacably toward his goal. Here the progress of the investigation isn't so briskly linear (or so predictable): we feel that it's bringing us closer to something that we, and Starling, would much prefer to keep at a distance. The suspense of *The Silence of the Lambs* is reflective, oscillating between approach and avoidance (and also between the narrative mode of the detective genre, which is all confident approach, and that of the horror genre, which is all avoidance: the innocent and unwary in constant flight from the monster). Starling, the trainee, draws near Buffalo Bill with the hovering, darting motion of a moth around a flame. It's almost too excruciating to watch, because her fluctuating responses mirror our own: we need the satisfaction of resolution, but we don't want to have to expose ourselves to an ungovernable and annihilating evil force.

The Silence of the Lambs is a brilliantly effective piece of filmmaking, but it's a difficult picture to resolve your feelings about. Although it cuts much closer to the bone than thrillers usually do, it doesn't have the precision, the sharp focus, of a work of art. Harris's odd genius derives from his single-mindedness, from the doggedness with which he explores his obsessions, rather than from especially acute psychological insight, and he's not always successful in reconciling his serious concerns with his appetite for the sensational. He seems to be trying to make literature out of the unwholesome fascination of pulp—to achieve profundity through morbidity—and the ambiguity of this project can make us queasy: we want to be entertained or enlightened, but sometimes we just feel as if we were being skinned. Jonathan Demme, whose sensibility is neither sensationalist nor obsessive, does his best to play down the exploitation in the material. He treats the story not as a series of crude shocks but as a single accumulating trauma: the plot unfolds with an inexorable smoothness, as a graceful long descent toward the unspeakable. The movie is, of course, a far cry from the loose, generous-spirited comedies that Demme is known for; the tight form of the thriller and the demands of maintaining suspense don't allow him much room for his customary digressions and eccentricities. What enables him to get his bearings in this unfamiliar territory is the richness of the central character, who—like most of the people in his other films— is someone who's changing, learning, trying to formulate an identity. He keeps our attention on Starling and her shifting reactions to the world, and his most striking achievement in this picture is his direction of Jodie Foster. Her clear, strong features—which have sometimes given her, in other roles, a slightly impenetrable look—have never seemed so expressive. Demme treats her to one closeup after another, and she rewards him with a steady flow of small surprises. With amazing delicacy, Foster shows us the constant tension between the character's emotions and her actions—the omnipresent self-consciousness of inexperience. When, at the movie's climax, Starling has to use all the moves she's been rehearsing in her classes, Foster gives every gesture a hint of tentativeness, and that subtle hesitancy makes the student's courage incredibly touching. We may not know quite how to feel about the fears and insecurities and nightmare images that *The Silence of the Lambs* makes us vulnerable to, but we know exactly how to feel about Jodie Foster's performance: the only adequate response is "Thank you."

The New Yorker, February 25, 1991

THE DOORS

Twenty years ago, Jim Morrison, the lead singer and main songwriter of the sixties band the Doors, died, at the age of twenty-seven, and thus became one of the enduring figures in the mythology of rock and roll. He wasn't by any means the most brilliant musician of the psychedelic era (Hendrix was) or the most talented writer (Dylan and Lennon were far more original), and he may not even have been the most self-destructive rock star of his time (the competition was fierce). What set Morrison apart was his powerful sexual aura: the unsmiling bad-boy handsomeness; the vocal style that alternated low crooning with long orgasmic cries; his writhing movements onstage; and the songs themselves, many of which featured highly charged erotic imagery. Morrison once referred to the Doors as "erotic politicians," and their platform was explicitly Dionysiac—a program of liberation based on the intoxication of the senses. He was an alcoholic, an enthusiastic and omnivorous experimenter with drugs, a dabbler in spiritual arcana, and a devotee of the literature of transgression—Rimbaud, Artaud, the Beats. Morrison presented himself as a combination of shaman and *poète maudit*, and he was a star in life and a legend in death because he made the physical, intellectual, and spiritual excesses of the counterculture sexy. He was, in a sense, the perfect pop-culture idol of a chaotic time, and his death—in a Paris flat, the ideal setting for a Romantic poet's demise—sealed his myth. He's the intellectual adolescent's

278

Elvis; there are members of his cult who believe that their idol is still alive.

He certainly isn't alive in Oliver Stone's *The Doors*, though. You don't have to have been a big Morrison fan to find this treatment of his life offensive. *The Doors* is pure exploitation: Stone gobbles up Morrison and the sixties and rock and roll as if they were drugs. He clearly gets a charge out of the sixties: this is his third film about that period (*Platoon* and *Born on the Fourth of July* were the first two), and they have been progressively more frenzied and incoherent; it's beginning to look as if he were interested less in interpreting the Vietnam era than in simply appropriating as much of its unruly, orgiastic energy as he can. *The Doors* offers no perspective on those strange days. It's an extended, self-important freakout, an exercise in disorientation, and Stone, with no apparent irony, resurrects the clichés of "psychedelic" movie technique: dreamy, soft-focus trip sequences; acid-flashback quick cuts; strobe lighting; distorting lenses. (In a couple of sequences, Stone has the camera rock back and forth and up and down for minutes at a stretch, and we feel not as if we were hallucinating but as if we had somehow wandered into a screening of *The Poseidon Adventure* by mistake.) These effects weren't very expressive even when they were in vogue. Now, out of their cultural context, they're worse than annoying; they seem cynical, coercive. One of the many differences between the sixties and the nineties is that what was then sold as expansion of consciousness is today called substance abuse; the substance that Oliver Stone abuses in *The Doors* is history itself.

The sixties, after all, were stimulating because their spirit was truly expansive, easygoing. All sorts of approaches to experience were available, but in the manner of a bazaar. You could stroll around in the cultural marketplace, linger over some items and pass by others, buy everything or nothing or, like most people, a little bit of this and a little bit of that: you could take the music and leave the drugs alone, explore radical political ideas and skip the Oriental philosophy. You could present yourself as a revolutionary (political or sexual or aesthetic, or any combination thereof), a spiritual adept (of any of dozens of belief systems), or just a happy hedonist. In *The Doors* Oliver Stone reduces the richly contradictory experience of the sixties to the myth of Morrison, and, in the process, reduces Morrison and the Doors as well: the movie restricts the viewer's freedom to imagine the sixties culture as anything but a movement with a single voice, or to imagine the Doors as anything but a metaphor. Stone portrays the crowds at the band's concerts as if they were a unanimous constituency—gatherings of the devout, all dying to be whipped into Dionysiac ecstasies. For most fans, however, the Doors were one good group among many, and people responded to their best songs—"Light My Fire," "People Are Strange," "Twentieth Century Fox"—as distinctive, exciting pieces of music, not necessarily as revelations of higher truth. (A lot of us took our Doors albums off the turntable when the heavy, message-bearing poetic stuff, like "When the Music's Over," came on.) And not everyone responded to the messianic intensity of Morrison's stage persona as if it were a life-changing spiritual force: for the majority of the audience, giving itself over to the frenzy of a Doors concert was more a theatrical experience than a religious one.

Morrison may have finally become so addled by drink and drugs that he didn't know whether he was a rock star or a true shaman, but in his lucid moments he showed more awareness of himself than this movie allows him. "It's all done tongue in cheek," he once said. "It's like if you play the villain in a Western it doesn't mean that that's you. That's just an aspect that you keep for show. I don't really take that seriously. That's supposed to be ironic." Stone doesn't provide even a glimpse of the Jim Morrison who could say something like that, or any suggestion that there was humor in the sixties aesthetic of deliberate, outrageous provocation—that virtually all the popular art of the era was conceived in the spirit of the put-on. The ponderousness of Stone's vision of the sixties and the relentlessness with which he pounds away at the most dubious symbolic aspects of Morrison's identity leave Val Kilmer, who plays Morrison, almost nothing to work with. Kilmer is physically convincing, but his performance can be only an impersonation: what the script (by Stone and J. Randal Johnson) gives him to play is the icon, not the man.

For a while, the movie's obviousness and flat-out vulgarity are sort of entertaining. (And Kyle MacLachlan, as the Doors' keyboard player, Ray Manzarek, has a few nice moments before he's shoved into the background.) It might be possible to enjoy *The Doors* as a kind of camp classic if you could ignore the mean-spiritedness that keeps breaking through—the fundamental hostility that Stone seems to feel toward his subjects, even while he's apparently celebrating them. For instance, his vision of the sexual revolution, of which Morrison is supposed to be an avatar, is like a *Playboy* fantasy of a world filled with bare-breasted hippie chicks, stoned and ready for love. (In this movie, only naked women seem to be admitted to Doors concerts.) In one particularly ugly sequence, the Doors attend a Warhol party in New York, and a beautiful blonde with a European accent introduces herself to Morrison: "Hi, I'm Nico." This is, of course, the Nico who sang on one of the great albums of the sixties, the first Velvet Underground record; the movie doesn't tell us that, though, and a few minutes later we see her going down on Morrison in an elevator, as if she were just another desperate groupie. (Nico—who did have an affair with Morrison—can't defend herself; she died three years ago.) The women in Morrison's life whom we see the most of in the movie are his longtime girlfriend, Pamela Courson (Meg Ryan), and a journalist named Patricia Kennealy (Kathleen Quinlan), who was also a lover: Pam is portrayed as an airhead and a nag, and Patricia as a practicing witch, who drinks blood. Journalists get a bum rap elsewhere in the picture, too, but Stone's own view of sixties culture betrays a prurient, tabloidlike sensibility: it trashes what it glorifies, punishes us for our attractions.

Watching *The Doors* is like being at a concert in an auditorium with a terrible sound system: the music is reduced to undifferentiated noise, a maddening throb of bass notes, as persistent as a migraine. And near the end of this two-hour-and-fifteen-minute bad trip Stone treats us to an unbearable, head-splitting blast of feedback, in the form of a video-image montage of the tragedies and atrocities of the late sixties: corpses on a road in Vietnam, the assassinations of Robert Kennedy and Martin Luther King, Jr. The sequence is the setup for a punch line: Morrison, in alcoholic decline, muttering, "I think I'm having a nervous breakdown." This is the movie's most unspeakable and most emblematic scene—the moment when its bad faith is most purely revealed. In *The Doors*, the sixties are just a hallucination, a jumble of images in which nothing is more important than anything else and the only point is the sensory excitement of seeing them flash before us. Stone seems to want to turn the audience, and himself, on by tapping into the energy of the Vietnam era, but the movie leaves us exhausted and depressed; it makes us feel like voyeurs of our own memories.

The New Yorker, March 11, 1991

PARIS IS BURNING

Jennie Livingston's *Paris Is Burning*, about gay black and Latino men who compete in drag balls, is a beautiful piece of documentary filmmaking—lively, intelligent, exploratory. The movie is an examination of the rituals of an American urban subculture (most of the balls we're shown take place in Harlem), and the subject is loaded with ironies of the sort that encourage heavy-duty sociological analysis, because virtually every aspect of this community of underdogs imitates some perceived value of the white middle-class heterosexual society from which they feel excluded. The drag queens of *Paris Is Burning* seem to be holding a mirror up to the world of the empowered as they see it in movies, TV shows, and magazines. In the ballroom (usually an Elks lodge or a YMCA hall), they appear in clothing that signifies strength, success, sexual desirability—in the armor of confident, unambiguous social identities. Some present themselves as elegant, glamorous women in designer outfits, and walk with the hip-swinging slouch of runway models, while others adopt more mundane personas: college students (of both sexes), wearing glasses, cardigan sweaters, and serious looks, and carrying textbooks and notebooks at their sides; military men in crisp uniforms; aristocrats at play, dressed for yachting or riding to hounds; Wall Street businessmen in impeccable three-piece suits. The criterion by which all these turns on the floor are evaluated (in the style of the Olympics or a slam-dunk contest, with a panel of judges holding up scorecards after each performance) is verisimilitude—"realness," in the idiom of the ball culture. Every man we meet in this picture is the product of a tireless, fanatically scrupulous art practiced on himself—each man his own Pygmalion and his own Galatea.

It doesn't take an advanced degree to recognize the paradoxes of the world described by *Paris Is Burning*, or to develop from its elaborate theories about reality and artifice, or the language of style, or the relationship of street culture to official culture, or the mechanics by which the dominant values of a society are internalized even by those whom they oppress—you could go on and on. The material is almost too rich, too suggestive. Everything about *Paris Is Burning* signifies so blatantly and so promiscuously that our formulations—our neatly paired theses and antitheses—multiply faster than we can keep track of them, and the movie induces a kind of semiotic daze. What's wonderful about the picture is that Livingston is smart enough not to reduce her subjects to the sum of their possible meanings, perhaps because she realizes that the way the drag performers manipulate images and fetishes and the iconography of popular culture is for many of them a sophisticated form of humor: a joke whose punch line, I suspect, is the intellectual vertigo it produces in outsiders who presume to explain it. The most self-aware of the gay men we see here revel in the ironies of their social and sexual identities, and the film makes us appreciate the comic grace and the strange wisdom of that approach; the ball veterans, the elders of the community, use their self-conscious theatricality to create a refuge for themselves—a forest of symbols in which they and their friends can play undisturbed and others just get lost.

Some of those inside the ball world get lost, too—the ones who are taken in by their own mimetic powers, for whom "realness" is no joke. In the process of reporting on this extraordinary society and presenting for our entertainment the rowdy and often hilarious theater of the ballroom competitions, *Paris Is Burning* (which is also the name of one of the major balls) manages to tell a fascinating story about generational differences. Part of the attraction of the ball subculture, what gives it its vitality as a community, is that its members have developed their own forms of social organization: everyone belongs to a particular "house," which functions as a kind of family. And within each house there's a structure, a hierarchy: the

younger members are known as "the children"; the more experienced, who have won trophies at the balls, are "legends"; the ultimate authorities, watching over everyone, are "the mother" and "the
father." As in any clan, the elders are the voices of prudence and
moderation, but in this world it takes us a while to catch on to that,
because the legends and the mothers and the fathers express their
essential conservatism through flamboyance—old-style flaming ef-
feminacy. They're men who came bursting out of the closet years
ago, dressed to the teeth and ready to dazzle. The first performer we
see in full drag in *Paris Is Burning* is Pepper Labeija, who appears
on the ballroom floor in an extravagant, billowing gold dress and
struts his stuff with outrageous, self-mocking assurance. Livingston
cuts from this out-there performance to a scene of Pepper at
home—a trim middle-aged man in men's clothes. He looks straight
into the camera and says, "Do you want me to say who I *am* and all
of that?" His voice as he says this has an exaggerated weariness and
an undertone of sarcasm: he seems amused both by the absurdity of
the idea that he could define himself simply and by the naiveté of
a filmmaker—or an audience—who thinks he'd give himself away
so easily. He answers with the equivalent of name, rank, and serial
number: "I am Pepper Labeija, the Legendary Mother of the House
of Labeija." Pepper is the presiding spirit of *Paris Is Burning*. His
campy bravura in the ballroom and his ironic detachment outside it
are the components of a remarkably sane, clear-eyed attitude toward
life. He enjoys himself, because he appreciates the value of play and
make-believe and knows them for what they are. His routines on the
ballroom floor are explicitly and unabashedly *performances,* as obvious and outsized as those of an old Shakespearean ham; he has the
wit to keep his distance from what he impersonates.

Later in the film, Pepper speaks directly to the heart of the issue:
"I've been a man, and I've been a man who emulated a woman. I've
never been a woman." He's making this statement as a warning to
the younger generation, to the children who seem to him to be
taking verisimilitude to dangerous extremes. Many of the young
ballwalkers we see in *Paris Is Burning* perform in a far more earnest
and more naturalistic style than that of the legends, and with an
almost frightening absorption in their roles; they're Method actors of
drag. A few have had breast implants; a handful have gone all the

way and had sex-change operations; and many more dream of such transformations. They dream, too, of breaking out of the safe, self-contained world of the ball subculture and gaining acceptance in the larger world—not as talented drag performers but as real women. We see one of them, an elegant young man who calls himself Octavia (of the House of Saint Laurent), nervously entering the Supermodel of the Year competition; his idol is the cover girl Paulina. Another, a slim blond ("petite" is his word) who goes by the name of Venus Xtravaganza, says flatly, "I would like to be a spoiled rich white girl." In a brilliant sequence, Livingston cuts back and forth between an interview with Octavia and one with Venus, each in his shabby-looking apartment, and their comments have the eerie repetitiveness of a litany: almost every sentence either of them utters begins with "I want." They're intensely focused on their fantasies, which have become their goals: they've crossed a line between the attempt to create an illusion and the belief that they can incarnate it in the world. These children don't think of what they do at the balls as play; they lack the humor and the self-awareness of the drag classicism that the legends practice—the protective irony that has enabled men like Pepper to survive in a hostile world.

Livingston and her editor, Jonathan Oppenheim, are terrifically deft at juxtaposing the near-hysterical party atmosphere of the ball footage with the more reflective mood of the interviews, and they don't hit us over the head with the contrast between the wild fun and the pathos: both qualities seem to emerge naturally from the material. And, like all the best documentaries, *Paris Is Burning* does its subjects the honor of not understanding them too readily—of allowing them to retain some of their mystery. The movie is a sympathetic observation of a specialized, private world; it doesn't feel like a violation or an intrusion (or, for that matter, a dissertation). We feel, instead, Livingston's curiosity about the way this little society works and her affection for its members. She's more interested in the differences between individuals than in the theoretical similarities, so she keeps picking up fresh nuances of behavior and performance: the movie packs a tremendous amount of information into its seventy-eight minutes. *Paris Is Burning* has its share of sobering, and even tragic, moments, but its spirit is buoyant, because it never strays too far from the crazy exuberance of the ballrooms. We see one amazing performance after another, from the spectacular light-ning-flash voguing of Willi Ninja (he's like Nijinsky's faun on fast forward) to the picture's final routine, a lip-synching turn by a fat man doing Patti LaBelle in a sequined gown: this huge queen wig-gles his hips and waves his arms and then, suddenly, breaks into a dead run for the center of the floor, where he flops down and begins to writhe ecstatically, kicking his big legs every which way. There's no accounting for this sort of theatrical transport. It is, perhaps, a joy that only the most abandoned of performers will ever know, and all we can do is gaze on it, in delight and awe; its sources are beyond the reach of our formulations.

The New Yorker, March 25, 1991

TRULY, MADLY, DEEPLY

The heroine of *Truly, Madly, Deeply* is a young woman named Nina
(Juliet Stevenson), who lives by herself in a large, cluttered, rat-
infested flat in North London. She's obsessed with the memory of
her lover, Jamie, who died suddenly and freakishly. When she's
alone, she hears him speaking to her; she feels as if he were following her home from the tube station, protecting her as she walks the
dark streets, and she has soothing little domestic chats with him
before she goes to bed. She guards her solitude jealously, because
she doesn't want to lose Jamie's voice: it's all she cares about. Her
grief has taken the form of fantasy, a refusal to accept that her life has
changed; the voice Nina hears is like phantom pain from an am-
putated limb. The first half hour or so of this picture shows us a
woman who isn't really connecting with her everyday life, who
moves through it without seeming to be a part of it. She's pleasant
with her neighbors and relatives and coworkers, and doesn't mope
ostentatiously, but we can sense how difficult it is for her to interact
with them, how disengaged she feels; when she's with other people,
she looks alien, slightly artificial, as if her presence among them
were just some sort of photographic trick, an optical effect done in
the lab. In these early scenes, Anthony Minghella, directing his own
screenplay, establishes an unusual, delicately varied mood. He does
justice both to the numbness of Nina's emotional life and to the
squalor of her material circumstances (everything in her flat is falling
apart, and the rats seem determined to crowd her out), but the

movie isn't oppressive or claustrophobic. We understand that Nina doesn't *want* to be miserable; it's just something that has happened to her, and she can't yet see a way out of it. We know that we're seeing a fundamentally sane, happy woman who's going through a very rough patch in her life.

These opening scenes have a fluid, gentle realism, a vivid sense of the textures of ordinary life, and it would be possible, I suppose, to mistake this picture, a BBC production, for one of those tastefully boring English domestic dramas, full of tiny, familiar emotions and whispered truisms about middle-class anguish. But Minghella's realism is more ambitious and more thorough than that; it's not just surface verisimilitude. In *Truly, Madly, Deeply*, the lovingly rendered details of the heroine's life always seem to point beyond themselves. There's an emotional unity to everything we see, a sense that even within the circumscribed world of Nina's flat, and even within the cocoon of reminiscence she has spun around herself, nothing has a fixed, immutable meaning—that her relationship to her most cherished objects and memories is subject to change. Although Nina is trying to hide from life, to remain suspended in the happier past, the world keeps breaking in on her, suggesting other possibilities. Minghella surrounds her with people who are coping, in various ways, with the small shocks of day-to-day existence and their own feelings of strangeness in the world: a Polish handyman (Christopher Rózycki), who misses his country and thinks he's in love with Nina; her boss, Sandy (the marvelous Bill Paterson), a linguist who's separated from his Spanish-speaking wife and can't read his son's postcards, because they're written in her language, which Sandy has never bothered to learn; a Chilean exile (Stella Maris), who was a filmmaker in her native country and now takes cleaning jobs to support herself; an elderly, widowed exterminator (David Ryall), who confesses that he still has conversations with his dead wife. Every one of these characters expands the context in which we see Nina's emotional state, casts a different sort of light on the disheveled furnishings of her life.

This shifting, unpredictable play of light allows Minghella to move gracefully from a realistic mode into a fantastic one. One night, Nina sits down at the piano and begins to play a Bach piece, and she's so transported by the music that she imagines she's hearing the cello part that Jamie used to play; she smiles, and the camera pans across the darkened room to reveal her dead lover, in the flesh, behind her. For the rest of the picture, Jamie (Alan Rickman) pops in and out of her flat, a ghost with a body, and his presence seems perfectly natural to us: he has emerged from a setting that is already charged with Nina's feelings for him. He's the embodiment, the literal manifestation, of the fantasy that she has taken refuge in since his death. And he's all too literal. After her initial euphoria at having him back, Nina's relation to him begins to change: she's forced to confront, in the most concrete way, what it would really mean to live the rest of her life with a dead guy as her significant other. By reappearing and reinserting himself in the irritating specificity of the everyday, the ordinary business of living, Jamie becomes just another possibility, another eccentric perspective on the world: reincarnated and constantly underfoot, he's something that Nina can at last start to distance herself from.

Nina and Jamie's estrangement is, like everything else in this movie, a gradual process, an unobtrusive accumulation of details and stray moments. The transformation in the heroine's relationship with her lover sneaks up on her, and on the audience, because it's achieved largely by means of a kind of weird domestic comedy. Jamie gets on Nina's nerves in the trivial ways that anyone who lives with anyone else does: he turns the heat up too high, because he's afraid of catching a cold; he interrupts her while she's taking a bath; he invites friends over without telling her, and she finds her living room filled with extremely pale men who watch videos far into the night. (Jamie's buddies from the afterlife are a hilarious group. They huddle intently around the television and mouth the dialogue of old favorites like *Brief Encounter*. They all seem to have gone straight to Heaven from the Everyman repertory cinema in Hampstead.) She still loves him, but his presence in her ordinary life soon loses its miraculous character: her fantasy becomes, in a sense, mundane, domesticated—something to *deal* with, as if it were one of those alarming surprises her flat keeps springing on her. With Jamie around, Nina recognizes, with inescapable force, the hermetic, stifling quality of her recent existence; she begins to feel the need to let some light and air in again, to reenter the disorder of reality.

This lovely, original comedy is the first film directed by Minghella, who is known in England as a writer of plays for radio, television, and the stage. *Truly, Madly, Deeply* is the work of a mature artist, one with the skill to draw us into a fresh and startlingly humane vision of modern urban life. Minghella writes dialogue that sounds casual but somehow takes us straight to the heart of his work's larger concerns, and he directs the actors beautifully. Rickman (the suave villain of the first *Die Hard* picture) is unexpectedly romantic here, and very funny besides. And Juliet Stevenson, who has worked with Minghella many times, gives a remarkable performance in an extremely demanding role. Nina could easily have been a drab, exasperating character—by virtue of either her unvarying grief or her basic liberal decency—but Stevenson makes her glow. She doesn't have a false moment, or a boring one, in the whole picture. Together, she and Minghella embody the movie's spirit of transformation: by giving each other room, and remaining alert both to each other and to the changing surfaces of the world, they seem to have discovered a new set of possibilities for movie realism.

The New Yorker, May 6, 1991

IMPROMPTU

James Lapine's *Impromptu* is an ebullient and absurdly entertaining account of the famous love affair of Frédéric Chopin and George Sand, the French woman novelist who made herself notorious by dressing in men's clothing. The script, by Sarah Kernochan (who is Lapine's wife), isn't terribly scrupulous about historical accuracy: it makes Sand's wooing and winning of frail, chaste young Chopin into a busy exercise in farce, with a full complement of deceptions and setbacks and misunderstandings—few of which, as far as I can tell, have any basis in fact. Celebrities of the Romantic movement—Delacroix, Musset, and Liszt among them—are put through their paces, along with George and Frédéric, in the salons and ballrooms and country houses of 1830s France; they issue florid declarations of love, hurl barbed epigrams at their rivals, challenge each other to duels, and, overall, make complete asses of themselves in their pursuit of the sublime. They're lively company. And for all its frivolity and whole-cloth embellishment, *Impromptu* seems truer to its subjects than the movies' previous treatment of this story, an insane 1944 Hollywood biopic called *A Song to Remember*. That movie, directed by Charles Vidor, gave us Cornel Wilde as a doltishly naive Chopin allowing himself to be the kept man of Merle Oberon's evil George Sand—Vampira in pants. She forces him to stay at home and compose silly études and nocturnes rather than the polonaises that, in the picture's bizarre ideology, represent his better self, as a man of the people and a foe of czarist oppression. She alienates him from his kindly old teacher (Paul Muni at his most unbearable), and even tries to prevent him from giving a series of concerts to benefit the Polish freedom fighters; despite his poor health, he defies her, though, and, in the movie's climactic sequence, leaves a trail of clammy sweat and bloody sputum through the great concert halls of Europe as he plays polonaises for his people. (The historical record does not provide a lot of support for this version of events.)

Impromptu is refreshingly free of high-minded impulses. It's content, for the most part, to show us the peculiar spectacle of nineteenth-century bohemians at play, and it's shamelessly eager to please. Kernochan's script embroiders the Chopin-Sand love story with motifs lifted from other tales of romantic intrigue, such as *Les Liaisons Dangereuses* and Jean Renoir's *The Rules of the Game*, for no better (or worse) reason than to keep the characters in constant furious motion. (There's a sly joke in her borrowing from Renoir's film. She gathers her Romantic all-stars in an opulent country house, where they give amorous chase to one another, in various combinations, and at the climax of this long sequence they put on a show for their aristocratic hosts; the author and star of their little performance piece is Musset—whose play *Les Caprices de Marianne* was the primary source of *The Rules of the Game*.) Lapine directs with broad theatrical flair: he wants every scene to be a showstopper, and he's not above throwing in some slapstick to perk things up. And the actors look as if they were having a wonderful time charging around in their elaborate costumes. Bernadette Peters, as Liszt's mistress, and Mandy Patinkin, as Musset, are especially uninhibited, and Emma Thompson, as the art-groupie duchess who presides over the bohemians' country revels, does some expert high-style mugging; there's a different sort of wit in Julian Sand's gaunt, fierce-looking Liszt.

The historical figures we see in *Impromptu* are cartoons, but they're cartoons with recognizable human qualities; their selfishness and jealousy and unscrupulousness are so exaggerated that the bad traits become rather endearing, like Daffy Duck's vanity or Wile E. Coyote's deviousness. Hugh Grant's Chopin is a brilliant caricature of the Romantic ideal of the artist. Grant, who is as beautiful as a cherub, gives his character an air of befuddled unworldliness, and he punctuates his readings with delicately timed tubercular coughs.

He plays Chopin as a besieged virgin, outraged by social impropriety and terrified of physical love; Sand's advances make him tremble and shiver, as if he were being exposed to a nasty draft. And Sand, as Judy Davis plays her, has a personality that would make stronger men than Chopin run for cover. This is a great role, and Davis, a prodigiously talented actress, attacks it ferociously; she blows through the picture like a strong wind, leveling everything in her path. Sand's passion for Chopin is the sort of ardor that makes people ridiculous, and Davis makes Sand's absurdities both funny and tremendously moving; this woman's willingness to embarrass herself seems a kind of romantic heroism. The ultimate surprise of *Impromptu* is how satisfying it is as a celebration of romantic (and Romantic) love. By the end of the picture, Sand, with her swaggering aggressiveness, and Chopin, with his maidenly modesty, look like a match made in Heaven.

The New Yorker, May 6, 1991

THELMA & LOUISE

Ridley Scott's *Thelma & Louise* is a crazily overstuffed Hollywood entertainment. Its heroines, played by Geena Davis (Thelma) and Susan Sarandon (Louise), are a couple of Arkansas women who set out for a weekend in the mountains and wind up speeding through the Southwest, on the run from the law. Following the tradition of movie outlaws, they're headed for the Mexican border; they cross a fair number of state lines, and genre lines, on the way. The act that puts the women on this reckless course is a murder. To get themselves in the mood for their carefree weekend, Thelma and Louise stop off at a roadside honky-tonk, where Thelma, elated at the prospect of a few days' freedom from her obnoxious husband, Darryl (Christopher McDonald), allows herself to be picked up by a smooth-talking cracker named Harlan (Timothy Carhart). After whooping it up on the dance floor for a while, Thelma, feeling sick, heads for the parking lot, and Harlan tries to rape her; Louise shoots him dead. They hop in Louise's convertible and flee the scene, because Louise is sure that the police won't believe the women's version of events; she thinks that Thelma's flirtatious behavior in the roadhouse would cast doubt on the story of attempted rape. Louise makes this radical decision, to go on the lam rather than face the skepticism of the authorities, instantaneously and with unanswerable conviction. For the audience, the moment requires a leap of faith that is far greater than the one the cops would have to make in order to believe the women's story. And it's only the first of a series of leaps that the script, by Callie Khouri, forces us to make if we want to stay with these unlikely desperadoes on their wild ride. The women have plenty of opportunities to turn back, but the movie is designed to keep pushing them farther and farther out there—past the point of no return, into the vanishing point of a vast Western landscape, and, finally, over the edge of the world.

Essentially, *Thelma & Louise* is an outlaw fantasy, and a mighty shameless one. The feminist justification that Khouri's script provides for the heroines' behavior doesn't make their actions any less preposterous: the characters would probably be more believable if the movie provided fewer explanations of their motives—if it allowed us to see their mad dash to the border as purely irrational (in the manner of, say, a Patricia Highsmith novel). The way the script is constructed, we sometimes feel, unfortunately, that the feminist ideas are being used opportunistically, just to keep the narrative moving—that every time Thelma and Louise have a chance to give themselves up, a man does something horrible and strengthens their conviction that they're better off on the run. The funny thing about *Thelma & Louise* is that you can recognize the crudeness of the script's devices and still have an awfully good time. The dopey ideas do at least give the picture some momentum: the heroines' flight is fueled (however implausibly) by impulses that are more powerful than the usual road-movie anomie. The movie has the hellbent energy of a drive-in exploitation picture, and it's eventful—it isn't just figures drifting dazedly through alienating landscapes. Thelma and Louise are lively, voluble good old girls, and they're not given to brooding; they keep each other's spirits up. The audience's, too. Davis and Sarandon are so vivid and likable that they carry us past the plot's most obvious contrivances; a little disbelief seems a small price to pay for being allowed to remain in their company.

Davis has the flashier role. Thelma is totally oppressed by her loudmouthed, beer-swilling, gold-chain-wearing husband, an irredeemable male-chauvinist goon. Despite her grim servitude to this pig, she manages to be pretty cheerful, in a girlish, spacey way. She seems never to have grown up; when she sneaks off, without telling Darryl, for her weekend with Louise, she giggles wickedly, like a teenager who has put one over on her parents. It's a wonderful role for Geena Davis: she gets to show off her (proven) talent for dizzy comedy, and to go through lots of emotional changes besides. In her best scenes, she does both at once. After a one-night stand with a sexy young hitchhiker (Brad Pitt, who has the sullen handsomeness—and the white cowboy hat—of the country singer Dwight Yoakam), Thelma sashays into the motel coffee shop with a big goofy grin on her face and tells Louise, "I finally understand what all the fuss is about." Davis's silly rapture makes this a classic scene, a sweetly funny image of sexual bliss. Throughout the movie, Davis's large, changeable features and her lanky frame serve the character beautifully; she seems to combine the malleability of a cartoon character—which isn't inappropriate here—with a kind of long-limbed Western grace. She gets terrific vocal effects, too: she produces a lovely comic music out of laughs and shouts and drawls. Davis is spectacular, but Sarandon, whose character has a less extreme emotional range, is every bit as good. Louise, a fortyish diner waitress who's involved with a kindhearted but unreliable musician (Michael Madsen), is steadier, world-wearier, and more practical than her young friend. She has a been-there look about her, and she doesn't trust people much; she's always scolding Thelma for striking up conversations with strangers. (And her suspiciousness always turns out to be justified.) In many scenes, Sarandon plays straight person to Davis, and does it with the skill and good humor of an extremely confident actress. She trains a penetrating, no-nonsense stare on her companion's antics; her looks of affectionate disbelief often mirror the audience's reactions. And when she breaks down and laughs, giving in to the craziness around her, her abandon is infectious. Sarandon holds our attention by not betraying her character's emotions too readily. Her held-in quality makes an effective contrast to Davis's overflowing exuberance, and it has its own power, too; in a sense, Sarandon's mysterious straight-ahead intensity is what propels the story forward.

There's an exhilarating ease and intuitiveness in the way these actresses work together; we feel, and share, their pleasure in surprising each other. *Thelma & Louise* is at its best in its most casual, most aimless-seeming moments, in the dawdling intervals between "important" scenes, while the women are just zipping down the highway and trying to figure out what to do next. (Or why they did what they did last. They often seem as dumbfounded by the story as the audience is.) And Ridley Scott provides an abundance of moments like these: scenes in which the women tease each other or get on each other's nerves or sing along with the car radio, as their hair blows all over their faces. The camera lingers on Davis and Sarandon as if it couldn't get enough of them: Scott seems to want to show us what they look like in every kind of light and every kind of mood. The director's entranced gaze slows down the rhythm of the narrative; quite a lot happens in this movie, but it has a leisurely, expansive air. Scott—the director of *The Duellists*, *Alien*, and *Blade Runner*—is known for his striking, even overpowering, visual style: the compositions in his films are meticulous, shiny, and elaborately textured. They frequently look too good to be true, and Scott has sometimes been seen as just another member of a school of filmmakers who developed a slick, manipulative craft in the British advertising industry—directors like Alan Parker (*Midnight Express* and *Mississippi Burning*), Adrian Lyne (*Flashdance* and *Fatal Attraction*), and Ridley's brother Tony Scott (*Top Gun* and *Days of Thunder*). Ridley Scott isn't really that kind of filmmaker, though. He has never been a cynical manipulator of audience reactions. He's a romantic, and rather an innocent and credulous one, at that, investing everything he works on with the passion and enthusiasm of an imaginative child. His images have a true believer's intensity, and if they're not always persuasive it's perhaps because Scott isn't terribly selective about what he believes in.

His fabulist's sensibility does wonders for *Thelma & Louise*. He dances attendance on the outlaw princesses who are his heroines, and treats every stage of their journey as an occasion for awe. Truck stops, mesas, motel pools, deserted country roads, messy kitchens, and the packed ladies' room of the honky-tonk all have a hyperreal gleam to them, a luminous expressiveness. When Thelma and Louise are on the road, the movie has the look of a mirage, a jeweled shimmer that keeps us half hypnotized. (The trance is broken periodically by the intrusion of banal plot mechanics: cutaways to the police investigation, under the direction of a sympathetic cop played by Harvey Keitel. These are the movie's clumsiest scenes; we can feel Scott's impatience to get back to the women.) Scott's love of the women and the landscape doesn't quite transform Khouri's gimmicky, rabble-rousing script into something profound, but it has the welcome effect of softening the hard edges of the story; it gives the whole movie a pleasantly dreamy quality. In the end, *Thelma & Louise* seems less a feminist parable than an airy, lyrical joke about a couple of women who go off in search of a little personal space and discover that they have to keep going and going and going to find a space that's big enough.

The New Yorker, June 3, 1991

EUROPA EUROPA

Every European Jew who survived the Holocaust has an amazing story to tell. The usual skills that human beings exercise in order to ward off the world's dangers didn't, in themselves, provide an adequate defense against the organized ferocity of the Final Solution. Courage, prudence, and guile were rarely enough, and every survivor's history has, necessarily, elements of the miraculous: unexpected, often inexplicable, acts of kindness; providential oversights on the part of the authorities; happy accidents of timing; one-in-a-million convergences of favorable circumstances. Among all these tales of wonder—of just-missed hiding places and impossible reprieves—none is more bizarre than that of Salomon Perel, a German Jew who spent much of the war passing for Aryan in an elite Hitler Youth academy. Perel's memoir, *Europa Europa*, was published in France last year (it hasn't yet been translated into English), and this improbable narrative of a Jew's coming of age among the Nazis is the basis of a superb new movie by the Polish director Agnieszka Holland. Her film, which retains the title of Perel's autobiography, dramatizes young Solly's wartime experiences with a surprisingly light touch. It bounds from one jaw-dropping episode to the next with the speed and the unnerving neutrality of a picaresque adventure, and never pauses to judge its ambiguous hero; it's content to let the ironies of his situation collect around him like reflections in dressing-room mirrors.

Right from the start, Holland adopts a magic-realist tone. The first images of *Europa Europa* are of Solly (Marco Hofschneider) underwater. As he flails and struggles in this undefined place, we hear his voice on the soundtrack telling us that he was born in Germany in 1925, and that he shares a birthday (April 20) with Adolf Hitler; and this coincidence, this bit of cosmic irony, seems to signify—in a literary way—that the hero is somehow singular, marked for a special destiny. From this skewed fairy-tale prologue the movie cuts to the scene of Solly's circumcision, which the narrator claims to actually remember. And from there Holland takes us swiftly forward to 1938; Solly, on the eve of his bar mitzvah, is enjoying a leisurely bath when a rock thrown by jeering bands of Nazis in the street below crashes through the bathroom window, and he flees the apartment to take refuge in a barrel. That night, our hero, who has left his clothes in the apartment, asks a neighbor to bring him something to wear; all she can find for him is a black coat with a swastika armband, and it's in this appalling getup that he returns home, to find that his sister is dead—she's laid out in the dining room, her blood dripping onto the very table at which Solly was circumcised. These brisk and beautifully controlled opening scenes have a poetic clarity that haunts us for the rest of the movie: Holland makes us conscious, from the outset, of the significance of water and blood, and of the terrible contrast between the Nazis' uniforms, covering their wearers with the armor of totalitarian iconography, and the exposed flesh of the Reich's victims. When, later in the film, circumstances force the hero to live in that uniform as if it were the full expression of himself, we remain constantly aware (as he is) of what the clothes conceal— the circumcised penis, the irreversible and unambiguous sign of Solly's identity as a Jew. By the time the movie is over, we understand why the hero believes that he can remember his bris. During the war, his circumcision acquires the unwanted status of the defining event in his young life. How could he forget the operation that left him so cruelly unprotected? The world he lives in from 1938 to 1945 won't let him forget it. Every time he has to urinate, or take a bath or a shower, he risks exposure, and the prospect of a sexual encounter generates emotional havoc: his feelings alternate, excruciatingly, between intense adolescent desire and abject fear. The movie shows us the thoroughness of Nazi terror in the pained expression of a teenage boy who doesn't dare allow himself to be seduced.

As Holland has constructed the story, this physical evidence of Solly's Jewishness is the fulcrum of the movie's delicately balanced narrative and moral tensions. She uses the ever-present threat that Solly will be caught with his pants down as a means of creating suspense, but she does a lot more with it than that. In the course of the film she makes us understand that the fact of Solly's circumcision is, in a sense, all that keeps him honest. If he could wish his missing bit of foreskin back into existence, he could get into bed with anyone, literally and metaphorically. He's an awfully adaptable kid. He's attractive, personable, good at languages, and deft at lying, and he isn't burdened with an excess of religious zeal: he has a talent for blending in with whatever surroundings he finds himself in, for becoming whatever the people around him want him to be. (His quick instincts in sizing up changes in a situation and his chameleonlike ability to change himself along with it are the qualities of a picaresque hero.) By the time Solly is initiated into the Hitler Youth, he has already run through several identities, and has proved himself capable of playing his roles with conviction and enthusiasm.

After his sister's death, his family fled to Lodz, in Poland, and when his parents heard that the German army was approaching they ordered Solly and his older brother Isaac (Rene Hofschneider) to pack up and head east, toward the Soviet Union. The movie shows us a few pointed scenes of Solly's life in a Soviet school: he becomes a star pupil, and is accepted—despite his petit-bourgeois origins— into the most prestigious Communist youth organization, the Komsomol. We see him stand before an assembly of his student comrades and give a fervent, impeccably Stalinist oration on the evils of religion; and then, after the Germans attack and he has been taken prisoner, we see him renounce his Communist ideology and reincarnate himself, on the spot, as an orphaned "pure" German, an Aryan child wandering in the barbaric eastern wilderness. His captors are so charmed and moved by his story that they ignore his lack of identity papers. By turning himself into the hero of a Nazi fairy tale, Solly stirs the tender emotions of the Wehrmacht soldiers and earns the privilege of accompanying them, as translator and mascot, on their march through Russia. He's very popular: one officer falls in love with him; the commander of the unit wants to adopt him.

So when Solly arrives at the Hitler Youth school he has had plenty of practice in conforming to the expectations of totalitarian institutions. And we have seen how skillful he is at disarming his enemies, how proficient he is at using his youth and beauty and glibness to dazzle and distract his pursuers. Putting on his Hitler Youth uniform for the first time, Solly breaks into a grin and does a silly little softshoe in front of the mirror, as if to loosen himself up for the twenty-four-hour-a-day performance he knows he's going to have to give. Everything that's most appealing in him is in this frisky, parodic dance—as well as everything that's most disturbing. The situation he's in won't allow him to sustain a playful attitude toward his latest act of impersonation: his youthful delight in getting away with something is attenuated by the intolerable pressure of never being able to rest—he's playing his part ceaselessly, without intermission.

In these circumstances, which would test even the strongest, most fully formed identity, this malleable teenager is often tempted to resolve his emotional tensions by surrendering to his role, losing himself in the embrace of the enemy's culture and ideology. In one terrifying scene, the film shows us the brown-shirted students' response to the news of the German army's defeat in Russia: they weep, and Solly, giving in to the collective emotion of the moment, weeps with them. His desire to reduce the cognitive dissonance of his existence—to live a "normal" life in the perverse and monolithic universe of the Reich—reaches a heartbreaking climax when he attempts, in the privacy of a bathroom stall, to alter the unalterable, to erase the last vestige of his Jewishness. Working, painfully, with bits of thread, he tries to extend the flesh of his penis into something resembling a foreskin. These scenes of self-mutilation—of exhausted surrender to the impulse to annihilate oneself in uniformity—are unbearably intimate. We know that Solly has undertaken this grotesque experiment in part so he can satisfy a fundamental human appetite: he wants to sleep with his girlfriend. (This blond beauty, played by Julie Delpy, is a passionately committed Nazi and a rabid anti-Semite; she wants to bear a child for the Führer.) Holland, sympathetic and yet pitilessly objective, makes these passages seem a kind of apotheosis of the ironies in Solly Perel's extraordinary story. In all the art and history of the Holocaust, there is no clearer image of the cost of survival—of the unnatural forms that even this most basic instinct can sometimes take. At such moments we see the hero of *Europa Europa* as a creature immersed in ambiguities, not drowning but not surfacing, either—a young man who can't allow himself simply to be. In dangerous circumstances, he manages to reach maturity, and that's a victory, but his sense of self is stillborn. He seems, at the end, an elusive, undefinable entity: a boy forever on the eve of his bar mitzvah.

In the movie's final scene, Holland shows us the real Salomon Perel: he's a bald, sixty-five-year-old man standing on the bank of a river in Israel (where he has lived since the war). As the camera rests on him, in closeup, we try to read his features, to find in them some clue to the meaning of his almost inconceivable experience. Like most faces, Perel's is ultimately inscrutable. He looks mournful and somewhat dazed, but it's difficult to attribute even these qualities to him with any certainty: we may be only projecting our own emotions and expectations onto him, as the Soviets and the Nazis did when he was young.

We can't imagine how this man could sort out all he has lived through. A couple of times in the course of the film, Holland presumes to enter young Solly's dreams. These sequences are grimly comic jumbles of images and ideas from the disparate experiences that have imposed themselves on his consciousness: Hitler and Stalin dance with each other, surrounded by a corps of Soviet baby ballerinas; Hitler hides from his own secret police in the closet of the Perels' apartment in Germany, then turns into one of Solly's Wehrmacht friends and is shot. Solly's dreams are no more legible, and barely more preposterous, than his waking life. (The most nightmarish passage in the film isn't a dream at all. Solly, on leave from the Hitler Youth academy, travels to Lodz and rides through the ghetto in a bus with whitewashed windows; through a tiny gap in the paint he sees a woman disappearing into an alleyway, and believes that it was his mother.) The way Holland tells the story of Salomon Perel in *Europa Europa*, no fuller explanation of his unlikely survival seems necessary, or even desirable. In the shimmering golden light of the movie's final shots, the old man on the riverbank looks faintly unreal: he could be a mirage, or the product of an illusionist's arrangement of mirrors. Whatever he is, he is undeniably *there,* before our eyes. Agnieszka Holland delivers him to us as a pure, absurd miracle of history.

The New Yorker, July 1, 1991

THE MIRACLE

The Miracle, the beautiful new film by the Irish writer and director Neil Jordan (*Mona Lisa, The Company of Wolves*), begins with a haunting, almost familiar melody and an enigmatic image of a woman's face floating toward us, in closeup, against the background of a milky sky. Her features are indistinct: dark glasses hide her eyes, and a shadow covers the rest of her face—a fringe across the top of the frame suggests that she's carrying a parasol. In any event, this half-lit face has a mysteriously old-fashioned, even archaic, quality. The obscurity of the image is tantalizing, alluring—an invitation to fill out our vague perceptions with sharper details, to turn these spectral traces of recognition into something known and loved. We want to imagine this woman as the heroine of an old, grand story, as a creature out of a fairy tale (a queen in exile, perhaps) or a tawdry pulp thriller (a femme fatale, a lady with a past, a nightclub siren). The ravishing image fades after a minute or so, and just in time—before our tentative speculations about the woman's identity have quite hardened into formulations. Jordan leaves that face suspended in our minds, still indefinite enough to promise any kind of story, while he resolves the smaller mystery of the music that we've been trying to put a name to. It's the introductory verse of "Star Dust," maybe the most famous and beloved of all romantic pop standards. A plangent trumpet solo (by Wynton Marsalis) states the theme over a very clean and unobtrusive arrangement of strings, and we recognize it right away. The tune is so firmly embedded in our memories that most of us probably can't recall a time when we didn't know it.

As we sink into the comfortable embrace of the old song, Jordan gives us a scene to orient ourselves in: a view of a beach, with the low buildings of a small town in the background and a weathered stone wall in the foreground. Against the wall, high above the beach, the camera catches first the shadow of a human figure and then its source, an old man strolling along the promenade; and then a teenage boy and a teenage girl, following the old gent at a discreet distance. The teenagers, Jimmy (Niall Byrne) and Rose (Lorraine Pilkington), speak to each other in conspiratorial tones about the drama that they imagine is taking place before them. As the old man walks by an elderly woman in a red hat, Rose intones, "Every time he passes her, her heart leaps," and Jimmy nods, admiring her skill at literary improvisation. This, we quickly realize, is how Jimmy and Rose spend most of their days—wandering through their home-town, Bray, in search of people to make up stories about. It doesn't take much to stimulate their cheap-fiction reflexes. The sight of a perfectly ordinary-looking stranger eating chips in a café provides Jimmy with a flash of inspiration: "The drabness of his life was so complete as to have its own fascination." He adds, "Write it down," and Rose does. The kids seem to enjoy an ideal rapport: taking off from the human material that presents itself to them in the seaside town, they trade verbal riffs with the gleeful competitiveness of jamming musicians. In their early scenes together, these teenagers bounce phrases and story fragments off each other with an almost magical ease, and give the movie a light, varied rhythm; they establish a groove.

Byrne and Pilkington aren't professional actors. Their gestures and readings have a fresh, unstudied quality that makes it impossible for us to find Jimmy and Rose obnoxious. The teenagers' fiction-making game seems outrageously presumptuous, and the formulations they arrive at are often fancy and unconvincing, but the young actors manage to persuade us that Jimmy and Rose aren't taking any of it too seriously—that they only half believe in the "truth" of what they make up. On some level, they seem aware that they don't yet know a whole lot about life. Besides, the object of their activity isn't really to understand the people they come upon but to impress each other: their conversations are mating dances in the guise of literary collaboration. There's a sweet, dry humor in these exchanges: we feel the pleasure that Jimmy and Rose take in their verbal play—and we feel, too, that their pleasure is freer yet thinner than it would be if they expressed it in the form of sex. Surrounded by old folks and old buildings, in a country that seems stuck in a mythic past, these young people aren't sure they want to act on the timeless impulses, to live the old story of men and women—to play the standards straight, so you can hear the melody.

Jazz musicians often speak of "telling a story" in their solos—improvising a line that's both shapely and evocative, coherent musically and emotionally. When we first see Jimmy and Rose, they haven't quite learned how to tell a story in this sense; they're just noodling, showing off their dexterity. In the way of the very young, they're proud of their facility in manipulating ideas and language; their flights of imagination are spontaneous, tossed-off, deliberately ephemeral. If there were any sweat involved in producing these inventions, the kids wouldn't enjoy them as much.

When Jimmy isn't roaming the promenade with Rose, he occasionally picks up a saxophone or sits down at a piano. His father, Sam (Donal McCann), repairs musical instruments and plays tenor sax in a group that appears nightly at a rather forlorn club: the band's book consists of hoary numbers like "Baubles, Bangles, and Beads," taken at tempos stately enough for senior citizens to dance to without fear. Jimmy has the natural talent that his father (by Sam's own admission) never had, but he never practices. Sam keeps trying to cajole his son into joining him on the bandstand; on the rare occasions when Jimmy allows himself to be persuaded, he blows a few desultory choruses and tries to get off the stage as quickly as he can. Jimmy's reluctance to do anything with his musical ability is, of course, a rebuke to his father: the prospect of surpassing the old man isn't worth the risk of becoming him. This father-son relationship is a complicated one, clouded by the absence of Jimmy's mother. Sam has told him that she's dead, and Jimmy knows nothing about who she was, because his father won't answer his questions. Jimmy hasn't the faintest idea how to feel about her. He won't assume his father's emotions toward her; he doesn't want anything secondhand.

Neil Jordan lives in Bray, and he spent part of his childhood there. This movie, his sixth, has the emotional fluency of memories that have sprung to life in a way that, finally, makes sense of them. *The Miracle* is a clear, complete vision of experience: everything we see (and hear) flows into everything else, with an unpredictable rightness. Jordan's camera moves with a kind of meditative grace, framing and reframing the characters as if to capture the most delicate momentary changes in their relationships. (The cinematographer, Philippe Rousselot, is a master of lighting and composition.) While Jordan has shown enormous talent in his previous pictures, he proves in this movie that he can tell a story in every sense. Learning to tell your own story—or, rather, learning to live the old stories as if they were your own—is the true subject of *The Miracle*, the theme that ultimately rises out of the artfully arranged background. The hero's story really begins when he and Rose spot a beautiful blond woman (Beverly D'Angelo) getting off the Dublin train. She's the woman we saw in the movie's suggestive initial image, and the kids latch on to her. For once, though, they disagree on who one of their characters should turn out to be. Rose's reaction is "She's looking for something"; Jimmy prefers to think that the glamorous stranger is running away from something, a terrible secret in her past. (They're both right.) They're out of synch in a more fundamental respect, too. Rose treats this latest find with her customary nonchalance: as soon as they've come up with the usual succinct characterization, she assumes, she and Jimmy can move on to something new. But Jimmy is inclined to linger. The mature, unapproachable-looking woman in dark glasses stirs him in a way he can't account for. She becomes for him an object of contemplation, even an obsession. He wants to follow her farther than the game with Rose allows, to go deeper and deeper into her story; where this woman's concerned, he can't be satisfied with a handful of deft phrases. He strikes up a conversation with her, and then pursues her, in Bray and in Dublin, with an ardor that's partly sexual and partly something else—a feeling so muddled and inchoate that he can't put a name to it. Jimmy keeps prodding this woman, who looks almost as confused as he does, to reveal her whole life to him; he seems to be acting out of an obscure sense that she can (in the words of Billie Holiday) tell him more and more, and then some.

The story she has to tell (but never quite does, not fully) is an ancient one. "The oldest," says Rose, who knows her archetypes. It's older than "Star Dust," the melody that haunts this movie: the song is played over and over again, by different people, in different settings, and expresses, with each new version, different shades of feeling. In one of the picture's most brilliant scenes, D'Angelo and Byrne perform an impromptu duet of the song at a party in a Dublin pub. She sings that unfamiliar introductory verse a cappella, and then, as she moves into the melody, Jimmy begins to accompany her on piano. She turns, startled, at the sound of his first, soft chord, but doesn't miss a beat, and the camera glides with her as she wanders back and forth between the piano and the microphone. Sometimes she's by herself in the frame, sometimes she shares it with Jimmy, and Jordan doesn't cut until their lovely performance is over. The music, the visual compositions, and the characters' emotions all seem to have come together, to have been gathered into the worn material of "Star Dust": we feel as if we'd never really heard the song before. Later, even Sam has a go at it. On a night in Bray when all the characters' stories are reaching their climax, he stands on the dance-hall stage and rips a heartfelt, powerful solo out of his horn: he produces sounds he didn't know he had in him. The last "Star Dust," played over the closing credits by the young English saxophonist Courtney Pine, is something else again: a slightly harsher-toned, more jagged version, in which a modern sense of dislocation mixes with old-fashioned romantic yearnings.

In *The Miracle* we sense the presence of a filmmaker who's on an incredible roll; every note Jordan tries for, no matter how wild, comes out pure and drops right into place. His imagery draws on some pretty outré sources: among the picture's recurring motifs are an acrobat who balances herself on one finger, a statue of a dreamy-looking Christ, a Ferris wheel, a rose, a bad stage production of *Destry Rides Again*, a bunch of chattering nuns, and the inscrutable eye of a circus elephant. (Jordan might be making a little joke about Yeats's characterization of the youthful imagination; in his early work, the old poet said, he put all his circus animals on display.) There are several dream sequences, each of them brief and shocking: in one, Sam is offered the opportunity to buy his own coffin, and the salesmen won't allow him to pay in installments; in another,

Jimmy watches his father burst into flames. And the movie's climax—the miracle of the title—is a daring, flamboyant gesture. It
springs not from any supernatural source but from an unlikely,
exhilarating convergence of nature and imagination: it's a human
wonder. Jordan manages to unite everything—the florid imagery,
the dark emotional undertones, the flaky comedy, the astonishing
physical beauty of the Irish seacoast—into a single, unbroken
mood, a smooth arc connecting the past and the present, the familiar
and the unforeseen. In the final scene of *The Miracle*, Jimmy and
Rose stroll together on the promenade and discuss their recent
experiences. On one side of them is the crumbling town; on the
other is the elegant, always changing curve of the coastline. And
they're surrounded by a swirl of chaotic activity: creatures of all
shapes and sizes dart past them, willy-nilly. The teenagers appear
serene, unfazed. They walk purposefully, as if they had found their
way through the world's muddle of passions and sensations—as if
they had discovered, after their separate improvisations, that they
had arrived at the same place, in unexpected harmony.

The New Yorker, July 15, 1991

THE NAKED GUN 2½: THE SMELL OF FEAR *and* TERMINATOR 2: JUDGMENT DAY

The hero of *The Naked Gun 2½: The Smell of Fear* is a middle-aged police lieutenant named Frank Drebin (Leslie Nielsen). He's the most dangerous man in American movies. In the picture's opening sequence, this white-haired, blandly handsome cop is a guest at a formal White House dinner: he's being honored for having killed his one-thousandth drug dealer. With becoming modesty, he admits that his last two victims were a couple of pedestrians he ran over while backing out of a parking space. ("Luckily, they turned out to be drug dealers.") Summer after summer, Hollywood moviemakers compete with each other to create ever more implacable, indestructible action-movie icons: enforcers and avengers capable of wiping out legions of evildoers with a stroke of advanced technology. But no one runs up as impressive a body count as Frank Drebin, and he accomplishes his prodigious feats of mayhem without the benefit of either state-of-the-art weaponry or excessive machismo; he works in more mysterious ways. At the White House dinner, Drebin, unawed

312

by the setting or the company (which also includes the Mandelas and several corporate big shots), pays no attention to the president's little speech; all his attention is focused on cracking open the lobster on his plate. His concentration on the task at hand is absolute, though it lacks a certain finesse, and the woman he's sitting next to—Barbara Bush—is felled by his exertions. She winds up flat on her back, her legs waving helplessly in the air; she's a casualty of Frank Drebin's lethal weapon, which is utter obliviousness. In this manner, he lays waste dozens of baddies in the movie's next eighty minutes or so, and emerges triumphant; in the stirring final scene, he even gets the chance to subject the Bushes to further indignities. He's the most convincing hero figure on American screens this summer, because he really stands for something, embodies the virtues we all know lead to success: blind luck, a total lack of imagination, and brazen, unearned self-confidence.

This great character rose from humble beginnings, as the protagonist of a short-lived 1982 TV series called *Police Squad!*—a half-hour comedy made by the team of David Zucker, Jim Abrahams, and Jerry Zucker, in the freewheeling parodic style of their 1980 hit movie *Airplane!* The series, which was canceled after only four episodes, had an irresistible dopiness, a loose-cannon approach to comedy, which at its best recalled *The Goon Show*, Monty Python, and early Mel Brooks. The show featured some inspired running gags: each episode began with the announcement of a "special guest star," who would invariably be killed off ten seconds later, and ended with a "freeze-frame," a tableau of Drebin and his colleagues laughing and congratulating each other in the station house; this effect was achieved, however, not by holding a frame of film but by the actors' remaining stock-still while the cameras kept rolling. (In the funniest of these endings, a suspect escapes while the cops are playing statues.) When, six years after the series, the *Police Squad!* idea was resurrected as the first *Naked Gun* movie, David Zucker, who directed the film, had the sense not to mess with the defiantly cheesy ethos of the original: even on the big screen, the adventures of Drebin and his cohorts had the look of cheap, hasty TV action drama. And *NG2½*, also directed by David Zucker, is, happily, guided by the same low-rent aesthetic. It's oblivious of production values, narrative sense, and all the higher, finer aspects of the human spirit—of everything, that is, except the impulse to spray us with jokes and knock us out of our chairs.

The plot has to do with a conspiracy of energy-industry executives (headed by Robert Goulet) to silence an environmental expert (Richard Griffiths) who is about to deliver to the president a report recommending conservation and the development of alternative energy sources: the villains kidnap the idealistic scientist and substitute a double. There's a hint of a message here, but Zucker and his cowriter, Pat Proft, never allow it to slow down the picture's relentless barrage of slapstick, movie parodies, outrageous double-entendres, and cracked musical production numbers. When Griffiths finally gets to present his enlightened recommendations, at a huge Washington banquet, his speech puts all the assembled dignitaries to sleep; he's able to rouse them only by reading aloud a steamy passage from a paperback porn novel. Zucker's odd mixture of liberal decency and adolescent goofiness is surprisingly winning, and, in a way, the environmental theme is perfectly appropriate to the movie's form. *The Naked Gun 2½* is compact, unassuming, and speedy; it's energy-efficient.

Zucker's approach to humor is that of a committed recycler. For him, nothing's ever too trashy or worn out to be used again; what he practices is, in the truest sense, pulp comedy. The material of this picture is all abject, faded, discarded stuff, which he reclaims with tremendous affection and enthusiasm. The picture wallows in cop-show and action-movie conventions, and scatters pop-culture allusions indiscriminately. (Nielsen plays a parody version of the pottery-wheel lovemaking scene from *Ghost*, and he also gets to sing a lusty rendition of "Besame Mucho," in full gay-caballero regalia.) And Zucker lifts comic ideas from everywhere, as needed. There's one sequence that's taken directly from Monty Python, and at least a couple of Zucker's jokes are self-plagiarized—re-creations of sight gags from the *Police Squad!* series. The cast consists almost entirely of television and B-movie actors who look as if they had seen better days, or had never seen a good one: in addition to Nielsen and Goulet, the performers include Priscilla Presley (of Elvis and *Dallas*), George Kennedy (of the *Airport* movies), and O. J. Simpson (of car-rental ads and the NFL). The movie uses these junk-culture journeymen expertly and sort of respectfully. They've been selected, clearly, for their experience in maintaining straight faces while speaking ludicrous dialogue, and their game professionalism is very appealing.

Leslie Nielsen is the incarnation of the movie's redemptively silly values. This is an actor who before *Police Squad!* spent better than thirty years of hard labor in television and forgettable movies, usually cast as a smooth villain or an uninteresting second lead. In those roles, he used his soothing deep voice to project either menace or nice-guy sincerity, whichever was required; nothing more exciting was ever asked of him. By the time the role of Frank Drebin came around, Nielsen had become one of those actors who are so familiar that they're virtually invisible: ubiquitous presences in functional, old-fashioned entertainments. His ability to blend in with the middle-aged textures of series TV turns out to be the key to his success in the Zucker style of comedy. The genius of Nielsen's performance is that it evokes a type that just about everyone has run into at one time or another. He's the respectable, conservatively dressed businessman who sits next to you on an airplane, nods politely, makes some innocuous small talk, and then, having broken the ice, begins to ramble disconnectedly about whatever comes into his head—to drop his problems, his fantasies, and his crackpot opinions right in your seat-belted lap. In *Police Squad!* and the *Naked Gun* movies, Leslie Nielsen is—and plays Drebin as—a straight arrow who's finally letting go, giving in to his repressed impulses: he sings, he dances, he loves, he shoots to kill. This avuncular upholder of the public good is profoundly crazy. Nielsen combines B-movie earnestness, exuberant mugging (he has a terrific "uh-oh" expression), and a trouper's slightly desperate cheerfulness: he turns this rather alarming character into a sweet, ebullient lunatic—albeit one who's hell on innocent bystanders. We can feel the actor's joy at getting this opportunity to recycle himself. In one of the picture's most hilarious scenes, Goulet, who has captured the hero, declares, "I want the pleasure of killing him myself," and Nielsen, with inane aplomb, announces, "The pleasure is all mine." What Leslie Nielsen does with lines like that in *Naked Gun 2½* is beyond recycling; it's practically alchemy.

* * *

Even David Zucker would be hard-pressed to come up with a notion as ridiculous as the premise of *Terminator 2: Judgment Day*. The killer cyborg who was played by Arnold Schwarzenegger in the original *Terminator* (1984) has returned—only, this time he's the hero. In the first movie, Arnold's "character," the T-800 Terminator model, is sent back in time—from the year 2029 to 1984—with orders to kill a Los Angeles waitress named Sarah Connor (Linda Hamilton). The machines of the future, who rule the world, know that she will give birth to a son, John Connor, who will one day lead a guerrilla movement against them. The dominant machines don't want to take any chances: they want to nip this resistance thing in the bud, and the most efficient way is to make sure that John never gets born. Enter the Terminator, a hulking android with sophisticated programming: a smart bomb with muscles. He appears unstoppable—by either strength or cunning or conventional weapons—and he pursues Sarah with terrifying, inhuman doggedness. *The Terminator* is essentially a long chase picture, but the writer and director, James Cameron, varies the action ingeniously, and he manages to make Schwarzenegger both frightening and funny—funny *because* he's so frightening. Made on a relatively modest budget, *The Terminator* is one of the genre-movie classics of the eighties: a lean, witty science-fiction movie without great pretensions to significance.

The sequel, also written (with William Wisher) and directed by Cameron, is far less satisfying. It's an even longer chase than the first *Terminator*, and there isn't much tension this time. T-800 has joined the good guys; his mission now is to protect young John Connor (Edward Furlong), who has managed to get born and to become a pint-size juvenile delinquent. Sarah's in a mental institution, where she spends her time raving about murderous androids from the future and developing her upper-body strength. A more advanced Terminator model, the T-1000 (Robert Patrick), has just arrived in L.A. to have a go at eliminating John and ensuring that the future will continue to belong to the machines. This new Terminator isn't a brute: he's made of some sort of liquid metal, with shape-shifting properties, and he's sleeker and more versatile than the old Arnold model. The movie is full of spectacular action sequences and dazzling special effects, but the narrative doesn't have the snap of the original's; it's lumbering and monotonous, and it carries a heavy-handed antinuke message. The effects (by Stan Winston, among many, many others) are used like steroids—to turn an ordinary frame into something that can pass for powerful.

Even if the plotting were defter, *Terminator 2* wouldn't work, because the whole movie is based on the insane conceit that Arnold Schwarzenegger is the *underdog*. T-800 is almost human here: since he's been superseded by the spiffier model, we can see him as a vulnerable guy (or guyoid), and shed a tear when he sacrifices himself to save humanity from nuclear holocaust. (The alteration of history removes the need for John Connor to lead the resistance, and, presumably, leaves him free to become a common criminal.) This mutation of Schwarzenegger's screen persona is, to put it mildly, something of a stretch. It's probably a concession to his superstar status: he can't play a villain anymore, he wants to be a lovable giant. But the old-Terminator-as-martyr motif also seems to reflect James Cameron's sentimental sense of himself. Since the first *Terminator*, his movies (*Aliens*, *The Abyss*, and now this) have become unwieldy, leaden-footed behemoths, and he must be looking over his shoulder—both at the meaner, more agile B-movie self that made *The Terminator* and at the new-model pretenders who might be gaining on him.

The New Yorker, July 29, 1991

TRUST

Trust, the new movie by the young writer and director Hal Hartley, takes place entirely in a white, middle-class neighborhood of a forlorn-looking Long Island town. The kitchens and bedrooms and TV-dominated living rooms in which Hartley's characters spend most of their time have an odd anonymous quality, like spaceship cabins in a science-fiction movie. These rooms may be oppressive, even claustrophobic, but people huddle in them anyway, because what's outside seems worse: an atmosphere that's thin, inhospitable to life. The Long Island we see in *Trust* and in Hartley's previous film, *The Unbelievable Truth* (1990), is a bleak, featureless, neither-here-nor-there milieu. It's a place where anything can happen and almost nothing does—where parents and children, living together in tight quarters, torment and negotiate with each other just to create some drama for themselves. The landscape's as flat as a petri dish, and weird stuff grows in it: obsessions, stubborn neuroses, spectacular personality disorders, persistent low-grade anomie, and, very occasionally, some amazing bloom of imagination. Hartley's Long Island is a laboratory of identities, with all sorts of mutants and hybrids crowded together in insane profusion, and every now and then one of these fantastic creatures gets strong enough to attempt an escape. Perhaps only someone who grew up on Long Island, as Hartley did, would dare to present its middle-class culture as a kind of (wholly inadvertent) experiment in freedom. He seems to know that these drab, rootless suburban small towns can force people to define themselves—to invent themselves from scratch, if need be. In this sort of environment, any sense of what you're doing and why you're doing it—even if the action is destructive and the reasons are provisional—constitutes a moral triumph. Hartley's movies don't say that explicitly. They don't have to; their confident, fiercely original style is all the proof we need that it's possible to make something out of next to nothing—to create a self out of the suburban vacuum.

Like most truly distinctive styles, Hartley's is an amalgam of borrowed ideas. A given scene in *Trust* may remind you simultaneously of, say, early Godard, Robert Frank, a TV sitcom, and the no-budget horror classic *Carnival of Souls*, and yet seem like nothing you've ever seen before, because of the sheer improbability of the combination. Hartley mixes his disparate influences in an unmistakably personal way: no one else could have precisely this collection of stray notions in his head. Hartley's style is at once self-conscious and bizarrely innocent—allusive but never academic. And the heroes and heroines of his pictures are invariably young people who share his idiosyncratic approach to culture. Both *The Unbelievable Truth* and *Trust* are romantic comedies in which the lovers are passionate autodidacts: guys who have acquired specialized technical knowledge, random bits of philosophy, and impressive vocabularies while doing time in prison or reform school; and teenage girls who don't like school but read constantly, in their bedrooms and on the street, greedy for something they can use to help them make sense of their lives. In Hartley's world, these moody ex-cons and earnest high school girls are the only really interesting people around, because they're relatively unformed. They haven't settled into their personalities, like everyone else—the bitter housewives, the exhausted clock-punchers, the weaselly strivers. Their identities are still works in progress.

The hero of *Trust*, a thirtyish electronics whiz named Matthew (Martin Donovan), is a rumpled, chain-smoking depressive who lives with his widowed father (John MacKay). Matthew has the look of someone who doesn't care about anything; his job, at a plant that assembles low-quality computers, and his father, a macho domestic tyrant, keep him beaten down and dispirited. But there's an edge to his despair—traces of anger and humor, indicating that he hasn't yet been totally numbed by circumstances. In the refuge of his bedroom, he reads books on theoretical physics and fondles a hand grenade (a war souvenir of his father's), which, if the time came, could send him out of this life in a suitably sensational and ironic style. The movie's heroine, Maria (Adrienne Shelly, who was also the star of *The Unbelievable Truth*), looks at first like a typical Long Island teenager, and at first that's exactly what she is. She's a cartoon adolescent bimbo, strutting down the high school corridors in garish makeup, high heels, and a neon-orange mini. Her boyfriend (Gary Sauer), the quarterback of the school's football team, has made her pregnant, and on the day she breaks the news to everyone she begins to realize that the persona she's adopted isn't going to be much use to her in this situation. Her father calls her a tramp; she yells back at him and then slaps him, and as she walks out the door he collapses, dead of a coronary. (Maria doesn't learn of his death until later in her very bad day.) The quarterback, who's a self-infatuated hotshot with dreams of major-college stardom and an NFL contract, doesn't respond much more satisfyingly. He makes it clear that marriage to Maria isn't part of his career plan, and to drive the point home he tells her how he imagines her after childbirth: as a slovenly housewife, spending her days with one eye on the brat and the other on the tube. (She wouldn't, he thinks, be a stimulating enough mate for an ace like him.) This cruel vision shakes Maria up, and by the time she meets Matthew, a few hours later, she's had some further jolts. Her mother (Merritt Nelson), who holds Maria responsible for her father's death, has kicked her out of the house; a convenience-store clerk has tried to rape her; she has witnessed the abduction of a baby. These dire events mount up with preposterous speed, and Maria bounces from one to another like a pinball. When Matthew comes upon her, sprawled in an abandoned building with a spent six-pack of beer at her side, she looks like a young woman who's ready to change her life in a big, big way.

Maria has hit bottom fast; Hartley's accelerated exposition contrives to give her a lifetime of traumatic experience in about half a day. Having opened the movie with a tight close-up of Maria's face, set in the rock-hard attitude of someone who knows just how she wants to present herself to the world, Hartley spends the next half hour or so dismantling her, blowing that initial image (which is also her self-image) to bits. These early passages, which intercut the adventures of the heroine and scenes of Matthew's slightly more mundane troubles at work and at home, require some patience of the audience: the tone wobbles, the minor characters' heartlessness seems overscaled, and we're afraid that the movie is going to consist entirely of semisatiric humiliation scenes. But when Maria and Matthew find each other and begin to develop their losers' alliance—part romance, part tutorial, and part vaudeville act—the picture becomes fascinating. The story moves by surprising leaps (not all of them forward), with the rhythm of the main characters' erratic, uncertain progress toward an awareness of possibilities beyond their limited, cramped Long Island experience. *Trust* draws its narrative energy from their unpredictability. They're building themselves up from the flattest, lowest point imaginable, with unpromising materials, and on spongy ground. They have to do a lot of improvising.

To Hartley's credit, the story never turns inspirational. It never even comes close, because, although the movie respects its characters' impulse to make something better of their lives than what they've been offered, it doesn't define that something in any concrete way. There's no specific goal that they're trying to reach, no job, no relationship, no dream home for them to aspire to—nothing in sight, anyway. Hartley sets Maria and Matthew down in a world of negative possibilities—stifling families, soul-destroying workplaces, dreary tract houses—and watches while his young lovers try to figure out if there's anything in this environment that's worth salvaging. He's alert to the absurdities of their situation; he keeps the movie's tone dry, and makes the threatening, pervasive nothingness of the milieu grotesquely funny. Mostly, *Trust* plays as a series of twisted skits in which defenders of the Long Island way of life, like Maria's mother and Matthew's father, try to bully and manipulate their kids into being more like them. The parents and the children seem to be inhabiting different universes—they're rarely even in the same frame—and the disparity between the generations' worldviews becomes ludicrously, comically extreme. In this picture, ordinary domestic strife takes on a heightened, mock-epic quality.

Hal Hartley's manner in *Trust* is a risky blend of formal abstraction and dramatic realism, and it demands subtle, resourceful actors. Some of the supporting players here aren't quite equal to the challenge; they produce a few awkward, puzzling moments. But his stars are remarkable. Martin Donovan gives Matthew a gangling, disheveled charm. He shambles about like a junior Rodney Dangerfield and yet manages to be an attractive, romantic presence. He has a nice casual air about him—a wonderful nihilistic insouciance—when he knocks people off barstools or puts a coworker's head in a vise, and his bummed-out line readings are superbly timed. Adrienne Shelly brings off Maria's transformation from teenage temptress to serious young woman with extraordinary ease. Shelly has changeable, childlike features: she has the ability to look either intelligent or utterly vacant, either fragile or wiry-tough. It's difficult to imagine another young actress who could make this character's rapid about-face seem so natural. Under Hartley's direction, Shelly and Donovan invent an acting style for a genre that appears to have materialized out of nowhere. *Trust* is, of all things, an existentialist comedy of manners. It comes from the nowhere that its maker grew up in.

The New Yorker, August 12, 1991

BARTON FINK

The Coen brothers' *Barton Fink*, a macabre comedy about a blocked writer in 1941 Hollywood, is densely packed with allusions, clever dialogue, ingenious visual jokes, startling plot twists, and imaginative atmospheric effects, yet it feels thin. It's an empty tour de force, and what's dismaying about the picture is that the filmmakers (Joel Coen directed, Ethan Coen produced, and they wrote the script together) seem inordinately pleased with its hermetic meaninglessness. The Coens started out, in *Blood Simple* (1983) and *Raising Arizona* (1987), as genre-movie parodists and cynical wits—smart-alecky connoisseurs of trash. But in *Barton Fink*, as in last year's *Miller's Crossing*, the Coens appear to be taking their lack of seriousness seriously: they've become nihilist showoffs. The new film, which won the top prize at the most recent Cannes Film Festival, is the story of the disillusionment of a left-wing New York playwright, Barton Fink (John Turturro). On the strength of one successful play, called *Bare Ruined Choirs*, he's offered a contract to write screenplays for Capitol Pictures. He goes to L.A., checks into the seedy, depressing Hotel Earle, has a meeting with the head of the studio—a fat vulgarian named Lipnick (Michael Lerner)—and then tries to settle down to work on his first assignment, a wrestling picture for Wallace Beery. Understandably, Fink has a hard time finding anything to inspire him in this project; he sits in his hotel room, stares morosely at his typewriter, and feels defeated. For some reason, the studio hasn't provided him with an office, so Fink and his stalled

323

imagination are at the mercy of the thick, rotting ambience of the Earle: no sunlight or street noise ever seems to penetrate his solitude, but strange voices from adjoining rooms reach him with disconcerting clarity; the ornate, faded wallpaper keeps peeling off, and viscous paste drips down toward him; the staff consists of an ancient elevator operator and an ominously overeager desk man; the corridors are silent, deserted, and impossibly long, and the camera tracks along them slowly, as if to savor their voluptuous creepiness.

The setup of *Barton Fink* is tantalizing. The combination of the cheap, overdrawn Hollywood satire of Fink's initial scene with Lipnick and the luxurious horror-movie mood of the hotel scenes is potently weird. And the absurdity of the hero's situation has nice comic possibilities. Even the Coens' shameless movie in-jokes have, at first, a pleasantly disposable quality: the movie begins with a parody of a famous shot from *Citizen Kane*, which was released in 1941; the twisty, berserk dialogue in the Lipnick scene plays like an homage to Preston Sturges, whose 1941 comedy *Sullivan's Travels* was about the uneasy relationship between social consciousness and Hollywood entertainment; and the hotel sequences explicitly recall Stanley Kubrick's *The Shining*, whose monstrous protagonist is a man driven insane by his inability to write. There's no real weight to any of these allusions. They're sly, intricately constructed jokes, with delayed-action punch lines; if you get a Coen gag, you feel smart, but if you don't you haven't missed anything important. The minor amusements of the first twenty minutes or so of *Barton Fink* don't last, though. At a certain point, the filmmakers' playfulness begins to make us uncomfortable, because the Coens seem to be flaunting their facility and their lack of conviction, using them to ridicule the values of the movie's intense, idealistic hero.

The political fervor of writers like Clifford Odets, upon whom Barton Fink is obviously based, is easy enough to make fun of. The plays that Odets wrote in the thirties for the Group Theatre (the most well known are *Waiting for Lefty* and *Awake and Sing!*) are awkward, untidy mixtures of Chekhovian melancholy and agitprop speechifying. His language, which is a heightened rendering of Depression-era slang, sounds dated, and his ideology, which is founded on the hope that oppressed workers would liberate themselves through collective action, now feels naive. But Odets wasn't a phony, or a buffoon, or a talentless hack. Barton Fink is all those things, and the Coens treat this emblematic figure of thirties culture with merciless contempt. The movie is designed to visit ever more grotesque indignities on a character who's pitiful from the outset, and there's not much fun in that. At first, Fink seems merely a wimpy, distracted intellectual, a head-in-the-clouds type who's easily befuddled by the bluster and vigorous pragmatism of men like Lipnick. But when Fink starts trying to write the Wallace Beery vehicle, he comes across as a fraud, too—not even enough of a professional to bang out a routine B-movie script. And then the film exposes him as a self-absorbed poseur: in his first conversation with his next-door neighbor, an affable insurance salesman called Charlie (John Goodman), Fink condescendingly refers to his new acquaintance as a "common man," and launches into a didactic rant about politics and theater, ignoring Charlie's every attempt to get a word in edgewise. This pompous jerk Fink, we're given to understand, is interested in the common man only as an abstraction; with the real thing sitting three feet away from him, he'd rather lecture than listen. It's at this point that the humor of *Barton Fink* starts turning sour. For the rest of the picture, the Coens devote themselves to the project of punishing their hero for his fatuousness, his incompetence, his intellectual vanity. It's a cruel exercise, and the glee with which the filmmakers invent torments for Fink is disturbing. The idea seems to be that Fink, the monastic theorist of social realism, needs to have his nose rubbed in some unpleasant realities. The Coens' notion of reality, however, is as abstract as their hero's idealized conception of the common man. When the movie gets violent and ugly, the gruesomeness is less shocking than simply alienating. Joel Coen's smooth, precisely choreographed, decorative camera style gives even the most horrifying events a high gloss; the movie makes its argument, proceeds from its hypothesis to its conclusion, with the polished, haughty manner of a professor delivering a lecture that he's been trotting out for years.

In effect, the Coens, whose interests are purely academic, take it upon themselves to convict and sentence their protagonist for the crime of isolation from the real world. Or perhaps Barton Fink deserves his comeuppance solely on the basis of taste: it's gauche to proclaim belief, in anything. *Barton Fink* is just a joke, a game with the audience, but bad faith curdles the humor, and the Coens set things up so that the last laugh—a dry, knowing one—is theirs. Their prankish formalism becomes very irritating in the course of this picture. The style of *Barton Fink* is all curlicues and embellishments: we feel as if we were sitting in a bleak room and staring at the intricate patterns of the wallpaper. (At times, Joel Coen's baroque technique—his meticulous arrangement of overhead shots and zooms and blackouts and tracks in and out—achieves the insufferable elegance of Alain Resnais.) And John Turturro, who is in every scene, performs in a style that matches the filmmakers', gimmick for gimmick. His Barton Fink is the most fanatically detailed caricature of a nerd since the heyday of Jerry Lewis. The way Turturro plays this leftist intellectual, the movie might as well have been called *The Nutty Pinko*: he gapes and blinks and stammers and contorts his body into ungainly poses, and his mouth never seems to close. Like the Coens, he's an inexhaustible inventor of bizarre, arresting shtick. And his inventions, like theirs, are essentially pointless and diversionary—doodles in the margins of a page with no text.

Maybe the best way to understand the Coens—to put their intellectual agility and their fundamental coldness in perspective—is to think of them as jaded graduate students amusing themselves by working up rarefied, wittily erudite interpretations of their favorite authors. *Miller's Crossing* is like a deluxe, annotated edition of the collected works of Dashiell Hammett. *Barton Fink* seems to be trying to give the same treatment to Nathanael West, whose short, ferocious satiric novels were published in the thirties, the time of Odets's greatest success. It's not a by-the-numbers pastiche, as *Miller's Crossing* is, but neither film does justice to its source. West's novels—*A Cool Million*, *Miss Lonelyhearts*, and *The Day of the Locust* (which is set in Hollywood)—are strange fables of innocence and corruption, in which naive heroes are invariably crushed by the world's pitiless indifference to their good intentions. West presents the defeat of his hapless innocents with swift, cruel humor, which makes him seem more modern than someone like Odets; there's nothing inspirational, or even vaguely hopeful, in Nathanael West. But there is in him, as in all genuine satirists, a core of moral outrage. His protagonists are *true* innocents, not highbrow fakers, and we sense his anger that these poor fools are destined to get ground into little pieces by the harsh social machinery of Depression-era America. What the Coens give us in this picture is a version of West in which the style has been refined (West's was brisk, clipped, and inelegant) and the sensibility has been coarsened. *Barton Fink* is just a fancy metaphysical splatter movie, and it's unsatisfying in every way. There's nothing at stake in the filmmakers' systematic dismantling of their hero and all he stands for—except, perhaps, their desire to demonstrate their superiority to the ethics and aesthetics of an earlier time. (Even Faulkner, in the guise of an alcoholic Southern novelist played by John Mahoney, takes his licks from the Coens.) It's tempting to imagine the response of Clifford Odets to the Coens' smug, preening jokiness. The first line of his first play, *Waiting for Lefty*, would do nicely: "You're so wrong I ain't laughing."

The New Yorker, September 9, 1991

FRANKIE & JOHNNY

Frankie & Johnny, the movie version of Terrence McNally's 1987 play *Frankie and Johnny in the Clair de Lune*, is a sweet-tempered romantic comedy whose main characters are a New York coffee-shop waitress (Frankie) and a short-order cook (Johnny). The names, of course, recall those of the couple in the famous song, but McNally's characters don't resemble the tragic lovers in any other way. For the cook, however, this trivial coincidence is loaded with significance: it's an indication, he keeps telling the skeptical object of his desire, that he and she were meant to be lovers, and why fight destiny? In Johnny's highly selective interpretation of this sign from the heavens, fate does not ordain that he's going to do her wrong and she's going to shoot him dead: the song's first line says "Frankie and Johnny were lovers," and as far as he's concerned the rest doesn't count. This is only one of many dubious but tenaciously argued positions that Johnny takes in his campaign to win Frankie's undying love. He bombards her with charm, jokes, romantic rhetoric, quotations from Shakespeare, auto-biographical pathos, beautiful music, and heartfelt (though not terribly rigorous) philosophizing. He's the most eclectic and exhausting suitor imaginable, and he's too much for Frankie, who's determined not to expose herself to the pain and uncertainty of a serious relationship. The play, in which Frankie and Johnny were the only characters and all the action took place in one night and on one set, was essentially a long sparring match, a comic clash between sharply opposed attitudes toward romantic love—Johnny's let's-do-it optimism versus Frankie's stubborn, defensive pessimism. In a sense, the play was an exercise in stripping down romantic comedy to its most basic component—two people sizing each other up and trying to figure out whether they want to be together.

The form of the play is much too stark for the movies. McNally, adapting his work for the screen, has expanded and drastically rearranged his original story. He and the film's director, Garry Marshall, have attempted to place Frankie and Johnny in a variety of settings and situations, to stretch the narrative out over a longer period, to surround the lovers with lots of other people—and to incorporate all this extra material without dissipating the emotional tensions of the main characters' relationship. Romantic comedy isn't really a complex genre. All the writer has to do is keep our attention focused on a single question: Will they or won't they? The only tricky part is sustaining the illusion that the outcome isn't inevitable—inventing obstacles and diversions to scatter over the course of true love. The guiding principle of the genre is perilously extended anticipation; the best romantic comedies make us laugh at the pleasure of delayed gratification. McNally's screenplay keeps that principle in view. In giving a fuller narrative shape to Frankie and Johnny's relationship—making explicit the events that were only implicit in the play's all-night postcoital negotiating session—McNally actually enhances the story's romantic suspense. The movie shows us the lovers' initial meeting, Johnny's persistent efforts to get Frankie to go out with him, their first date (and first sex), a tense cooling-off period, and, finally, a long night of conversation in which the lovers, popping in and out of Frankie's sofa bed, fumble their way toward a sort of understanding. The dramatic structure of the movie is more conventional than that of the play, but it almost has to be; in a film, the stylized, concentrated form of the theater piece would seem a tedious conceit, a distraction. The strength of the play was its simplicity and its directness; the movie preserves those qualities by telling the story in the ordinary, straightforward Hollywood manner. *Frankie & Johnny* is now a vehicle for Al Pacino and Michelle Pfeiffer, and that's as it should be, too; in the movies, there's nothing simpler and nothing more direct than the sight of actors we love pretending to fall in love with each other. Pacino and Pfeiffer are more glamorous than the characters they're playing, but, in a weird way, their star power is perfectly appropriate here: it's the meat-and-potatoes stuff of big-budget movie entertainment.

Besides, the presence of Pacino and Pfeiffer guarantees that our interest in the main characters' relationship won't be overwhelmed by all the supporting characters and peripheral activity that McNally and Marshall have added. The film takes us outside the room where Frankie and Johnny argue and make love, and into a densely populated world. The coffee shop has a full cast of characters: an amiable Greek owner (Hector Elizondo) with a huge supply of relatives, some of whom he recruits for brief, unsatisfying stints behind the cash register; a bizarre crew of veteran waitresses, of whom the most prominent are a cynical flirt named Cora (Kate Nelligan) and a chain-smoking old maid named Nedda (Jane Morris); an assortment of cooks, kitchen helpers, and busboys, each of them with his own special quirk; and a constant flow of customers, as crazily diverse as you would expect the clientele of a Manhattan coffee shop to be. The movie also provides Frankie with a sympathetic neighbor: a wry, wisecracking gay man, Tim (Nathan Lane), who appears to have unrestricted access to her tiny apartment. It's tempting to think of him as the Rhoda figure here—and, for that matter, to think of the coffee shop as the equivalent of the *Mary Tyler Moore Show* newsroom. The style that McNally and Marshall have adopted for the picture is a kind of sitcom classicism, whose indispensable elements are a wacky workplace filled with benign eccentrics and an apartment building with at least one resident capable of bursting into the main character's apartment and reeling off a string of tart one-liners. Before Marshall became a movie director (*The Flamingo Kid*, *Pretty Woman*), he spent years writing, producing, and directing television comedies, and he knows how to make this sort of thing work. He's almost too proficient. Even as you're enjoying the deft timing of the jokes and the expert handling of the bit players (Nelligan and Lane are both hilarious), you may get the uncomfortable feeling that what you're watching could, with virtually no alteration, be spun off into a half-hour weekly series; at times the picture gives you the even more disturbing sense that it was designed for that.

But the stars' performances elevate the material; they supply *Frankie & Johnny* with movie-scale authority and resonance. Pacino's Johnny is a terrifically funny and persuasive portrait of a pesky, in-your-face romantic. At one point in his continuing argument with Frankie, Johnny shakes his head in disbelief at her mulishness and says, "This all should be so easy. Why does it have to be so damn hard?" He just can't believe how much energy it's taking to convince her that she should surrender herself to him, body and soul, forever and ever. (His attitude could be summed up in a line from Frank O'Hara's poem "Meditations in an Emergency": "I am the least difficult of men. All I want is boundless love.") To him, the romantic scenario in his head—marriage, kids, endless bliss—is clear, complete, and blindingly obvious, and he doesn't see any reason not to lay the whole thing on Frankie immediately; it doesn't occur to him that a more patient, less pressuring approach might be more effective. Johnny is in his late forties; he's divorced and he rarely sees his children; he has just been released from prison, where he spent eighteen months for forging a check. He's eager to make a fresh start in life, and he isn't inclined to waste time. Meeting Frankie gets him so excited that he can't help blurting out his feelings for her, whether she's ready for them or not: he has a problem with premature articulation. Johnny is an antsy ex-depressive; his amazing, overbearing intensity is the manic enthusiasm of someone who knows what it's like to feel utterly defeated. This is a wonderful role for Pacino. He brings out the comedy and the ambiguity of a middle-aged man's sense of emotional rebirth: he's exuberant, touching, and a little scary.

Pfeiffer is extraordinary. In this picture, she doesn't appear to be wearing any makeup, and her hair just hangs there, and her wardrobe is unglamorous (mostly jeans and a frumpy waitress's uniform); she still looks smashing. (McNally's description of Frankie in the play script—"striking, but not conventional, good looks"—is apt if you read "not conventional" to mean "supernatural.") Her Frankie is beautiful in the way of a woman who doesn't know that she's beautiful, or doesn't want to know. Pfeiffer makes us understand that being attractive to men hasn't, so far, done Frankie a lot of good—that she'd rather play down her looks than risk attracting more trouble. The actress seems to bring together in this character the different qualities of several of the women she has portrayed onscreen in the past few years: the tough cookies of *Married to the Mob* and *The Fabulous Baker Boys*; the reluctant Mme. de Tourvel of

Dangerous Liaisons, trying desperately to repel the advances of an implacable suitor; the honest, reserved Soviet heroine of *The Russia House*. And this is a role that requires her to use everything that she has learned from her previous work. Frankie is, in her closed-off way, a far more volatile character than Johnny, because, unlike him, she's never quite sure how she feels or who she wants to be: she veers between the urge to surrender to her lover's vision of her and the impulse to resist that temptation at all costs. Her feelings change course very quickly, and Pfeiffer, without doing anything showy, makes every one of these emotional shifts lucid and thrillingly natural. Frankie isn't a happy woman, but Pfeiffer never lets the character become drab or mopey. The story wouldn't work at all if Frankie weren't, in some sense, as passionate and willful as Johnny: we have to feel that there's as much energy and vigor in her defensiveness as there is in his aggressiveness. Although it's perfectly apparent to us that Frankie has allowed herself to settle for a life of low expectations and modest rewards, there's something perversely bracing in the way she fends off Johnny's attempt to invade her narrow emotional turf. Her ferocity is a sign of life, and Pfeiffer does full justice to it. This is a superbly detailed rendering of a woman with a fanatically conservative heart.

What makes *Frankie & Johnny* such an enjoyable picture is that the relationship of its battling lovers is a striking (but not conventional) representation of the fundamental tension that drives romantic comedy. Johnny, with his inexplicable certainty that he and Frankie are destined to love each other for the rest of their lives, speaks to the part of us that *knows,* as we follow this sort of story, that everything's going to turn out fine. Frankie speaks to the part of us that wants to postpone the inevitable. She won't just give in to Johnny's fully developed romantic script, accept the whole package on faith; she has to study it, to figure out how its details add up, to decide—in her own sweet time—whether this story makes sense for her. (She has the temperament of an extremely demanding critic.) The classic Hollywood romantic comedies of the thirties usually delayed the gratification of the happy ending by external means: they used the plot mechanics of farce to generate the mishaps and misunderstandings that would keep the lovers apart for ninety minutes or so. In *Frankie & Johnny* McNally produces the exquisitely attenuated pleasure of romantic comedy by a different method: the obstacles in the path of love are all internal. That's why, despite the new characters and settings that the writer has invented for the movie, *Frankie & Johnny* is still essentially a two-character piece. The machinery of farce—the opening and closing doors, the unlikely hiding places, the hastily assembled disguises—is felt rather than seen, because it's inside Frankie and Johnny. As we watch them, we can sense the thoughts and emotions that are scurrying across the private movie screens in their heads. And when the farce is played out and the lights come up, for Frankie and Johnny and for us, we understand why romance and comedy make an ideal, inevitable couple.

The New Yorker, October 21, 1991

LIFE IS SWEET

Over the last twenty years, the prolific English writer and director Mike Leigh has created an extraordinarily rich body of work for television, the theater, and the cinema, and very little of it has been seen by American audiences. Most of us on this side of the Atlantic became aware of Leigh only a couple of years ago, when his feature *High Hopes* was released here. That film, which was simultaneously a riotous satire on British class consciousness and a rueful meditation on the Thatcherite transformation of everyday life, showed a startlingly original sensibility. *High Hopes* was loose, playful, exploratory; it felt, that is, more like the work of an enthusiastic first-time filmmaker than like that of a mature, established artist. And Leigh's new movie, *Life Is Sweet*, has the same youthful quality—the exuberance and the autobiographical-seeming emotional intimacy of a first film. In the past couple of weeks, I've seen, on videotape, Leigh's actual first feature, which was shot in 1971, as well as seven of the TV films he made between the early seventies and the late eighties, and these films, along with *High Hopes* and *Life Is Sweet*, trace a pattern of artistic development unlike that of any other contemporary filmmaker. It's just about impossible to detect any advance in technical sophistication from his earliest works to his most recent ones; neither his visual ideas nor his sense of dramatic structure has become noticeably more "professional" over the years. One film, from whatever period, looks much like any other. Most of them carry the peculiar credit "Devised and Directed by Mike Leigh," because

334

his pieces are the products of workshop-style collaboration with his casts: the stories evolve from the actors' improvisations on the characters that the director has given them. This is, of course, a risky method of making feature-length films, and other directors who have tried it have usually produced drab, aggressively tedious works, with a lot of shouting and encounter-session truthtelling. Mike Leigh has succeeded in avoiding the pitfalls of the group-improvisation approach to dramatic composition, because he refuses to force meanings out of the situations that he sets up. He proceeds from genuine curiosity about how people live and how they manage to get along with each other, and his filmmaking method is a way of ensuring that each new set of characters and circumstances will be looked at from a fresh, unbiased perspective. He's interested not in demonstrating general, abstract truths but in discovering small, particular ones, so he could go on making this sort of film forever without having to worry about repeating himself. Every time, Leigh and his actors are starting from scratch, and he shapes the films so that the initial excitement of exploring characters can still be felt in the finished product.

In *Life Is Sweet* Leigh takes us into the domestic life of a lower-middle-class family in Middlesex. The characters are, by conventional standards, ordinary people, but they aren't dreary, and their actions aren't predictable; the movie doesn't treat anyone as a type. Wendy (Alison Steadman) is an attractive, ebullient middle-aged woman who works in a children's-clothing shop and conducts dance classes for little girls. She's always on the move, always doing something, and she accompanies her activities with a steady stream of chatter and jokes and high-pitched nasal laughter. Wendy is hilariously tireless, but she doesn't wear her family (or us) out. She isn't self-important; she buzzes around without insisting that anyone pay special attention to her. Her husband, Andy (Jim Broadbent), a chef who supervises the staff of a huge institutional kitchen, has a more phlegmatic sort of charm. He's an amiable dawdler, a guy who starts ambitious home-improvement projects and never quite gets around to finishing them. On his days off, he sets out, with the best of intentions, for his shed at the back of the yard, and then spends a bit of time meditating on the junk and bric-a-brac that he's accumulated over the years; then, maybe, a pal drops by, they chat awhile, have a beer, go for a quick ride; and when they get back it's time for tea and another day has somehow slipped away. Wendy and Andy are the parents of twins, Natalie (Claire Skinner) and Nicola (Jane Horrocks), who live at home. The twins are probably a year or two out of school, and they're ludicrously unalike. Natalie is a quiet, serious, dignified girl with a tidy short haircut. Sensibly, she has learned a trade: she's a plumber. Nicola, however, is a parents' nightmare. Her only occupation seems to be to make everyone aware, at every moment, of how much she hates her life. Hiding behind glasses and a mess of straggly hair, she responds with snarls and contemptuous epithets to even the most innocuous attempts at conversation; she generally refuses to eat, because she has a horror of fat (she's excruciatingly thin); and although she doesn't appear to derive any pleasure from the company of her parents and her sister, she never leaves the house—she's always hanging about, looking sullen and neurotically alert, waiting for the opportunity to blurt out something shrill and horrible and bring everybody down. Nicola also has an impressive array of nervous tics: hair-tugging, face-scratching, the works.

At the beginning of *Life Is Sweet*, Leigh just plops us into the middle of this family's unruly everyday life. He doesn't give us an obvious narrative hook—a clear sense of what the story is going to be or what sort of dramatic revelations he may have in store for us. And, despite Nicola's relentless negativity, the tone is light and casual. We sense right away that her bratty outbursts are simply accepted as part of the normal texture of life in this household; they're annoying, but they don't spark the flaming rows that Nicola seems to hope for. We find ourselves laughing at her strenuous efforts to get a real rise out of her parents and her sister, and laughing, too, at how unruffled they are by her provocations. In Leigh's world, the ordinary and the bizarre often live under one roof, and not as uncomfortably as one might imagine: there's a comic wisdom in the way this family accommodates the alien presence of an inexplicably unhappy child. Whatever Wendy and Andy may have expected of a daughter, Nicola certainly isn't it; they don't spend a lot of time fretting about what went wrong, though—they're well past that point. In a sense, *Life Is Sweet* is a naturalistic examination of one of the primary sources of British humor: the insouciance with which people accept the incongruous, and proceed as if nothing unusual were going on. And Leigh's muddling-through characters are easy for us to identify with, because, as we feel our way into the movie, we, too, are sorting out jumbled impressions—measuring this leisurely, almost haphazard experience against our expectations of proper dramatic form—and at a certain point we can feel ourselves giving in to the erratic flow of events, and taking things as they come.

Leigh's unconventional storytelling gives his movies a strange kind of suspense. Every scene and every new character seems to give rise to a fresh set of narrative possibilities, and there's no way to predict which of them will be elaborated upon and which will remain, to the end, suggestive diversions. When, about half an hour into the picture, an oddball family friend named Aubrey (Timothy Spall) comes visiting and joins the ensemble, we have no idea what to make of him. He's an outlandish caricature: a pudgy, balding lonely guy who dresses and speaks as if he were the coolest of young bachelors. (His averted-gaze manner suggests, however, that this act isn't entirely convincing even to him.) Aubrey is immediately and explosively funny; he seems to have come out of nowhere, and we have every reason to believe that after a brief scene or two this broadly conceived character will drop out of sight. Instead, Aubrey dominates the movie for long stretches. He's preparing to open a small restaurant, called The Regret Rien, which will embody his highly original idea of upscale, trendy cuisine. The menu promises exotic delights for the jaded yuppie palate: tripe soufflé; black-pudding-and-Camembert soup; pork cyst; liver in lager; tongues in a rhubarb hollandaise sauce. This absurdly wrongheaded enterprise provides opportunities for extended sequences of wild slapstick; Leigh isn't timid about juxtaposing radically different tones. Although the Aubrey sequences should probably have been trimmed by a few minutes, there are some big laughs in them, and they have the effect of keeping the audience off balance: we're never able to settle into a single mood, to allow ourselves the comfort of knowing what sort of reaction will be demanded of us next.

Leigh doesn't manipulate our responses; he roughs them up a little, though. By means of a dense texture of tiny behavioral details and disconcerting shifts of style, he attempts to reshuffle our emotions. He prepares us to accept the moments of piercing, almost miraculous clarity that arise, as if by happy accident, at the end of his best films. These moments are modest, unspectacular: if we were primed for a grand dramatic climax, we would be disappointed. *Life Is Sweet* ambles along for nearly an hour and a half without seeming especially concerned about where it's headed, and then, long after we've given up trying to figure out what the whole thing is supposed to mean, Leigh comes up with a stunning scene in which Wendy and Nicola discuss Nicola's dissatisfaction with life. This isn't a conversation that either of them has appeared to be building up to, or perhaps ever expected to have, but as it progresses we sense how this moment of mutual unguarded honesty has emerged from the apparent chaos of the women's recent experiences. And we realize, too, that Mike Leigh's unusual filmmaking process is designed to generate scenes like this, to bring forth acting that is as pure and direct as Alison Steadman's and Jane Horrocks'. Leigh's conception of dramatic structure has nothing to do with resolving elaborate plots, or teasing out shattering revelations of dark secrets, or engineering life-changing confrontations. What he's searching for in his movies is the possibility of seeing the world through someone else's eyes—someone specific, whose life can be shared only through patient observation of its random and stubbornly idiosyncratic details. His art consists of making such moments of sudden, profound understanding seem worth any amount of pain, muddle, and slapstick catastrophe.

The New Yorker, November 4, 1991

BLACK ROBE

The title of Bruce Beresford's unusual and absorbing new film, *Black Robe*, refers to the long cassocks worn by Jesuit missionaries in North America in the seventeenth century. The zealous priests were part of the early days of French exploration in the New World; while explorers like Champlain plunged into the wilderness, claimed land, and established settlements, the Jesuits who traveled alongside them were out to claim the souls of the Algonquian, Huron, and Iroquois Indians who inhabited that wilderness. The priests considered these people savage and godless, and the Indians called the missionaries "Blackrobes"—an ominous, mythic-sounding name for figures who were of all the white intruders surely the most disturbing and the least comprehensible. *Black Robe*, which is based on Brian Moore's 1985 novel of that name (Moore himself did the screenplay), is a culture-clash drama in which the most important conflicts take place in the realm of the spirit. The hero is a pale and excruciatingly pious young Jesuit called Father Laforgue (Lothaire Bluteau), who sets out from the Quebec settlement on a journey up the St. Lawrence and Ottawa rivers. His destination is a remote mission among the Hurons. Father Jerome, the Jesuit in charge there, hasn't been heard from for too long, and his superiors in Quebec are worried. Laforgue is to find out what's going on; it's understood that he will take over the mission if Father Jerome is dead.

As Laforgue heads upriver with a reluctant escort of Algonquians, we begin to understand why the Indians and the priests are so

fearful and suspicious of each other. The differences between Laforgue and the Algonquian chief, Chomina (August Schellenberg),
aren't matters of social organization or moral codes. The world
views of Laforgue and Chomina are so radically opposed that at
times the two men seem unable even to acknowledge each other as
human. The priest and the Indian, making their way together to the
distant mission, are sharing experience in only the most literal, limited sense. We feel at every moment that Laforgue and Chomina
aren't seeing or hearing the same things—that they aren't living the
same history. These characters don't engage in philosophical de-
bates; there's nothing to talk about. Most stories of this sort are
framed so that the characters can "learn" from each other: people
from different cultures wind up looking into each other's eyes and
thinking, These people have something good. Often, though, this
cross-cultural understanding seems to have been accomplished in a
facile way—by treating the features of complex, integrated cultures
as if they were merely life-style choices. *Black Robe* offers no easy
way out of the spiritual impasse between the Jesuits and the Indians,
and the characters are presented without concessions to twentieth-
century sensibilities. Laforgue and Chomina are as alien to us as they
are to each other.

Laforgue is the strangest, most difficult hero in recent movies.
Looking at him, you do not think of a modern Jesuit—not the
fiendishly ingenious intellectuals who befuddle students in American high schools and universities, and not the liberation-theology
activists who work in the Third World. The Jesuit in *Black Robe* is an
old-fashioned true believer. He prays, he reads Scripture, he struggles to resist fleshly temptations; he lives only to serve the one true
God of Catholicism. For him, the material world is nothing, an
illusion: all nature is just the antechamber to Heaven, and the body
is the cell in which the soul counts the days until its release. Aspiring
to a state of pure, incorporeal spirituality, Laforgue often seems
inhuman, lifeless, spectral. He's a spooky guy, and it's easy to see
why the Indians he means to convert find his values so resistible;
many of them think he's a demon. Laforgue, the Father from another
planet, is so bizarre that any other world view should, by contrast,
look pretty attractive. Chomina and the rest of the Algonquians do
at least live by a philosophy that allows for sensual pleasure; they

don't deny the reality of the physical world or reduce day-to-day existence to the status of diligent, joyless preparation for a blissful afterlife. Their vision of nature is animistic—the spirits of the dead speak through birds and animals and rivers and trees—and they believe in the truth of dreams. The movie's portrayal of the Indians' mysticism is straightforward, unromanticized; it has an anthropological detachment. The signs and portents that come to Chomina are always ambiguous and often unreliable: disturbed by dream images, he consults his wife and his friends and a shaman (a nasty-spirited dwarf) for their interpretations, and the ideas that they give him are confusing and contradictory. He's never quite sure how he should act on his visions. If the priest's world seems thin and insubstantial, the Indian's is perhaps too rich; Chomina often appears to be wandering uncertainly through a blizzard of meanings.

Moore and Beresford show extraordinary respect for the stubborn, almost impenetrable otherness of their historical characters. *Black Robe* dares to build a story around people whom contemporary audiences couldn't possibly identify with. This is a movie we have to feel our way into—tentatively, gradually—and it accumulates emotional force as it goes along. It's an adventure story in the truest sense: the filmmakers lead us into unknown territory, and keep pushing us farther and farther on, until, by the end, we find ourselves deep in the wilderness of the seventeenth-century consciousness. We're not entirely at home there, but at least we're able to figure out where we are—to recognize some of the moral and philosophical coordinates of this strange new world. Despite the movie's rigor, it never feels austere or merely academic. The story has plenty of action, in the James Fenimore Cooper manner—ambushes, escapes, tense confrontations. Even when nothing dramatic is happening, the movie is suspenseful: we're constantly aware of danger—and aware, too, that the Huron mission at the end of the journey might be the scene of an appalling catastrophe. And the late-autumn and winter landscapes in which the action is set are piercingly lovely: the river is broad and sinuous, and it cuts through tree-covered mountains; the skies have the mysterious dull-gray beauty of pewter; and the snow, when it comes, gives a kind of radiance to everything. Beresford and his cinematographer, Peter James, have provided *Black Robe* with a voluptuous surface, and the movie's visual splendor is more than decoration. These views of natural phenomena have a clarity that's almost unreal: paradoxically, they seem to justify both the Indians' animism and the Jesuits' sense of the world as illusion. Beresford (*Driving Miss Daisy*, *Mister Johnson*) puts his characteristic pictorialism to good use here. *Black Robe* has real sweep, and its beauties are expressive; this is the best filmmaking he has ever done.

By the end of the picture, Moore and Beresford have accustomed us to the peculiar terms in which the characters understand their lives. Without ever feeling that Laforgue or Chomina or any of the other people on the screen are "just like us," we begin, nonetheless, to respond to their struggles wholeheartedly. The intensity of their beliefs becomes very moving, and the irreconcilable disparity between the Blackrobes' philosophy and the Indians' becomes unbearably sad. In the movie's greatest scene, near the end, Laforgue stands over a dying Algonquian and searches for something to say to him. The priest tries to bless the old Indian, to tell him, "My God loves you," and the dying man's daughter is outraged. It's a complex, disorienting moment. In a sense, the blessing is obscenely irrelevant: it's no solace to the Algonquian, who doesn't believe in the Jesuit's God and, for that matter, isn't entirely sure that Laforgue isn't some kind of sorcerer. The gesture can be seen, too, as a confirmation of the spiritual colonialism of missionary activity—the impulse to collect souls the way trappers bag pelts. (The Jesuits were keen on baptizing dying Indian babies and sending their souls straight to Heaven.) And yet Laforgue's awkward words are touching; we sense that they come from a genuine desire to do good and a real affection for the dying man. The priest has no choice but to speak, and no other way of expressing himself fully, and his absurd invocation of his God is somehow an act of bravery: he has to trust that the Algonquian will hear honest feelings rather than meaningless words.

Black Robe moves on a steady, powerful flow of ideas and emotions. Moore's superbly intelligent script and Beresford's confident direction carry us past the movie's one serious weakness, which is Lothaire Bluteau's enervated performance as Laforgue. Fortunately, August Schellenberg's Chomina is magnificent, and the movie is so strongly conceived that its themes come through despite

Bluteau's passivity. (Repressed characters should look as if they might once have had some impulse vital enough to be worth repressing.) In every other respect, the picture is a triumph. *Black Robe* isn't about anything so simple as lost innocence, but its freshness gives us an intimation of how audiences must have responded when movies were a new world: it stirs in us a sense of discovery.

The New Yorker, November 18, 1991

CAPE FEAR

Martin Scorsese's *Cape Fear* is a remake of a bluntly effective 1962 thriller about a middle-class family—husband, wife, teenage daughter—who are terrorized by a devious, implacable psychopath. This looks like Scorsese's attempt to make a crowd-pleasing commercial film, to apply his intense, kinetic style to the relatively undemanding job of scaring audiences out of their wits. The movie is a disgrace: an ugly, incoherent, dishonest piece of work. The original picture, directed by a skillful journeyman, J. Lee Thompson, is memorable without being especially artful. Thompson's movie (adapted, by James R. Webb, from a John D. MacDonald pulp novel called *The Executioners*) is no-frills suspense. The story couldn't be simpler. An ex-con named Max Cady arrives in a Southern town in search of the man he holds responsible for his imprisonment, the lawyer Sam Bowden. There's no doubt that Cady is out for revenge. We understand that his dedication to his task is utterly single-minded, but he's too smart to do anything that would allow the authorities to lock him up or run him out of town; he conveys his intentions to Bowden through suggestions and insinuations rather than explicit threats. Calmly and cruelly, he does everything he can to undermine Bowden's sense of security. From the moment Cady appears in town, Bowden is constantly aware of him. Cady is furtive and unscrupulous, and he has the unnerving quick-strike elusiveness of a guerrilla fighter—the now-you-see-it-now-you-don't quality that can give human malevolence the aura of the demonic. He's a mon-

344

ster, a bogeyman, and the original *Cape Fear* has the straight-ahead construction of a horror movie. It aims low, meaning only to produce the most fundamental, uncomplicated sort of tension: there's something out there; we don't know how to stop it; here it comes again. Bowden (played by Gregory Peck in his best pillar-of-rectitude manner) is so civilized and rational that initially he is almost helpless against Cady's animal cunning; as the movie goes along, though, his rock-solid principles erode, and what replaces them is a fierce, basic instinct to defend himself and his family by whatever means may be necessary.

Like all truly scary movies, the original *Cape Fear* is essentially conservative, even reactionary. It works by evoking the childish, primal fears that are strong enough to override reason, moral discrimination, faith in the social contract—to make every consideration other than that of survival seem irrelevant, effete. A good part of the horror that movies of this sort induce is horror at the baseness and violence of our own reactions; we feel as if we had regressed to some primitive state of consciousness. For an educated middle-class audience—those of us, that is, who are meant to identify with the besieged Bowden family—the original *Cape Fear* is the guiltiest pleasure imaginable, more shameful than pornography; it brings out the vigilante, the redneck, the caveman lurking inside our liberal-humanist selves. There's a strange purity to the dishonorable intentions of Thompson's picture: it frames the conflict in the starkest terms and proceeds inexorably from there, without bothering to provide the distractions of wit, imagination, or psychological nuance. Its terrifying momentum is fueled by our fascination with Robert Mitchum's Cady. Mitchum is amazing; he uses all his customary mannerisms for profoundly disturbing effects. The danger that Cady poses to the Bowden family is largely sexual: the crime he was sent up for was the rape of a teenage girl, and his plan for revenge clearly includes the violation of Bowden's daughter. Mitchum's characteristic air of relaxed masculine confidence takes on really foul overtones in *Cape Fear*. His star power has always depended on the hint of sexual threat expressed by his drawling, ambling, heavy-lidded presence. Here his lazy machismo is appalling, and yet, unsettlingly, he's still attractive. He is the sole source of excitement in *Cape Fear*, and a constant reminder that the pleasure we're deriving from

this brutal thriller is corrupt, helplessly perverse. There's a remarkable scene near the end of the picture in which Cady, who has traced
the Bowdens to a houseboat on the Cape Fear River, peels off his
shirt and slips quietly into the water, hoping to sneak up on his prey.
In the moonlight, he looks simultaneously like a gleaming, bare-
chested stud, a grimly determined commando, and some sort of
prehistoric reptile—a cold-blooded predator that we thought had
disappeared from the earth a few geological ages ago.

The 1962 *Cape Fear* isn't complex—morally, psychologically, or
cinematically. The picture makes a mockery of the very notion of
complexity; it's constructed to dissolve all emotional and intellectual
distinctions, to throw everything back into the undifferentiated primal ooze of terror and survival. This is not an admirable aim, but the
movie certainly has the courage of its low convictions: it never
pretends that what it's doing is good for us. Scorsese's remake
muddies the waters with self-consciousness. He has loaded *Cape
Fear* with apparent moral ambiguities, facile ideas about guilt and
redemption (themes that link the movie, forcibly, to his previous
work), and explicit attempts to portray his scuzzy villain as a mythic
nemesis. In the new script (which is credited to Wesley Strick), the
Bowdens aren't innocent victims of an irrational evil. The seeds of
evil are within them, and Cady no longer seems to have come out
of nowhere like a hurricane, an unforeseeable natural disaster; in
this picture, he appears to have sprung forth from the Bowdens'
dirty little souls. Sam Bowden (Nick Nolte) isn't quite the straight
arrow he was in the first movie. He once almost wrecked his marriage with his philandering, we learn, and it's not clear that he has
entirely reformed: he's enjoying a heavy flirtation with a law clerk
named Lori (Illeana Douglas)—a relationship teetering between
friendship and romance. And he isn't a paragon of legal integrity,
either. The basis of Cady's grudge against him has been changed
from that of the original story. In the novel and the 1962 film,
Bowden witnessed Cady's assault on the teenager and gave testimony in court. In the new version, Bowden has not witnessed the
crime; he was Cady's defense attorney in the rape trial, and he
suppressed evidence that could have led to his client's acquittal.
Bowden's wife, Leigh (Jessica Lange), is now an edgy, unhappy-
looking woman; she hasn't forgiven her husband for his past in-

fidelities, and she's quick to accuse him of new ones. Fifteen-year-old Danielle Bowden (Juliette Lewis), Cady's ultimate prey, has been given a sullen, pouty teenage sexuality, and she's alienated from her parents. She's more repelled by the hostile vibes between Sam and Leigh than she is by Cady's advances to her. In one long, loathsome scene, Cady, posing as Danielle's new drama teacher, comes perilously close to seducing her. Halfway into the sequence, she sees through the impersonation and realizes that this man is her family's tormentor, but she isn't turned off; she kisses him anyway. And this Cady (Robert De Niro) is more than a sadistic, amoral cracker; he is also an avenging angel (his body is covered with tattooed Biblical quotations like "Vengeance Is Mine" and with Christian symbols like the Cross) and the trickster figure common to many of the world's mythologies.

Of course, educated middle-class moviegoers like a little subtext in a genre picture: it adds spice. Picking up intimations of dark psychological "truths," identifying mythic patterns and narrative archetypes—these are ways of making ourselves feel smart while we enjoy dumb movies, of asserting our superiority to gut-level, cheap-thrills storytelling. They're also ways of neutralizing the visceral, wholly irrational kick of powerhouse trash like the original *Cape Fear*: they enable us to dismiss the damning evidence of our emotional reactions—to deny that we've been lured, momentarily, into wholehearted acceptance of some pretty crude notions. Thompson's *Cape Fear* turns the audience as well as the hero into yahoos, and it doesn't supply us with any convenient excuses for our feelings. It ends, after a climactic battle in which Sam vanquishes the monster, with a brief, bleak shot of the Bowdens, their faces expressing exhaustion and degradation rather than triumph. The new *Cape Fear* is all excuses. You couldn't say that Scorsese's treatment is a desecration of a great, pure work of the human spirit; it's more like a consecration of something debased and profane. This *Cape Fear* is much flashier and more assaultive than the original (and it's also, at two hours and eight minutes, a hell of a lot longer), but the Christian/mythological subtext that Scorsese dredges up and places in the foreground has the effect of increasing our emotional distance from the story. And it isn't true subtext; it's stuff that has been imposed on, rather than discovered in, the material. The idea that

Cady is a monster who has bubbled up out of the unconscious of a "dysfunctional" family seems at first to be just glib, fashionable pop psychology. As the movie goes along, though, Scorsese keeps hammering away at the Bowdens' frailties, and it becomes harder and harder to ignore the implication that they somehow *deserve* the vengeance that's being visited on them. There's a gruesome sequence in which Cady picks up Lori, the law clerk, in a bar and then handcuffs her in bed and beats her senseless, and the movie gives us to understand that Sam is indirectly responsible for this atrocity: Lori allowed herself to be seduced by Cady because she was frustrated by the unsatisfying ambiguity of her relationship with Sam. In this movie, flirting with a coworker can leave a guy with blood on his hands. And what makes the long scene between Cady and Danielle so surpassingly ugly is that it turns the normal confused sexuality of a teenage girl into something unclean: as Danielle begins to respond to the advances of her would-be rapist, the movie unavoidably suggests that she, like the unfortunate Lori, is *asking for it.*

There's no way to recast this story in Christian terms without reducing it to moral (and aesthetic) nonsense. The stain of original sin on the Bowdens' souls seems to justify Cady's viciousness. Sam's breach of legal ethics in his conduct of Cady's defense makes the lawyer's later descent, first into shady extralegal tactics and then into plain violence, seem far less dramatic. The whole story is now constructed to illustrate the Christian idea that suffering is good for the soul: battling Cady provides a kind of spiritual catharsis for the Bowdens. In the end, they've been reborn: they've wrestled with the demons of their corrupt natures and exorcised them, spewed the poison out of their mouths. If that devil, that tattooed man, had not come along, Lord knows what might have become of these lost children; they would still be wandering in the wilderness of sin. The Christian implications that Scorsese lays on this elemental story actually serve to make the message more reactionary: violence is no longer just a matter of survival—it's now the instrument of salvation. (If Scorsese were making *Taxi Driver* today, would he present Travis Bickle's spooky calm in the aftermath of the massacre without irony, as if this serenity were a sign of grace?) These ideas may be among Scorsese's most deeply held convictions, but they aren't integral to this kind of movie or this particular story. The new *Cape Fear* is still, at heart, a picture whose sole aim is to give its audience huge, bowel-loosening shocks; the veneer of moral seriousness and psychological complexity that Scorsese brings to the enterprise feels like an attempt to convince himself that he's not doing what he's doing.

It's hard to find the pleasure, or value, in a horror picture that keeps providing us with high-toned justifications for our basest reactions—insisting that the gruelling experience it's putting us through is really meant to edify us. De Niro's frenetic but thoroughly uninteresting performance is emblematic of the movie's inadequacy. He's covered with tattooed messages and symbols, but he doesn't seem to have a body. We could feel Mitchum's evil in all its slimy physicality; De Niro's is an evil that we merely read. Despite the movie's relentless pace and the ingenious staging and editing of its violent sequences, *Cape Fear* has a peculiarly antiseptic quality. It drags us into the mud and then tells us that we haven't got dirty. Our messy primitive responses have been cleaned up, rationalized away; we're guilt-free—washed in the blood of the bogeyman. The pretense of moral purity in Scorsese's *Cape Fear* is far more sordid than the honest, unself-conscious shock-mongering of the original. Scorsese seems to want to make a gut-wrenching thriller and yet duck the responsibility for the sleazy thoughts it might churn up in us. He's asking absolution for the wrong sin. He shouldn't be ashamed of having made a mass-audience horror movie; he should be ashamed of having made one that sends its viewers home feeling morally complacent and intellectually superior.

The New Yorker, December 2, 1991

FOR THE BOYS

In the opening sequence of *For the Boys*, Bette Midler presents herself to the audience as a crusty octogenarian. The old-age makeup has been applied so thickly that her head appears massive; she seems to be wearing padding under her bathrobe, too. She looks as though she had as many layers as the earth itself. There's something strangely appropriate about this effect. In *For the Boys*, Midler piles persona on top of persona on top of persona for two and a half hours in an attempt to overwhelm us with the sheer force and infinite variety of herself: she is the world. The movie, which was produced by her own company, has been constructed to serve as the Portable Bette—a boxed set of Midler moments, remixed and repackaged for Christmas giving. The elderly tough-broad behemoth we meet in the movie's first scene is, of course, a narrative device—a flashback-generator. This woman, Dixie Leonard, is a singer-dancer-comedienne who became famous in the early days of the Second World War, when she teamed up with an established star named Eddie Sparks (James Caan). In the framing story, Dixie and Eddie have been invited to an awards ceremony intended to honor them for their many years of entertaining troops on USO tours. Dixie refuses to appear onstage with her old partner, and the producers of the shindig dispatch a polite young man (Arye Gross) to call on her and get her to change her mind. The emissary listens worshipfully as Dixie recalls key episodes in the history of her up-and-down relationship with Eddie. Most of the dramatic high points of her reminiscences take place in wartime, and the picture's big sequences are organized around four USO shows: one in London and one in North Africa during the Second World War; one in Korea in the early fifties; and, finally, one in Vietnam in 1969. This structure allows Midler to perform musical numbers from different eras and to attempt the acting tour de force of playing a character at several distinct stages of life. Her performance is a stunt, a shameless display of virtuosity, and it's not nearly as much fun as it should be; it's too calculated.

Midler gets off to a nice start, though, in the initial flashback sequence, in which Dixie and Eddie do their act together for the first time. The setting is London during the blitz. Dixie, wearing nothing but an officer's jacket and high heels, takes the stage to an excited chorus of cheers and wolf whistles, and proceeds to steal the show from Eddie: she improvises some raunchy patter, sings a couple of songs, flirts with the servicemen, and does it all with an endearing lack of restraint. As a singer, Midler is a belter in the Merman style, and her way with sexual innuendo is barely less blatant than Mae West's. When she's at her best, as she is in this long sequence, she wins the audience over with a combination of there's-no-business-like-show-business ebullience and I'm-no-angel vulgarity. It's pure chutzpah: we sense an iron will to entertain. In this mode, she pushes herself to the brink of self-parody, and then beyond; she doesn't take herself seriously, doesn't mind looking ridiculous, just as long as she gets a rise out of the audience. This is the persona—the campy, retro, forties-style trouper—that made Bette Midler a star in the seventies. The London scenes in *For the Boys* are deliberate reminders of her early appeal, and for a while the picture has a certain trashy charm; the director, Mark Rydell (who also directed Midler in her first starring vehicle, *The Rose*, in 1979), isn't shy about milking our goodwill toward her old, raucous style.

But when the movie gets past the "Boogie-Woogie Bugle Boy" era the party's over. Dixie and Eddie keep singing and hoofing and trading double-entendres, but they also begin to gather around them an unwelcome aura of significance. The scenes in Korea and Vietnam feature "realistic" combat footage. Eddie's professional-patriot style starts to take on evil overtones: during the McCarthy era, he fires an old friend who has exhibited some faintly leftist tendencies; in Vietnam, he cheerleads for the Pentagon, and the movie wants us to believe that he shares responsibility for the war's casualties. He starts off as a creep, and sinks lower with each new historical development. But Dixie just seems to get nobler and nobler as the bodies pile up around her. She weeps over dying soldiers, scolds Eddie for his cowardice in the blacklist episode, and worries about her son, whom she has brought up by herself since he was five or six. (Her husband was killed in action in the Second World War.) We realize, with mounting horror, that Midler is recapitulating her entire career in this picture, from the exuberant tackiness of her seventies act right through the self-aggrandizing sentimentality of recent movies like *Beaches* and *Stella*—and that this strenuous exercise in image-consolidation is, in fact, the movie's sole reason for being. The picture itself has a kind of life-achievement-award feel to it: when it's over, the words "a great entertainer and a wonderful human being" seem to have acquired a new, unprecedentedly berserk meaning.

One of the many unintentional ironies of *For the Boys* (whose screenplay is signed by Marshall Brickman, Neal Jimenez, and Lindy Laub) is that its antiwar sentiments seem every bit as cynical as Eddie's enthusiastic militarism: they're both pristine specimens of show-biz piety—ways for entertainers to whip up some easy, ego-gratifying applause. The movie's phoniness reaches its peak in the Vietnam scenes. Dixie and Eddie are playing to a difficult crowd here, a bunch of exhausted, unsmiling young men who don't have much in common with the neatly groomed, superbly receptive audiences of the Second World War shows; these guys look like bikers in a really bad mood. Eddie's flag-waving and corny one-liners elicit a stony response. And, as in virtually every scene in the picture, his failure sets up Dixie's triumph. She talks tough and dirty to her audience, and then croons a maudlin rendition of "In My Life," and the grunts are visibly moved; the camera pans slowly across them as they listen reverently, their faces shining with gratitude. Once again, Dixie has upstaged her partner, professionally and morally. In acting terms, though, Caan walks off with the movie. Every time Midler stops the show with a flashy musical number or a heavy emotional scene, Caan quietly gets it going again. He knows better than to try to be ingratiating; the screenplay wraps Midler in so much virtue that there's none left for him anyway. He just bears down on the character and turns it into a witty, precise portrait of a cheerfully opportunistic entertainer: Eddie's a heel, but he's a recognizable human being—the only one in the movie. Of course, Caan doesn't have to carry the picture; it's Midler's vehicle, not his, and the magnitude of this vanity production takes its toll on the star. After two and a half hours of accumulating flattering images of herself and lugging them, along with the rest of the baggage of her career, across the battlefields of several decades, she looks, in the end, as if she could barely move anymore. (She has only enough energy left, we sense, to totter onto a stage and accept an award.) In *For the Boys*, Bette Midler begins as a red-hot mama and winds up as Mother Courage. And the movie is such an ordeal that it turns into a demonstration of a startling thesis: war is bad, but entertainment is hell.

The New Yorker, December 16, 1991

HOOK *and* BUGSY

Steven Spielberg's *Hook* means to give a contemporary spin to *Peter Pan*, the classic J. M. Barrie story about a boy who refuses to grow up. The movie is a failure in almost every way, but it's unmistakably of our time: its lack of conviction and its panicky eagerness to please are depressingly up-to-the-minute. Barrie's Peter Pan embodies the freedom and beautiful lightness of children's imaginations. He flies, he's immortal, and he lives on a "delectable island" called Neverland, a paradise of endless play. He ventures into the real world only occasionally; one night Peter, as insidious as a draft, steals into the London house of a middle-class family called the Darlings and carries off its dreaming children, Wendy, Michael, and John. The simple, compelling idea of the original story is that kids when they play or fantasize really are (as parents often say they are) "off in another world." Barrie makes us feel the vast distance that separates children's minds from those of their parents. Imaginative boys and girls can seem exasperatingly remote: absorbed, transported, unreachable. Barrie's Peter Pan story (written first as a play, in 1904, and later as a novel called *Peter and Wendy*) is a wonderful fable for youngsters, and it's also a peerless guidebook for puzzled grown-ups. Here, the writer tells us as he leads us on a tour of Neverland, is where the children go when they get that lost, faraway look in their eyes, or when their faces, transformed by sleep, take on that beatific opacity—*this* is the place that they've flown off to.

354

Neverland as Barrie imagined it is a world in which the laws of nature and the rules of ordinary civilized life do not apply. It's inherently chaotic: this enchanted realm is populated by an impossible collection of figures from bedtime stories and juvenile adventure tales—pirates, fairies, mermaids, and "redskins." Peter is, of course, named for the Greek god Pan, and there's more than a little Robin Hood in him, too: he lives in the forest with a band of pint-size Merry Men called the Lost Boys. Barrie has tremendous respect for the random, willy-nilly quality of kids' imaginations. He jumbles up all these exotic creatures with a fine heedlessness, as if he were unaware of their incongruity. *Peter Pan* gives us every kind of story at once, and Barrie seems to know that children will find this perfectly natural: the whole thing goes down as easily as a pudding.

Hook is just a lumpy mess, and it's served up in a whopping portion. This vastly expensive ($80 million is the most popular guess about the cost), 135-minute picture adds truckloads of new ingredients to the original mixture, which was already pretty rich; if you were feeling generous, you might see the wild profusion of notions and effects in *Hook* as an extension of Barrie's blithely inclusive, why-not approach to storytelling. But the movie's inventiveness has a desperate quality. Spielberg, who once had the ability to turn the junk-fed imagination of the American middle class into the stuff of soaring pop fantasies, seems to have lost confidence in his own gifts. *Hook* is meant to be "magical," like *E.T.* and *Close Encounters of the Third Kind*, but its tricks feel strained; we're constantly aware of the anxiety and the backbreaking effort it's taking to produce them, and that's no kind of magic at all. Spielberg rushes from one effect to another, casting about frantically for something that will win the audience over for good. Nothing works, but he keeps throwing ever more elaborate (and more laborious) illusions at us, and *Hook* becomes so cluttered and so frenzied that it's nearly unwatchable. The magician's nervousness makes us squirm: the movie seems drenched in flop sweat. If this picture had been made by anyone else, it would be easier to dismiss. The Neverland of *Hook* feels joyless and claustrophobic, and its oppressiveness is disheartening not only because it violates the expansive spirit of Barrie's story but also because it betrays a profound weariness in Steven Spielberg's attitude toward his art and his audience. In this version of *Peter Pan*, the imagination seems like a burden—a terrible, crushing obligation.

The script, by Jim V. Hart and Malia Scotch Marmo (from a story by Hart and Nick Castle), presents Peter Pan as a grown-up American family man named Peter Banning (Robin Williams), who returns without enthusiasm to the scene of his glorious adventures. Peter, it seems, renounced his eternal boyhood and entered the real world of mortality and adult responsibility because he fell in love with the granddaughter of Wendy Darling. As the movie begins, he's a cutthroat yuppie lawyer, specializing in mergers and acquisitions, and he has no idea that he was ever Peter Pan. He's so wrapped up in making money that he neglects his wife, Moira (Caroline Goodall), and his kids, Jack (Charlie Korsmo) and Maggie (Amber Scott). His selfishness is dramatized by his failure to show up for an important Little League game: he promises his son that he'll attend, but business keeps him away, and young Jack, with a forlorn eye on Dad's empty seat in the stands, comes to the plate in the bottom of the ninth and despairingly strikes out with the winning run on base. The Bannings travel to London to visit Granny Wendy (Maggie Smith), and the two children, who have been given the bedroom that the Darling children used to sleep in, are kidnapped by Pan's old nemesis, Captain Hook (Dustin Hoffman). Hurriedly, Wendy fills Peter in on his legendary past; the fairy Tinker Bell (Julia Roberts) turns up and spirits him away to Neverland to rescue his children. To get them back, he has to become Peter Pan again; the Lost Boys whip him into shape for a climactic battle with Hook and his scurvy band of pirates.

The movie seems unable (or unwilling) to keep its mind on the business of telling a rousing, fantastic adventure. It uses up its energy and our patience in scattershot attempts to appeal to every conceivable audience. At its most abject, *Hook* ladles on boomer-generation sentimentality about parenthood: the "happy thought" that enables paunchy, middle-aged Peter to fly again is "I'm a daddy." The whole sorry spectacle turns out to be a kind of self-help fairy tale, an illustrated lecture on finding the inner child. Peter, having reacquainted himself with the boyish side of his nature, emerges from his Neverland excursion a changed man. We know he's going to be a better father now. In the end, the Bannings look at one another with a renewed sense of love and respect, a deeper understanding of what binds them as a family. A wider, brighter world has been revealed to them; these, we feel, are people who will soon be making popcorn and watching *Field of Dreams* together.

For kiddie appeal, the movie relies heavily on the Lost Boys, a large multicultural aggregation whose woodland lair now has an urban-playground feel to it: the Boys shoot hoops and zip around on skateboards; their leader, Rufio (Dante Basco), is a teenage tough guy who sports a punkish haircut and a permanent Elvis-like sneer. The "contemporary" trappings have the disastrous effect of making Neverland look ordinary, overfamiliar: this is Secondhandland. The intent of the interminably frolicsome Lost Boys sequences is transparent: the filmmakers are obviously worried that the younger viewers won't be sufficiently turned on by pirate-story action (who knows from pirates anymore?) or the emotional problems of a Peter Pan in midlife crisis. When concerns like those are dictating the shape of a movie, everything winds up seeming cheesy and halfhearted. The inner-child theme has no real resonance or urgency; the Lost Boys passages are as banal and perfunctory as Saturday-morning television; and the pirate scenes aren't nearly as rousing as they ought to be—the duels and battles that take place on Hook's ship have the rote, mechanical quality of hourly demonstrations at a theme park. At a crucial moment in the original play, Peter turns to the audience and asks them to clap if they believe in fairies. The people who made *Hook* don't try to re-create Barrie's *coup de théâtre*. They don't dare, because this picture's relationship to its audience is much dodgier and less straightforward than Barrie's relationship to his. Spielberg and the screenwriters are too timid to stake their success on actually requiring our belief in fairies, pirates, or anything else. Like Peter Banning, they're neither here nor there—corporate types who have been dragged kicking and screaming into an imaginary world that no longer feels like home to them.

The actors hit their marks and strive gamely to give the impression that they're having a rip-roaring time. As you scan their faces, you can almost see the performers racking their brains for the happy thoughts that might allow them to rise above the picture's clunky

script and elephantine production. The only actors who look as if
they had really found a workable happy thought, though, are Dustin
Hoffman and Maggie Smith, and it's probably the same thought for
both of them: "I have more technique than anyone else on this set."
In filmmaking terms, Spielberg should be able to say something like
that to himself, but his work here doesn't express even the pleasure
of craftsmanship. The audacious, effortless-seeming wizardy of *Jaws*,
Close Encounters, *E.T.*, and the best parts of *1941* isn't in evidence
in *Hook*. If Spielberg's delight in moviemaking has deserted him, it
may be because he senses that his rapport with the audience isn't
what it used to be. He once told stories and created images with the
confidence of an artist who knew that his imagination and ours had
the same coordinates—that any Neverland he chose to take us to
would be a place we'd recognize. Barrie, who developed the story
of Peter Pan out of fantasy games he played with a neighbor's
children, wrote a play and a book that achieved this sort of magical
complicity between the storyteller and his audience. His intimacy
with the dream worlds of Victorian and Edwardian children was
profound and wholehearted. The real horror of *Hook* is that it
shakes our faith in the very idea of popular art—of stories that grow
out of imaginative empathy and shared cultural values rather than
out of demographic calculation. Even today, Barrie's *Peter Pan* has
the power to convince us that everything is possible. *Hook* brings us
back down to earth. It doesn't believe in itself, and it doesn't trust
the audience; it says that nothing is possible. Not a happy thought.

A blockbuster fiasco like *Hook* can make big-budget Hollywood
filmmaking seem absurd, pointless. The great beasts, we feel, can
never walk the earth again. (Fittingly, Spielberg's next project, *Juras-
sic Park*, is about dinosaurs.) Every now and then, though, one of
these huge, plush, Oscar-ready creatures heaves into view looking
startlingly vigorous. Barry Levinson's *Bugsy*, an opulent period gangster movie, is as long as *Hook* (virtually to the minute), but it's much
lighter on its feet, and it gives the tradition of high-gloss studio
entertainment at least a temporary reprieve from extinction. The
movie is largely a showcase for the old-fashioned star magnetism of
Warren Beatty, who plays the title character, the legendary Benjamin
(Bugsy) Siegel. Siegel, a Brooklyn street kid who became a leader of

a powerful New York mob, moved to Los Angeles in the late thirties, and—to the dismay of his East Coast partners, Meyer Lansky and Lucky Luciano—made himself a highly visible figure, a celebrity who hung out with Hollywood actors and liked seeing his picture in the paper. The screenplay, by James Toback, portrays him as a charming, mercurial psychopath with a rather touching taste for glamour. Although we're free to take him as a metaphor for the Hollywood sensibility at its craziest, the movie doesn't really try to do anything more than reflect his contradictory personality as accurately as possible. Beatty, Toback, and Levinson don't waste time chasing after the meaning of Bugsy Siegel's life. Bugsy is a vivid, unpredictable, one-of-a-kind guy, and the filmmakers seem to realize that they can't take their eyes off him for a second—that if they didn't concentrate hard on the everyday details, if they stopped following all the little hairpin turns of his erratic behavior, they'd lose him. They can't afford to pull back and look at the big picture. Besides, they don't need to. Bugsy Siegel is a fascinating monster; we don't want to take our eyes off him, either.

For a gangster movie, *Bugsy* doesn't have a lot of violent action. It also lacks the sweep and the tragic weight of genre masterpieces like the original *Scarface* and the first two *Godfather* films. Toback's sensationally agile script treats Bugsy's life in crime as an occasion of dark, bold comedy, and the movie finds all the violence it needs right inside its main character. Bugsy Siegel is the funniest and most volatile hood since the migraine-plagued killer played by James Cagney in *White Heat*. Instead of headaches Bugsy has brainstorms: watching his old friend George Raft (Joe Mantegna) at work on a movie set, the hero decides to arrange a screen test for himself; on the same set, he spots a gorgeous bit player named Virginia Hill (Annette Bening) and immediately falls in love with her; he buys a Hollywood mansion on impulse, and pays cash for it; and after meeting a slimy Italian count in a night club he hatches a plan to assassinate Mussolini. The assassination scheme is the movie's looniest running gag, and it's also an ideal expression of the hero's personality: it's fantastic and grandiose, and Bugsy's obsession with it comes and goes—it has so many other strong momentary passions to compete with. In any event, most of Bugsy's fierce desires don't remain unsatisfied long enough to become full-blown obsessions; he's swift, decisive, and utterly unscrupulous about getting what he wants. Long-range thinking is not his modus operandi. His megalomania is instinctive, appetitive. He's happy to let his boyhood friend Lansky (Ben Kingsley) do all the fretting about business strategy and administrative problems.

As the movie goes along, though, Bugsy's greedy imagination becomes increasingly dominated by two shining objects of desire that even he can't just reach out and grab. One is Virginia, a courtesan who is attracted to dangerous men but isn't intimidated by them. She's tough, wily, independent-minded, and not very trustworthy, and she keeps the love-struck gangster on his toes. She walks out on him regularly, taunts him with other lovers, past and present, nags him to leave his wife (whom he has stashed, along with two daughters, in a suburban house back East). When she's out of Bugsy's sight, he keeps her under surveillance—there's no telling what she might do. The other glittery thing that occupies his mind is a vision—it came to him in the Nevada desert—of a grand hotel-casino that could draw millions of suckers to the dusty frontier town called Las Vegas. He intends to build this gambling palace, which he names the Flamingo (Virginia's nickname), with money staked by Lansky and Luciano (Bill Graham), and he oversees the gigantic project with his customary recklessness, authorizing ever larger expenditures without thinking twice about the consequences; by the time the Flamingo is finished, the cost has grown from $1 million to $6 million, and the investors are not amused. Virginia and her namesake in the desert together bring about Bugsy's downfall. The sly joke that informs the screenplay's structure is the central contradiction of the hero's character: he's a visionary with a fatally short attention span.

This is a rich role for Warren Beatty (who commissioned the script and served as one of the film's producers), and he tears into it hungrily. It's the best kind of star performance; Beatty seems entirely himself, but in a new way. Although he has often been wonderful, he has never been as forceful and alert as he is here. He's ferociously, mesmerizingly funny. Beatty holds the performance together by emphasizing Bugsy's childlike sense of invulnerability—the quality that makes the character so attractive, so ridiculous, and so dangerous, all at once. In the great Hollywood tradition, Beatty has supplied himself with a ravishing siren to share the screen with, and Bening (who benefits from superbly glamorous lighting by the film's cinematographer, Allen Daviau) more than holds her own in her scenes with the star: Virginia's express-train personality is a perfect match for Bugsy's. And the movie is filled with pungent, memorable supporting performances. Kingsley brings a surprisingly dry, elegant sense of comic timing to his portrait of sober Meyer Lansky. Harvey Keitel, as Mickey Cohen, Bugsy's right-hand man in Los Angeles, spits out his profane lines as if they were live firecrackers; he's hilarious. And, perhaps best of all, there's Elliott Gould, who plays the tiny role of Harry Greenberg, an aging, flabby mob schlemiel—a dazed henchman with an alarming propensity for doing the wrong thing. Gould's gentle comic style seems absolutely inspired here: he plays Harry as a Willy Loman who has wandered too far from the old territory. *Bugsy*, despite its lavish surface, is essentially a movie of small, lovingly crafted pleasures. It's smart, swanky fun.

The New Yorker, December 30, 1991

JFK

Oliver Stone's *JFK* is a movie with a mission: it means to demonstrate that the assassination of John F. Kennedy, in Dallas in 1963, was not the act of a disturbed Marxist loner named Lee Harvey Oswald but the result of a vast, complex right-wing conspiracy that involved (at the very least) members of the intelligence community and the defense establishment. According to the movie, this wide-ranging plot to kill the president was developed primarily in response to a White House decision to withdraw some advisers from Vietnam. Stone and Zachary Sklar, who collaborated on the screenplay, tell us that Kennedy was committed to making sweeping changes in United States foreign policy: he meant to get us out of Southeast Asia, to rein in the covert activities of the Central Intelligence Agency, and, ultimately, to end the Cold War altogether. What happened in Dallas was therefore (in Stone's view) more than a murder: it was a coup d'état. And the movie thus purports to provide not only a solution to the specific mystery of who killed John Kennedy but also a key to unlock the secrets of every political crime in the past twenty-eight years of American history. Since the narrative of *JFK* is organized around the investigation conducted by the New Orleans district attorney, Jim Garrison, between 1966 and 1969, the events that the movie can cite as "evidence" of the continuing effects of the coup are necessarily limited—to the escalation of the Vietnam War under LBJ and the assassinations of Robert Kennedy and Martin Luther King, Jr., in 1968. But Stone's interpretation of history is clearly intended to supply a framework for understanding the major scandals and outrages of the seventies and the eighties, too: Watergate, Iran-Contra, the alleged "October surprise" deal—Stone has mentioned them all in the many interviews he has given to promote this picture. His success in putting over the grand, vague conspiracy theory proposed in *JFK* depends, of course, on his ability to tap into the audience's inherent distrust of the powers that be—its sense that the government officials, military brass, and covert-action cowboys fingered here are the sort of people who are capable of the most heinous crimes, the most devious cover-ups, the most arrogant contempt for the democratic process. Since our direst suspicions about the way the government operates frequently turn out to be justified, Stone knows that in 1992 very few members of the audience are likely to reject his conspiracy scenario out of hand. The assassination could have happened the way *JFK* says it did, and for this filmmaker "could have" is good enough. Platoon leader Stone carries out his mission here with his characteristic indifference to intellectual niceties. *JFK* is a guerrilla raid on our sensibilities. Stone doesn't bother to try to win the hearts and minds of the audience with coherent, rational argument; he simply takes them prisoner.

According to Gallup-poll results included in the press materials for *JFK*, only 16 percent of the American people now believe that Oswald acted alone; 73 percent endorse the view that "others were involved." Among the majority there are presumably some who subscribe to the idea that Oswald didn't fire even a single shot on November 22, 1963, either at the president or at the Dallas police officer who was killed a mile from the suspect's rooming house less than an hour later. *JFK* accepts this thesis: that the alleged assassin was, as he loudly proclaimed after he was arrested, "a patsy," someone set up to take the fall for the real murderers. That's far from a new theory. It's just one of many variations that can be found in the hundreds of volumes of research and speculation produced over the years by students of the assassination. Nearly three decades of mostly independent, nonofficial examination of the event have turned up virtually no answers: the researchers all agree that the inquiry conducted by the government-appointed Warren Commission (which concluded that Oswald was the sole culprit) was deeply flawed, but, once past that common starting point, they scatter, each heading off in a different direction and no two ending up in exactly the same place.

The whole assassination-theory field is a nightmare of ambiguity and contradiction. If you don't accept the Warren Commission's findings—and there are plenty of good reasons not to—you're still in the dark. The case for Oswald as lone-wolf killer is far from airtight, but no one has yet managed to construct a chain of evidence that leads inevitably to a more satisfying solution. There are plausible conspiracy theories implicating the CIA, the Mafia, military intelligence, anti-Castro Cuban exiles, and mix-and-match combinations thereof (sometimes with Oswald as triggerman, sometimes without). No one, though, can honestly claim to have the goods, the hard data that make sense of everything. The information necessary to arrive at the truth always proves to be incomplete; every case, no matter how persuasively argued, collapses for lack of some crucial piece of evidence. Even the forensic data are maddeningly inconclusive. The Dallas doctors and nurses who examined Kennedy's body immediately after the shooting reported seeing a massive exit wound in the back of the head, but the report of the official autopsy, performed later that day in Bethesda, Maryland, places the exit wound in the right temple; the discrepancy is irresolvable, because the president's brain, which was supposedly preserved for further research in the National Archives, has been missing since at least 1966.

In the late seventies, a House committee probing the assassination seemed to have—at last—discovered irrefutable proof that not all the shots fired at JFK came from the direction of the Texas School Book Depository, where Oswald worked. Experts in acoustics, studying the recording of a police-radio transmission which was apparently made at the precise time of the shooting, determined that one shot had been fired from a different direction—from the famous Grassy Knoll. A few years after the committee stated its official conclusion, based primarily on the acoustical analysis, that there *was* a conspiracy to kill the president, this evidence, too, began to look shaky: closer study of the tape revealed the voice of a sheriff giving an order that was in fact issued after the shooting, not during it, so the sounds that the experts identified as gunfire could have been bursts of static. In the Kennedy-assassination case, nothing is solid, no one can be relied on: whatever looks like part of the solution always turns out, sooner or later, to be part of the problem.

Delving into the literature of the Kennedy assassination can be an unhinging, vertigo-inducing experience. Every conspiracy book should bear the legend "Abandon all hope." To maintain sanity in this murky underworld, you need a patient, judicious guide—someone like the British journalist Anthony Summers, whose 1980 book *Conspiracy* (revised and updated in 1989) is a thorough, sober, clear-eyed evaluation of the available evidence. Oliver Stone, with his overheated temperament and his propulsive, cut-to-the-chase filmmaking style, is not ideally suited for that role. *JFK* is more than three hours long, and it packs in an extraordinary amount of assassination lore: the motorcade route, the geography of Dealey Plaza, mock newsreel footage of eyewitness testimony to the shooting, portraits of suspected associates of Oswald, a graphic (and tasteless) reconstruction of the Bethesda autopsy, and a frame-by-frame analysis of the Zapruder film—the home movie, filmed by an onlooker in Dealey Plaza, that is the most detailed visual record of the killing. As if all these data weren't enough for us to assimilate, the movie adds a ton of speculative material about governmental misconduct and quite a few invented (Stone would say "composite") characters; and the whole wrenching spectacle climaxes with a thirty-five-minute courtroom oration by Garrison (Kevin Costner), in which fact, fiction, and ideology are indistinguishable from each other. For all its apparent meticulousness, *JFK* finally seems as muddled and as hastily thrown together as the Warren Commission Report. It's a thick gumbo of truths, half-truths, unverifiable hypotheses, and pure rant, and Stone ladles it out indiscriminately.

I don't think Stone is simply a victim of assassinationologist's syndrome—the confusion and derangement that overtake even the most sensible people when they pursue this mystery. There are clear indications that the movie's elisions and distortions have been carefully thought out, and that the sensory overload *JFK* produces is a deliberate strategy. The choice of Garrison as hero is significant. The script is based largely on his 1988 chronicle of his investigation, *On the Trail of the Assassins*, which is a well-written, exciting book. It's easy to understand why a filmmaker would be attracted to Garrison's story: the district attorney and his staff tracked down leads and gathered evidence and eventually brought an alleged conspirator—a local businessman named Clay Shaw—to trial. The story has a dramatic shape that is familiar to movie audiences, and a kind of procedural suspense that we're comfortable with. Garrison portrays himself as a lonely fighter against hostile institutional forces—government, the media—that set in motion a well-orchestrated effort to stymie his inquiry. That's a movie-friendly concept, too: the combative DA can be seen as a Capra-style populist hero, a champion of the little guy against the big-bully establishment. More specifically, Garrison is the sort of character that Oliver Stone has always been drawn to: tenacious, obsessive, and, let's say, not averse to calling attention to himself. He would be an ideal vehicle for exploring the assassination controversy if it weren't for the embarrassing fact that the case he brought against Shaw was a shambles: the jury reached a "not guilty" verdict in less than an hour of deliberation, and it's almost impossible to find a conspiracy theorist today who thinks that Shaw had anything to do with the assassination.

Garrison tried his case mostly in the press and on television, regularly issuing wild pronouncements about evidence in his possession which would establish beyond doubt the identity of Kennedy's murderers. What he produced in court, however, was skimpy testimony from highly impeachable witnesses. Shamelessly, he turned the paucity of evidence for the conspiracy into evidence of a cover-up, and he wasn't shy (or particularly selective) about assigning blame for the supposed obstruction of his investigation. The CIA, the Justice Department, and Lyndon Johnson all took their licks from Garrison in the media, and in one televised interview he suggested that Robert Kennedy was working against him, too.

Garrison's contradictory, intemperate, inflammatory public utterances, in fact, lend support to the idea that an institutional campaign to "discredit" him was never necessary: he discredited himself every time he opened his mouth. This blustering, intimidating loose-cannon prosecutor is not the Garrison of *JFK*. Stone's Garrison is bespectacled and soft-spoken—a scholarly-looking seeker of truth. But even if you allow Stone the dramatic license of enhancing Garrison's reputation with Kevin Costner's aura of moral authority and regular-guy decency, you have to be suspicious of the way the movie handles the details of the Shaw case. The lengthy, expensive prosecution was a smoke-and-mirrors job, and Stone appears to know it. Garrison's shaky principal witnesses are nowhere to be found in *JFK*; the script replaces them with an invented character (played by Kevin Bacon) who tells a "composite" story that's far more compelling than anything the real Garrison elicited from his real witnesses. That is to say, when Stone comes up against a piece of material that seems inconveniently ambiguous, he fictionalizes it. Cutting a few corners here and a few more there, airbrushing the flaws in his hero's character, coloring in the sketchy outlines of the historical record, he manufactures a collage that tries to pass as a perfect, undoctored photograph of the assassination.

Stone's approach to historical truth is based on some very odd premises. In interviews, he has responded to attacks on the movie's accuracy by saying that his intention in *JFK* is to create a "counter-myth" of the assassination—in opposition, that is, to the official myth represented by the Warren Commission's version of events (a myth that nearly three-quarters of the American public doesn't buy, anyway). Another myth is, I should say, pretty much the last thing most of us want from a purported investigation of the J.F.K. murder; in this field we've had a surfeit of myth. Stone has also been saying that he's less interested in the "who" and the "how" of the conspiracy than in the "why"—that the answer to why Kennedy was killed will lead us to the truth about everything else. The most charitable interpretation of that statement is that Stone isn't a rigorous logician: how, exactly, would someone determine why a president was murdered without first knowing who did it and how it was done? You might begin to search for leads in a simple domestic crime on the basis of a hypothesis about motivation, but political assassination presents too wide a range of possibilities: there were plenty of people and groups who hated Kennedy in 1963, all for different reasons. Stone simply selects a "why" that sounds good to him, and he makes a poor choice. Yes, Kennedy had approved an order to withdraw a few American advisers from Vietnam, but there's no evidence that this limited move signaled a fundamental change in Cold War foreign policy, or even, for that matter, in policy specific to Southeast Asia.

In essence, the conspiracy case that Stone makes in *JFK* amounts to a series of inferential leaps proceeding from a speculation. It's all bombast and misdirection, like a courtroom summation by a lawyer who knows that he can't win on the evidence. Stone comes on like a fearless radical, but his attitude toward the audience is firmly in the Hollywood tradition: he tries to bypass the intellect and go straight for the gut. *JFK* has the fevered tone of tabloid television; it plays like an endless episode of *America's Most Wanted*. The movie's hysterical manner and its slipshod handling of the facts actually have the effect of diminishing the credibility of the case for conspiracy. The clearest sounds we hear in *JFK* are those of Oliver Stone shooting himself in the foot.

The New Yorker, January 13, 1992

THE PRINCE OF TIDES

Barbra Streisand's *The Prince of Tides*, adapted from Pat Conroy's 1986 novel of that name, is a big, earnest psychoanalytic soap opera. The book takes 664 pages of smallish print (in the paperback edition) to tell the story of a screwed-up South Carolina family. Conroy's fulsome pseudoliterary prose inflates everything—the most trivial perceptions, the most unremarkable emotions—to epic size, but his strenuous huffing and puffing can't disguise the banality of his ideas: *The Prince of Tides* is a novel in which people come to terms with their past, make peace with the demons that have haunted them since childhood, learn how to let go of the "dysfunctional" emotional patterns inflicted on them by their parents, and become sensitive, caring human beings. Traumas are dredged up; harsh truths are faced; crippling neuroses are conquered; lives are changed. Conroy's insistent mythicizing of magazine-article psychology gives the story a peculiar quality of unreality; the florid soul-searching of the narrator, an unemployed high school English teacher and football coach named Tom Wingo, makes ordinary scenes of domestic strife seem fantastic, hysterically overimagined. This family saga should have been called *One Hundred Years of Solipsism*.

Compressing Conroy's bloated opus to feature-film dimensions automatically improves it. Streisand handles the material affectionately, even reverently, but the demands of movie storytelling force her to get to the point a lot quicker than the novel does. Her direction is smooth and canny: she sets up the fundamental dramatic conflicts clearly and economically, and she keeps the narrative moving along at a satisfying pace. *The Prince of Tides* plays better on the screen than it does on the page partly because Streisand is such a skillful director and partly because in this context the triteness of the content doesn't feel quite so jarringly disproportionate to the style. Streisand distills Conroy's story to its corn-based essence: the film's strong Hollywood brew of pop uplift, soft-focus romance, and middle-class melodrama seems the ideal form for *The Prince of Tides*.

The fumes of Conroy's terrible ideas linger in the air, though, along with pungent whiffs of his prose. (Conroy wrote the screenplay, in collaboration with Becky Johnston, and we're treated periodically to brief passages of voice-over narration taken directly from the book.) The movie retains both the structure and the underlying philosophy of its source. The story incorporates frequent flashbacks to Tom Wingo's childhood and is designed to build to a Freudian analytic breakthrough—the moment when he reveals the deep, dark secret that has prevented him from reaching full emotional maturity. After a lyrical prologue in which the narrator breezes through some benign childhood memories, the story proper begins, and we see the adult Tom (Nick Nolte) at home, on the South Carolina coast, with his edgy-looking wife, Sallie (Blythe Danner), and their three young daughters. He's a middle-aged ex-jock who seems to respond to everything with jaunty, self-conscious wisecracks. We're meant to sense the desperation underneath his forced heartiness, and the movie doesn't take long to bring his unease to the surface. His mother, Lila (Kate Nelligan), whom he obviously detests, gives him the news that his twin sister, Savannah (Melinda Dillon), is in the psychiatric ward of a New York City hospital recovering from a serious suicide attempt; Tom makes plans to go to New York and consult with Savannah's shrink, and before he leaves, Sallie tells him how unhappy she is with their marriage. In this flurry of plotting, the movie contrives to bring its hero face to face with all the unresolved emotions that he has been repressing— the anxieties, the long-nursed resentments, the persistent sense of failure. When Tom gets to New York, he moves into Savannah's Village apartment and goes to see her psychiatrist, Dr. Lowenstein (Streisand); the doctor persuades him to tell her the Wingo family history, with the idea that he might lead her to the source of Savannah's misery.

The narrative is organized around Tom's reminiscences, which he doles out in daily sessions with Dr. Lowenstein. At her instigation, he recounts, reluctantly at first, the horrors of his upbringing: the abuses heaped on the Wingo kids by their bullying, macho father, Henry (Brad Sullivan); the face-saving dishonesty imposed on them by their vain and rather crafty mother. As the flashbacks pile up, we're given to understand that this oral-history project, undertaken on behalf of Savannah, is doing Tom a terrific amount of good. He's becoming more confident, more open, less guarded. He quits smoking, starts jogging daily, and tutors the doctor's moody teenage son (Jason Gould) in the art of football. By the final forty minutes or so of the picture—after Tom has, at last, opened his psychic bomb bays all the way and dropped the Big One—he's a new man: man enough to take Lowenstein to his bed, giving her everything she hasn't been getting from her slimeball concert-violinist husband (Jeroen Krabbé), and then man enough to renounce her. The movie ends in a blaze of healing, wholeness, and midlife acceptance of self; the sun sets, the credits roll, the music (by James Newton Howard) swells like an abscess. The emotional wealth that Tom Wingo acquires in the course of *The Prince of Tides* does not, however, trickle down to enrich the audience. Tom's memories strike him with the force of huge cathartic revelations, but they're not nearly distinctive enough to move us in the same way. The childhood scenes quickly lose their power to surprise us, because they're just variations on a set of crude archetypes: brutal Dad, manipulative Mom. The static, repetitive quality of these sequences is inevitable, given Conroy's conception of the Wingo parents: Henry is intended to represent some essential principle of masculinity, Lila its feminine counterpart. Their orbits are fixed.

In fact, everything in *The Prince of Tides* has that sort of predictability. Conroy's narrative method consists of establishing characters who embody common stereotypes, setting them in motion around each other, and then watching them follow the courses that he's mapped for them. The inherent, irreparable flaw in both the book and the movie is that Conroy's message of openness and change and emotional liberation is belied by his manner: the overdetermination of the characters and the plot reveals his desire to create something universal, eternal, immutable. If the movie feels a lot less oppressive than the novel, it's largely because the actors sometimes manage to break out of their assigned places in Conroy's grand design—to violate the stereotypes with traces of their own mysteriously particular human qualities. Sullivan's snarling Henry Wingo remains a gross caricature throughout, and Streisand never quite gets the hang of the Lowenstein role (which seems, unfortunately, a repository for the author's highly conflicted feelings about New Yorkers, Jewish intellectuals, and professional women), but most of the cast performs heroically. Danner, who has rarely had a movie role large enough for her extraordinary talents, makes the most of her few scenes here. As written, Sallie Wingo is barely more than a plot function, a trigger for her husband's midlife crisis, but Danner's deceptively simple gestures and readings evoke depths of pain and confusion that the role seems inadequate to contain. The emotional power of her acting is so direct and so suggestive that it stays in your mind even when she's not onscreen; no matter what's going on in New York, we're always aware of Sallie, wondering how she's doing—we can't forget her any more than Tom can. Nelligan brings a comparable quality of spilling-over inventiveness to the difficult role of Lila Wingo. She thoroughly transcends the narrow Southern-belle terms of the part, and thus almost subverts one of the story's crucial premises: that Lila's deviousness and her willingness to cover up unpleasant truths are the sources of Tom's inability to confront his emotions. The way Nelligan plays her, the character seems far too complex to deserve such facile condemnation. When Tom reveals the incident that really sealed his grudge against his mother, we aren't nearly as shocked as we're meant to be. Nelligan has made us understand this difficult woman, and sort of like her; even at her worst, Lila doesn't horrify us.

The Prince of Tides is primarily Nick Nolte's show; he bears the weight of all Conroy's and Streisand's ambitions, and, for the most part, he carries his burden with miraculous grace. He's a marvelous actor and a great screen presence, and he's well cast as Tom Wingo. Tom is intended to embody several stereotypes at once: the rugged masculinity of the football coach, the sensitivity of the English teacher, the easy jocularity of the Southern good old boy. Nolte comes close—closer, perhaps, than any other actor could—to making human sense of this grab bag of clichés; for long stretches of the picture, we actually believe in Tom Wingo. Nolte lends a touch of unforced irony to the character's insufferable self-absorption; without his ease and charm, *The Prince of Tides* would be impossible to sit through. But even he can't redeem the movie's showstopper emotional scenes: the fuzzy-headedness and the grandiose bathos of the material defeat him. There's an overwhelming current of self-pity running through the story, and it culminates in what is supposed to be the picture's climactic sequence—Tom's account of his most traumatic memory. By the time he's ready to tell all, both he and we have just about forgotten that the purpose of his recollections is to help his sister. She's the one who tried to kill herself, the one who seems to have suffered most from the sins of the Wingo family, but we're entirely focused on *his* pain now. He breaks down weeping, in close-up, and then the camera pans to Lowenstein's face, and tears are rolling there, too. The scene is classically unplayable, because the flamboyant anguish of Tom and the sympathetic shrink feels like a false emotional resolution: they seem to be having Savannah's therapeutic breakthrough, and she's nowhere in sight. Whose catharsis is this, anyway? Savannah does surface briefly later in the picture, looking tenuously healthy; while no one was watching, Dr. Lowenstein must have passed along the gist of Tom's liberating revelation to her patient.

The comforting fantasy of *The Prince of Tides* is that being honest with yourself wipes out all your problems in a swift, bold stroke: face yourself, and you're cured. The movie, however, is proof that things aren't so simple, either in art or in life. For all the intelligent craft and sincere effort that have gone into the picture, for all the emotional "truth" that it parades before us, it leaves us unconvinced, uneasy, unchanged. Streisand has done an admirably scrupulous job of adaptation, but the movie never manages to transform its imperfect material. Both as a work of the imagination and as a design for living, Conroy's story remains stubbornly and fundamentally dysfunctional.

The New Yorker, January 27, 1992

AMERICAN DREAM

Barbara Kopple's documentary *American Dream*, about a strike in a Minnesota meat-packing plant, is a lucid and unfussy piece of movie journalism that manages to be as complexly affecting as a great novel. It's a masterpiece of social art: you can't shake off the experience this picture gives you. The story that Kopple tells here is a terrifying one, and the plainness and straightforwardness of her narrative manner accumulate force as the movie goes along. At first, the flat reportorial precision of her style may not feel satisfying—it's not like the stirring, balladlike lyricism of *Harlan County, U.S.A.*, her celebrated 1976 documentary about a coal miners' strike in Kentucky—but by the end it has become piercingly expressive. Events unfold with the unaccountable headlong awfulness of a developing nightmare, and we begin to understand that Kopple's apparently even tone has nothing to do with objectivity or resignation—that it is, rather, the exaggerated calm of deep shock. *American Dream* speaks to us in the careful, measured voice of utter disbelief, the voice of an eyewitness to a smashup on the highway. Kopple saw the whole thing, as it was happening; we sense the anguish in her painstaking reconstruction, the desire to get the details right, the need to make some sense of the catastrophe.

In the fall of 1983, Geo. A. Hormel & Company announced that it intended to roll back the wages and benefits of the workers in its Austin, Minnesota, plant. The union, Local P-9 of the United Food and Commercial Workers International Union, refused to make the concessions. The workers were outraged at being asked to accept $8.25 an hour for jobs that had been paying $10.69 an hour, especially since the company had reported profits of $29.5 million in that year. The P-9 members, who had been forced in recent years to give up a lucrative work-incentive plan, were determined to hold the line: they weren't buying Hormel's argument about its need to remain competitive with lower-paying companies in the industry. The president of the local, a deceptively soft-spoken and unassuming man named Jim Guyette, was a militant, a leader who inspired his constituency by his unyielding adherence to principle. Guyette's blunt personality was not ideally suited to the intricate art of collective bargaining, and Hormel's negotiators obviously felt that the company's position was so strong that they didn't have to compromise much. Against the advice of the international union, P-9 hired a free-lance New York consultant named Ray Rogers, whose organization, Corporate Campaign, espoused an unorthodox approach to labor disputes. Rogers's strategy consisted mainly of generating negative publicity about the company and its major corporate stockholders, and maintaining that sort of constant pressure until the harassed employer would be compelled to settle on the union's terms.

In *American Dream*, the arrival of Rogers kicks off a period of euphoric solidarity for the rank and file of P-9. He's a fantastic cheerleader: when he speaks at a union meeting, it turns into something like a high-school pep rally before the big game. Whatever doubts the workers may feel about the course that the local is taking are pushed out of their minds by his ringing optimistic rhetoric. He creates a terrific spirit of community and resolve in the local, and these sequences early in the movie lift our spirits, too: we feel as if we were watching a miraculous resuscitation of the energy and courage that fueled the labor movement in the thirties. For the past couple of decades, labor has hardly seemed to be a movement at all. The international unions have, for the most part, become bureaucratic and institutional rather than militant and democratic, and in the early eighties Big Labor was being routed in battle after battle, by the anti-union policies of the Reagan administration. Throughout the country, unions threatened with layoffs and plant closings were accepting concessionary contracts, and seemed powerless to halt the retreat. There wasn't much public support for their struggles, either. The unions had lost their aura of romantic populism, and the Republicans had managed to impart a wicked semantic spin to the concept of the labor movement: from the time Reagan took office, the unions, representing millions of people, were defined as a "special interest" (a distinction they shared with racial minorities and women). In this sort of atmosphere, the rah-rah enthusiasm of Rogers has the effect of sunshine after weeks of rain: he makes everything look possible again.

American Dream is unabashedly on the side of the workers. Kopple doesn't give the Hormel executives a lot of screen time to explain their position, and there's no reason she should. The company's argument isn't difficult to understand. Hormel wants to reduce the expense of operating its (new, multimillion-dollar) Austin plant; the simplest way to achieve the reduction is to slash wages and benefits; and the company feels that it has the power to extract such concessions from the union. Yes, there were trends in the meat-packing industry which influenced Hormel's decision. (A 1989 book by Dave Hage and Paul Klauda, *No Retreat, No Surrender: Labor's War at Hormel*, gives a more detailed picture of the economic background of the strike.) But morally the conflict between Hormel and P-9 is a no-brainer: the workers are right. Kopple probably brought her cameras to Austin in the hope of capturing images of a rank-and-file labor revolution. In the months before the expiration of P-9's old contract (in August of 1985), Guyette and Rogers looked like the prophets of a newly vigorous style of unionism— men who might be capable of shaking labor out of its lethargy and timidity and defeatism, of reversing the apparently irreversible decline in the fortunes of American industrial workers. At the beginning of *American Dream*, both the quietly righteous Guyette and the fiery Rogers are charismatic, galvanizing figures: they're leading the rank and file back to the promised land. The buoyant revivalist spirit of the P-9ers is inspiring: despite the bitterness uniting them against Hormel, they actually look as if they were having fun. And, thanks to Rogers, they're even getting some coverage from the national news media. It's easy to see why an activist filmmaker like Barbara Kopple would want to go to Austin and help spread the word, as she had done with the brave struggle of the Harlan County miners. When the movie turns its attention to the international union, then, the UFCW officials who object to P-9's tactics sound like killjoys—scared-rabbit bureaucrats, whose caution undermines their locals' will to fight. We see Lewie Anderson, the chief negotiator in the international's meat-packing division, tell the members of P-9 that Rogers's strategy is "doomed." Anderson knows that the local doesn't have the clout to bring Hormel to its knees; he clearly believes that they're going to have to settle for less than $10.69 an hour. The P-9ers think he's a jerk, and so, at first, do we.

What makes *American Dream* so emotionally involving, so wrenching, is that after the local's confrontation with Anderson the movie gradually begins to shift its attention from the clearly mapped moral ground of P-9's dispute with Hormel to the more ambiguous territory of the local's relations with the international. The tactical disagreement between Guyette and Anderson turns into a battle that's as fierce as the workers' battle with the company. We watch in horror as the P-9ers' feeling of isolation, fanned by the heated oratory of Guyette and Rogers, becomes a kind of raging paranoia. They begin to believe that they're waging war on two fronts, and the tenuousness of their position only makes them dig in harder. As the situation deteriorates, we see a bunker mentality developing among the leaders and the rank and file of P-9. The local rejects management's final offer, and on August 17, 1985, the workers, cheering and defiant, go out on strike. The company, unfazed, continues to run the plant, at reduced capacity, and makes up for the loss of production in Austin by transferring its functions to other plants and buying meat from other companies (some nonunion). Rogers continues to stage media-ready demonstrations, Guyette insists that his members won't go back to work for less than $10.69 an hour, and there's no progress toward a settlement. The walkout isn't hurting the company, and the Rogers-Guyette strategy is bogged down in stasis and futile repetition. The international, despite its reservations, has sanctioned the strike and is paying the P-9ers its standard strike benefit (forty dollars per person per week), but the local's leaders aren't working with Anderson or anyone else at the UFCW; it's a standoff on that front, too. The valiant members of P-9 are stranded on a narrowing strip of no man's land; when winter comes, they walk picket lines in below-zero cold with nothing but their sense of local solidarity to keep them warm.

As the strike wears on, our reactions to what we're seeing become more volatile—as irresolvable, we sometimes feel, as the contract dispute at the center of the drama. Our hearts are with Guyette and the pumped-up rank and file of P-9: the movie has provided us, invigoratingly, with a share in their enthusiasm and their hope, and we're reluctant to give back what we've gained. But our heads, increasingly (and surprisingly), are with the pragmatic Lewie Anderson. His initial analysis of the local's chances against the company proves accurate in virtually every particular. With each new turn of events, we come closer to the realization that Hormel has always been holding all the cards—that the only thing P-9 can do is keep bluffing until its small stake runs out. It's as agonizing to watch as a classical tragedy. (The oracles usually came off as jerks, too.) Rogers begins to look like a well-intentioned but dangerous blowhard, and Guyette seems to crumble before our eyes: his moral rectitude and his rhetorical fervor remain constant throughout, but his voice sounds weaker and less confident as the strike's momentum slows to a stop and the company's defenses grow more formidable. Twenty weeks into the walkout, Hormel starts hiring replacement workers, and there's nothing P-9 can do about it. The strikers' attempts to deny the scabs access to the plant are swiftly rebuffed. The National Guard appears on the scene to keep the gates open, and as the troops arrive Kopple cuts to a bleak, heartbreaking shot of Guyette, haggard and sunken-faced, looking on from the backseat of a car: he's wearing a cowboy hat, as if he were ready to ride to the rescue, but he just sits there, immobilized, impotent, watching the men and women he has led into battle scatter in disarray.

At moments like that—and there are many of them—the movie tears you up inside. In one scene, Guyette says, "Belief is something that will carry you a long ways." Kopple's vivid and sympathetic portrayal of the P-9ers has made us believe in them, but the disastrous course of the strike tests that belief relentlessly. We admire them, we understand what they're fighting for, and yet the doubting, weary voice of Lewie Anderson keeps breaking into our thoughts: maybe they're going too far; maybe, in their frustration and their righteous anger, they're collaborating in their own destruction. *American Dream* makes us feel, deep within ourselves, the terrible confusion in the minds of the country's embattled industrial workers: the paralyzing ambivalence about what to do, whom to trust, where to draw the line between the need to stand up for principle and the prospect of economic annihilation. By the time the movie is over, Kopple's level, unflinching gaze has become our way of seeing. She takes us past shock and into a more profound state of empathy, where our rage and our sorrow are keener and yet our judgment, somehow, seems sharper, too. The complex emotional responses this movie evokes can lead us, if we allow them, to a kind of tragic understanding of American life—tragic in the original and the fullest sense, in which the spectacle of unspeakable calamity produces pity and terror and then an unforeseeable and penetrating clarity.

Barbara Kopple couldn't have predicted when she arrived in Austin that several months later she would be setting up her camera in the front seat of a van in order to film the reactions of unhappy P-9 members crossing their own union's picket line. In the movie's most extraordinary sequence, Kopple shows us exactly how it feels to become a scab. Shortly before going back to work, John Morrison—a Guyette opponent, whom we've seen being shouted down at union meetings—and three other men talk to Kopple about their decision, and a couple of them end up weeping: the union and the company together have put them in an impossible bind, and they're about to do something that devastates their sense of themselves. The next day, we ride with them to the plant gates and beyond. The drive seems to take forever, and we hear and see the same things they do: the jeers and angry faces of their friends on the picket line, and then the strange emptiness and silence on the other side of the gate, where they're alone with the consequences of their action. It's a shattering sequence. You don't want to see the world through the eyes of a scab, but for a few minutes you do, and you realize that you have to: you can't understand anything if you don't understand these men. Soon afterward, a title card—white letters on a black background—delivers the news that in the twenty-fifth week of the strike the Hormel plant in Austin is fully staffed: "No jobs remain." My father (who's now retired) belonged to a union. I thought of him, and my eyes blurred with tears.

The New Yorker, March 23, 1992

WHITE MEN CAN'T JUMP

Ron Shelton's *White Men Can't Jump* is a resourceful, sneaky-fast comedy about playground basketball. Like his sublimely funny *Bull Durham* (1988), whose background is minor-league baseball, *White Men* focuses on grown men trying to make a living at a boys' game, and it does full justice to the sweet absurdity of that enterprise. Most sports movies stink, because they aren't really about sports. Their only true subject is winning, and they're generally designed to build up to a Big Game in which the underdogs squeeze out a narrow victory over their mean, arrogant, and more talented opponents. In these movies, it's always Shea Stadium in 1969, and the message always appears in giant, scoreboard-size letters: "You gotta believe." Probably the only audiences that respond wholeheartedly to these pictures are small children (who like fairy tales) and businessmen (who like motivational lectures). Shelton's approach is bracingly different. He doesn't worry much about big games, and when his characters are engrossed in play he barely bothers to keep score. The heroes of *White Men*, Sidney (Wesley Snipes) and Billy (Woody Harrelson), don't play basketball for glory. They play because they're good at it: their physical skills are the source of intense pleasure, a kind of feeling that nothing else can give them. They do play for money, but there are easier ways to make a buck than venturing into tough, hostile inner-city neighborhoods and trying to hustle the kings of the local courts. Sidney and Billy are addicted to the game—hooked on the deep contentment of making a jumper

over an outstretched hand, or hitting a teammate with a perfect pass
as he breaks free along the baseline, or spinning past a defender and
taking it to the hoop.

In Shelton's movies, playing ball doesn't function as a character-
builder; it's pure hedonism. Shelton knows (maybe because he was
an athlete himself, a baseball player whose career ended at the top
level of the minors) that the most extraordinary joy can come from
talents that are, in every practical sense, useless. Professional ath-
letes, the lucky few, can justify what they do: they have salaries and
benefits, like normal people. Sidney and Billy and the other playground hot shots we see in *White Men* have a harder time rationaliz-
ing their ballplaying, to themselves and to the women in their lives.
Sidney, who has a wife, Rhonda (Tyra Ferrell), and a child, tells his
family that he's "going to work" when he steps on the court; Billy,
who has a cocky, commanding presence as a player, turns nervous
and furtive when he comes home to his live-in girlfriend, Gloria
(Rosie Perez). In domestic contests, the men are overmatched: the
women play tight, in-your-shorts defense, and the guys don't have
the verbal moves to get around them. When their mates challenge
them to account for themselves, Sidney and Billy lose their cool, and
for a very good reason. They—and the women, and everyone in the
audience—know that the primary object of their basketball hustling
is the childlike, irresponsible delight it gives them. The money they
win buys them time: it keeps the heat off at home, and enables them
to live the playground life for a little longer.

The movie begins with Billy hustling Sidney on an outdoor court
at Venice Beach, in Los Angeles. Sidney is the reigning star there, but
the challenger catches him off guard. Billy works a diabolical con: he
blinds his opponents with the color of his skin. Because he's a white
guy—and a goofy-looking, miserably dressed one, at that—everyone assumes he can't play the speedy, shake-and-bake style of black
playground ball. And, in fact, he doesn't run or jump as well as
players like Sidney, but he's a superb passer and a deadly jump
shooter, and he starts every contest with a huge psychological edge:
by the time the opponent realizes that he isn't a pushover, most of
the damage is done. Although Sidney gets beaten—and it's humiliating to lose on your own court to a white dufus in baggy shorts and
a turned-around cap—he's smart enough to smell the possibility of

a fantastic scam. He and Billy begin to roam the courts of Los Angeles together, but always traveling separately. Arriving in a new neighborhood, Sidney gets into a game and starts taunting the local players with boasts about his prowess. Before long, everyone on the court is shouting at everyone else, and Sidney, apparently deranged by anger and bravado, issues the challenge: he'll stake everything he has on a game of two-on-two, and the opponents can pick his teammate. They choose the white guy every time. It's great fun watching the deception develop. We get the intellectual satisfaction of witnessing an impeccably executed con, and then we get some fine, fierce basketball action. Roping the suckers into the bet is, after all, only half the battle: Sidney and Billy still have to win the game.

Shelton, working with the cinematographer Russell Boyd and the editor Paul Seydor, has put together basketball sequences that capture the free-flowing rhythms of the playground game. Under the hot California sun, players fake and shuffle and jockey for position to the steady beat of the ball hitting the asphalt, and then, suddenly, the decisive move is made and someone is streaking toward the hoop and starting to rise. What's so breathtaking about playground ball is the split-second creativity it demands. Shelton has a sure feel for the game's exhilarating unpredictability; the thrill of basketball played at this level is its capacity for surprise, for out-of-nowhere feats of inspiration. When Sidney and Billy are really cooking on the court, even they don't know what they're going to come up with next, and every idea, no matter how wild, turns into effective action—a score—with magical immediacy. The two-on-two contests in *White Men Can't Jump* give us the delicious feeling a basketball player gets when he's *almost* out of control: flying but lucid. It's no wonder that Sidney and Billy are hooked on this stuff.

The movie takes its style from its subject: it's focused but relaxed, ready to move in any direction. Shelton's script has a slightly raggedy, one-thing-after-another structure, which allows him to try out all sorts of comic notions. There's a hilarious subplot about Gloria's attempts to become a contestant on *Jeopardy!* She declares, "It is my destiny that I triumph magnificently on that show," and to that end she spends her days packing her brain with trivia. Her mnemonic ability is a nice match for Billy's basketball skills: like her boyfriend, she has a freakish and not obviously lucrative talent that she feels (or hopes) will somehow pay off in the end. The *Jeopardy!* motif is something that Shelton seems to have plucked out of thin air, but it manages, unobtrusively, to fit into the movie's larger concerns: it's a flashy move that also accomplishes something. Not everything in the movie has that sort of effortless-seeming rightness. There's an occasional lull in the narrative momentum, and the important character of Sidney's wife feels underimagined. The picture would be stronger if Ferrell had a few more scenes and if Perez (who's often sensationally funny here) were a bit less shrill; the women are meant to be wiser and more honest than the men, but sometimes they just seem like nags.

The lapses are easy to forgive, though, because the movie has a generous spirit and a deep appreciation of play, and it moves with a distinctive funky grace: it takes things as they come and trusts itself to handle them. Although there's a lot of aggressive energy in the action on the screen, the picture itself never feels overbearing. Shelton doesn't get in the audience's face, even in a showstopper sequence like that of the tournament in which Sidney and Billy compete against two-man teams from all over the region. Billy, whose life has not been going well, turns into a genius of trash-talking: he heaps baroquely inventive verbal abuse on every player he faces. The beauty of the scene is that Billy's put-down lines aren't just crowd-pleasing zingers: they tumble out in a great vulgar rush, one after another—an eruption of hostility (and, of course, gamesmanship) that gets funnier as it gets more extreme. Throughout the picture, Shelton keeps his eye on the fine points of playground culture and lets the story's meanings—and its humor—emerge from the details. Refreshingly, he doesn't bear down too hard on the racial significance of the heroes' partnership. He treats the differences between blacks and whites mostly in basketball terms, as matters of style. Racial stereotypes, like the one embodied in the title, function as rules that are waiting to be broken, occasions for comic anomalies. Billy, for instance, holds the common view that black players care more about looking good on the court than about winning, while white players know how to win. Billy's game does rely on strategy and guile; Sidney's moves are more spectacular. The joke, which dawns on us slowly in the course of the movie, is that Sidney is an intelligent player, too, and his smarts, unlike Billy's, extend to the decisions he makes off the court. Snipes and Harrelson do a superb job of bringing out the witty contrasts of the script. The timing of their exchanges is as miraculously exact as their teamwork on the court: they pass lines back and forth as if they had been doing this sort of thing forever. Harrelson's Billy shambles through the picture like a dazed kid, but he turns steely and determined when he's playing ball; this is a rich, subtle, and delicately funny perform-ance. And Snipes is just amazing. He's both loose and explosive: everything he does seems to leap right off the screen.

White Men Can't Jump is a terrifically original mixture of patience and flash. Shelton orchestrates the action like a veteran point guard. He's a wily pro with a streak of playground showmanship, and that's an ideal style for movies as well as for basketball. This is a sane, savvy picture that's also unpredictable enough to produce more than a few moments of comic euphoria. American studio movies have been so plodding and unimaginative in the past few years that an entertaining picture like *White Men Can't Jump* seems as unlikely as the last play we see Sidney and Billy make—an over-the-shoulder alley-oop pass leading to a clean dunk. You gape, and ask yourself, "Where did *that* come from?" And then you start to grin.

The New Yorker, April 6, 1992

THE PLAYER

The title character of Robert Altman's *The Player* is a young Holly-wood studio executive named Griffin Mill (Tim Robbins), who, for no very good reason, murders an aspiring screenwriter. The picture is a brilliant dark comedy about the death of American filmmaking, and the protagonist, charming and smart and impeccably turned out, is a pure incarnation of the forces that squeeze the life out of adventurous moviemakers. The idea that corporate smoothies like Griffin are killers—and proud of it—isn't a surprising one, but the screenplay, by Michael Tolkin, who also wrote the 1988 novel on which the film is based, embellishes this obvious joke with wickedly ingenious riffs. You can sense the vengeful pleasure Tolkin takes in building the case against Griffin. The novel is a writer's lovingly detailed portrait of an enemy, and it's frighteningly acute: it has the obsessive precision of nursed paranoia. An adversary who wields power as skillfully and as unscrupulously as Griffin Mill does is impossible to beat: the only small satisfaction available to the bruised loser lies in understanding the beast out of existence— dissecting it, classifying it, handling it (mentally) like a laboratory specimen.

And Tolkin has this character nailed. He seems to know things about studio executives that they don't know about themselves, and that's not because he's more intelligent than they are or because he has a finer moral sense but because Hollywood is a mirror world, a culture in which every encounter is an intricate dance of images projected and reflected. In the opening sequence of *The Player*—an insolently elaborate eight-minute tracking shot—we see a succession of writers nervously pitching story ideas to Griffin, and they're all trying to speak what they imagine is the executive's language. "It's *Ghost* meets *The Manchurian Candidate*," one of them babbles. They want to demonstrate that they know how to think in his terms, and they seem to have put a lot of effort into figuring out how to make their stories play in the theater of Griffin Mill's consciousness: they've spent more time prowling the inside of his head than he has. The goal for each of them is, in a sense, to *become* him: to internalize the essence of Griffin Mill so thoroughly that the mimicry doesn't show at all. At this point, theoretically, the participants in the meeting will have achieved such sublime rapport that the writer's ideas will strike the executive as his own. (Fundamentally, they are.) And that's how a writer like Tolkin can know the mind of a movie executive with uncanny intimacy: Hollywood screenwriters and directors learn to negate themselves and reinvent themselves in the image of their enemy. In *The Player* Tolkin and Altman turn this depressing process into a kind of nightmarish slapstick. The insular, constantly self-regarding culture of the movie community here combines the sinister ambiguity of the hall-of-mirrors shootout in *The Lady from Shanghai*, in which bullets shatter image after image in silvered glass as the opponents search wildly for their real targets, with the deep silliness of the scene from *Duck Soup* in which Harpo imitates Groucho's gestures so precisely that Groucho thinks he's watching himself in a mirror.

The Player is like a documentary about a mirage. The world Altman shows us is sunlit and shimmering, and the people have the thin presence of holograms. That's their reality, and Altman looks at them with the same sort of playfully inquisitive gaze he trained on the country singers of *Nashville* and the political campaigners of the HBO series *Tanner '88*. In this picture Altman is doing one of his specialties: exploring an odd American subculture—revealing its distinctive textures and explicating the peculiar principles of social intercourse which keep it functioning. But when his idiosyncratic style of anthropological realism is applied to the tight community of Hollywood "players" it has an almost hallucinatory effect. Part of the movie's verisimilitude is that wherever Griffin goes—every chic restaurant, every charity banquet, every cocktail party—he runs into movie stars. Cher, Jack Lemmon, Nick Nolte, Anjelica Huston, Burt Reynolds, and dozens of other famous faces pop up throughout the picture, most of them for just a few seconds. These people are the everyday cast of characters in the protagonist's life, the people that a man in his position would naturally move among; but, even as we're saying "Of course" and admiring the ease with which Altman weaves the celebrities into the social textures of the movie, we're jarred every time one of these well-known figures materializes in the background of a scene. There seems to be a glaze on them, a light protective shield of perfectly achieved artifice. We laugh at how completely the stars fill the outlines of our images of them, how conscientiously they satisfy our expectations. They look as if they were doing dead-on impersonations of themselves, and after a while we begin to get an eerie, unsettled feeling. In this way (and many others), the picture seems to take us through mimetic realism, as through a looking glass, and out the other side: we find ourselves, without knowing how we got there, in a fairy-tale world of seductive apparitions and ominous doubles.

Altman isn't just playing fancy reality-and-illusion games. He's describing, with hilarious exactness, a milieu in which extreme self-consciousness—neurotically close attention to the appearance you present to society—is the norm, the quality without which survival is virtually impossible. The protagonist of *The Player* is a virtuoso of self-image calculation. Every gesture he makes, every word he speaks, every tiny nuance of personality seems to have been thought out carefully, and by an unusually subtle and flexible mind. Griffin is so good at orchestrating the impression he wants to make in any given situation that in a sense he doesn't really exist. There *is* no essence of Griffin Mill, no core to his personality: he's no more than the sum of his acquired and meticulously arranged traits, an automaton that has programmed itself, with exquisite adaptability, for success. At the beginning of the film, we see him at his most likable: he's sympathetic because he's in a bit of a panic. The machinery isn't functioning as efficiently as he wants it to, and he can't put his finger on what's wrong. A rival executive is maneuvering to usurp his power at the studio, and he has also received threatening anonymous postcards from an embittered writer. In his confusion—his inability to make the adjustments necessary to reestablish control over his life—Griffin seems almost human. He's clearly upset by the wrath of the nameless writer, who has announced, rather grandly, his intention of killing Griffin in the name of writers everywhere. This venom is especially puzzling to Griffin because he has cultivated the reputation of being a "writer's executive": the postcards violate his image of himself. Searching his files for a suspect—or, at least, for a comparable "nobody" writer to whom he can make some sort of symbolic amends—he finds the name David Kahane, and he contrives an accidental-seeming meeting at an out-of-the-way revival cinema. In the course of this awkwardly engineered encounter, Kahane (Vincent D'Onofrio), who has a rude, abrasive manner, taunts Griffin mercilessly and finally goes too far: in a dark parking lot, the executive loses his cool and kills the writer. The murder is the most beautiful, the most profoundly funny joke in the movie. It's the only spontaneous, unrehearsed act the hero performs, and we realize, gradually, that the crime is the moment when Griffin Mill finds his essence: the core of his being is his hatred of writers, his fear of the unruliness of imagination. In a story meeting the next day, his colleagues muse aloud about the possibility of eliminating the writer from the moviemaking process. Griffin has actually done, in the most concrete way, what they only dream of, and that knowledge makes him a stronger, more confident corporate manipulator. At the start of the movie, he strikes us as a clever, amiably superficial young man. By the end, his features seem to have acquired greater definition, to have taken on a different and much scarier look—the look of a winner.

Tim Robbins, a wonderfully inventive actor, makes that progression feel utterly believable. His Griffin Mill is a layered, richly suggestive comic creation: the sort of performance that Robert Altman's filmmaking style, at its best, produces without obvious effort. *The Player* has the exhilarating nonchalance of Altman's seventies classics, and its tone is volatile, elusive. With breathtaking assurance, the movie veers from psychological-thriller suspense to goofball comedy to icy satire: it's Patricia Highsmith meets Monty Python meets Nathanael West. When Altman is in form, as he is here, everything seems to meet in front of his cameras: the most disparate personalities and voices come together, in combinations as unexpectedly right as the gathering at the end of *Nashville*, with stars and impassioned amateurs and a huge audience and a killer all crowded on or around a great stage in the open air. *The Player* resists every attempt to pin it down: there's too much life in it, too much movement, too many flickering changes of mood to sort out. The movie turns the self-reflective world of Hollywood into a fun house in which every grotesque distortion somehow appears to us as a newly discovered, paradoxical truth. In this comedy-thriller, even the most familiar genre elements become their opposites: the humor has the satisfying inevitability of a superbly constructed thriller plot, in which every clue clicks right into place, and the suspense has the giddy, unpredictable rhythms of improvisational comedy.

One of the ironies surrounding *The Player* is that the movie has given Altman some credibility in Hollywood, for the first time in years: the studio people are impressed by this not at all flattering portrait of their values and life style. Go figure. Maybe they are happy to see any reflection of themselves and are so narcissistic that they don't now how bad they look, or maybe they really are proud of being killers. The joke will be on them, though, if this picture reminds the audience, as it should, of how invigorating movies can be when they're made freely, when the ideas haven't been shaped to fit the limited contours of the executive mind. *The Player* is in itself a peerless reproach to the studio system, a vindication of the joys of imagination. It's the work of a man who makes movies with the grace of a master, and who hasn't yet learned how to be anyone but himself. At sixty-seven, Robert Altman is still the youngest filmmaker in America.

The New Yorker, April 20, 1992

Index

About the Author

Terrence Rafferty studied comparative literature at Cornell University and creative writing at Brown University. He has written extensively for *Sight and Sound*, *The Atlantic*, the *Village Voice*, *The Nation*, and *The New Yorker*, where he is currently film critic. He received a Guggenheim Fellowship in 1987. Mr. Rafferty lives just outside of New York City, with his wife, Diane, a writer; two cats; and Louis, a German shepherd.